CAMBRIDGE

Books of enduring scholarly value

Maritime Exploration

This series includes accounts, by eye-witnesses and contemporaries, of voyages by Europeans to the Americas, Asia, Australasia and the Pacific during the colonial period. Driven by the military and commercial interests of powers including Britain, France and the Netherlands, particularly the East India Companies, these expeditions brought back a wealth of information on climate, natural resources, topography, and distant civilisations. Their detailed observations provide fascinating historical data for climatologists, ecologists and anthropologists, and the accounts of the mariners' experiences on their long and dangerous voyages are full of human interest.

A Voyage to New Guinea and the Moluccas, from Balambangan

In 1770, Thomas Forrest (c.1729–c.1802) was involved in establishing a new free port at Balambangan, Malaysia, which would improve the British East India Company's trade routes eastwards. In 1774 he agreed to lead an expedition on the Company's behalf to find out more about the waters between Malaysia and New Guinea. This 1779 publication (reissued in the Dublin edition) tells the story of Forrest's fifteen-month voyage in a small local vessel crewed by Malaysians, exploring the archipelago between the Philippines and present-day Indonesia. A French translation appeared in 1780, and linguist Wilhelm von Humboldt referred to the book fifty years later. Forrest describes the islands, their populations, and their vegetation, including different spices. He discusses relations between local rulers and the rivalries between the British and the Dutch, particularly as regards control of the spice trade. The book also contains a substantial vocabulary of the Maguindanao language.

Cambridge University Press has long been a pioneer in the reissuing of out-of-print titles from its own backlist, producing digital reprints of books that are still sought after by scholars and students but could not be reprinted economically using traditional technology. The Cambridge Library Collection extends this activity to a wider range of books which are still of importance to researchers and professionals, either for the source material they contain, or as landmarks in the history of their academic discipline.

Drawing from the world-renowned collections in the Cambridge University Library and other partner libraries, and guided by the advice of experts in each subject area, Cambridge University Press is using state-of-the-art scanning machines in its own Printing House to capture the content of each book selected for inclusion. The files are processed to give a consistently clear, crisp image, and the books finished to the high quality standard for which the Press is recognised around the world. The latest print-on-demand technology ensures that the books will remain available indefinitely, and that orders for single or multiple copies can quickly be supplied.

The Cambridge Library Collection brings back to life books of enduring scholarly value (including out-of-copyright works originally issued by other publishers) across a wide range of disciplines in the humanities and social sciences and in science and technology.

A Voyage to New Guinea and the Moluccas, from Balambangan

Including an Account of Magindano, Sooloo, and Other Islands

THOMAS FORREST

CAMBRIDGE
UNIVERSITY PRESS

CAMBRIDGE
UNIVERSITY PRESS

University Printing House, Cambridge, CB2 8BS, United Kingdom

Cambridge University Press is part of the University of Cambridge.
It furthers the University's mission by disseminating knowledge in the pursuit of
education, learning and research at the highest international levels of excellence.

www.cambridge.org
Information on this title: www.cambridge.org/9781108082846

© in this compilation Cambridge University Press 2018

This edition first published 1779
This digitally printed version 2018

ISBN 978-1-108-08284-6 Paperback

The original edition of this book contains a number of oversize plates
which it has not been possible to reproduce to scale in this edition.
They can be found online at www.cambridge.org/9781108082846

A

VOYAGE

TO

NEW GUINEA,

AND THE

MOLUCCAS,

FROM

BALAMBANGAN:

INCLUDING AN

Account of MAGINDANO, SOOLOO, and other Islands;

ILLUSTRATED WITH COPPER-PLATES.

PERFORMED IN THE

TARTAR GALLEY,

BELONGING TO THE

HONOURABLE EAST INDIA COMPANY,

During the YEARS, 1774, 1775, and 1776,

By CAPTAIN THOMAS FORREST.

TO WHICH IS ADDED,

A VOCABULARY

OF THE

MAGINDANO TONGUE.

IGNOTIS ERRARE LOCIS, IGNOTA VIDERE
LITTORA GAUDEBAT, STUDIO MINUENTE LABOREM.
OVID. MET. IV. 294.

D U B L I N:

Printed for Messrs. PRICE, W. and H. WHITESTONE, SLEATER,
POTTS, WILLIAMS, MONCRIEFFE, WALKER, JENKIN,
HALLHEAD, BEATTY, EXSHAW, and WHITE.
M,DCC,LXXIX.

GENTLEMEN,

HAVING early devoted myfelf to your fervice, and been many years employed in it abroad, I cannot but feel myfelf peculiarly interefted in the profperity of this great Company, whofe approbation has been the ambition of my life.

When you were pleafed, in the year 1770, to confer upon me, by a fpecial commiffion, the command of your marine, on the Weft-coaft of Sumatra, I repaired thither, with the zeal fuch confidence muft infpire, and in the hope of opportunity to prove myfelf not quite unworthy of it.

Sometime after my arrival at Fort Marlborough, your plan of a fettlement on the Ifland of Balambangan, afforded me fuch opportunity : by permiffion of the Governor and Council, I embarked with Mr. Herbert, who was appointed Chief on that Service.

I had not been long at Balambangan, when that Gentleman communicated to me your orders for exploring Iflands to the eaftward, and propofed to me the honor of executing the arduous tafk.

To

To the profitable command of the Britannia, vacant by the death of Capt. Wilmot, I relinquifh-ed my unqueftionable right, in order to undertake the delicate as well as dangerous voyage; to which I could have no motive, but the ardor of juftifying Mr. Herbert's choice of a perfon moft likely to accomplifh the important defign of You, my ever honored employers.

How I have by kind Providence been enabled to do this, I here fubmit to the candor of the Honorable Company: nor could the reward, on which I rely, be claimed before the fpecification of the Service. In the whole, I have the honor to be,

GENTLEMEN,

LONDON,   Your moft obedient,
Feb. 1ft, 1779.

As moft devoted Servant,

THOMAS FORREST.

INTRODUCTION.

THE firſt diſcovery of New Guinea,* or Tanna (Land) Papua, was made ſo long ago as the year 1511, by Antonio Ambreu, and Francis Serrano. †

By the Portugueſe names given to certain harbours, bays, and iſlands, that we find on the north coaſt of New Guinea, between what is called Schouten's iſland and Solomon's iſlands, it would ſeem that nation had in former days much frequented thoſe parts. Nicholas Struyck, in a book publiſhed at Amſterdam in 1753, gives a particular account of places and iſlands on the north coaſt of this country, with Portugueſe names ; and ſays, the Dutch endeavoured to conceal the knowledge of them. ‡ New Guinea is alſo ſaid to have been diſcovered by Alvaro de Saavedra in 1527, who ſo called it, as being oppoſite on the globe to

* Littora Novæ Guineæ, inſulæ Salomonis, inſulæ de Los Ladrones, omnium harum inſularum et regionum, ſi communiter ſpeƈtentur, temperies humida eſt, et moderate calida.

DE BRY, fol. 34.

† Galvano Baros.—Dalrymple's Chron. Tab. of Diſcovery

‡ Hiſtoire des navigations aux terres Auſtrales.

Guinea

INTRODUCTION.

Guinea in Africa. Antonio Urdanetta faw New Guinea in 1528.*

Ruy Lopez de Lobos, in 1543, fent from Tidore, towards New Spain, by the fouth fide of the line, a fhip commanded by Ortez de Rotha. That Captain failed to the coaft of Os Papuas, and ranged it; but, not knowing that Saavedra had been there before him, he challenged the honour of difcovery. He called it New Guinea,† from the frizzled locks of the inhabitants: for the memory of Saavedra's voyage was almoft loft. ‡

Lopez Vaz relates, that fometime about the year 1567, Lopez de Caftro, governor of Peru, fent a fleet to difcover certain iflands in the South Sea. Alvarez de Mendanio was general. At the diftance of 800 leagues, they difcovered between 9° and 11° of S. latitude, fome large iflands; together, eighty leagues in compafs. The greateft ifland was, *according to the firft finder*, called Guadalcanal. Here they landed, took a town, and found fmall grains of gold. He farther fays, " now at the time they thought of fettling thefe iflands, Captain Drake entering the South Seas, command was inftantly given, that the iflands fhould not be fettled, left the Englifh or other na-

* Hiftoire des voyages, par l'Abbé Prevot, tome 42 de l'edit. in-douze.

† Nova Guinea a nautis fic dicta, quod ejus littora locorumque facies Guineæ Africanæ admodum funt fimilia. Ab Andrea Corfali videtur dici terra Piccona. LINSCHOOTEN, p. 328.

‡ Lord Oxford's continuation, vol. II. p. 402.

tions,

tions, who paffed the ftraits of Magellan for the
South Sea, fhould find there any fuccour but from
the Indians." *

It is not impoffible, that purfuant to this, the
Spaniards, in their pofterior charts, mifplaced
Solomon's iflands, and caft them far eaft into the
South Sea. But Mr. Dalrymple, to whofe refearches and furveys navigation is deeply indebted,
by collating Dampier's map of New Guinea, with
what fketches are found in Herrera, and in the
collection of voyages by de Bry, has evinced, that
Dampier's New Britain and Solomon's iflands are
the fame. This has fo far been verified by Captain Carteret's difcovering a ftrait pafs through the
middle of New Britain. But, a map publifhed by
Linfchooten in 1695, puts the matter beyond all
doubt, as in that map the iflands at the eaft extremity of New Guinea, are abfolutely named
Solomon's iflands.

It is to be regretted, that Dampier, who failed
to New Britain in the Roebuck 1699, had not feen
Linfchooten's map, publifhed but four years before. Such a guide might have induced him to put
into harbours which he did not vifit, not knowing
they exifted : for the leaft additional light to a dif-
coverer may be productive of important confe-
quences.

As Lopez Vaz mentions gold found there, and
the Spaniards unwilling the Portuguefe fhould
have any fhare in it, that circumftance might far-

* Hakluyt, vol. III. p. 802.

ther

ther induce the former (if they were indeed induced) to misplace those islands; that these might not appear in the portion of the globe which the Pope had assigned them; the other half having been given to the Portuguese by virtue of the famous meridian * of partition his Holinefs drew on the occasion. Lopez Vaz asserts, that the Spaniards carried back gold from Solomon's islands to New Spain.

Schouten † and le Maire, in 1616, after leaving an island they called St. John, and the Green islands, came to the coast of New Guinea, and sent their shallop in shore to sound. She was attacked by several canoes, whence they threw stones at the boat with slings. Next day, the 26th of June, the ship was attacked, the enemy throwing stones and darts. This they were obliged to resent. They killed ten of the assailants, took three more, and four canoes. The canoes they destroyed, and ransomed two of the three prisoners for a hog and a bunch of plantains. Next day, they got another hog for some nails and trinkets. On the 28th, a handsome large canoe came on board, with twenty-one persons, who admired the ship much, and

* Some say, the first meridian is drawn through Fayal; but the following accompanies de Bry's maps.

Quicquid spatii intra duos illos meridianos, signatos terræ Americæ, est navigationibus detectum, aut detegetur in posterum, Castiliensibus assignatum est.   De Bry.

In the above map, one meridian goes through the banks of Newfoundland; the other through Java.

† Harris's Collection, Vol. I. p. 60.

brought

brought betel nut and lime.* Thefe called themfelves Papuas, and did not offer to exchange the
third prifoner ; upon which they put him afhore.

Continuing their courfe weftward, on the 7th of
July, they paffed an ifland called 'Vulcan's ; no
doubt, one of the burning iflands in the map. On
the 13th, they anchored within half a league of the
main land, in 2° 54' S. latitude ; and, finding the
country abound in coco nuts, fent the boat, well
provided for an attack, with orders *to land and get
fome*. But fuch was the reception, from the arrows
of the inhabitants, that fixteen being wounded, the
invaders were forced, notwithftanding their mufkets, to retire.

On the 16th, they anchored between two iflands,
landed, burnt fome houfes, and brought off as
many coco nuts as dealt three a man.

In failing along the coaft, they faw a very pleafant ifland, named in the map, Horn ifland. The
crew changing its name, called it Schouten's ifland, in compliment to their commander. As the
fouth coaft of it is in Dampier's chart, left indefi-
nite by a dotted line, I have fome reafon to think,
the promontory of Dory may be the fame land, but
not fufficient evidence to afcertain it.

Abel Tafman, in 1642, after failing round New
Holland, and fo difcovering it to be an ifland, returned by New Britain and New Guinea. He then

* Ufed by moft Eaft Indians with the areka nut and betel
leaf.

paffed

paffed a burning mountain, in the latitude of 5°
04' S. and afterwards got refreſhments from the
iſland Jama, which lies a little to the eaſt of Moa.
The natives brought him 6000 coco nuts, and 100
bags of plantains. The ſailors, in return, making
knives of iron hoops, bartered theſe awkward in-
ſtruments for thoſe refreſhments. Taſman had no
quarrel with the inhabitants. They ſeemed, at
Moa and Arimoa, to be afraid of him; for, one
of his ſailors having been accidentally wounded, by
an arrow from the bow of one of the natives, the
man was delivered up.

Captain Dampier, in the voyage of the Roebuck, already mentioned, being on the weſt coaſt
of New Guinea, bought, near an iſland, called by
the natives Sabuda, three or four nutmegs in the
ſhell, *which did not ſeem to be long gathered.* This
agrees with what I found at Dory. The dreſs of
the people alſo near Pulo Sabuda, is exactly that
worn at Dory; the men wearing the rind of the
palm-tree, and the women calicoes.

Dampier touched no where on the coaſt of New
Guinea, but ſailed near ſeveral iſlands cloſe by
New Britain, Wiſhart's Iſland, Matthias, and Squally Iſland; alſo Slinger's Iſland, whence he was in-
ſulted with vollies of ſtones. Had he anchored
behind any of theſe iſlands, which, I apprehend, he
might have done; or, if he had not fired ſmall
and great ſhot at the inhabitants of the large bay,
where he did anchor, *to ſcare them,* as he owns, he
might have doubtleſs had intercourſe with them,
and not been reduced to the hoſtility of taking, by
violence,

violence, fome of their hogs. Thus the whole difcovery, from impatience or fear, was fruftrated.
By his account of the appearance of the country,
it is well inhabited and cultivated; much better than
the places I vifited farther weft.

Captain William Funnel, 1705,* obferved feveral iflands in 0° 42' N. latitude, near the coaft of
New Guinea, inhabited; but by a feemingly hoftile people: which prevented all intercourfe with
them. He faw the coaft only at a diftance; and
fays, it appeared to him mountainous, black, and
rocky. Being afterwards in diftrefs for provifions,
and unacquainted in thofe feas, he was, by the mafk
of friendfhip, decoyed to Amboyna, where he fuffered very rough ufage from the Dutch.

Commodore Roggewein † coafted the north part
of New Guinea, in 1722, and touched at the iflands Moa and Arimoa; whence came to him with
provifions 200 canoes, with whom he dealt. He
then paffed by what he clufters in the name of the
Thoufand Iflands; where, he fays, the inhabitants
had their heads covered with thick curled wool,
and were called Papuas. Some of them had a bit
of ftick piercing the griftle of the nofe, as I remarked in a flave who was brought to Dory, to
be fold.

Roggewein's people landing on the ifland Moa,
began to fell the coco nut trees; and the Indians,
who lay in ambufh, defervedly let fly at them a
fhower of arrows. Injuftice is always imprudence,

* Harris's Collection.   † Ibid.

and

and ingratitude is the worſt ſpecies of injuſtice. The natives had, juſt before this invaſion of their property, brought the ſtrangers all manner of re-freſhments. The latter, however, perceiving Moa thinly inhabited, had fallen upon this ſcheme of ſeizing proviſions; thinking, to carry off, at once, ſtock ſufficient for the proſecution of their voyage. To this conduct they were animated by the conſi-deration, that the arrows of the natives did them little or no hurt; whereas, the diſcharge of their ſmall arms laid abundance of their entertainers on the ground.

The next I can find, was Captain Carteret, who diſcovered, as has been ſaid, New Britain to be di-vided into two parts at leaſt; by a ſtrait, which he names St. George's Channel. He found in Eng-liſh Cove, near Cape St. George, the nutmeg tree; but the fruit not ripe. He had only a diſtant in-tercourſe with the inhabitants. Mr. Bougainville, who paſſed that ſtrait ſoon after found them trea-cherous.

Captain Cook ſailed much about the ſame time to the ſouth of New Guinea, through the Endeavour ſtrait; where, by his account, the land is low. He had no friendly intercourſe with the inhabitants.

To this hour, I do not find, that any European has had friendly intercourſe with New Britain, which is well inhabited: and ſince Roggewein, no-body we know of, has had any with New Guinea. Monſieur Sonerrat, in his *Voyage à la Nouvelle Gui-née*, lately publiſhed, went no farther eaſt than the
island

ifland Gibby,* near Patany Hook, on Gilolo. Gib-
by is often mentioned in the following fheets.
What little connexion I had with the Papuas in
New Guinea, will alſo there appear.

The account of the cinnamon tree is taken from
the Acta Phyſico-Medica Academiæ Cæſareæ,
vol. I.

Since my own enquiries and conjectures about
the people called Badjoos, mentioned chap. xviii. I
have met with a curious account of them in Valentine. He ſays, the Oran Badjoos or Wadjoos, are
fiſhermen ; and that Mr. Padderburg at Manado
on Celebes, had them under his charge in 1675.

Mr. Padderburg imagines the Badjoos have been
driven from Macaſſar, Java, Bantam, and Japara.
They have about 700 boats, in which they live
moſtly on fiſh. He adds, they have a king, to
whom they pay homage. They have a ſtrange
ſqueal in their voice, with a very wild appearance ;
and, were it not for the freedom which their boats
afford them of going from place to place, they
would not remain in any particular quarter, as they
have a diſlike to the ſhore.

Padderburg is of opinion, they muſt have come
either from China or Japan, where multitudes live in
boats ; and their departure from that country muſt
have been occaſioned, he thinks, by the inroads of

---

* The Author· does not ſay, whither he went ; but this I
learned from a perſon who deſerted him, and whom I ſaw at
Sooloo, in 1773.

the

the Tartars, who conquered China, and expelled the Badjoos, who may then have found their way amongft thefe iflands. Thofe about Manado, Ma-caffar, Borneo, and the Philippines, are a medley of different nations; fuch as Chinefe with long plaited hair, Javans with bare throats, plucked beards and whifkers, and Macaffars with black fhining teeth.

The religion is chiefly Chinefe or Mahometan. They have in different parts many veffels; and, what is remarkable, their women are capable of managing thofe veffels even in heavy feas. Thefe people are very ufeful to the Dutch Eaft India Company, in carrying intelligence fpeedily from place to place, and giving information of what-ever happens.

CON-

CONTENTS.

BOOK I.

CHAPTER I.

CHAP. II.

CHAP. III.

C O N T E N T S.

C H A P.

C H A P. XII.

B O O K II.

C H A P T E R I.

C H A P. II.

C H A P.

CHAP. III.

CHAP. IV.

CHAP. V.

CHAP. VI.

CHAP. VII.

c

C H A P.

CHAP. XVI.

CHAP. XVII.

CHAP. XVIII.

A VOYAGE

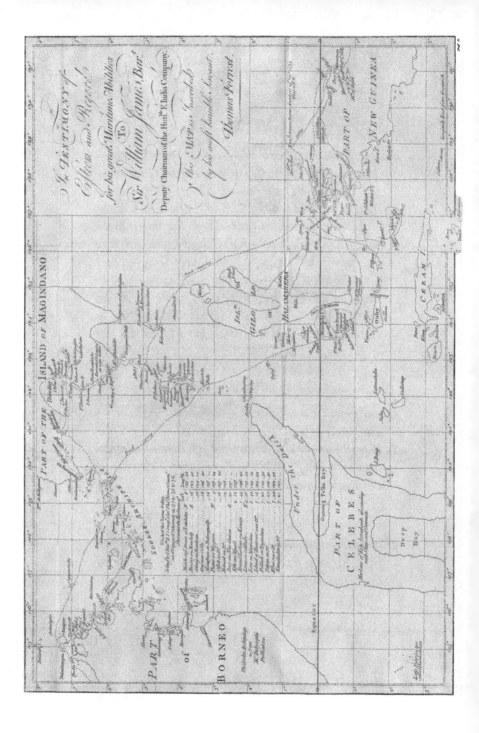

The material originally positioned here is too large for reproduction in this reissue. A PDF can be downloaded from the web address given on page iv of this book, by clicking on 'Resources Available'.

A

VOYAGE

TO

NEW GUINEA.

BOOK I.

CHAPTER I.

Intention of the Voyage—Sailing Orders—Reasons for undertaking it in a small Vessel—Description of the Tartar Galley—and list of the Crew.

THE intention of the voyage I am about to relate, was to forward what the Honourable East India Company had recommended by the ship Britannia, that went from England, to settle Balambangan, * an island situated near the north promontory of Borneo. The following is an extract from their general letter, dated June the 12th 1771, to the Chief and Council of that place.

* See Dalrymple's plan for extending the commerce of the East India Company, 1769.

B   " Having

" Having good authority from the experience
" and inquiries of Mr. Dalrymple, to be affured
" that cinnamon, cloves, nutmegs, pepper, and
" clove bark, may with proper management be
" eafily introduced into Balambangan, as fome of
" thofe articles are produced in the Sooloo diftricts,
" and others in the adjacent iflands, as the inclofed
" paper of inquiry, mentioned in a preceding pa-
" ragraph, will fhow : the acquifition and cultiva-
" tion of thofe valuable articles, muft be fpecially
" recommended to the moft diligent attention of
" the Chief and Council, as an object of the higheft
" importance, with promifes of a very favourable
" notice on our part, on its being made apparent
" to us, that their endeavours for that purpofe
" have been effectually and advantageoufly exe-
" cuted. Thefe articles, if obtained, we particu-
" larly direct, fhall be made part of our confign-
" ment to the China Council, until we fee occafion
" to fignify our further pleafure therein."

About the latter end of Auguft 1774, Ambaf-
fadors came from the hcir apparent of the Sultan
of Mindanao, to Balambangan, in whofe train
was an inhabitant of the Molucca's, called Ifhmael
Tuan Hadjee, who having been long employed
there by the Dutch, had gained an accurate knowledge of the Molucca iflands ; and having alfo
been to the eaftward of them, beyond Pitt's
Straits, as far as the coaft of New Guinea, called
Papua, had feen, and confequently reported that
nutmegs grew there.

Mr.

Mr. Herbert, the chief, had frequent confer-
ences with this man; and, defirous to profit from
his intelligence, in the fcheme which he had in
view, of forwarding the honourable court's in-
junctions by the Britannia, as above related, to
endeavour to obtain fpices from parts which had
no connexion with the Dutch fettlements, he was
pleafed to confult me on the occafion. As I had,
from other accounts, found that there was great
probability in the relation of Tuan Hadjee, I offered to go, accompanied by him, on a voyage
to New Guinea, if Mr. Herbert thought proper,
in order to afcertain the truth of his affertion, and
propofed to attempt it in a fmall country embark-
ation.—This was approved by Mr. Herbert and
his Council, and they left the management of it
entirely to my direction.

Inftructions from the Chief and Council of Balamban-
gan, to Captain Thomas Forreft.

S I R,
The knowledge you have acquired from experience of all the departments of marine bufinefs in
general, to which you was trained from your
earlieft years, together with a competent fhare of
commercial tranfactions in this quarter of the world,
were fufficient inducements for the chief to accept
of your offer to attend him on the expedition to
Balambangan. From the fmall number of fervants, moft of whom were unexperienced, he
knew there would be fufficient field to difplay
your talents, abftracted from the official bufinefs

of thofe brought up in the regular line of the fervice.

He perfectly knew your attachment and turn for difcovery; and though nothing has been undertaken hitherto in the purfuit thereof, we would not have you imagine that we have thought lightly of fuch matters; or, that the chief has taken in bad part the feveral anecdotes and remarks you have at various times furnifhed him with.

We have juft received a copy of a paragraph of a letter from Bombay, wrote by the Honourable Court to that Prefidency, which feems to imply very ftrongly, that it is their intention, to keep affairs in this quarter in as circumfcribed and narrow limits as poffible. A favourable opportunity however offering, without incurring heavy expences, we are unwilling to let it flip; as it is an object of the firft confequence, and may, if accomplifhed, turn out extremely beneficial, not only to our honourable employers in particular, but alfo to the Britifh nation in general.

You muft be fenfible, as we are, how important the monopoly of fpices is to the Dutch company, and the States of Holland; and equally fo, how incompatible it is, as well with the dignity of our company, as their advantage, to carry on a trade in thefe articles furreptitioufly obtained, as they annually are, from the Dutch territories, and tranfported to Bencoolen, Rhio, and other places in the Straits of Malacca. The Molucca's being generally underftood in Europe to be folely fub-

ject

ject to the Dutch, joined to the invariable commands of our fuperiors, not to interfere where any
other European nation is engaged, are motives
fufficient for us to reject the application that has
been made, or any other that we may receive
hereafter, which we may efteem to have the leaft
tendency towards creating a controverfy between
the two companies.

We have thought it neceffary to premife thus
much, that our intentions, and our conduct may
appear as clear to you, as they will to the world,
fhould the public be led ever to inveftigate the one
or the other.

From the many converfations we have had here
with Tuan Hadjee Cutchil, we are confirmed in
opinion that cloves and nutmegs are produced in
many places which the Dutch are, or affect to be,
ftrangers to; where the inhabitants are not fubject
to any prince or potentate in alliance with, or tributary to them ; and on iflands, even where there
are no people. As he has very readily confented
to embark with you in a fmall country veffel (a
Sooloo Prow) and his accounts and reprefentati-
ons give us a latitude to hope for fome favourable
difcoveries; we think we fhould not deferve the
appellation of faithful fervants, if we delayed our
refearches into an object of the firft magnitude,
when it can be profecuted with no heavy charge,
and wears the profpect of terminating to the
greateft national good.

It would be abfurd to lay reftrictions, or to pretend to impofe rules in a bufinefs of this nature.

It

It is an undertaking that requires prudence, difcre-tion, and perfeverance ; therefore, we have thought it beft to leave it to yourfelf.

Under this cover come fome information and remarks, to which you are no ftranger; likewife fome extracts from Mr. Dalrymple's Memoirs, which we recommend to your perufal.

If the object in expectation fails of the wifhed-for fuccefs, yet your voyage may have a very good effect towards the improvement of navigation. You muft therefore be as accurate as poffible, in laying down all fhoals, &c. as well as explicit in your remarks and obfervations. Charts and draw-ings thereof muft be taken, minutely marking every thing that may conduce to the above pur-pofe. We wifh you a good voyage, and remain,

Your affectionate friends,

and humble fervants,

BALAMBANGAN,   JOHN HERBERT,
12th October, 1774.   EDWARD COLES,
                 THOMAS PALMER.

The Dutch feem to claim a right to all the Mo-lucca iflands, more from the forbearance of other European nations, than from any juft title. I am not certain whether the iflands of Waygiou, Myfol, Batanta and Salwattay, may not alfo be claimed by them; but I refolved, from Tuan Hadjee's report, and what I had learned of others, to go beyond thofe iflands, as far as the coaft of New Guinea, where furely the Dutch can have no exclufive pretenfions.

Senfible

Senfible of the jealoufy and watchfulnefs of the Dutch in the Molucca iflands, near which it was neceffary for me to pafs on my way to New Guinea, no lefs than of the danger of navigating in narrow feas, in a veffel that drew much water, I preferred a fmall one of ten tons burden.

In a large veffel we muft have been cautious of coming near land. The crew I had (Malays chiefly) make bad failors in fquare rigged veffels; and, having never been accuftomed to lie in an open road, or be in a harbour, without the indulgence of going on fhore, they would not have had patience to remain on board, which even in a floop of thirty tons, would have been neceffary : and, in a veffel no larger than thirty tons, with fuch a crew, I muft have frequently run the rifk of being wrecked, had I made free with the fhore. This I was enabled to do boldly, in a boat of fmall burden, that rowed, and drew little water; and, when fhe touched the ground, which often happened, part of the crew, by jumping overboard, could pufh her off again ; and, when in harbour, every body had free accefs to the fhore.

In a large veffel, I muft have carried with me a ftock of provifions, which the fettlement we fitted out from, could not well afford; befides, when at places that afforded provifions, in a veffel of any fize at anchor, I muft have fent my boat afhore, which would be liable to infult. I have known many fuch things befall fhips boats in Malay countries, where defigning people entice the

crew

crew or commanding officers to be off their guard, by a treacherous fhew of civility. Commodore Watfon, in the Revenge, loft his boat going through fome ftraits, by the ifland Salwattay. Many voyages have failed, many trading country vef-fels have been cut off, and fome wrecked, from unexpected accidents of this kind.

The veffel I had, and which fhall be hereafter defcribed, was perfectly fuited, in her conftruc-tion and manner of working, to the crew, who were moftly Malays, or natives of thofe iflands that lie eaft of Atcheen Head : feveral were Bi-fayans, that is, natives of the Philippines, and were chriftians ; fome were Magindano and Mo-lucca Mahometans, vaffals and flaves to Tuan Hadjee ; two were from Bencoolen and Pulo Nays, and three were Indoftan failors (lafcars).

Fearing, that, if I carried many Europeans with me, quarrels might arife between them and the Malays, who cannot (unlefs indeed properly trained) be fuppofed fubject to difcipline, ac-cording to our ideas of it; I therefore engaged only two white men to go with me, who were plain good feamen, David Baxter, mate, and Laurence Lound, gunner. They knew not a word of the Malay tongue, at leaft for many months after they embarked ; confequently, could not well quarrel with their Mahometan fhip-mates. However, they foon learnt to fpeak Malays, and at the fame time they learnt how to behave towards them, that is, never to hurry or abufe them. To enfure fobriety, I carried

with

with me very little wine, or ſtrong liquor: my
Malay crew never required any, and my two
Europeans ſoon reconciled themſelves to tea and
coffee.

I had one perſon of rank, education, and
good behaviour with me, Tuan Hadjee. He
had ſeveral of his own country with him, his
ſlaves and vaſſals, for whom he drew pay; and
who often took liberties, againſt which I found
it imprudent to remonſtrate. This perſon had
made a pilgrimage to Mecca. He was a relation of the Sultan of Batchian, and was well
rewarded before he came on board, by Mr.
Herbert, who made him a captain of Buggeſſes, having beſides great expectations. I knew
I could depend on his fidelity, and that he
would be of great ſervice in the voyage, having formerly been at Dory harbour, on the
coaſt of New Guinea. Without ſuch a perſon
I ſhould have been in danger from a Malay
crew; eſpecially as I had property on board to
bear the expence of the voyage, victualling, &c.
I made my account from the beginning, that
wherever I found people, I ſhould there find proviſions; and, I thank God, we were not diſappointed.

The veſſel, in which I made the voyage, was
called the Tartar-Galley. She was a Sooloo
boat, or prow, about ten tons burthen. Her
keel was twenty-five feet long, and ſhe had a
kind of gallery built on each ſide, from ſtem
to ſtern, projecting about thirty inches over each
gunnel.

gunnel. Here fat the rowers, fometimes twenty in number. She overhung fo much forward and abaft, that fhe was forty feet long. Her draft of water was generally three foot and a half. We had four fwivel guns, two blunderbuffes, ten mufkets, and fix piftols, befide lances, bows and arrows.

She had for a maft an artillery triangle * (gin or tripod) made of three ftout bamboos, which could be ftruck with the greateft eafe by three men. On this was hoifted a large four cornered fail, called by the Malays, lyre tanjong (pointed fail), becaufe the upper corner appears fharp or pointed. I fixed to her a foremaft clofe forward, and a bowfprit; and gave her a lateen, or three cornered forefail. I alfo gave her a lateen mizen; but, when it blew frefh, I took down the lyre tanjong from the tripod maft, as it was a very large fail, and put in its place a lateen fail. The fails then refembled thofe of the galleys in the Mediterranean. One very great advantage attends the lyre tanjong, which is this; that when the wind frefhens, it can, without lowering, be inftantly diminifhed or made fmaller, by eafing or flacking the fheet, and at the fame time winding up the fail, by two men turning the crofs bar or winch that is fixed to the in-

* A great improvement might be made in navigation by means of the tripod maft. It would be a very good fubftitute for a mizen maft to cruizers; becaufe, when ftruck, they would appear at a diftance like brigs, and deceive an enemy. Lafh two London wherries together, and give this double veffel the tripod maft and lyre tanjong, it will beat the faft failing boats, at leaft three to two.

ner

ner end of the boom, and which spreads the lower part of the sail. By this means, the sail may be entirely rolled up until the boom touches the yard; the sail being always in this compact manner, as seamen call it, *taken in*. In the same manner, it may be set again instantly, or let out, by turning the winch back the other way; or half set, according to the weather. The galley steered with two commoodies (rudders), a sort of broad paddle; but one generally served.

She was covered almost entirely with the leaves of a certain Palm tree, called Nipa, such as the natives cover houses with on the south west coast of Sumatra, and in almost all Malay countries; it being a light kind of thatch, which keeps off sunshine and rain. One small part abaft was covered with boards; and this made a little apartment, called, by the Malays, Koran. *

At Tomoguy, one of the Molucca islands, I hauled her ashore to clean her bottom; and there I raised her one streak or plank, about fifteen inches high, as I found her rather too low to proceed down the coast of New Guinea, she being apt to ship water in bad weather. I also new roofed or thatched her there.---At Magindano, (as I had leisure) I decked her, and turned her into a schooner.

* The reason why the Malays, who are Mahometans, call it the Koran, is, that they seldom travel by sea without the Alcoran; which they always deposit in the best and safest place, from that custom terming the cabin, Koran.

List

Lift of the Crew of the Tartar Galley.

Captain THOMAS FORREST,	Commander.
David Baxter,	Mate.
Laurence Lound,	Gunner.
William Hunt,	{ Paffenger to Sooloo. Left at Sooloo.
5 Ifhmael Tuan Hadjee,	Pilot.
Tuan Imum, Ifhmael Jerrybatoo,	} Helmfmen.
Matthew,	Steward.
Jaffier,	Serang.
10 Saban, Marudo, Abdaraman, Dya, Andrew, 15 George, Mungary, Diego, Jacob, Rum Johny, 20 Gibalu,	Seamen.
Panjang,	Cook. *
Strap,	Boy.

* He died at Magindano—being the only perfon I loft during the voyage.

CHAP,

C H A P. II.

Departure from Balambangan—Touched at the Iflands of Cagayan Sooloo, and Pangatarran—Arrived at Sooloo, where we found a Molucca Prow loaded with Nutmegs.——Touched at the Ifland Tonkyl —Left it unexpectedly—Saw the Ifland Sangir— Paffed Karakita, Palla, and Siao——Paffed the Iflands Ternate and Tidore—Arrived at Malaleo Harbour, in the Straits of Latalatta—Sailed thence and arrived at Biffory Harbour—Tuan Hadjee vifits the Sultan of Batchian.

ON *Wednefday* the 9th of *November*, in the morning I rowed out of the North-eaft harbour of Balambangan with the aforementioned crew; faluting the fettlement with five guns, and having three returned. About noon we had rain and calms; then light foutherly winds. Towards evening we anchored in four and a half fathom water, muddy ground, clofe to the Ifland of Banguey; the fhips at Balambangan being ftill in fight. Here we fent afhore our canoe, which brought fome water out of a fmall river on the ifland of Banguey. In the evening we weighed, and rowed on. We foon got a frefh breeze at fouth-weft, and about midnight anchored; but, finding the current fet to the eaftward, weighed again.

On *Thurfday* the 10th, at funrife, we had calms and light breezes from the north-weft. We then

had

1774. November.

had paffed the iflands called the Salenfingers, but
juft faw them.   At feven we rowed with fourteen
oars, and continued fo moft part of the day, flacking at times when it was very hot.   In the night
we had a fquall from the north eaft, with thunder,
lightning, and rain.   The night was dark and
gloomy ; but this, being common in low latitudes,
little affects thofe who are accuftomed to it, as it
feldom does harm : and, had our veffel been tight
overhead, we might have paffed the night tolerably ; for during thefe tornado's, it is the cuftom of
Malays to lie to at fea, as they are generally accompanied with uncertain gufts of wind.   This
we did for feveral hours, dropping a wooden anchor from the weather-bow, which kept the veffel's
head to the fea and made her lie eafy.   But the
rain beat through the Palm leaves with which the
veffel was covered, fo violently, that we Europeans
found it very uncomfortable : the crew did not
much mind it.

Friday the 11th, at funrife, we faw the Ifland of
Cagayan Sooloo, bearing eaft, diftant about eight
leagues.   It is of middling height, and covered
with trees ; but not quite fo much as Malay Iflands
generally are ; fome fpots upon it appearing from
fea clear of wood, and cultivated.   A frefh wind
fpringing up from the fouth-weft, and increafing,
we fixed the lateen mizen for a forefail.   At three
P. M. I difcovered in the road, or harbour, a prow,
with many people on board, and canoes going
backwards and forwards to her from the fhore.
At four, I anchored pretty near this veffel, and
found her to be a Mangaio prow, or armed
                                    veffel

veffel that goes a cruifing, generally amongft the
Philippine iflands, called Bifaya. She was not
above four tons burthen, looked very fmart, having
a gallery fore and aft for the rowers to fit on, as we
had ; having alfo the tripod maft and lyre tanjong,
and mounting four brafs fwivel guns called Ran-
takers, carrying each a four-ounce ball. She belonged to the Rajah of the ifland ; and I apprehend
from the hurry they were in, when we firft appeared that they were a little afraid.

When we were at anchor, the weftermoft part
of the ifland bore W. by S. two miles diftant, and
the eaftermoft part of a reef, that lay off the faid
weft part of the ifland, bore S. by W. one mile diftant. This formed a good road, if not a harbour;
being fhut in from the eaftern fwell, by a reef of
rocks : two fmall iflands bearing at the fame time,
E. by S. three leagues diftant, called the Mambalu
iflands, in Mr. Dalrymple's maps. Early in the
morning of the 12th, I went on fhore, and waited
on the Rajah, who fpoke good Malays. I enquired
the deftination of his privateer ; he anfwered, *Dio
Pigy Mangaio, de Nigri Bifaya :* " She is going a
" cruife amongft the Philippines." I carried with
me a tea-kettle, fome tea and fugar candy—and he
drank tea with me, furnifhing tea-pot and cups.
I told him tea was *(Englifh punio Ciry)* Englifh
Beetle, alluding to the beetle leaf, which all Eaft
Indians chew. He laughed, and faid it was very
good Ciry.

The Rajah who was very civil and facetious—
afked after Tuan Hadjee, who he had heard was

on

on board. I told him, he would pay his respects to him that afternoon. I was accompanied by Tuan Imum, one of my helmsmen, a kind of a Muffelman priest, and a great favourite with Tuan Hadjee, who deferred his visit, as we did not choose to be both out of the veffel together, for my two Europeans did not as yet know a word of Malays.

The Rajah ordered a very good fowl to be dreffed in a curry, of which Tuan Imum and I partook, after walking about and bathing in a fine pool of fresh water.

I prefented him with a pocket compass, two pieces of courfe chintz, and a little tea and fugar candy, which Malays are generally fond of; and of which I had laid in a pretty good stock at Balambangan. In return, he gave me a goat, fome fowls, fruits, &c. and immediately after dinner, I returned on board.

About two in the afternoon, Tuan Hadjee, who was very well pleafed to hear of the civil treatment I had received from the Rajah, went on fhore. He returned at fix, with fowls, fruits, &c. which the Rajah had given him, in return for fome prefents he had made. During our fhort stay here, I repaired, and made at least water tight, the leaky roof of the veffel.

In the cool of the evening, I founded the harbour, and found the most water in it fix fathom, the least three, with three fathom on the bar at
half

half flood. The tide rifes fix feet on the fprings, and a rifing and fetting moon makes high water. The bar is coral rocks, about thirty yards in width, and ten yards acrofs, or over : within and without the bar is clean fand, free from rocks; and it will admit with fafety, veffels drawing fifteen feet water.

Cagayan Sooloo is a pleafant looking ifland, the foil is rich, and the vegetation is fo luxuriant, that I found every where the grafs called (Lallang) Couch Grafs, grown to the height, even of fix feet; the foil being black mold. The Rajah told me there was another harbour on the eaft coaft of the ifland; which is about twenty miles round, lies in the latitude of 7° N. and longitude 116°, 45' and its diftance from Balambangan is 100 miles E. by S.

The ifland is dependant on Sooloo, the Rajah being a Datoo * there, and is much frequented by Mangaio Prows in general. Even the fmall Mangaio Prows, of the Oran Tedong (men of Tedong) a barbarous piratical people, who live up certain rivers, on the north-eaft part of Borneo, are admitted here, as the Rajah is, I fuppofe, too weak to dare to refufe them. Thefe Oran Tedong, are not Mahometans : this circumftance, and their country being under the dominion of Sooloo, may be the reafon why the Sooloos will not permit them to come into any of their ports on that ifland, as they difcountenance their piracies. Something more of the Oran Tedong will be faid hereafter.

* Datoo, fignifies baror—nobleman.

C

On

On *Sunday* the 13th, we rowed out of Cagayan harbour, early in the morning, and found a ſtrong current ſet to the ſouthward. At ſun-ſet, Cagayan bore north, five leagues diſtant, we having been retarded by calms. A freſh breeze ſpringing up ſoon after from the N. N. W. ſteered E. by N. ſome iſlands that lye to the northward of Cagayan being in ſight; and the Mambalu iſlands to the ſouthward bearing S. S. W. ſeven leagues. Our latitude, obſerved at noon, was 6° 40′ N.

On the 14th, at ſunriſe, we had a fine breeze from the northward : at ten it ſhifted to the weſt-ward, and blew freſh; hoiſted our mizen for a foreſail, and ſet a lug main ſail. At the ſame time, our canoe broke looſe; and, as it blew ve-ry freſh, we could not recover her. At noon, it being more moderate, we ſet our proper ſails. At 4 P. M. there being little wind, we rowed with all our oars, being eighteen in number; and, at three in the morning, we had ſome ſevere ſqualls, followed by heavy rain. Our courſe to day was E. by N. It being cloudy, we had no obſervation.

On the 15th, at three P. M. we ſaw the iſland of Pangatarran.* At ſunſet, we were within three leagues of it, and kept rowing and ſailing

---

* Pangatarran, a long flat iſland, has no freſh water; nor is any good anchoring neaɪ, except in ſome few places. It abounds in Coco nuts, and a fruit called Guava. Tappool, Seaſſee and Pangatarran, are the only iſlands of the Soolod Archipelago to which the Spaniards have preſerved a title, by conſent of the Sooloos. Tappool and Seaſſee are of middling height, well cultivated and inhabited.

all

all night; we ſtruck all our ſails in a ſquall, within a cable's length of the ſhore, but had no ſoundings. At midnight anchored, in two fathoms water, ſandy ground, abreaſt of an old ruined fort;
but ſaw no people.

On *Wedneſday* the 16th, finding nobody here,
I weighed and rowed more to the northward. I
then ſaw ſome people belonging to the iſland, and
ſome Sooloo people. From thoſe I learnt, that
there were two Molucca Prows at Sooloo, loaded
with nutmegs and mace; and, at Tuan Hadjee's
ſuggeſtion, I reſolved to go thither, as it was not
out of our way, to endeavour to perſuade the
Noquedahs (commanders) to carry their nutmegs
to Balambangan. I therefore immediately got under way, rowed and ſailed towards Sooloo. At
midnight could ſee lights aſhore, in the town of
Bowang, which is the chief town of Sooloo. As
Pangatarran abounds in Coco nuts, I laid in a
good ſtock.

On *Thurſday* the 17th, I anchored in Sooloo
road, juſt before ſunriſe. I found riding here
the Antelope, Captain Smith, a ſhip belonging to
the Honourable Company, and only one Molucca
Prow, beſide many ſmall prows and veſſels belonging to the Sooloos. As I anchored cloſe to
the Molucca prow, the Noquedah came on board,
and informed me, that the other prow, after diſ-
poſing of her cargo, had ſailed; he likewiſe told
us, that he had ſold, or at leaſt bargained for his
nutmegs with the Sultan: therefore he declined
going to Balambangan. He was very glad to ſee
Tuan Hadjee.

As

As I was anxious to fee this eaftern veffel, I went on board; I found her about thirty tons burthen, high built, and fitted with the tripod maft, and lyre tanjong. I bought from one of the crew, about twenty pounds of very good mace for a red handkerchief: I alfo bought fome fago cakes. The people belonging to this prow were exceeding civil, and lent me their canoe (fampan) to fetch water.

Captain Smith perceiving I was without a boat, very politely fent his to attend me; in which, after vifiting him, Tuan Hadjee and I went afhore, and paid our refpects to Mr. Corbet, the Englifh refident, who received me with great civility, and entertained me at his houfe. I then went and paid my refpects to the Sultan, whofe name was Ifrael: he was fon to the old Sultan Amiralmoomine, and had his education at Manilla, where his father and he had long been prifoners, and were relieved laft war from their captivity, by the arms of the Englifh. Amiralmoomine being old, had given up the reins of government to his fon Ifrael.

After dining with Mr. Corbet, in company with captain Smith and his officers, I went and paid my refpects to Datoo Alamoodine, who was intended to fucceed Sultan Ifrael, as he had no children. I alfo vifited the Datoos Almilbahar the admiral, and Almilbadar the general. I found the Sultan, and all thefe gentlemen, concluded I was going to Magindano;* nor did I undeceive them.

* The Englifh ufed to call it Mindano, and I fhall often call it fo.

In

In the cool of the evening, I had the pleafure of feeing the Sultan's niece Potely (princefs) Diamelen, and the general's daughter Fatima, ride on horfe-back, accompanied by feveral Datoos and others. Their manner is, to ride backwards and forwards, the length of a long broad ftreet, upon fandy ground, forcing their horfes on a quick trot, and checking them when they attempt to gallop. The horfes accuftomed to this, trot very faft.

Thefe two ladies were remarkably handfome, and were reckoned fair; which they certainly were by comparifon. They wore waiftcoats of fine muflin, clofe fitted to their bodies; their necks to the upper parts of the breaft being bare. From the waift downwards, they wore a loofe robe, girt with an embroidered zone or belt about the middle, with a large clafp of gold, and a precious ftone. This loofe robe like a petticoat, came over their drawers, and reached to the mid-dle of the leg; the drawers of fine muflin, reach-ing to the ancle. They rode acrofs with very fhort ftirrups, and wore their hair clubbed, atop, Chinefe fafhion. Before the exercife was over, Diamelen's hair fell loofe, and hung in black fhining ringlets, moft gracefully down her back, as far as the fad-dle. They often put fweet oils on their hair, which gives it a glofs. The ladies fat their horfes remark-ably well; and this is an exercife women of fa-fhion indulge all over the ifland. Their faddles have in the middle a vacancy, which muft make it eafy for the horfe, like thofe recommended for troopers by marfhal Saxe in his Reveries.

Here

Here I got excellent refreſhment : oranges full
as good as thoſe in China, and all kinds of
the beſt tropical fruits—very good beef, fowls,
&c.

On *Friday* the 18th, we had ſqually weather,
the winds at S. W. At noon we parted from our
grapnel, and let go another, by which we held
faſt. Captain Smith aſſiſted me in the evening
very readily with his boat and people, to ſweep
for the loſt grapnel, to no purpoſe, the ground
where it happened to be dropt being rocky. I
had from Mr. Corbet a ſtout bamboo for a fore-
maſt, alſo two Engliſh enſigns. I ſhould have
ſtayed here longer, at leaſt until I had got a canoe ; but, the road being expoſed to the north
weſt wind and ſwell, tho' ſheltered from all other
winds, and this being the time of the ſhifting of
the monſoon, I thought proper to be gone.

On *Saturday* the 19th, I ſailed from Sooloo road,
with the wind at N. W. blowing freſh, and ſteered N. E. At noon we ſaw the two iſlands of
Duoblod ; the northermoſt is the ſmaller. At four
in the morning we ſaw the iſland of Baſilan. It
is an iſland belonging to Sooloo, and about the
ſame ſize ; the weſt end of it bore E. by N. diſtant
ſix leagues. Here I found the ebb tide ſet very
ſtrong to the eaſtward, much ſtronger than the
flood tide ſets to the weſtward : this is the caſe during the S. W. monſoon, and the current had not
yet changed.

Sunday

Sunday the 20th. Next to Duoblod, in an eaſt direction, is an iſland with a large hummoc or hillock upon it ; it is called Tantaran in Mr. Dalrymple's map. As the weather threatened, I attempted, but in vain, to get to it, the current and tide ſetting ſtrong to the eaſtward, betweeen it and two very ſmall iſlands called Dippool, which lie ſouth of it, and are ſhaped like ſugar loaves ; the one much larger than the other. I therefore bore away for a low iſland, lying farther eaſt. At eight A. M. I reached it, and found it ſurrounded with coral rocks, yet I came to amongſt them, with a wooden anchor, in three fathom water, the weather looking very unſettled, and the wind blowing freſh at N. N. W.

On *Monday* the 21ſt, about noon, I ſpoke with a ſmall fiſhing boat, or prow, with only one Sooloo man in her ; who told us, that further on, was a harbour, into which we might go ; and informed me that the iſland was called Tonkyl. I accordingly weighed, but obſerving that it was a dry harbour, I did not chuſe to go into it. However, I anchored in three fathom water, on a ſmall ſpot of ſand, juſt without the harbour. Here I bought ſome very good fiſh, exceeding cheap, of ſome of the natives who were out in their boats. Notwithſtanding I lay under the lee of the iſland, cloſe to the ſhore, yet I gave a reward to ſome of the natives for bringing fire-wood on board, not chuſing to truſt my people on ſhore to cut it, as I perceived many armed men, of whom I was

ſuſpicious ;

suspicious; and who calling out, endeavoured to persuade me, but to no purpose, to go into the harbour.

The weather still having a very unsettled aspect, I was unwilling to put to sea, to continue our voyage, but thought of going over to the island Basilan, which was then in sight, and where I was told by Tuan Hadjee's people, there was choice of good harbours ;— at the same time, the fisherman, of whom I had bought the fish, offered to come early next morning, and conduct me to a very good harbour on that island ; I accordingly engaged him.

About eleven at night the wind came from the eastward, along shore, and blew fresh. We got up our grapnel, but the vessel casting wrong, touched upon the rocks. As she forged on without any sail, I instantly took out the piece of wood which secured the fore bamboo of the tripod mast, near the stem, and let the mast fall. Luckily it fell aslant against the mizen mast, which broke its fall and saved it. We then, with poles, set the vessel's head round, got up the mast, and made sail to the S. E. with the wind at E. N. E. I was apprehensive that had I been cast away upon this island, the Sooloos might at least have plundered us.

In the morning the weather was more moderate. We found one of the flooks of the grapnel straightened a little, probably by having caught hold of a rock. At noon we were in latitude 5° 30′ N. having run forty-eight miles on a S. E. by E.

courseA

courfe fince morning. The fea was now fmoother, and ran in a more even manner than it did, when we left the land ; it being then very irregular, and the veffel making water.

On *Tuefday* the 22d, we had moderate weather, and ran eighty-two miles on an E. S. E. courfe : and at noon we were in the latitude of 5° 3′ N.

To-day Tuan Hadjee told me, that it was highly imprudent to go to the coaft of New Guinea, whither we were bound, being only one veffel; and that we ran the rifk of being cut off by the Papuas. He faid nothing of this at Balamban-gan. We had there propofed to go to the north-ward of Morty (which ifland lies near the north part of the ifland Gilolo or Halamahera, the largeft of the Moluccas) in the veffel we had , and now for the firft time he ftarted objections. I confider-ed it imprudent to do any thing abfolutely oppofite to his opinion or advice, therefore agreed to go between the ifland Gilolo and Celebes, in order to purchafe, and fit up a Corocoro *, at fome con-venient

* A corocoro is a veffel generally fitted with out-riggers, with a high arched ftem and ftern, like the point of a half moon. They are ufed by the inhabitants of the Molucca iflands chiefly, and the Dutch have fleets of them at Amboyna, which they employ as guarda coftas. They have them from a very fmall fize, to above ten tons burden ; and on the crofs pieces which fupport the out-riggers, there are often put fore and aft planks, on which the people fit and paddle, befide thofe who fit in the veffel on each gunnel. In fmooth water they can be paddled very faft, as many hands may be employed in different ranks or rows. They are fteered with two commoodies, (broad paddles) and not with a rudder. When they are high out of
the

venient place thereabouts, that we might be two veffels in company. This pleafed him much. I found he had a ftrong inclination to vifit Batchian, the Sultan of which was his near relation.

On *Wednefday* the 23d, we had moderate wea-ther, and wefterly winds; fteered S. E. by E. fe-venty miles. At noon we were in the latitude of 4° 34', and one hundred and fifty miles eaft of the meridian of Tonkyl. This day we had many ripplings of currents, which I imputed to the mon-foon's changing.

On *Thurfday* the 24th, we had fair weather; fteered S. E. eighty miles: at noon our latitude was 3° 55' N.

On *Friday* the 25th, we had wefterly winds and fqually weather. Ran under a foul weather main-fail, and fteered as beft fuited the veffel's eafe, be-tween the fouth and eaft, as fhe laboured much, and fhipped water. Kept baling, as we had no pump, every half hour. Many of the rattan lafh-ings were alfo found broke. *

In the morning we faw the ifland of Sangir, ap-pearing large and high; the body of it, bearing about north-eaft, was covered with clouds. We

the water, they ufe oars; but, on the out-riggers, they always ufe paddles. Frequent mention is made of corocoros in the hiftory of Amboyna.

* The ends of the beams went through, or pierced the veffel's fides; the beams were tied to handles on the planks, which were nailed to the timbers.

fteered

steered to the northward of a cluster of five islands, which lie to the southward of Sangir; the two principal are called Karakita and Palla, as I was informed by Abdaraman, one of Tuan Hadjee's people, who had been there. Each of these two islands may be about five or six miles round. They are about three miles asunder, bearing N. N. E. and S. S. W. of one another; Karakita being to the northward, and are both cultivated; Palla, rather the largest, has a table land upon it. In passing Karakita, we saw a small canoe about two miles from us, which shunned us, paddling away very fast. On the north-west side of Karakita there is a bay, perhaps a harbour. Abdaraman could not particularly inform me about it. Opposite to the mouth of the bay there appears a beautiful row of coco nut trees on the ridge of a hill, as in the view.

Abdaraman told me there was a harbour at Pulo Siao; which island we saw bearing south from Karakita about ten leagues, and was partly wrapped in clouds, it being very high. To the westward of Karakita, and north-west of Palla, are three islands, one of them not above one mile round, which appeared like a gunner's coin or wedge. The other two are something larger. To the southward of Sangir, and near it, are also three small islands.

A small rocky island, with a few coco nut trees upon it, and many rocks, like sugar loaves, around it, bore E. S. E. from Karakita four miles, which, from its shape, we called the Rabbit. We passed

to

to the weftward of it within half a mile, the current fetting to the fouthward.   Karakita lies in the
latitude of 3° 16′ N. and longitude 122° 20′ E.
In my run from Tonkyl to Karakita, it was impoffible for me to be certain of my courfe and dif-
tances, as I fteered fo many different courfes to
keep the veffel eafy.   I expected to make Sangir
fooner than I did.   The currents at the beginning
of the north-eaft monfoon are uncertain, and fometimes very ftrong here, as they alfo are in the
China feas and Bay of Bengal at this feafon of the
year.   I had the greateft reafon to think I was fet
to the weftward ; and have, from my remarks
when I returned, chiefly, placed the ifland of
Sangir 2° 40′ E. of the meridian of Tonkyl ; although, by my run, I made it to be much
more.

On *Saturday* the 26th, we had moderate weather, with calms towards midnight.   We then
rowed a good deal, cheering up the rowers with
a difh of tea, which refrefhed them, and they
were fond of it, having no idea of fpirituous li-
quors; neither did any of them fmoak opium,
which Malays often do, thereby rendering themfelves unfit for duty.   In the morning the high
land of Siao bore N. W. half N. and at noon we
were in the latitude of 2° 16′ N.   To day, expect
to fee Myo and Tyfory, two fmall iflands near
Ternate, as we fometimes rowed three knots an
hour.

Early in the morning of *Sunday* the 27th, by
the light of the moon we faw the ifland Myo,
which

which is of middling height. Prefently after we faw the ifland Tyfory, juft open with its fouth end, bearing weft; Ternate Hill bearing at the fame time fouth-eaft, diftant about ten leagues. Myo lies in latitude 1° 23′ N. and longitude 122° 50′ E. Tyfory is a flat ifland, not fo large as Myo, and lies about W. by S. from it, five or fix miles diftant.* There is faid to be a good road on the coaft of Myo, and that many wild goats are upon it. It was formerly inhabited, when the Spaniards had the Moluccas; but the Dutch will not now permit any body to live there, left it fhould be convenient for the fmuggling of fpices. Tuan Hadjee told me he has been affured that fome few fpice trees grow upon it, which the Dutch know nothing of, being perfuaded they have long ago been rooted out.

On *Monday* the 28th, we had moderate weather, and in the night we rowed a good deal. I found Tuan Hadjee in high fpirits, cheering up the rowers with a certain Tactic fong, to which a man beat time with two brafs timbrels. This fong was in the Mindano tongue, and is much ufed by Mangaio boats, not only to amufe and cheer up the mind, but to give vigour to their motions in rowing. This I encouraged, that we might foon get paft the Dutch fettlements of Ternate and Tidore. I alfo gave each man a red handkerchief for their encouragement. The current was much

---

* Myo and Tyfory, in former days, furnifhed four hundred men as militia to the Sultan of Ternate. At Myo there is a harbour; and it produces cloves.
HISTOIRE GENERALLE DE L'ASIE PAR D'AVITY, p. 904.

in our favour. To day we paſſed Ternate and Tidore, and at four P. M. were abreaſt of Macquian, having moderate weather, with northerly winds. At ſunſet we paſſed Macquian, and ſailed within three miles of the weſtermoſt of the five Giaritchas, lying in latitude 00° 25′ N. The Giaritchas are a cluſter of five ſmall iſlands, lying about ſix leagues S. S. W. of Macquian. They are of middling height, with many bare rocks, intermixed with green ſpots and trees. When the ſouthermoſt bears S. by E. about ten miles diſtant, there appears a ſmall rock to the weſtward.

On *Tueſday* the 29th, having paſſed the Giaritchas, we ſteered ſouth for the ſtraits of Latalatta. At ten at night we got into a little harbour, called Malaleo, which is on the north-weſt part of the iſland Tappa; and off the ſaid north-weſt part of Tappa, are three ſmall iſles, or large rocks, about twenty-five feet high, with ſome buſhes upon them. I was told that thoſe rocks have ſome caves in them which produce birds neſts.* I therefore call them the Bird-Neſt iſlands, as none of
                                                    Tuan

---

* Edible birds neſts, built by certain birds like ſwallows in caves cloſe to the ſea, and into which the ſea flows. I have taken them from the face of a perpendicular rock, to which they ſtrongly adhered, in rows like ſemi-cups, the one touching the other. Captain Tattam at Tappanooly, told me, he has watched thoſe birds, and that they rob other birds of their eggs, part of which (the white perhaps) they mix up with ſomething elſe; and of this they form their neſts. The beſt are white and pellucid, worth five or ſix dollars per pound. There is another kind got in caves inland: they are dark coloured, full of feathers, and of very little value. Great quantities of the white kind are carried from all Malay coun-
                                                    tries

Tuan Hadjee's people could give me their proper names.

To fail into Malaleo harbour, fteer for thefe
iflands, if you come from the northward, and
leave them on the right hand. The harbour,
which is a kind of cove, will foon fhew itfelf;
and in going into it, you muft keep the right-hand
fhore on board, to avoid a fhoal on which the fea
breaks, that is on the left hand, at the entrance of
the harbour. A fhip may lie in this cove in four
fathom water perfectly land-locked, within twelve
yards of the fhore, to which it would be proper to
have a hawfer carried and made faft to a tree.
Here we found a very fragrant fmell come from
the woods. The latitude of Malaleo is oo° o6′ N.
and longitude 123° 35′ E.

On *Wednefday* the 30th, at funrife, we weighed
and rowed out of this fnug fmall harbour; we
turned to the right, and entered the ftraits of
Lalalatta, which divide the ifland Lalalatta from
the ifland Tappa. Thefe ftraits are about one

tries to China, where they are in great efteem, very defervedly,
as when ftewed, they are exceeding delicate and nutritious.
The Chinefe have a trick of moiftening them, to make them
heavy for fale.

It is very probable the birds ufe that glutinous fea plant
called Agal Agal, in making their nefts, as Mr. Dalrymple, in
his account of the Sooloo curiofities, fays the natives reported
to him.

I have feen in fmall iflands, in the Sooloo Archipelago,
under overhanging rocks at the fea fide, a glutinous fubftance
fticking to the rock, yellow and pellucid, and of an infipid
tafte. The fifhermen (Badjoos), that frequent thofe iflands in
covered boats, told me, the birds ufed it in building their nefts.

mile

mile and a half in length, and in some places not above forty yards broad, with good soundings in them. At the end there is a little island like an ordinary dwelling-house in size. Opposite to it, and not fifty yards from it, across the channel, on the island Tappa, we found a charming pool of fresh water, where, after filling our jars, we all bathed: we then weighed, left it on the right hand, and suddenly came out of the narrow straits, already mentioned, into the wide straits from Latalatta and the island of Mandioly, which may be eight miles across. We lay to part of the night, and at daylight passed a rock within thirty yards of the island Mandioly, like a pigeon-house in size and shape, with a bush or two atop. We left it on the left hand, as we steered into the harbour of Biffory. When the said pigeon-house rock bears north, or even long before that, the peninsula of Biffory, which forms the harbour, will shew itself as in the view. Look out for the reef that lies off the peninsula to seaward, and giving it a reasonable birth, you may steer in eighteen, sixteen, and fourteen fathom muddy ground into the harbour. There you lie perfectly smooth in twelve fathom water: fresh water is to be got in a small river, the bar of which is smooth. The harbour of Biffory lies in latitude 00° 18' south, and longitude 123° 40' east. About ten miles south of the Pigeon-House Rock, there is another rock, nearly of the same size, and as near to the land. I call it from its shape, the Obtuse Cone. It has also a bush or two atop.

On the 31st, we had fair weather and westerly winds; we saw no boats, nor any people all day long

long. Tuan Hadjee prepared to go to vifit his
relation, the Sultan of Batchian, accompanied by
my fervant Matthew. They had about fifteen
miles to walk.

C H A P. III.

*Account of the Ifland of Gilolo, from the Information of
Ifhmael Tuan Hadjee and others—Of the Sago Tree,
and the Method of baking the Sago Bread, with a
Comparifon between the Sago, and Bread Fruit Trees.*

I Can fay nothing of the ifland of Gilolo* from my
own experience, having never been upon it. But
the following account I learnt from Tuan Hadjee,
at leifure hours during the voyage; and I have
thought proper to introduce it in this place.

The great ifland of Gilolo, or Halamahera,
which feems to divide the Indian ocean to the
eaftward from the great fouth fea, extends from
the latitude of 3° 10' north, to 00° 50' fouth;
the ifland Morty extending northward of it, to 3°
35' north latitude.

Gilolo was once under one fovereign, Serif,
who came from Mecca, and who was brother to
the Sultan of Magindano, as alfo to the Sultan
of Borneo.

---

* The Chinefe are faid to have poffeffed the Moluccas firft,
then the Javans, Buggeffes, and Malays, then the Arabs.
   BARTHOLOMEW D'ARGINSOLA's Conqueft of the Moluccas.

D   On

On the weft fide of this ifland, lie the fmall iflands of Ternate and Tidore, which give title to two princes, in ftrict alliance with the Dutch.

On Ternate the Dutch have a ftrong ftone caftle, with a garrifon of three hundred and fifty Europeans; and on the ifland refides the Sultan, who lives in great ftate.

The Dutch, in order to compenfate their allowing the Sultan no power to interfere with their plan of curbing all kind of free and open trade (not only with Magindano and other more diftant parts, but with any adjacent country) fhow him great attention and refpect, becaufe, if this were not clofely watched, and put under fevere reftrictions, it would foon affect their monopoly of the clove and nutmeg, the former of which they permit to be cultivated at Amboyna, and the latter at Banda only.

In order to effect this, or rather to approximate towards it, the Dutch, with great wifdom, difcourage the inhabitants of Gilolo from trading with Celebes, Bouro, Ooby, Ceram, Myfol, Salwatty, and other parts. Such prows or veffels, as clear out regularly for thofe iflands, with grain, fago, or other articles permitted, muft have a pafs, which is not only expenfive, but got with difficulty, and muft be renewed every voyage. This ftrictnefs is to prevent their trading in fpices, growing in abundance, in many retired fpots of the large and woody ifland of Gilolo. They are generally cut down in places of eafy accefs, and near the

sea;

fea ; but what may be thus deftroyed, is not, perhaps, the hundredth part of the trees, producing
this precious fruit.

The parties fent out on fuch bufinefs, confift
generally of a military officer, or fome civil fervant
belonging to the Dutch, with three or four European attendants, and perhaps twenty or thirty Buggefs foldiers, with their officer. They generally
make it a party of pleafure ; and the Buggefs officer (while the chief is regaling himfelf in the heat
of the day) fets off to the woods with fome of his
men, where he executes his commiffion juft as it
fuits his convenience ; taking care to bring back
plenty of branches, to fhow his affiduity, when,
perhaps, they are all from one tree.

Sometime a ferjeant at an out-poft, to get into
favour with his chief, fends an account of his having difcovered on a certain fpot, a parcel of fpice
trees ; with news, perhaps, at the fame time, that
he has deftroyed them all—this gets him into favour. Poffibly the chief's domeftics might inform
him of many more fuch fpots at hand ; but they
are too wife to fay much on fo delicate a fubject.

A Dutch governor of Ternate, once travelling
on the main of Gilolo, ftopped at a Malay village,
where he faw a long notched ftick made of the
clove tree *. The inhabitants (whofe houfes, as

* The clove tree I never faw : but on the ifland Tappa I faw
a nutmeg tree, and gathered the unripe fruit, which exactly refembles our peach. The thick unripe coat that covers the
mace, we ftewed in our difhes.

in

in other Malay countries, are built on ftilts or poits,
about five or fix foot from the ground) ufe fuch
notched fticks as ladders to afcend by, about the
bignefs of a man's leg.   Unfortunately, however,
for the poor people of the village, this ftick or
ladder, was longer than fufficient to mount to any
of their houfes ; and being of the clove tree, they
were deemed guilty of having fomehow dealt in
that forbidden fruit.   The Dutch are fevere upon
thofe occafions.   Tuan Hadjee told me, the Sultan of Batchian applies frequently to the governor
of Ternate for fpices, to fhow his zeal, though they
grow in abundance near his houfe ; fpices being
regularly fent to Ternate by the annual fhip from
Batavia.

The dominions of the Sultan of Ternate *,
comprehend the greateft part of the north of
Gilolo,

* The kingdom of Ternate drew militia from the following
countries and iflands under its dominion in former times :

From the fixteen burgs of Ternate	3000
Ifland Motir	300
Gazia	300
Xula	4000
Bouro	4000
Veranulla near Amboyna	15,000
Buana and Manipa	3000
Myo and Tyfory	400
Bao and Jaquita on Gilolo	1000
Bata China on ditto	10,000
The north-eaft part of Celebes gave from Tetoli and Bohol	6000
Kydipan	7000
Gorantalu and Ilbolo	10,000
Tomine	12,000

Dondo

Gilolo, which, for a Malay country, is pretty well inhabited. Under his dominion, is alſo a great part of the north eaſt quarter of Celebes, where are the Dutch ſettlements of Manado and Gorontalu, which they maintain for two reaſons ; firſt, as frontiers to Gilolo, on the weſt and north weſt ; and ſecondly, as producing much gold, which the Dutch receive in exchange for the cotton cloths of Indoſtan, and opium from Bengal, whilſt the Sultan has only certain revenues from the lands. To him alſo belongs the iſland of Sangir, with the adjacent iſlands of Siao, Karakita, Tagulanda, Banka, and Telluſyang, of which more will be ſaid hereafter.

The iſland Morty belongs alſo to the Sultan of Ternate ; it is very poorly inhabited, and is ſaid to have many groves of the libby or ſago tree, amongſt its woods. Parties go often thither from Gilolo, for no other purpoſe than to cut them down for the flour or pith. Morty looks very pleaſant from the ſea, gently riſing from the beach. The Dutch ſtrictly guard the ſtraits between Morty and Gilolo, with Panchallangs (veſſels of one maſt, and the lyre tanjong) and with Corocoros ; but, the guarda coſ-

Dondo	———	———	700
Labaque	———	———	1000
Japua	———	———	10,000
Iſland Sangir or Sanguir		———	3000
		———	90,700

The fort of Ternate was taken from the Portugueſe in 1606. There were found in it forty pieces of braſs cannon.

DESCRIPTION GENERALLE DE L'ASIE PAR PERE
D'AVITAY, p. 904.

tas

tas of Gilolo, are chiefly panchallangs and floops.
Twelve panchallangs are kept at Ternate. The
guarda coftas of Amboyna and Ceram, are chiefly
Corocoros, and at Banda, floops. Prows often go
a trading from Sooloo to Ternate; they carry many
Chinefe articles, and bring back rice, fwallo or fea
flug, fhark fins, tortoife-fhell, a great many loories,
and fome fmall pearls; but no fpices, except perhaps a very few by ftealth. Buggefs prows (called
paduakans, fitted with the tripod maft) go alfo to
Gilolo; but they muft have a Dutch pafs : and I
have been told, that notwithftanding the protection
of this pafs, fometimes a rapacious Dutch cruifer
meets them, trumps up a ftory againft them, and
makes prize of them.

If the Sultan of Ternate or Tidore fits out a
prow of any fize, and it is fufpected fhe is going to
fome diftance; the Dutch will expect to know the
place of her deftination : and, if the Sultan fays
it is to the Buggefs country, or to any diftant
place, for cloth or fuch merchandize, the reply will
be, that the Company's warehoufes contain every
thing of that kind he can want, and all is at his
fervice. If he ftill perfifts, and fays, I am an independant prince, and will fend my veffel whither I
pleafe; the governor at laft fends him perhaps
a valuable prefent of various calicoes, fuch as he
knows will be acceptable to his women, who may,
at the very fame time, be fecretly bribed to divert
the Sultan from his purpofe : fo cautious are they
of bringing matters to extremity, and they generally fucceed, or at the worft, have leave to fend an
officer in the veffel.

The

1774.
November.

The Sultans of Ternate and Tidore * have often had bloody wars with each other: and the Dutch have known how to profit by them.

On the ifland of Ternate, are three Miffigys (mofques) ferved by two Caliphas and four Imums, and many other inferior clergy, called Katibes, Modams and Mifimis. There is one church for the Dutch, but none for the Portuguefe, of whom many remain on the ifland, but they are grown as black as the natives.

The country is divided into five nigris (a certain diftrict) over which are five Synagees, as they pronounce †, a kind of chief. There is alfo a Captain Laut, who commands the Sultan's prows; and a Gogo, an officer who fuperintends the police : amongft other parts of his duty, it is his bufinefs to fee that the inhabitants keep the fences of their gardens in repair, againft the wild hogs and deer ; and that houfes be provided with pots of fand to extinguifh fire. This regulation, well intended, is badly executed amongft the natives; while the Dutch economy within, and near their fort, is admirably exerted in this, and in every other part of India.

The Dutch have a civil Governor and council, befides a fabandar and fifcal, whofe power is often

---

* The prefent Sultan of Ternate is named Mahutajine Jillil Woodine—The Sultan of Tidore is Immel Loodine—and the Sultan of Batchian is Mahmood Sahowdine.

† Sangiac, poffibly from Senchaque, which fignifies, in the Turkifh language, commander. BARTHOLOMEW ARGINSOLA, CONQUEST OF THE MOLUCCAS, p. 15.

feverely

ſeverely felt, not only by natives, but alſo by Europeans, who are prohibited trade with all foreign parts, but Batavia.

No Chineſe junk or veſſel is allowed to come to Ternate from China; but Chineſe junks trade from China to Macaſſar, which may be conſidered as the weſt frontier to the Moluccas; in ſhort, the Dutch contrive to make Ternate as dependant as poſſible on Batavia, for what they want; and although, as I have ſaid, the Sooloos ſend veſſels to Ternate, no Dutch burgher, or Chineſe inhabitant, can ſend a veſſel to Sooloo.

Neither can any Dutch burgher trade to the coaſt of New Guinea for Miſſoy bark, the powder of which is much uſed by the Javans for rubbing their bodies, as the Gentoos on Coromandel uſe ſandal wood—the diſcreet Chineſe only having acceſs to New Guinea.

The iſland of Tidore is but two or three leagues from Ternate; being very populous, it has no fewer than twenty-five moſques. The capital moſque is at the Sultan's, and is ſerved by one Caliph, and four Imums The Sultan poſſeſſes great part of Gilolo, to the ſouth and eaſt; the chief towns there are called Maba, * and Weda, and Patany. † On Patany hook or point, is a

* The French are ſaid to have got cloves from Maba.

† The people of Patany ſupplied with clove plants, the French, who went no further eaſt than the iſland of Gibby. Voyage à la Nouvelle Guinée.

                                            very

very ftrong and capacious natural fort or faftnefs,
acceffible only by means of ladders, up the face of
a perpendicular rock. The top is flat ground, containing many houfes, gardens, &c. the whole being
about three miles in circumference. The Sultan of
Tidore, befides his proportion of Gilolo, claims
the iflands of Waygiou, Myfol, and Batanta. Salwatty is governed by its own Rajah, who at prefent is at variance with the Dutch : his predecef-
for was banifhed to the Cape of Good Hope.

The Sultan of Batchian is the leaft dependant
of the three Gilolo princes, for he will not truft himfelf in the power of the Dutch, ever fince they fent
a great force to his town, on the ifland Mandioly,
to furprife him in the night. A captain of Buggeffes having apprized him of it in time, the Sultan
got off in fmall canoes with his family and moft
portable effects, through creeks, and narrow arms
of the fea, with which his country is divided into
many iflands. Next morning the Dutch wreaked
their vengeance on his houfe and furniture. This
happened ten or twelve years ago ; fince then,
matters have been fo far made up, that he admits
eight or ten Dutch foldiers about his perfon, at his
houfe, which is not far from Fort Barnevelt, in the
ftraits of Batiang or Labuhat.

The Sultan of Batchian once offered to fearch
for gold in his country, where it certainly abounds :
but the Dutch fignifying to him that they expected
the monopoly of what he fhould find, in exchange
for calicoes, iron, &c. which he might want, and
that he fhould not fend to other parts for thofe
neceffaries,

neceffaries, he declined encouraging his people to make the fearch he had propofed.

The Sultan of Batchian is fovereign not only of the ifland fo called, but of the iflands Ooby, Ceram, and Goram—Goram has thirteen Mofques.

I have been told that on the iflands of Ternate and Tidore, but on Ternate efpecially, European garden ftuff grows in as great perfection as at Batavia. Both thefe iflands are exceedingly well watered, by ftreams from their refpective peaks, which are generally covered with clouds, and the peak of Ternate fometimes emits fire. On the ifland Motir was lately a great eruption, attended with an earthquake. I had an account of it from a Buggefs, who, during the eruption at Motir, fet off in his prow, into which he affured me fome hot ftones fell.

The ifland Gilolo * abounds with bullocks and buffalos, goats and deer, alfo wild hogs; there are but few fheep, and no wild beafts. The wild hogs frequent the places where fago trees have lately been cut down, and the flour or pith has been taken out. They there feaft and fatten on the remains, and thofe who have feen them, have defcribed them to me, as appearing with their young black pigs, like flies upon a table.

* The Dutch forbid the manufacturing of cloth on the ifland Gilolo ; notwithftanding which, the natives do it, getting a great deal of cotton yarn from the ifland Bally, and the Buggefs country. The Buggeffes make exceeding good chequered cloth, very ftrong.

The

The fago or libby tree, has, like the coco nut tree, no diftinct bark that peels off, and may be defined a long tube of hard wood, about two inches thick, containing a pulp or pith mixed with many longitudinal fibres. The tree being felled, it is cut into lengths of about five or fix feet. A part of the hard wood is then fliced off, and the workman, coming to the pith, cuts acrofs (generally with an adze made of hard wood called aneebong) the longitudinal fibres and the pith together; leaving a part at each end uncut; fo that, when it is excavated, there remains a trough, into which the pulp is again put, mixed with water, and beat with a piece of wood; then the fibres feparated from the pulp, float atop, and the flour fubfides. After being cleared in this manner by feveral waters, the pulp is put into cylindrical bafkets, made of the leaves of the tree; and, if it is to be kept fome time, thofe bafkets are generally funk in frefh water.

One tree will produce from two to four hundred weight of flour. I have often found large pieces of the fago tree on the fea fhore, drifts from other countries. The fago, thus fteeped in the falt water, had always a four difagreeable fmell; and in this ftate, I dare fay, the wild hogs would not tafte it. The leaf of the fago tree makes the beft covering for houfes, of all the palm * kind : it will laft feven years. Coverings of the nipa or common

* Thofe trees of the palm kind, have all got a heart like what is called the cabbage tree; even the head of the common rattan has a fmall cabbage, of which I have eat.

attop,

attop, fuch as they ufe on the fouth weft coaft of
Sumatra, will not laft half the time.   When fago
trees are cut down, frefh ones fprout up from the
roots.

We feldom or never fee fago in Europe, but in
a granulated ftate.   To bring it into this ftate from
the flour, it muft be firft moiftened, and paffed
through a fieve into an iron pot (very fhallow) held
over a fire, which enables it to affume a globular
form.

Thus, all our grained fago is half baked, and
will keep long.   The pulp or powder, of which
this is made, will alfo keep long, if preferved from
the air ; but, if expofed, it prefently turns four.

The Papua oven, for this flour, is made of
earthen ware.   It is generally nine inches fquare,
and about four deep : it is divided into two equal
parts, by a partition parallel to its fides.   Each of
thofe parts is fubdivided into eight or nine, about
an inch broad ; fo the whole contains two rows
of cells, about eight or nine in a row.   When the
cell is broad, the fago cake is not likely to be well
baked.   I think the beft fized cell is fuch as would
contain an ordinary octavo volume upon its edge.
When they are of fuch a fize, the cakes will be
properly baked, in the following manner.

The oven is fuppofed to have at its bottom, a
round handle, by which the baker turns the cells
downward upon the fire.   When fufficiently heated, it is turned with the mouths of the cells up ;
                                                    and

and then refts upon the handle (which is now become the bottom) as on a ftand.

Whilft the oven is heating, the baker is fuppofed
to have prepared his flour, by breaking the lumps
fmall; moiftening it with water, if too dry, and
paffing it once or twice through a fieve, at the
fame time rejecting any parts that look black or
fmell four. This done, he fills the cells with the
flour, lays a bit of clean leaf over, and with his
finger preffes the flour down into the cell, then covers all up with leaves, and puts a ftone or piece
of wood atop, to keep in the heat. In about ten
or twelve minutes, the cakes will be fufficiently
baked, according to their thicknefs; and bread
thus baked, will keep, I am told, feveral years.
I have kept it twelve months, nor did vermin deftroy it in that time. It may not be amifs to mix
a little falt with the flour.

The fago bread, frefh from the oven, eats juft
like hot rolls. I grew very fond of it; as did both
my officers. If the baker hits his time, the cakes
will be nicely browned on each fide. If the heat
be too great, the corners of the cakes will melt into a jelly, which, when kept, becomes hard and
horny; and, if eat frefh, proves infipid. When
properly baked, it is in a kind of middle ftate, between raw and jellied.

A fago cake, when hard, requires to be foaked
in water, before it be eaten, it then foftens and
fwells into a curd, like bifcuit foaked; but, if
eat

eat without foaking (unlefs frefh from the oven) it
feels difagreeable, like fand in the mouth.

No wonder then, if agriculture be neglected in
a country, where the labour of five men, in felling fago trees, beating the flour, and inftantly baking the bread, will maintain a hundred. I muft
own my crew would have preferred rice ; and,
when my fmall ftock of rice, which I carried from
Balambangan, was near expended, I have heard
them grumble and fay, *nanti makan roti Papua,* " we
muft foon eat Papua bread." But, as I took all
opportunities of baking it frefh, being almoft continually in port, they were very well contented.

The fago bread intended for immediate ufe,
need not be kept fo long in the oven as what is intended for fea ufe, which may be faid to refemble bifcuit.

I have often reflected how well Dampier, Funnel, Roggewein, and many other circumnaviga-
tors might have fared, when paffing this way in
diftrefs for provifions, had they known where to
find the groves of fago trees, with which moft
iflands here in low latitudes abound ; Morty, near
Gilolo efpecially. Frefh bread made of fago flour,
and the kima (a large fhell fifh like a cockle) would
have been no bad fupport among the Moluccas.
The kima is found in abundance, of all fizes, at
low water, during fpring tides, on the reefs of coral rocks. From experience, I equal the frefh
baked fago bread to our wheat-bread ; and the
kima ftewed, is as good as moft fifh, nor does one
                                        tire

tire of it; but it muſt be ſtewed ſome time, or it will not be tender.   Its row will ſometimes weigh ſix pounds; the fiſh altogether, when cleared of the ſhell, weighing twenty or thirty pounds.

Neither is the kima cockle * the worſe for being large.   Sometimes the kima in the ſhell may endanger ſtaving a ſmall canoe, getting it in.   The beſt way is to put a ſtick under water, into the gaping ſhell, which then cloſes and holds faſt; then drag, or lift it towards the ſhore, and ſtab it with a cutlaſs; it dies immediately, and can be taken out.   Small kimas, about the ſize of a man's head, are very good: they will keep long alive if wetted frequently with ſalt water.

Large ſhips, navigating in thoſe ſeas, muſt naturally dread the reefs of rocks, which might produce ſo much good to them, if in diſtreſs for proviſions: but to profit from them, they muſt hit the time of low water ſpring tides.   The vaſt fleets of Mangaio boats that ſet out from Sooloo and Mindano, to cruize among the Philippine iſlands, againſt the Spaniards, truſt to the reefs of rocks, which may be ſaid to ſurround all thoſe iſlands, producing them fiſh for their ſubſiſtence; as they only lay in rice or ſago bread.

The account I have given of the ſago tree, ſhews how eaſily the inhabitants of thoſe countries may find ſubſiſtence.   They have alſo all

* Dampier mentions in his voyage to New Britain, his having got a cockle ſhell 278 lb. weight, on the weſt of New Guinea. Harris's collection, p. 124.

over

over the Moluccas, and on New Guinea, the
rima, or bread fruit, which is the chief food
of the inhabitants of Otaheitee, in the South Sea,
where (according to Doctor Forfter's * curious
computation) ten or twelve perfons live eight
months upon the produce of an acre, planted with
this tree. I fhall therefore endeavour to fhow
how many perfons may live on an acre, planted
with fago trees which, growing more upright, and
the roots not fpreading fo much, will confequently
take up much lefs room than the rima tree.

I fhall allow a fago tree to take up the room of
10 feet fquared, or 100 fquare feet. Now, the
contents of an acre are 43,500 fquare feet, which
being divided by a hundred, allow 433 trees to
grow within that fpace. But, to give ample room,
I fhall fay 300 trees only; and fuppofing that, one
with another, they give 300 weight of flour; then
three trees, or 900 weight may maintain one man
for a year, and an acre to be cut down, would
maintain 100 men for the fame time. Now as
fago trees are 7 years a growing, I divide 100 by 7,
which will then allow 14 men to be maintained for
a year, on the produce of one feventh part of an
acre, immediately; or, on the produce of a whole
acre, progreffively cut, one feventh part at a time,
allowing frefh trees to fprout up.

So far the inhabitants of the globe, in low latitudes, may be juftly confidered as happily

* Obfervations in a voyage round the world, p. 220.

fituated;

fituated ; fomething like what is faid of the golden age, they may live almoft without labour. But certain evils, in a great meafure, counterbalance this feeming happinefs : the faculties of the mind are blunted, and the body is fo enervated by indolence, that thefe petty ftates are fubject to be overcome, by what Europeans would call a very defpicable enemy, as they know nothing of the polity of great focieties.

The inhabitants of the Moluccas in particular, not being able to maintain their independence againft Europeans, (whatever they did before hiftory gives an account of them) have had their country continually in a ftate of war, as the monopoly of the clove and nutmeg has been fucceffively a fubject of contention between the Portugueze, Spaniards, and Dutch.

I choofe to draw a veil over that part of hiftory which informs us that our own country ever had any fhare in that trade.

E   CHAP.

C H A P.   IV.

*Tuan Hadjee returns on Board with a Meſſenger
from the Sultan of Batchian—Sailed from Biſſory
Harbour—Had an accidental Interview with the
Sultan of Batchian, on the Iſland Bally—Sailed
thence for Tomoguy—Put into Selang Harbour—
Deſcription of it—Sailed thence, and put into a
Harbour on the Iſland Gag—Deſcription of it—
ſailed thence, and arrived at Tomoguy, where we
narrowly eſcaped Shipwreck——Hauled the Veſſel
aſhore to repair.*

1774.
December.

O N *Thurſday* the firſt of *December*, a fiſhing
boat came on board. She was the only embark-
ation I had ſeen ſince we left Tonkyl, excepting
the ſmall canoe off Karakita. At night I lay off
in twelve fathom water, muddy ground ; but, in
the day I hauled cloſe to the peninſula : I was then
hid from the ſea. This I did to avoid being ſeen by
any Dutch cruiſer in the offing, that might be paſſing this way. A large ſhip might lie cloſe to the
peninſula, in five fathom water, muddy ground,
and heave down conveniently, as it is ſteep.

On *Friday* the 2d, it blew very freſh from the
N. W. ſaw nobody all day——gathered, near
the ſea ſhore, ſome ripe limes from the tree.

On Saturday the 3d, about noon, Tuan Hadjee
returned by ſea ; he came in a ſmall prow or canoe,
mounted with outriggers, and had three prows
besides

besides with him.   He was accompanied by a mef-
senger from the Sultan of Batchian, with a prefent
of fowls, fruit, rice, &c. and about twenty pounds
of cloves in a bafket.   The meffenger's name was
Tuan Bobo.   In return, I prefented him with a
whole piece of Englifh fcarlet broad cloth, for the
Sultan ; and two pieces of gingham for himfelf.   I
obferved Tuan Hadjee fent moft of the fine goods
he had got from Mr. Herbert, at Balambangan,
afhore at this place, by Tuan Bobo.

At four in the afternoon we rowed out of Biffory
Harbour, and ftood to the fouthward : at midnight,
we anchored behind a fmall ifle, called Pulo Bally,
in two fathom water, fandy ground.

On *Sunday* the 4th, in the morning, we had a
hard fquall of wind from the N. W. with rain.
About ten in the forenoon, came on board in a canoe three perfons, who faid they were Rajahs on
the ifland Ceram.   After Tuan Hadjee and I had
a little converfation with them, concerning that
ifland and other matters, in which they told me
that cloves certainly grew on many parts of it,
they went afhore to the ifland Bally.   We then
weighed, and got under fail, intending to touch
at the ifland of Waygiou, or fomewhere near it, in
order, as I had agreed with Tuan Hadjee, to purchafe, and fit up a corocoro, to enable us to pro-
fecute our voyage to New Guinea ; for we thought
Batchian was too near Ternate to do that bufinefs
there.

Prefently after we faw a boat ftanding towards us,
with a white flag.   Tuan Hadjee told me it was

the

the Sultan of Batchian. As it then blew frefh, and the wind came round from the N. W to the weft, and W. by S. I put back to regain the ifland. I found the veffel work very ill, being hard to veer; and I regained the anchorage with difficulty. The Sultan had many fmall prows attending him; one of them came very opportunely to tow us in behind the ifland.

I then went afhore with Tuan Hadjee, to pay my refpects to the Sultan of Batchian. He fat under the fhade of a covered canoe, that was hauled up, upon fome boards laid acrofs the gunnel; and, when I came within ten or twelve yards of him, he ran forwards and embraced me.

After being feated in the canoe, I told him in Malays, which he fpoke very well, that I was going to Tanna Papua (New Guinea) and afked the favour of him to affift me with a linguift. He very readily confented to my requeft, and defired me to go to the ifland Tomoguy, near the large ifland Waygiou, where he would give direction, that one captain Mareca fhould accompany me to New Guinea, and be my linguift. In the converfation I had with the Sultan, I told him the Englifh wifhed him very well, but, would have nothing to fay to the Molucca iflands; and I advifed him to keep on good terms with the Dutch. When I had ftaid with him about an hour, I took my leave. I found I was the firft Englifhman he had ever feen.

The Sultan is a handfome man, about forty-four years of age. Tuan Hadjee, whilft we were with

the

the Sultan, fat on the ground, and every time he
fpoke to the Sultan, nay almoft at every word,
lifted his hands clofe together to his head, it being
the Molucca cuftom to do it frequently, and much
oftner than in Indoftan.

Pulo Bally is an ifland about two miles round,
and lies in the latitude of 00° 30′ S. There is good
anchorage to the eaftward of it in twelve and thirteen fathom water, muddy ground. It has abundance of wood and frefh water; and as I went
behind it from the S. W. I believe there is no danger that way. A fmall ifland, called Siao, lies near
it. About three leagues S. W. of Bally are fome
dangerous breakers, which I faw very high, as it
was ftormy this morning. About two in the afternoon, we weighed and ftood on to the fouthward,
the weather being moderate: but we found a large
fwell from the weftward, and paffed within the fhoal
which has been mentioned. The breakers were
exceedingly high upon it. The channel between
it and the oppofite fhore of Batchian is about five
miles wide. About ten at night it fell calm, during which I found a great fwell again from the
weftward, and the fea broke feveral times; owing,
I fuppofe, to a ftrong current. On the fouth-weft
point of Batchian is a long low point, which I call
Flat Point. We paffed it in the night, about three
miles off, and had no foundings with feventy fathoms of line. It lies in latitude 00° 38 S. and
longitude 123° 38′ E.

On *Monday* the 5th, in the morning, Flat Point
bore N. W. by N. and the high hill of Labuhat

on

on the eaft fide of the ftraits that divide Batchian from it, bore E. by S. At the fame time we could fee the ifland Ooby very plain, and Pulo Tappa bore S. S. E. Had no ground within half a mile of the fhore. About noon we were abreaft of the ftraits above mentioned: they are called fometimes the ftraits of Betyang; and we could fee within the ftraits a hill with a flat top, like what is called the fruftum of a cone. The Dutch fort Barnavelt is faid to be at the foot of it.

At noon we were in the latitude of 00° 45′ S. Labuhat Hill bearing E. half N.

Converfing with Tuan Hadjee about Batchian, he informed me, that a great deal of cloves might be had from thence, and from Gilolo alfo, if any fhip fhould think of trading that way; the Dutch being much off their guard to what they were formerly. He alfo told me, pearls were to be had amongft the Moluccas.

On *Tuefday* the 6th, we had fqually and rainy weather, with W. and W. N. W. winds; fteered eaft. About ten in the morning, the wind coming to the S. E. ran into the harbour of Selang.

In fteering along-fhore, the ifland Selang, that makes the harbour, may be eafily perceived. It is not flat and low, neither is it very high; but the eaft part flopes down to where it feems to join the main land of Batchian; the ftraits there being narrow, and not five foot deep. The ifland forms two harbours with the main land; an outer and

an

an inner harbour. There is no danger in running into either, but what is plainly feen. I would advife to keep near the ifland. In going into the inner harbour, keep ftill near the ifland, and you will pafs between two reefs, both of which may be feen even at high water, as they will then be only covered with three foot and a half water, and the coral rocks fhew themfelves very plain under water in fo fmall a depth. The width between the reefs is about 100 fathom, and the depth twelve fathom, foft muddy ground; the inner harbour being about two miles broad and three long, and the general depth ten fathom. The latitude of Selang harbour is 00° 50′ S. and its longitude 124° 10′ E.

In the evening we rowed out of the harbour; but the wind coming to the eaftward, we put back, and anchored behind the fecond point, in the outer harbour.

On *Wednefday* the 7th, in order to compleat our water, as I did not immediately find any on the ifland, we rowed behind a reef of rocks, in the outer harbour, and anchored in feven fathom good holding ground, clofe to the main land of Batchian.

Here I found frefh water very acceffible; a reef of coral rocks fheltering this little harbour from the S. and S. W. fwell, the point of Labuhat (the extreme to the weftward) being then fhut in with what I call Attop Point, as many nipa or attop trees grow there. To day it blew very frefh from the weftward. Between this and the ftraits of Labuhat, or Betyang, which we have paffed, lies, as

Tuan

Tuan Hadjee told me, a moft commodious harbour, called Wyoua; but we did not go into it.

Hitherto we faw no boats, houfes, or people.
Sent a little way into the woods in fearch of clove
trees, but none were found. The people, however, difcovered many nutmeg trees very tall. There
was no fruit vifible on the branches; but many old
nutmegs were lying on the ground, and moft of
them had fprouted.

Here all hands bathed, which we generally did
when frefh water was acceffible. We alfo got on
Attop Point many kima, which made excellent
curry.

On *Thurfday* the 8th, we weighed in the morning, and failed out of the harbour of Selang with
a firft land wind: it then fell calm. About ten A.
M. the wind came frefh from the fouth-weft; fteered S. E. Paffed a fpot of coral rocks with five fathom water on fome parts of it, lying S. E. by S.
from the eaft point of Selang ifland, and about two
miles diftant from it. I was told by fome of Tuan
Hadjee's people, that there was a paffage for fhips
within it, and I found upon it a great rippling of
a tide or current. At four P. M. we faw the
iflands that are faid to lie to the fouthward of Pulo
Dammer, and are called Gorongo. They bore
eaft. In the night we fteered S. E. to avoid fome
rocks, which Tuan Hadjee faid lay to the eaftward of us.

In the morning of the 9th, we could fee Pulo
Pifang bearing eaft about eight leagues; it is covered

1774.
December.

vered with trees; and two iflands called Liliola and Tapiola, covered alfo with trees; the iflands Gorongo, that lie fouth of Pulo Dammer, (mentioned yefterday) bearing north. They lie in 1° 10′ S. latitude; Pulo Pifang lies in latitude 1° 30′ S. and longitude 125° 40′ E. At funfet Pulo Pifang bore S. by E. half E. We could then fee the high land of Ceram very diftant: hauled up N. E.

On *Saturday* the 10th, in the morning we could fee the iflands of Bo, bearing S. S. E. At the fame time Pulo Pifang bore S. W. by S. We had very fmooth water, with the wind at N. W. and N. W. by W. fteering N. E. I had no obfervation at noon, Pulo Pifang then bore S. W. 16 leagues. Pulo Bo, bore fouth, and Pulo Popo fouth eaft; could alfo fee an ifland called Gag, of middling height, bearing north eaft. There was little wind, fometimes it was calm.

Sunday the 11th. All night we fteered north eaft, with the wind at weft, and rowed a good deal. In the morning feveral fmall iflands, flat and low, bore from E. by N. to E. S. E. they were about four in number; one in particular, called Piamis, had a pointed peak, might be three or four hundred feet high. At noon, Pulo Gag bore N. N. E. five or fix leagues. We were then in the latitude of 00° 35′ fouth.

At one P. M Pulo Gag bore from N. half E. to N. E. by N. about four leagues diftant. Another ifland, in appearance, as high as Gag, bore N. W. by N. half N. about ten leagues diftant: this we found afterwards to be Gibby. Two fmall iflands,
one

one of them with a hummoc upon it, lay S. by W.
from Gag; they are named Doif.   Some high land
appeared to the eaftward, which I was told to be
the ifland Waygiou.

At funfet, a boat with three Papua men came on
board; I hired them to tow us into a fine bay on
the fouth eaft quarter of Pulo Gag.   Here we anchored in eight fathom water, muddy ground,
within fifty yards of the ftrand.

At eight in the evening, Tuan Hadjee went to
Tomoguy, whither we had been directed, (a place
near Gibby Monpine, on the weft coaft of the
ifland Waygiou) in the fame boat, leaving her owner, who was a Papua man, and fpoke good Malays,
on board of the galley.

On *Monday* the 12th, in the morning, I went
afhore upon Gag, and found a fmall clear rivulet,
where we watered.   We alfo fupplied ourfelves
with wood, then weighed and rowed out, intending
to proceed to the ifland of Tomoguy; as we expected Tuan Hadjee, by this time, had been
there.

At the mouth of the harbour we met a boat with
four Papua men, and two women, which I hired
to tow us out, there being little wind, and we
therefore rowing at the fame time.   I obferved the
two women plied their paddles more than the
men : their hire was a red handkerchief.   Having
got out of the bay, we found a tide or current fet
ftrong to the northward : fo we continued all night
fteering north eaft, thinking the tide fet then to
                                              the

the fouthward. At noon we were in the latitude of 00° 10′ fouth.

The 13th was calm in the morning ; a little be-fore noon, we faw a boat ftanding towards us. At noon, Pulo Gag bore from W. by S. to S. W. by W. fix leagues; and the fouth part of Gibby, bore weft half north; our latitude was then 00° 10′ fouth. A high ifland called Ruib, at the fame time, bore N. by E. half E. and part of Waygiou, which re-markably figures a cock's comb, being a long in-dented ridge of a hill, with fome white chalky fpots upon it, bore E. N. E.   At this time, we were within fight of the beach of a long flat ifland, called Yew, which bore from E. by N. to E. by S. And we faw ten fmall low iflands to the fouthward. But, before I go farther, I muft fay fomething of the ifland Gag, and then return to Tuan Hadjee, who came on board a little after noon, in the fame boat wherein the night before he had left that ifland.

Pulo Gag, in latitude 00° 18′ fouth, and longi-tude 126° 40′ eaft, is an ifland of middling height. When plainly feen, it looks very like land of Eu-rope, not being loaded with wood, as iflands in Malay countries generally are.   From this circum-ftance, I judge it to be rather barren in general; tho' the valley where I landed, and which ap-pears in the view, had a rich foil, with a moft luxuriant vegetation; and that part of the ifland, on the north fide of the bay, is covered with tall timber trees; whereas, the trees on thofe other parts that appear in the view, to the fouth weft, are rather dwarfifh.   I was told that a good many
fago

fago trees grew upon it. This island is not inhabited, tho' travellers by water, in their way from
Patany-hook, on the island Gilolo, and from the
island Gibby to Waygiou, often put into the
bay where I did, to pafs the night, and fometimes ftay there a fifhing for feveral days; the Ifland
Gag being about half way betwixt Gibby and
Waygiou, and almoft in the track. To go into
the bay, fend firft a boat to lie upon the fpots of
coral rocks, that are on each hand in the entrance,
which is fufficiently broad. Thefe rocks fhow
themfelves by their bright colour under water;
but never above water, even at the loweft. Off
Pulo Gag lie feveral banks, with ten and twenty
fathom depth, fandy ground: on thofe banks is
good fifhing.

A little after noon, as I have faid, Tuan Hadjee returned on board in the fame boat that carried him from Gag; he brought captain Mareca
along with him, who was to be our linguift to
New Guinea. We therefore immediately bore
away for the ifland of Tomoguy, where captain
Mareca lived, and which was not yet feen, it being hid by the larger iflands of Batang Pally.

We paffed the fouthward of Batang Pally, by the
north fide of a fmall low ifland, not half a mile round,
covered with trees, leaving it on the right hand,
and ftill fteering round Batang Pally. After funfet, we arrived at Tomoguy ifland, and paffing
fouthward, anchored to the eaftward of it, in
eighteen fathoms muddy ground, pretty clofe to
fhore: it was then near eight o'clock, and very
dark.

dark. On the Papua man's going aſhore, I re-
warded him handſomely for the uſe of his boat.

On *Wedneſday* the 14th, in the morning it began
to blow at north eaſt ; being a lee ſhore and very
ſteep, we rode for ſome time in great danger. We
diagged our grapnel from the mud ſoundings, but
it luckily hooked the coral rocks, and held faſt,
while the ſea broke under our ſtern. I could not
but be vexed Captain Mareca had brought us to
an anchor in ſo bad a place, when many ſafe harbours were near ; and the darkneſs, when we
anchored the night before, prevented my ſeeing
the badneſs of our birth. About noon, when the
gale had moderated a little, Captain Mareca came
to us in a corocoro, with ten men and paddles.
They preſently carried out a wooden anchor, and
rattan cable, which by floating, made an excellent
warp ; they alſo towed us, and we got out of our
danger.

I immediately made ſail for a place called Manafuin, about two leagues from Tomoguy ; and
there I anchored in a ſmooth bay, in twelve fathom
water, clean ſandy ground. The people, who
aſſiſted us ſo opportunely, were rewarded to their
wiſh.

On *Thurſday* the 15th. In this bay, I paſſed the
night very happy with the thoughts of having juſt
eſcaped ſhipwreck. Tuan Hadjee and I had agreed
to haul the veſſel aſhore at Tomoguy, or ſome
where near it, not only to clean, as I feared the
worms had got into her bottom, but to raiſe her

one

one ftreak or plank, as I found her, in croffing from Tonkyl to the Moluccas, rather too low, the fea often coming over her gunnel, which was no higher than her gallery beams, and getting into the hold through the thatch. I had not been afhore at Tomoguy; and, from the danger I had experienced near it, I imagined we could not there do our bufinefs with fafety. I therefore propofed to haul afhore, where we were. To this Tuan Hadjee objected, as did moft of the people that belonged to him: fo I did not infift upon it.

About noon, Captain Mareca came on board in the corocoro that had fo greatly affifted us yefterday. He faid, we might haul afhore at high water, clofe to his houfe, the veffel being previoufly lightened, to enable her to float over the coral rocks. To this I confented: fo we weighed, and rowed back to Tomoguy, Captain Mareca's corocoro towing us at the fame time. We anchored in fifteen fathom, oppofite his houfe, until the tide ferved; and having taken up fome of the coral rocks, as well as lightened the veffel, we hauled her afhore at a village, confifting only of Captain Mareca's houfe, the houfe of the Papua man, whofe boat carried Tuan Hadjee from Pulo Gag, and three more little habitations.

Tomoguy is an ifland about two miles round, fhaped like a horfe fhoe; the hollow being that bay, where I had lately made fo narrow an efcape. On the ifland rifes a hill, which takes up about three-fourths of its compafs; and on the fide of this hill, which may be a hundred and
fifty

fifty foot high, are plantations of tropical fruits and
roots. The hill towards the weſt, is rather ſteep,
the Horſe Shoe bay lying to the eaſtward. From
the hill I could ſee, to the ſouthward, many low
iſlands, of which I took ſome notice the day before I came to Tomoguy. I could alſo ſee diſtant
land to the ſouthward; they called it Batanta and
Famiay. The iſland Tomoguy lies in latitude
00° 15′ S. and longitude 127° 4′ E.

C H A P. V.

*Sent a Boat to the Iſland Salwatty, to purchaſe
Sago Bread—Was viſited by the Synagees of the
Country—Had my Houſe robbed—A Corocoro
arrives from Batchian with Tuan Bobo on Board,
and another Officer, who bring a letter from the
Sultan to Tuan Hadjee—Farther Tranſactions
there—Prepare to depart—Account of the Inhabitants.*

ON *Friday, December* the 16th, the veſſel hauled up and ſecured, we were moſt of the day
employed in waſhing and cleaning her inſide, for
Muſſulmen are not very cleanly. At high water
we hauled her up a little farther. All day it blew
freſh from north weſt.

On *Saturday* the 17th, we had ſtill freſh north
weſt winds, with rain. Sent the people to cut wood
for burning the coral rocks we had gathered, in
order

order to make chenam (lime) for mixing with
oil to be put upon the veffel's bottom.

On the 18th, frefh north weft winds with rain.
Hired a corocoro to go to the ifland of Salwatty,
to purchafe fago bread. For this purpofe, I fent
red handkerchiefs and various calicoes. Tuan
Hadjee writ by the boat to fome of his acquaintance there, to affift the commander in his bufinefs.

On *Monday* the 19th, we had for the firft part of
the day moderate weather, with calms. Afternoon
brought hard gales from the N. W. with thunder,
lightning, and rain; a fwell came alfo in, which
made the veffel lie uneafy, and thump.

On *Tuefday* the 20th, with variable winds and
rain, came to vifit me, fome perfons, who Tuan
Hadjee faid were Synagees (certain chiefs) of the
country. They wore long hair, were Mahometans, and held their title from the Sultan of Tidore. They behaved civilly, in expectation of
prefents, which I made them; Tuan Hadjee, to
whom they paid great refpect, telling me it was neceffary. Two boats arriving, I bought from Papua
men, who were in them, fago flour, put up in
Cylindrical bafkets, made of the leaves of the
tree. Thefe Papua men had their frizzled black
locks fticking out a great way from their heads,
and were as black as African Coffres.

On *Wednefday* the 21ft, eafterly winds and
calms. This is the firft fair day we have had
fince our arrival.

To

To day, came in from Gibby feveral fmall prows or corocoros; for they call them by either name. I found it was expected I fhould make the mafters fmall prefents, which I thought prudent to do. Tuan Hadjee was much refpected by them, and loved to do things genteelly, to which I was not averfe.

On *Thurfday* the 22d, the weather was moderate, but we had at times, feveral very hard fqualls from the N. W. In the night feveral, not all, of the Gibby prows failed. To day we made a new latteen mainfail, and breamed the veffel's bottom, into which I found the worm had juft entered. I purchafed alfo a corocoro, which we fet about fitting up, to affift us in our intended voyage.

On *Friday* the 23d, had wefterly winds, with heavy fqualls and rain in the night.

As I wanted to expedite our bufinefs, and get afloat, I embraced an opportunity when it was fair, to calk the ftarboard fide of the galley, above water. In the night my houfe was robbed of fome fhirts, and other wearing apparel. My fervant Matthew purfued the thief with a cutlas; but I was not difpleafed he did not catch him : Matthew being a lad of fpirit, there might have been bloodfhed.

On *Saturday* the 24th, we had N. W. winds, with frequent fhowers; towards the evening it was calm. While we lay here, we were accommodated with fifh (bonettas) and greens, from

F   Captain

Captain Mareca's garden; whence we were fupplied with pumpkin fprouts, the tops of the fweet
potatoe, and brinjals.*

On *Sunday* the 25th, the winds at W. and W.
N. W. employed ourfelves in covering the veffel
with fago leaves.

On *Monday* the 26th, we had wefterly winds
and rain. To day the boat returned from Salwatty,
with three thoufand cakes of fago bread, all in excellent order. Fixed two gunnel planks, fifteen
inches broad, the whole length of the veffel. Captain Mareca, who had contracted to do it, cut the
planks out of a tree. To day, the thief that
robbed me was taken, and brought to Captain
Mareca's houfe; but none of the ftolen goods
were brought with him. They afked how I would
have him punifhed; I replied, as the robbery was
committed afhore, they might punifh him their
own way. The fellow, who was a Papua Coffre,
did not feem much afhamed. I fufpected a trick
at the bottom, which made me aware of indulging refentment. I was told they did nothing
to him.

On the 27th, the former part of the day we had
variable winds, with rain; the latter part eafterly
winds. About noon arrived a corocoro from Batchian, with two officers, one of them (Tuan
Bobo) the perfon fent to me by the Sultan of Bat-

* A fruit which parboiled, and then roafted, eats like an
artichoak.

chian,

chian, at Biffory harbour, as has been related; the other called Tuan Affahan. I faluted them on their landing, with three fwivel guns. They brought a letter from the Sultan to Tuan Hadjee; but none to me. However they brought me, with the Sultan's compliments, fix bafkets, about fifteen pound each, of excellent fago bread, of a reddifh colour, and fix bafkets of fine rice. The officers told me they had orders from the Sultan of Bat-chian, to accompany me, whitherfoever I thought proper to go, to affift me with every thing in their power, and afterwards to proceed with me back to Balambangan. I kept them to drink tea with me in the evening. The veffel had eighteen men, befides the two officers, with two brafs fwivel guns, and many bows and arrows.

On *Wednefday* the 28th, we had eafterly winds, during the former, and north weft winds, the latter part of the day. The Batchian people affifted me in repairing the veffel.

On *Thurfday* the 29th, north weft winds began, and eafterly winds ended the day. Employed in finifhing the gunnel planks. Obferved the fun's amplitude afhore, and found the variation of the compafs to be one degree eaft.

On *Friday* the 30th, we had, for the former part, eafterly winds, during the latter, had winds from the N. N. W. with frefh gales. Employed as yefterday. To day feveral Patany prows ar-rived. About funfet, I went to the top of the hill, and took the bearings of Piamis Peak, as well as of the low flat iflands adjacent. From the

F 2

hill

hill I could fee to the fouthward, the diftant land of Famiay and Batanta.

To day, I employed a Papua man to make a wooden anchor; and advanced him a new Pulicat handkerchief, which was to be its price. About an hour after dark, feveral Patany men, lately from Gibby, which ifland lies in their way from Patany to Tomoguy, affembled at my houfe, and, in a very bold manner, afked me for Betel money. I got Tuan Hadjee, and Tuan Buffora, a man I had engaged to go with me to Tanna Papua, to affure them, that I intended to make them hand-fome prefents, they being Synagees of Patany Hook, on Gilolo, and of the ifland Gibby; that I had made prefents to fome perfons of rank, of Gibby-Monpine, on the ifland Waygiou, who had honoured me with a vifit; and, that if they would come next day, I fhould be glad to fee them. I kept, however, a good watch all night, not much liking the company I had got amongft.

Next day, *Saturday* the 31ft, about feven in the morning, I faw the wooden anchor, I had employ-ed the Papua man to make for me, lying on the ground, cut and defaced. I inftantly found out the man, who had got his fhield in his hand, his lance, bows and arrows, and was preparing to fet off in his boat, as on a journey; at the fame time, he feemed to be very much difpleafed, and fpoke angri-ly. I took him by the hand, and, pointing to the man-gled anchor, laughed, faying, it would do very well. With much difficulty, I got him into my houfe, where I appeafed his wrath, and gave him about ten

times

times its value.　Immediately after this, finding the Batchian officers did not come to breakfaſt as uſual, I went to them.　They looked very grave, and had all their people ready as if to launch their corocoro, that was hauled up, on hearing the anchor carpenter make a noiſe, which they left me to allay. A little while after this, they came to my houſe to breakfaſt.　Some days before, I had preſented the carpenter's father, whoſe boat carried Tuan Hadjee from Gag to Tomoguy, with a half worn ſcarlet waiſtcoat, and a fathom of new ſcarlet broad cloth. The father contributed much to appeaſe his ſon's wrath ; but, though I never could learn the truth, I ſuſpected the man ſet on to impoſe, or perhaps to pick a quarrel : all that day, therefore, I went with loaded piſtols, and kept others armed alſo.

About eleven, A. M. the Patany and Gibby men came to wait on me.　I treated them with a diſh of tea, and gave each ſome tea and ſugar candy, put up in paper ; which they accepted with a good grace.　I then preſented each of them (about eight in number) with two pieces of Surat, and various other calicoe goods, to the amount of ſixty dollars, with which they were ſatisfied.

To day we had eaſterly winds, the former and latter parts.　About noon we had N. N. W. winds and rain.　Finiſhed the ſtarboard ſide of the veſſel, and paid it with lime, mixed with water, in which certain leaves of trees had been ſteeped.　This afternoon arrived many ſmall corocoros from Warjow, which lies on the north eaſt part of the iſland Waygiou.　On board of them were only Papua people,

people, who feemed afraid of coming amongft the
Mahometans.   I bought from them thirty-fix rolls
of fago flour, very reafonable.   I alfo purchafed
from Captain Mareca an old prow, which I broke
up for boards, to lay acrofs the lower beams of
the veffel for the people to fleep on.

On *Sunday, January* the 1ft, 1775, had northerly winds.   To day I finifhed caulking the larboard
fide of the veffel, and paid it with lime, mixed with
the liquid already mentioned, our oil being done.
We were employed alfo in making attops, and
covering the veffel with them, being refolved to get
afloat as foon as poffible.

On *Monday* the 2d, we had variable winds.   Finifhed covering the veffel.   At three P. M. hauled
off, and anchored juft without the reef.

Tuefday the 3d.   Got our ftores, &c. very expe-
ditioufly on board, in a fmall new corocoro, I had
bought from Tuan Buffora the Molucca man,
whom I had engaged to go with me to the coaft of
New Guinea.   At fix in the evening, hauled farther off, then rowed on about a mile, and anchored
in twenty-three fathom, muddy ground, in Horfe
Shoe Bay.

On *Wednefday* the 4th, we had light variable
winds, with fo heavy rain, as penetrated the new
roof of the veffel, it being too flat.   To remedy
this uncomfortable circumftance, I raifed the middle of it, by driving a few wedges below.

Not liking our road in Horfe Shoe Bay, I rowed
on to a land lockt harbour in the eaftermoft of the
two

two iſlands that are called Batang Pally. It has no particular name, but lies about two miles from Tomoguy. The two Batchian officers came on board, and went back to Tomoguy in the evening, to look after their corocoro. There came alſo to pay me a viſit a Molucca man, named Abdul Wahead; who gave me ſome information about New Guinea; telling me, he had often gone thither a trading for ſlaves, and that the people were not ſo barbarous as he underſtood they had been repreſented to me. I made him a preſent; upon which he ſaid, that he would have told me ſo before, but never had a fair opportunity, as Tuan Hadjee and the Batchian officers were conſtantly with me; and he found by their converſation, which he had overheard, that they wanted to perſuade me not to go thither. This was really the caſe: The Batchian officers eſpecially, prompted, I ſuppoſe, by Tuan Hadjee, were continually telling me, that the people of New Guinea were fierce and hoſtile in their manners, and even ſaid there were cannibals among them.

On *Thurſday* the 5th, we had fair weather. The carpenter's father, who helped to make up the quarrel I was near having with his ſon at Tomoguy, came on board. He preſented me with a Loorequet of beautiful plumage, moſtly green and yellow. Captain Mareca came alſo with two of his ſons and three ſervants; one of them a female cook. Likewiſe came Tuan Buffora. We were pretty much crouded. Tuan Hadjee joined, in a corocoro of eighteen feet keel, and eight foot beam, which I had purchaſed and fitted up to aſſiſt us in

our

our intended voyage.   She was manned with fourteen people.

Tuan Hadjee, for his encouragement, had one
half of her ; and fhe was taken into the Company's fervice.   Such Batchians as chofe to go in her,
had pay : fome other failors were fhipped by me.
The two Batchian officers came along in their corocoro, with about twelve people.

We rowed from the land lockt harbour on Little Batang Pally to Manafouin Bay, where we had
once lain, and where I had wifhed to haul afhore.
It lies in latitude 0° 12' S. and longitude 127° 0' E.
We lay afloat clofe to the beach without any danger, and employed ourfelves in cutting rattans ;
which we found at hand, to fix the outriggers of
the corocoros ; the fixtures of thefe embarkations
being moftly made with rattans ; but their timbers
are tied to a kind of handle made in their plank,
with a black ftrong cord, called Gumaty, which
a certain palm tree produces, as the coco nut tree
produces coir.   Of this they alfo make good ropes.
At Malacca they manufacture cables of it.   At
night, a fon of Captain Mareca's, after I had made
him fome prefents to engage him to go the voyage,
went afhore, and I never faw him more.

Friday the 6th.   I named the corocoro, on board
of which Tuan Hadjee chofe to remain, (for I
durft not order him on board the galley), the Banguey ; and the Batchian corocoro, the Borneo.
Employed in getting them both ready for fea.

The

The inhabitants of the fmall part of the Molucca iflands, I had hitherto feen, were of two forts,
viz. the long hair'd Moors, of a copper colour,
like Malays in every refpeét ; and the mopheaded
Papuas. Thefe Papuas inhabit not only New
Guinea, but the inland parts of moft of the Moluccas ; and thofe we faw at Tomoguy came moftly from the ifland Waygiou, which lay near it.
The Moors had generally in their boats a few Papuas as flaves.

The fago bread already mentioned, and which
they make delicately at Batchian, is called by thofe
who fpeak Malays, Roti Papua (Papua Bread).
They fay the Papuas introduced the art of baking
it amongft the Mahometans, who came to the
Moluccas from parts farther weft. Many of the
Papuas turn Muffulmen, and then cut off their
bufhy locks, or at leaft comb them down as ftraight
as they can. The perfon who carried Tuan Hadjee from Gag to Tomoguy was a profelyte of this
kind, and was called Hujamat, a very civil man.
His fon the carpenter was a favage indeed, and
wore his bufhy locks.

Many of thofe Synagees who vifited me, were
no better than fturdy beggars, and paid great
refpeét to Tuan Hadjee, on account of the pilgrimage he had made. He feemed to court this
refpeét, and I was careful always to fupport him
in it, as we lived on the beft terms. He had his
own fervants to cook for him, and attend him at
Captain Mareca's, whilft I lived in an oppofite
houfe. We generally drank tea or coffee once a
day

day in company ; though we feldom eat together :
and, upon the whole, I found him (whatever he
might be in his heart) perfectly well bred, and a
moft agreeable companion.

From the refpect fhewn Tuan Hadjee, whofe
anceftors were of the Serifs that came from Mecca,
and gave kings to thofe parts, I could not help
remarking the advantage Muffulmen priefts have
over others, as defcendants from their great prophet (Nabbi) Mahomet. There is fomething ftriking, efpecially to the vulgar, in the certainty of a
very noble extraction ; and fo far eaft Hadjees
were feldom feen. It is perhaps remarkable, that
I never met with any Roman miffionary in Malay
countries.

C H A P. VI.

*The Batchian Officers refufe to proceed to New Gui-
nea—Sailed without them, but immediately put
back——Converfation with Tuan Hadjee on the
Subject ; who agrees to go to the Iflands off the
Coaft of New Guinea, but not to the Main Land—
Account of the Weft Coaft of Waygiou, and of the
Straits of Batang Pally—Sailed for the Iflands of
Yowl—Paffed Ruib and Pulo Een——Arrived at
Offak Harbour, on the North Coaft of Waygiou.*

BEING all ready for fea, in the evening of the
6th of *January*, Tuan Affahan came on board, and
afked me whither I was going ; I told him to Tanna

na Papua, and thence to Balambangan. He faid, very ferioufly, as that was the cafe, he could not go with me. I told him, he might do as he pleafed; but that he fhould not have promifed to go. We then parted.

Saturday the 7th. In the morning I fired a gun as a fignal for failing. When I had got under way, the other corocoro being left at anchor, the Banguey approached, and one Mapalla, (fon to a head man of Ceram) who belonged to her, cried out, that if the Batchian officers did not go with me, he would not. This man had been fpared to me by thofe officers, and was upon wages. By way of anfwer to what he faid, I afked, where his commander Tuan Hadjee was, as I did not fee him? Mapalla anfwered, he was fick. On this I faid no more, but immediately fufpected him of being the fecret caufe of what had happened, as alfo of the defection of the Batchian officers related yefterday. I therefore inftantly put about, being only half a mile from our former birth, and anchored clofe to the Borneo corocoro, on board of which the two Batchian officers had remained.

When we had got to an anchor, Tuan Hadjee came on board and breakfafted with me. Whilft at breakfaft, I flightly mentioned the Batchian officers having failed in their promife; but I was very cautious of touching upon what had happened that morning, waving whatever might be imputed to him, and rather laying it on the Batchian officers, to whom, I faid, we were certainly obliged, for fo far affifting us in repairing our veffel;

but,

but, as for going with us to New Guinea, it was what I had no right to expect. The contents of the Sultan of Batchian's letter to him, he always told me, were, that his officers and corocoro fhould accompany me whitherfoever I went, and that he (Tuan Hadjee) was to inforce thefe orders. But, replied he, what can I do, if they will not obey? Soon after he fent a boat alongfide, as if to put on board his baggage; but his fervant carried her back towards the fhore; where afterwards feeing that fervant, I bid him afk his mafter, if he intended to put his baggage on board; to which the man gave me no anfwer.

I really expected, from the reluctance Tuan Hadjee and the Batchian officers had lately fhewn of proceeding to New Guinea, that matters would turn out as they did: I was therefore on my guard, and that afternoon had a long converfation with Tuan Hadjee about our voyage, in order to found him. The feeming indifference which I put on at what happened, led him, I believe, to imagine he might have every thing his own way; and on his hinting that we had come a great diftance, and, were we to return, it might not be amifs; at the fame time, politely acknowledging, that I was commander, &c. I faid, that I dropt all thoughts of going to Tanna Papua, but begged of him to accompany me to fome of the iflands that lie to the N. E. of Waygiou, near which we were, and about which he had talked fo much at Balambangan; in order that we might have at leaft fomething to fay on our return. This pleafed him, and he confented with a good grace. But before
I proceed,

I proceed, it may not be improper to say something of the iflands on the weft fide of Waygiou.

On the weft fide of Waygiou is a pretty deep
bay, before which lie many fmall low iflands
called Ranfawar, Efnowan, Binfi, Gopi, Kubbon,
Waftib, Wafwa, Wafagy, Tapopo, and Piapis.
Thefe are low flat, and covered with trees to the
water's edge, as moft Malay iflands are, Ranfawar
and Piapis excepted. The largeft of them may
not be above a mile and a half, fome only half
a mile round. I have already faid Tomoguy has
a hill about a hundred and fifty feet high. On an
ifland three miles E. N. E. of Tomoguy, called
Ranfawar, already mentioned, is a hill rather higher. Thefe iflands keeping off the weftward fwell,
muft make fmooth water within them, on the coaft
of Waygiou, where I am told are fome harbours;
but I did not vifit them, nor quit the ifland Tomoguy, whilft repairing there, above half an hour at
a time, and that only twice. Therefore I can
give no account of thefe harbours, and have laid
down in the chart, only the bearings of the iflands,
from Tomoguy hill, with their computed dif-
tances.

Tomoguy lies near the two iflands of Batang
Pally, which are of middling height, and about
eighteen miles in compafs, reckoning round them
both. They form the ftrait, in which is the harbour of Manafuin, where we lay. The ftrait may
be called one continued harbour, four miles long,
with mud foundings throughout. Here are fome
fpots of coral rocks : but they give fair warning,
fhowing

showing themselves by their bright colour at high water, and at low water being dry.

On the northern extremity of the westermost Batang Pally, is a flat table land. Near the other Batang Pally lies the small flat island of Waglol; between which and the larger island is a safe and short passage, with good soundings. At Waglol, lives a Synagee, who honoured me with a visit, while the vessel was repairing at Tomoguy, and begged a present like the rest. One half of his coat and long drawers was clouded red, white, and yellow; the other half blue, white, and green clouded also, not unlike the whimsical dresses of masquerades; his turban made of coarse white calicoe was pinked. The Mahometan inhabitants of the Molucca islands, are much given to cloud the Indostan calicoes with many colours. Several Molucca men having touched at Tomoguy, I observed not only their turbans, but even their coats clouded and pinked in this manner.

I was told that, east of Gilolo, were no horses, no horned cattle or sheep; I saw only a very few goats at Tomoguy. On the adjacent islands are many wild hogs, of which the Papua people who sold me sago, brought me at times, some pieces dry roasted at a slow fire. On these also are some deer. At Tomoguy I bought three of the large crowned pigeons, very well represented by Dampier. The Molucca people call them Mulutu, and the Papuas Manipi. My pigeons grew tame, and eat Indian corn, called Jaggon. They strike hard with their wings, on which is a kind of horn. One of the three escaped at Dory harbour, the other two

I carried

I carried to Mindano, where they died. Some Papua people brought me land crabs, fhaped like lobfters ; their claws exactly the fame, but much ftronger ; and their bodies not fo large ; they are called Oodang. I was told they climb trees, and eat the fruit.

Whilft I lay at Tomoguy, Captain Mareca was breaking fugar canes, by putting them in a prefs, and driving wedges. The juice thus extracted is boiled into a fyrup for ufe. I filled a liquor cafe with the juice, which in a little time became good vinegar. The Mahometans here, live moftly upon fifh and fago bread. Sometimes they mix a co-co nut rafped down, with the fago flour ; and, putting this into a thin Chinefe iron pan, they keep ftirring the mixture on the fire, and eat it warm. I have alfo feen, not only the Mahometans, but Papua men, eat the ordinary white fwallo (Eiche de Mer) which is found almoft every where in the fand at low water. They eat it raw, cut up fmall, and mixed with falt and lime juice.

I faw here a peculiar way of drawing blood ; they put the rough fide of a certain leaf, about as large as a man's hand, on that part whence they want to extract blood ; then, with the tongue, they lick the upper fide of the leaf, and the under fide is prefently all over bloody.

Here grows a particular kind of green fruit, which they eat with the areka nut, as they do the betel leaf in Indoftan : it is as long as the hollow part of a quill, and almoft as fmall : they call it,

as

as the Malays call the betel leaf, Ciry. This fruit
is very good in a curry or ftew, having a fine aromatic flavour. Tomoguy lies in latitude 00° 20′ S,
and longitude 127° 10′ E. But to return to our
voyage.

After I had, as before related, agreed with Tuan
Hadjee, that I would not proceed to New Guinea,
and that, after vifiting the iflands of Aiou and Fan,
(which I underftood lay to the N. E. of Waygiou,
the former in fight of it) I would return to Balambangan, the two Batchian officers came very frankly
to fup with me, and faid they would go very wil-
lingly to the iflands that lie off New Guinea, but
not to the main land. I told them I did not mean
to go to the continent; on which we parted, they
promifing to have every thing ready to fail in the
morning.

Saturday the 8th. At break of day, fired a gun,
as a fignal for failing; got under way, and rowed
through the ftrait between Batang Pally and
Waglol, where we found good foundings. This
ftrait is about half a mile broad at the narroweft
part. We had light and variable winds from the
fouth and fouth eaft, fteering north eaft, along the
north weft part of Waygiou. About noon came
on board a canoe with fix people, who had long
hair, were dreffed like Malays, and all fpoke the
Malay tongue. They belonged to a Dutch Chinefe floop, then in harbour, at a place called
Ilkalio; where is a deep ftrait (I was told) that
divides the ifland of Waygiou: the houfes of
Ilkalio being vifible with a glafs. They converfed
                                        much

much with Captain Mareca; and at going away
left him fome Cocaya mats, as a prefent. I fufpected they were very curious and inquifitive with
him, though they afked me no queftions. I fhowed
them, however, all manner of civility: but to in-
timate that I was not alone, the Banguey corocoro,
in which Tuan Hadjee was, being then about a
league to windward, I made a fignal to fpeak with
her; which fhe inftantly obferved, by bearing
down. Tuan Hadjee had then fome little converfation with the people in the canoe.

We left to the northward the ifland Ruib, which
confifts of one high hill, not peaked, and is higher
than the cock's comb of Gibby Monpine. The
diftance of Ruib from Waygiou, may be about
fix leagues. Ten fmall iflands, five pretty high,
and five fhaped like buttons, lie in the ftraits: I
left them to the northward. In paffing thofe
ftraits, between Waygiou and Ruib, I could get
no foundings. We faw alfo an ifland, with a
table land upon it, bearing about N. N. E. it is
called Pulo Een, or Fifh Ifland; and lies to the
eaftward of Ruib. Every ifland in thofe ftraits
feemed to be fteep. I kept fome times within half
a league of the ifland Waygiou, and found ftrong
tides, with a great fwell: the coaft of Waygiou
appeared likewife to be bold. Ruib lies in latitude
00° 15′ N. longitude 127° 10′ E. In the different
views I have given of Ruib and Pulo Een, they
cannot but be known. At funfet, the extreme part
of the coaft of Waygiou bore E. by S.

On *Monday* the 9th, had but little wind all night,
the current fet us to the eaftward. In the morn-

G   ing

ing Ruib bore weſt half ſouth, ſeven leagues:
found we had paſſed, in the night, ſeveral iſlands
ſhaped like buttons, near the coaſt of Waygiou.

In the morning we ſaw an iſland of middling
height, flat atop ; or rather like the flat of a plate
turned bottom up.* It bore eaſt by north, half
north. We alſo ſaw a remarkable peak like a
buffalo's horn, upon the iſland Waygiou, about a
league in-land.

In the evening we had the mouth of a good
looking harbour open : it is called Offak. The
peak or horn above mentioned, then bore S. S. E.
The wind immediately came round to the eaſtward, and it looked very gloomy to the northward ; which, however, came to nothing.

On *Tueſday* the 10th, lay to moſt part of the
night ; fired a gun, and ſhowed ſeveral lights for
the corocoros. In the morning, ſaw them both to
the weſtward ; ſtood on to the eaſtward, all three
in company, until P. M. The wind coming then
from the eaſt and north eaſt, we bore away for the
harbour Offak, and got into it by five o'clock ;
about ſunſet had a great deal of rain. I am of
opinion there is much rain on this iſland ; for the
hills are not exceeding high, but are above what
may be called middling height ; and the clouds,
as they paſs, often break, and diſſolve into rain.

Wedneſday the 11th. Employed in fitting our
commoodies, which did not move well ; alſo compleated our water. We ſent our boat to fiſh at

* Manouaran.

the

People of New Guinea and their Boats

the mouth of the harbour. She foon returned with nine bonettas. The people feemed all very well contented. Among the Batchian people, were four perfons, whom I called Manteries, by way of civility and diftinction : they belonged to certain head men on the ifland Ceram, who really had the title of Mantery ; and Ceram was under Batchian. I thought proper to keep thofe perfons in good humour, as well as Tuan Bobo and Tuan Affahan ; therefore, I promifed each of them a coat of Europe broad cloth.

C H A P. VII.

Defcription of the North Coaft of Waygiou, and of the Harbour of Offak—Paffed Manouaran---Arrived at the Iflands of Yowl---Account of them---Sailed for the Iflands of Fan---A Gale, in which we were feparated from the two Corocoros---Obliged to bear away---Arrived at Dory Harbour on the Coaft of New Guinea---Some Account of the Papuas there---Directions to get into the Harbour---Conjectures about Schouten's Ifland.

As I had the fatisfaction of finding all the people contented and in good humour, I took the opportunity of vifiting and furveying part of this fpacious harbour, whilft others were occupied, as I have faid, in fixing our rudders. At the fame time I employed four ovens on fhore, in baking bread from the fago flour, which I had bought at

G 2   Tomoguy,

Tomoguy, in order to fave our fea ftock, confifting of three thoufand bifcuits, which I had got
from Salwatty. Thefe bifcuits were hard, being
well baked; and few from that ftore had been
ufed. The view of fome of the hills on the left
hand, going into Offak harbour, is not only picturefque from without, but from within the harbour, as they are not overloaded with wood. On
the contrary, there were many clear fpots covered
with grafs; and fome appearing barren, even gave
pleafure, as they promifed eafe in travelling that
way : for it is almoft univerfally the cafe in Malay
countries, that too much wood, or too much long
grafs, called Lalang, and fometimes tall reeds, &c.
difappoint the traveller : he cannot walk on, far
lefs gain a fummit, not very diftant, or fo much as
the brow of a hill, which, feen from on board his
veffel, perhaps appears clofe by. Several groves
pointed out to me, were, I was told, fago trees :
but, as I ftaid only one day, I had not time to
make any excurfion. I was alfo told that the Papua
inhabitants hereabouts, often lurked in fecret places,
and fhot arrows at the unwary traveller ; but, this
my people poffibly faid to indulge their own lazi-
nefs, or perhaps their timidity.

The north coaft of the ifland Waygiou is about
fifteen leagues in length, from that fmall ifland on
the north weft extremity, and juft under the line,
to Rawak ifland and harbour, on the north eaft
part of the ifland. The hill on Gibby Monpine,
(a particular quarter of Waygiou) which I call the
Cock's Comb, from its fhape, may be feen about
twenty leagues off, and is not quite fo high as
Ruib.

Ruib. Some white fpots appear on it, as has been faid. Going along the coaft, abreaft of, and near to Piapis harbour, (which fhall be hereafter defcribed) we perceived a remarkable hill; I call it the Firft Peak; and, confidering it as a cone, the angle at its vertex is a right angle. Farther on, about five leagues, is juft fuch another hill: the angle of its top is alfo nearly a right angle; and it is the fame in fhape, which is that of a fugar loaf, though fomewhat higher than the Firft Peak: I call this laft the Second Peak. It is abreaft of a fmall ifland, which, from its fhape, I name the Shoe. Onward, in an eaft direction about three leagues, rifes a very remarkable peak, which I call the Third Peak, or Buffalo's Horn. In fome attitudes its top is blunt and rounding; in others, fharp and pointed: yet it is moftly covered with trees, and is very fteep.

Coming from the northward, the voyager muft defcry one of thefe three peeks. The middle one, as I have faid, is higher than the firft; it is alfo fomewhat higher than the third, and may be feen above twenty leagues off.

To go into Offak harbour, from the eaftward, you pafs a pyramidical naked rock, within half a mile of the entrance on the left. The entrance is bold, and half a mile wide, with twenty fathom mud foundings in mid channel. In the entrance, you leave on the left, two iflets, each no larger than a houfe: the larger has bufhes atop, and around both are breakers. A little farther is another iflet, that joins vifibly to the main, by a reef

of

of rocks. It will be neceffary to give all thefe a
reafonable birth, as well as the point on the left.
When you have paffed this point, on which is
three fathom water, you find a fandy bay ftill on
the left, with a ftream of frefh water, where you
may anchor in twelve fathom fand. From the
entrance into the harbour, the third peak, or buffalo's horn, bears fouth half weft, about three
miles in-land.

Oppofite to, or almoft fouth from the entrance,
are two little iflands, one fhaped like a fugar loaf,
the other with a hilloc on it. At the bottom of
this hilloc is a pond of frefh water, and behind,
or clofe to the iflet, is water five or fix fathom
deep. This would be a good place for a fhip to
heave down. The two iflands are joined by a reef
of coral rocks dry at low water.

On the eaft and weft, the harbour goes far into
the ifland of Waygiou; but, as I have been told,
the weft bay goes farther. At the bottom of it,
is faid to be a fmall neck, or carrying place, over
which canoes may be eafily tranfported into a
large lake,* where are many iflands. On the
largeft refides a great Rajah: all over it are
foundings, and it communicates with the fea at
the fouth part of the ifland. Captain Mareca told
me there were about 100,000 inhabitants upon
the ifland, that they were continually at war with
one another, and that it might be about forty
leagues round. Offak lies in latitude 00° 10' N.
longitude 127° 44'.

* This may be the deep bay, that in the charts is laid down on
the fouth fide of the ifland.

Thurfday

Thurfday the 12th. Got under way before dawn, having firft fired a gun, as a fignal to the two corocoros, which did not immediately follow : at feven in the morning, being then a good way from the harbour's mouth, we faw them in-fhore. About noon had very frefh gales at N. N. W. fteered E. N. E. and paffed Manouaran, an ifland of middling height. We foon after difcovered the higheft and largeft of the iflands Aiou. It is called by way of diftinction, I fuppofe, Aiou Baba, Father Aiou ; and bears from Manouaran, N. E. by N. eight leagues.

We had fine weather all night. The Borneo corocoro kept far ahead.

Friday the 13th, at funrife, could fee the high mountains of New Guinea : I inclined much to fteer for them ; but durft not, as I knew Tuan Hadjee would not confent.

We had fine weather until about eight A. M. it then began to rain, and the wind came to the eaftward. Steering for the largeft of the Aious, I found a reef run weft of it fix or feven miles.

The Borneo corocoro, in which was one of the Batchian officers, got over the reef, and fent us a boat with eight Coffres and a pilot, who was alfo a Papua Coffre. After lying by, until the tide ferved, he carried us over the edge of the reef, in one and a half fathom coral rocks ; and then we had barely one fathom. Immediately we came into a large found of five, four, three, and two
fathom

fathom clear fand, with fpots of rocks here and
there.   Anchored in one and a half fathom, at low
water (clean fand) within a fhort mile of fhe fhore.
Befide the pilot boat, came two others to tow us
in, the wind being againft us : for we went over
the edge of the reef at leaft four miles to the weftward of Aiou Baba.

Saturday the 14th. Had in the morning much
rain ; notwithstanding which, the three head men
of thofe iflands, ftiled the Moodo, the Synagee
and the Kymalaha, came on board about eight,
in a large corocoro, with fix banks of paddles,
three banks of a fide. They were Papua men,
and prefented me with feveral birds of paradife,
which they had got from New Guinea ; in return,
I gave each fome calicoes. I faluted them, when
they went away, with one gun, which they returned.

A fifherman, amongft various fifh, brought me
two, of which the heads were remarkable, by a
horn that projected from between their eyes. The
horn was about four inches long, equal in length
to the head. Altogether, the head was that of a
unicorn : the people called it Een Raw, that is, the
fifh Raw. The fkin was black, and the body
might be twenty inches long ; its tail was armed
with two ftrong fcythes on each fide, with their
points forward.*

* Mr. Banks found the fame kind of fifh on the coaft of
New Holland, of which he did me the favour to fhow me a
print—I preferved the heads of my two fifh ; they are now in
the Mufeum of Charles Boddam, Efquire.

On

On *Sunday* the 15th, went round Aiou Baba in the pilot's boat, and found it about five miles in compafs. Coming back, I went to the little harbour, where the Moodo, the Synagee, and Kymalaha lived; finding it very fnug for veffels of fix foot water, I chofe, however, to lie in the fmooth road without. To day Tuan Hadjee vifited the Moodo. On my return from the circuit of the ifland, I found him finely dreffed, with a number of attendants. Perceiving he had been on a vifit of ceremony, I regretted he had not fignified his intention, that I might have given orders for the proper falute on his going afhore, which he took in very good part.

Monday the 16th, fair weather for the firft part of the day, but much rain in the afternoon. About breakfaft time the Moodo paid me a vifit, accompanied by two of his wives, who, I learned, had been taken at Amblou, a Dutch fettlement, on an ifland near Amboyna, by the Papua people. Both had long black hair, and were of the Malay colour; whereas every one I faw here, men and women, were Coffres. By one of thefe female captives, the Moodo had a little boy, who came along with them. The corocoro that brought them on board, was not near fo large as that in which the Moodo came to make his firft vifit. The mother of the boy had a fettled melancholy in her countenance; fhe fpoke good Malays, and was cheared by the fight of Europeans. The other captive feemed more reconciled to her condition. I treated them with tea, and gave them a little to carry afhore
with

with them ; alfo fome fugar candy, for which they
were very thankful. I made them likewife prefents of calicoes.

In the evening, my mate, being ill of an inter-
mitting fever, went afhore to the Moodo's houfe :
the Serang * being fick, had been the day before
conveyed thither. To day I fent to the woods,
whence I had a new foremaft, and made a wood-
en anchor.

I was curious to enquire how fuch a perfon as
the Moodo, who was under the king of Tidore,
and had little power of his own, durft venture to
purchafe the fubjects of the Dutch. I was anfwered that here people did not mind the Dutch,
as they were far away ; but, whenever the Dutch
threatened vengeance to any Papua chiefs, and
fent to take off their heads, they, on fuch occafions, to reprefent the chief, dreft up a flave, who,
being really executed, fo far deceived the governor of Ternate.

On *Tuefday* the 17th, wefterly winds with fome
rain, until afternoon ; then N. E. winds, with much
rain. Notwithftanding it blew frefh, I lay fmooth :
for the huge fea, without, broke its violence on the
edge of the reef, with which this clufter of iflands
is furrounded. However, I became fenfible when
it was high water, by the veffel's pitching a little :
at low water the fea was perfectly fmooth, the
depth nine foot. A rifing and fetting moon makes
high water, and the fpring tides rife five foot.

* Serang, boatfwain.

The

The Papua people, in their boats, continued to bring us abundance of excellent fiſh ; alſo turtle, which my Mahometans would not eat ; but they ate the eggs. The natives had a way of ſtuffing the guts of the turtle, with the yolks of its eggs. So filled, they rolled it up in a ſpiral form, and roaſted it, or rather dried it over a ſlow fire ; it proved then a long ſauſage. They alſo brought us limes, and ſmall lemons. We found near the Moodo's houſe, the green, called by the Malays Aſſimum. It is about an inch and half long, and a quarter of an inch broad ; it breaks ſhort, being thick ; and has a ſalt taſte, when ate raw. It becomes very palatable with oil and vinegar, proving alſo very good boiled. This green ſprings abundant in the Soolco Archipelago, on ſmall iſlands, at high water mark.

Wedneſday the 18th. Fine weather : our people in the boat caught much fine fiſh in the night.

On *Thurſday* the 19th, went to the iſland of Abdon, accompanied by the Moodo and the Synagee : found it lie 00° 36′ north latitude : we returned at night. Abdon I diſcovered to be about three miles round, and about two hundred foot high. Konibar may be about the ſame height, and ſize : it lies north of Abdon. The reſt of the ſixteen iſlands, that form this cluſter, are flat and low, except Aiou Baba, near which we lay, and which riſes about five hundred foot. On Konibar, are ſaid to be plantations of yams, potatoes, ſugar canes, and other tropical productions. On the iſland Abdon, I was in a rude plantation of

papa

papa trees, lime trees, and chili or cayenne pepper : the foil was rich, as it is alfo on Aiou Baba.
Near the little harbour, where the Moodo's houfe
ftands, the foil is fandy and low ; and about two
hundred yards from his houfe, is a pond of frefh
water. But the three iflands of Aiou Baba, Abdon, and Konibar, are too thinly inhabited to produce much, though almoft every thing would
grow upon them. The Papua inhabitants have fifh
and turtle in fuch abundance, that they neglect agriculture. When they want bread, they carry live
turtle, and faufages made of their eggs, dried fifh,
&c. to Waygiou, where, in the harbours of Rawak,
Offak, Warjow, &c. they truck for fago, either
baked or raw ; nay, perhaps go to the woods and
provide themfelves, by cutting down the trees.
On thefe voyages, they often carry their wives
and families. They bring tortoife fhell and fwallo,
to fell to the Chinefe, who trade here in floops, that
muft always be furnifhed with Dutch paffes, many
Chinefe being fettled at Ternate and Amboyna.

Friday the 20th.. Frefh gales at N. W. until the
afternoon : then variable winds, and more moderate weather. Went in a boat to found the neareft paffage out, it being the eaftermoft, and within
two miles of Aiou Baba. I found it much better
than the channel, by which we entered ; fixed a
pole in the fand as a beacon. In the night we had
frefh gales and fqualls from the N. E. quarter.

Saturday the 21ft, much rain. The pilot came
on board, but, as the weather looked bad, and I
did not choofe to move, he went afhore again.

In

In the night the wind was at N. W. with frequent fqualls.

Sunday the 22d, moderate weather. The pilot returned on board; alfo Mr. Baxter, and the Serang, who had been kindly treated afhore, for fome trifling prefents to the Moodo. The Kymalaha came likewife, and affifted us very readily with a boat, and people, in towing the veffel over the reef, at the near, or fmall paffage. I gave out that I was going in fearch of the iflands of Fan, which I was informed lay about twelve hours fail to the N. E. of where we were. I difmiffed Captain Mareca, and his three fervants: he feemed very glad to get back to his family, efpecially as I rewarded him with ten bars of iron, and various piece goods. The reafon I parted with him was, I had bought from the Moodo, a Mulatto, who fpoke Malay and the Papua tongue: he was called Mapia. I fufpected alfo a jealoufy between Mareca and Tuan Hadjee, who, immediately on the captain's leaving the galley, came on board with his baggage. About half an hour paft eight in the morning, we got over the reef; and found twenty-five fathom water, fandy ground, not above half a cable's length from it. At parting, I prefented to the Moodo a pocket compafs, with three bars of iron, and one to the Kymalaha. I gave another pocket compafs to the pilot, and one bar of iron. When I told the Moodo and others, that I was bound for the iflands Fan, they furmifed (as I was told), that we were going thither in the view of catching certain yellow coloured people with long hair, who refort frequently

to

to Fan from other iſlands farther north for turtle, poſſibly from the iſlands named Palaos, * in 50° N. latitude ; amongſt ourſelves we called them Mapia, which ſignifies good, in the Magindano tongue.

The reef that ſurrounds theſe iſlands is about fifty miles in compaſs, divided by a deep ſtrait one mile broad, and about five long, into two parts. The ſmaller part incloſes the iſland of Aiou Baba, which is the largeſt of them all, and is high, with the ſmall iſlands Popy and Mof. The larger reef incloſes the iſlands of Abdon and Konibar, which are pretty high, and the low iſlands of Muſbekan, Sebemuky, Capamuky, Rutny, Rainy, Popy, Cafoly, Yowry, and three ſmall iſlands called Wiriſoy. A deep ſound is ſaid to be on the N. W. ſide of the larger reef. Viſiting Abdon, I paſſed over ſmooth water in this ſound eight and ten fathom deep ; and from this ſound the Moodo, who accompanied me when I viſited it, aſſured me, there was a good egreſs to the open ſea ; but I had no opportunity of examining it, and went only where the depth is marked. Amidſt theſe ſoundings, I frequently found little ſpots of coral rocks, ſteep, even with the water's edge. From a little height upon Abdon, I could not ſee the fartheſt iſlands called Wiriſoy : ſo they are put down only by report : all the other iſlands I ſaw. Aiou Baba lies in latitude 00° 32′ N. longitude 128° 25.

* Harris's Voyages, vol. 1. p. 691.

If

If it be true that there is an entrance into this found, which, as I have faid, has a good depth, fhips might lie there very fecure, and the fituation muft be healthy. They would find plenty of turtle and fifh, and fome tropical fruits. Water is alfo to be got, I am told, by digging even on the low iflands: but Waygiou being fo near, where are many good harbours, it would perhaps be more eligible to go thither; though, in point of health, Waygiou, being fubject to frequent rains, cannot compare with the iflands Aiou.

Having got over the reef, and taken leave of our Papua friends, who had behaved exceeding civilly, I fteered along the fouth edge of it. About noon, the Banguey corocoro keeping rather too near the reef, I fired a gun, and made her fignal. We then proceeded all three together, fteering N. N. E. wind at W. N. W. At funfet, the ifland Abdon bore weft, five or fix leagues,; the current fet eaftward. Lay to beft part of the night, feeing neither of the corocoros. It blew hard from N. W. which caufed a great fea.

Monday the 23d. In the morning Pulo Waygiou bore S. S. W. and the iflands of Aiou were out of fight. About eight in the morning, the Borneo corocoro (in which was Tuan Bobo, one of the Batchian officers, the other Tuan Affahan, being on board the galley) made, by firing a gun, a fignal of diftrefs. I found fhe had carried away her commoody or rudder. Luckily provided with two, a large and a fmall, I fpared her the latter, and with difficulty got it conveyed by a

rope,

rope, as there was a great fea. At noon I found myfelf in the latitude of 00° 52′ N.

On obferving the diftrefs of one of the corocoros, I had put about and fteered S. W. with the wind at N. W. willing, if poffible, to regain Waygiou; which, however, I did not expect; though Tuan Hadjee, feeing it right ahead, thought otherwife. At fix, P. M. it blowing very frefh, the veffel fprang a leak, and near three foot water got into her hold, before we could gain on her. We ftarted water, and hove overboard whatever came to hand; fago, firewood, and our cooking place; alfo a great many iron hoops: in doing of which, I cut my right hand, being in a hurry, while the black people ftood aghaft. My two Europeans were inceffantly employed in baling over each gunnel, and both the corocoros were in fight, and near us. At laft, in about an hour and a half, we began to gain, but kept one man conftantly baling all night, as the veffel continued leaky. So I kept her fometimes before the fea, and fometimes lay to, as fuited beft her eafe.

Tuefday the 24th. In the morning the gale had much abated, but, to my great concern, had driven out of fight both corocoros. I could fee Waygiou bearing weft, about fourteen leagues: at the fame time, I could difcover the high mountains of New Guinea.

I told Tuan Hadjee, there was an abfolute neceffity to bear away for Dory harbour on the coaft of New Guinea; to which he made no objection.

So

So we fteered S. E. and E. S. E. for the ifland of
Myfory, * to the fouthward of which, Tuan Hadjee told me, the Harbour of Dory lay.   At noon
we could juft fee Waygiou, from which I reckoned
myfelf above one degree eaft.   We could alfo fee
the Cape of Good Hope : it bore E. S. E. about
twelve leagues from us, then in 00° 13 N. latitude, which lays the Cape nearly under the line.

At funfet, the Cape bore E. S. E. four leagues.
We were then about feven miles from the neareft
fhore, and it clearing up weftward, I had fight of two
flat iflands, which Tuan Hadjee told me were
called Mifpalu : they bore weft, and were about
five leagues diftant.   During the night the weather was moderate, with the wind a little off fhore.
This part of the coaft of New Guinea, joining on
the weft of the Cape of Good Hope, confifts of
two, fometimes three, ranges of very high hills,
one behind the other.   About midnight we
doubled the Cape.

Wednefday the 25th.   In the morning the Cape
of Good Hope bore W. N. W. half N. feven
leagues, being then about feven miles off fhore.
I perceived many clear fpots on the hills which
were neareft the fhore, with afcending fmoke.
Tuan Hadjee told me, thefe were the plantations
of the Haraforas †.   At three in the afternoon we

---

* Which, by Tuan Hadjee's defcription, I took to be Schouten's ifland.

† People who live in land, and cultivate the ground.

H   could

could difcern the Cape of Good Hope to the weit-
ward, bearing W. by N. half N. and a certain bluff
land to the eaftward, bearing on the oppofite point
of the compafs E. by S. half S. we happening at
that inftant to be exactly on the rhumb line that
went between them. I then took the Cape to be ten
leagues, and the Bluff Land feven leagues diftant.
Immediately after, I faw land of middling height
appearing like an ifland, bearing E. by S. I concluded this was Schouten's ifland. Tuan Hadjee
afferting that it was, and that to gain Dory harbour
we muft fteer round the forementioned Bluff
Land ; but, luckily, before night, I perceived the
land I took to be Schouten's ifland, to be part of
the main land of New Guinea ; that the Bluff
Head already mentioned was a hill refembling a
bee-hive, and that it joined to the land I have er-
roneoufly called Schouten's ifland, by a low neck
covered with trees of equal height, excepting one
clump in the middle of the neck, which is higher
than the reft. This low neck not being feen
when the land without it firft appeared, made me
the rather believe it to be Schouten's ifland, and
fo far confirmed the miftake ; but, on finding it,
I hauled off. The wind then frefhening, I lay to
fome hours, left I fhould overfhoot the harbour of
Dory. Many years had paffed fince Tuan Hadjee
had been there : I was therefore not furprized at
his having been miftaken.

In the morning, faw a flat point of land bearing
S. E. fix leagues. Found the extremity of the land
mentioned yefterday at Schouten's ifland, but which
was the land of Dory, to bear E. by N. half N.
from

from the hill I have called the Bee-hive : fo that
the neck of land, with the low trees and the
clump of trees upon it, already mentioned, form
a bay. Steered E. S. E. for a little low ifland like
a bonnet, clofe to the fhore. About noon, it
blowing hard, and there being a great fea, when
we had run about twelve leagues from morning,
we hauled in round this ifland, leaving it to the
right. When it bore S. S. W. within lefs than
piftol fhot, we had fourteen fathom water, fandy
ground. It is called Yowry. We anchored behind it in three and a half fathom water, with a
wooden anchor, and made a rope faft to the fhore
of the ifland. We lay pretty fmooth. At night,
let go our iron grapnel, and foon after parted from
our wooden anchor, the cable being cut by the rocks.

I believe this to be a very good harbour farther
in ; but I had no opportunity to examine, as, it
blowing very frefh, I did not go afhore. I obferved a reef of rocks from the main land, projected fo far, as to overlap (if I may fo fay) the paffage to the north weft of the ifland Yowry ; and
no fwell came in that way, except a little at high
water.

Tuan Hadjee, Tuan Buffora, and Tuan Affahan, went directly afhore ; the firft was extremely
affected with the bad weather, and faid very little.
Tuan Affahan was a fmart feaman, and had been
very ufeful in the late gale. Coming along this
coaft, within four miles of the fhore, I would have
often founded ; but durft not bring the veffel to. In
rolling before the fea, I found the projecting

H 2   gallery

gallery of great ufe; for, when it took the water, it buoyed the veffel up like an outrigger. We fhipped water over the gunnel feveral times. On this little ifland Tuan Buffora found a nutmeg tree, which, however, had no fruit. The ifland Yowry may be about three quarters of a mile in compafs. Latitude 00° 15 S. longitude 130° 45' E.

Friday the 27th. At eight in the morning weighed, and ftood along fhore, about E. by S. the coaft lying nearly E. S. E. the wind ftill at N. W. blowing frefh. A flat point, like that mentioned yefterday, lies about fix or feven leagues from the ifland Yowry, in an E. S. E. direction: when we got abreaft of it, I found the bay of Dory open; and another flat point bore from it S. by E. about five leagues, the bay being between. Here the wind moderated a little. The veffel got into what I imagined to be a ground fwell, and the fea had like to have pooped us; but we prefently got out of it, hauling round into the bay. About noon came to an anchor, in a fandy bay, clofe to the land, well fheltered from the north weft and north. The wind (drawn by the land, no doubt) then came from the fea; upon which we weighed, and ftood on towards Dory harbour.

Off the mouth of the bay, before the harbour, but out of the fwell, a boat with two Papua men, came on board, after having converfed a good deal with our linguifts at a diftance: fatisfied we were friends, they haftened afhore, to tell, I fuppofe, the news. Soon after, many Papua Coffres came

came on board, and were quite eafy and familiar:
all of them wore their hair bufhed out fo much
round their heads, that its circumference meafured
about three foot, and where leaft, two and a half.
In this they ftuck their comb, confifting of four
or five long diverging teeth, with which they now
and then combed their frizzling locks, in a direction perpendicular from the head, as with a defign
to make it more bulky. They fometimes adorned
their hair with feathers. The women had only
their left ear pierced, in which they wore fmall
brafs rings. The hair of the women was bufhed
out alfo; but not quite fo much as that of the
men. As we were rowing along, one of my
crowned pigeons efcaped from its cage, and flew
to the woods.

We anchored about four in the afternoon, clofe
to one of their great houfes, which is built on
pofts, fixed feveral yards below low water mark;
fo that the tenement is always above the water: a
long ftage, fupported by pofts, going from it to
the land, juft at high water mark. The tenement
contains many families, who live in cabins on each
fide of a wide common hall, that goes through the
middle of it, and has two doors, one opening to
the ftage, towards the land; the other on a large
ftage towards the fea, fupported likewife by pofts,
in rather deeper water than thofe that fupport the
tenement. On this ftage the canoes are hauled up;
and from this the boats are ready for a launch, at
any time of tide, if the Haraforas attack from the
land; if they attack by fea, the Papuas take to
the woods. The married people, unmarried
women,

women, and children, live in thefe large tenements, which, as I have faid, have two doors;
the one to the long narrow ftage, that leads to the
land; the other to the broad ftage, which is over
the fea, and on which they keep their boats, having outriggers on each fide. A few yards from
this fea ftage, if I may fo call it, are built, in ftill
deeper water, and on ftronger pofts, houfes where
only batchelors live. This is like the cuftom of
the Batta people on Sumatra, and the Idaan or
Moroots on Borneo, where, I am told, the batchelors are feparated from the young women and
the married people.

At Dory were two large tenements of this kind,
about four hundred yards from each other, and
each had a houfe for the batchelors, clofe by it:
in one of the tenements were fourteen cabins,
feven on a fide; in the other twelve, or fix on a
fide. In the common hall, I faw the women
fometimes making mats, at other times forming
pieces of clay into earthen pots; with a pebble in
one hand, to put into it, whilft they held in the
other hand alfo a pebble, with which they knock-
ed, to enlarge and fmooth it. The pots fo formed,
they burnt with dry grafs, or light brufhwood.
The men, in general, wore a thin ftuff, that comes
from the coco nut tree, and refembles a coarfe
kind of cloth, tied forward round the middle, and
up behind, between the thighs. The women wore,
in general, coarfe blue Surat baftas, round their
middle, not as a petticoat, but tucked up behind,
like the men; fo that the body and thigh were
almoft naked; as boys and girls go entirely. I
have

have often obferved the women with an ax or chopping knife, fixing pofts for the ftages, whilft the men were fauntering about idle. Early in a morning I have feen the men fetting out in their boats, with two or three fox looking dogs,* for certain places to hunt the wild hog, which they call Ben : a dog they call Naf. I have frequently bought of them pieces of wild hog ; which, however, I avoided carrying on board the galley, but dreffed and eat it afhore, unwilling to give offence to the crew.

At anchor, I fired fome fwivel guns : the grown people did not regard this, or feem frightened, while the boys and girls ran along the ftages, into the woods.

Saturday the 28th. Frefh winds, with fqualls, but no rain. The clouds feemed to gather, and fettle over the mountains of Arfak, which lie fouth of this harbour : they are exceeding high ; higher than any of the mountains we had hitherto feen, to the weftward, on this coaft.

After paffing the Cape of Good Hope, the promontory of Dory, from a large fhip's deck, may be feen fifteen or fixteen leagues off, disjunct from New Guinea, and like an ifland. To get into Dory harbour, coaft it along, at a reafonable dif-

---

* Among fmall iflands, the wild hogs often fwim in a ftring, from one ifland to another, the hog behind leaning his fnout on the rump of the one before. The hunters then kill them with eafe.

tance :

tance: the flat points and the island Yowry will appear very plain. Having got beyond the laſt Flat Point, which is near the eaſtermoſt part of the promontory, you ſuddenly perceive an iſland (Manaſwary): this muſt be kept on the left. Steer mid channel, in fourteen and fifteen fathom water, ſandy ground. Farther in, and to the weſtward of Manaſwary, is a ſmaller iſland, called Maſmapy, which muſt alſo be left on the ſame hand. When abreaſt of the iſland Maſmapy, that is, when the body of it bears about ſouth, you will have fourteen fathom water, ſandy ground: then look out for a ſunk ſhoal of coral rocks, two foot deep, at low water, and at high water ſix: it is bold to Keep it alſo on the left, and ſteer into the inner harbour, which will hold any number of ſhips, in ſoundings from twelve to five fathom water, muddy ground. Freſh water may be had in many places; wood every where. Dory harbour lies in latitude 00° 21′ S. longitude 131° E.

Schouten's iſland, as laid down by Dampier, bears E. S. E. from the Cape of Good Hope, and has its ſouth coaſt undetermined by a dotted line. The coaſt of New Guinea oppoſite to it is undetermined alſo.---As the promontory of Dory bears from the Cape in the ſame direction, and I can find no voyager has gone to the ſouth of Schouten's iſland, I am apt to think it is the ſame land, which time alone will ſhow.

Having opened the hold, about which we lately had been in great pain, we found our proviſions greatly damaged. A tight cheſt ſaved many of
my

my piece goods. The damaged I wafhed directly in frefh water, and was lucky in getting them well dried. It often threatened to rain, but did not; unlike the climate of Waygiou, where, as has been faid, the clouds often break, and fall in rain unexpectedly.

C H A P. VIII.

Arrival of the Banguey Corocoro—Fate of the Borneo—Arrival of a Corocoro from Tidore—Molucca Method of fifhing—Arrival of a Boat from an Ifland called Myfory—Harbour of Manfingham—Apprehenfions of the Inhabitants of Offy Village—Farther Account of the Papuas—Strictnefs of the Dutch—Search for the Nutmeg Tree, to no Purpofe; find it at laft, on the Ifland of Manafwary —Account of the Haraforas—Give up to the People of Dory the Debt they have contracted—Account of Dory—Account of the Coaft of New Guinea, Eaft of Dory Harbour, and of the Iflands near the Coaft—Alfo of the Places on the Coaft, Weft of Dory Harbour.

W E had hitherto been very uneafy about the two corocoros, with which we parted company the twenty-fourth; but, juft after funfet, news was brought, to our very great joy, that one of them had arrived. Tuan Hadjee immediately fet off, in our boat; and returned with the Banguey, at feven in the evening. They informed us, that the

Borneo

Borneo had foundered in the bad weather, the next day after fhe parted with us; but, that the Banguey, by keeping near her, had faved the people, who were twelve: they loft, however, all their cloaths, and a bafket of cloves belonging to the Sultan of Batchian.

The Banguey corocoro had then twenty-five people: they hove overboard a cafk of water, and many cakes of fago. By what I could learn, the Borneo carried too much fail, juft before fhe foundered; and took in a fea forward, which water-logged her. The Serang being fick, I, at his requeft, fent him afhore, to the houfe of a Papua man, who, for fome Surat blue cloth, took great care of him. A boy brought me for fale, a fmall brown pig, which made me expect to find a breed of hogs; but I was difappointed, this being a very young pig caught in the woods, and fo tamed, that it eat fago flour.

Saturday the 29th. Had ftill north weft winds, with fome rain; fhifted our birth from the lower Papua tenement to the upper, and moored in two fathom fand, with a rope to the poft of the tenement. Prefented to each of the Batchian Manteries, as well as the two officers, a fcarlet coat, and gave each private man a frock and long drawers of chintz. I enquired much about nutmegs among the Papua people: one man faid, he would fetch fome nutmegs from Mandamy, a place to the eaftward. I made him a fmall prefent; but faw no more of him.

Monday

Monday the 30th. Fair weather, with winds at north weft; got out our fago bread to dry; founded part of the harbour. The Jerry Baffa (linguift) of Manfingham came on board, and was very talkative with Mapia, the linguift I had purchafed at Yowl. The name of the former was Mambeway; and he fpoke a little broken Malay.

Tuefday the 31ft. Variable winds at three P. M. We faw a large corocoro coming in, with Dutch colours flying. This put us on our guard; I found fhe came from Tidore: I then muftered fifty people, moftly armed with bows and arrows.

On *Wednefday* the 1ft of *February*. The No- quedah (commander) of the Tidore corocoro, made me a vifit. I treated him civilly, and prefented him with a pocket compafs and a palampore or counterpane.

Thurfday the 2d. Moderate weather: went a fifhing in company with the Tidore Noquedah. We tied coco nut leaves to a ftone, about a pound weight, then hooked to it the falfe flying fifh. This being let down fourteen, fifteen, or more fathoms, in deep water, the line is fuddenly pulled up with a jerk, to fever it from the leaf. The ftone goes to the bottom, while the falfe flying fifh, rifing quickly to the top, is fnapped at by albecores, bonettas, &c. However, we caught nothing. A boat, with outriggers, came pretty near us to day. Of the four men in her, two had, each about his neck, a ratan collar, to which, hung backwards, by the top, a log of wood, fhaped
ped

ped like a fugar loaf, and of about five or fix
pound weight.   They were flaves, offered to me
for fale.   I might have had them very cheap ; but,
being crouded, I did not choofe to purchafe them.
If I had, Tuan Hadjee and others would
have expected the fame indulgence.   Thefe objects of traffic had the griftle between the noftrils
pierced with a bit of tortoifefhell, and were natives
of New Guinea, a good way farther eaft.

Friday the 3d. South from Dory, is another harbour, called Manfingham ; willing to vifit it, went
to day in our boat ; the Tidore Noquedah went
with us.   I found it a very good harbour, but the
entrance rather narrow ; and altogether, it is not
of fo bold and fafe accefs as Dory harbour.
Returning, we put afhore, at a village called Offy,
on a fmall frefh water river, about five miles from
where the galley lay.   The houfes were built as
Malay houfes generally are : the great Papua tenements, already defcribed, being erected only on
the ftrand, where is no river.   I obferved the people of this village were fhy of us, moft of them
running away.   When we had breakfafted, we
embarked.

In the night a Papua corocoro came near
us, and alarmed the large Papua tenement oppofite which we lay ; the ftrangers being in fearch
of their wives and children, who had taken to the
woods, from the village of Offy, when we were
there, and after we had left it, afraid, not only
of us, but of the Tidore people.   In the boat
were about twenty perfons.   Tuan Hadjee wanted

ed me to fire upon them, which I would by no means do: in the morning the miftake was cleared up, and they went away fatisfied. I believe the Papuas did not like the Tidore men, who, I often obferved, make free with the coco nuts from the trees. To day we fhifted our birth from a rocky fpot, on which we had driven, to a fpot of clear fand.

On *Saturday* the 4th, variable winds, and fair weather; at noon the Tidore corocoro failed. The commander faid he was going farther eaft, to the iflands of Sao and Saba to trade. This being the firft day that the Papua people faw the new moon, they fang, and played on a fort of drum, the beft part of the night.

Sunday the 5th, winds at N. W. with fair weather; to day a fwell from the fea, having brought our grapnel home, we carried it out again. Several Papua people afhore, offered to go amongft the Haraforas in order to purchafe provifions; but wanted goods to be advanced for that purpofe. I therefore advanced them ten pieces of Surat blue cloth, and one bar of iron.

Monday the 6th, fine weather, no fwell, the winds moftly from the N. W. From Manfingham came a boat with fifteen Papua men, fome of them jabbered a little Malay. Iffued twenty pieces more, blue Surat baftas for provifions.

On *Tuefday* the 7th, fine weather: built a fhed houfe afhore, and railed it in. Sowed a quantity of muftard feed.

Near.

Near to where we built our fhed houfe, was an old tree, of which, left it fhould fall, I thought proper to cut the roots, and fixed a rope to it, to pull it down. In falling, it took a direction quite oppofite to the one intended, and fmafhed the fkeleton of the houfe. Tuan Hadjee, unlike a Fatalift or Predeftinarian, which Mahometans generally are, faid it was ominous, and defired me not to build there; but I perfifted.

To day I faw many of the Papua men fet off in their canoes to fetch provifions, as I was told. Part were thofe, to whom I had advanced cloth . they left their wives and children, under the care of fome of the old men. In each boat was generally a fmall fox looking dog.

Wednefday the 8th, fair weather, and foutherly winds. Arrived to day, a corocoro from the ifland Myfory; with a perfon who faid he came from the Rajah of Munfury, a portion of that ifland. It feems he had heard of a ftrange veffel's being at Dory. The corocoro went back in the evening, after promife to return. I prefented the mafter with one piece of baftas for himfelf, and a bar of iron for the Rajah. Tuan Hadjee informed me of the ifland Myfory's abounding with kalavanfas, (beans) but having no rice; alfo of its being populous; which was now confirmed by the mafter of this boat. They told me it lay towards the N. E. one day's fail.

Loft out of our houfe, laft night, a china jar: on my complaining to a Papua man, about the theft, it was next day put into its place.

On

On *Thurſday* the 9th, fine weather, and foutherly winds. Two ſmall boats returned from a place they called Wobur, with ſago, plantains, &c. for their families: they were therefore unwilling to diſpoſe of any. They alſo brought ſome birds of Paradiſe, which I purchaſed from them. To day I repaired to the large tenement, near which the veſſel lay. I found the women in the common hall, making cocoya mats as uſual; alſo kneading (if I may ſo term it) the clay, of which others formed the pots, with two pebble ſtones, as before deſcribed. Two of them were humming a tune, on which I took out a german flute, and played; they were exceedingly attentive, all work ſtopping inſtantly when I began. I then aſked one of the women to ſing, which ſhe did. The air ſhe ſung was very melodious, and of a ſpecies much ſuperior to Malay airs in general, which dwell long on a few notes, with little variety of riſe or fall. Giving her a fathom of blue baftas, I aſked another to ſing: ſhe was baſhful, and refuſed; therefore I gave her nothing: her looks ſpoke her vexed, as if diſappointed. Preſently, ſhe brought a large bunch of plantains, and gave it me with a ſmile. I then preſented her with the remaining fathom of baftas, having had but two pieces with me. There being many boys and girls about us as we ſat at that part of the common hall, that goes upon the outer ſtage of the tenement, I ſeparated ſome of the plantains from the bunch, and diſtributed to the children. When I had thus given away about one half, they would not permit me to part with any more; ſo the remainder I carried on board. I could not help taking notice

tice that the children did not fnatch, or feem too eager to receive, but waited patiently, and modeftly accepted of what I offered, lifting their hands to their heads. The batchelors, if courting, come freely to the common hall, and fit down by their fweethearts. The old ones at a diftance, are then faid often to call out, well, are you agreed ? If they agree before witneffes, they kill a cock, which is procured with difficulty, and then it is a marriage. Their cabins are miferably furnifhed ; a mat or two, a fire place, an earthen pot, with perhaps a china plate or bafon, and fome fago flour. As they cook in each cabin, and have no chimney, the fmoke iffues at every part of the roof : at a diftance the whole roof feems to fmoke. They are fond of glafs, or china beads of all colours ; both fexes wear them about the wrift, but the women only at the left ear. *.

They are exceeding good archers, and fome of their arrows are fix feet long ; the bow is generally of bamboo, and the ftring of fplit ratan. They purchafe their iron tools, chopping knives, and axes, blue and red baftaes, china beads, plates, bafons, &c. from the Chinefe. The Chinefe carry back Mifoy bark, which they get to the eaftward of Dory, at a place called Warmafine, or Warapine; it is worth 30 dollars, a pecul (133lb.) on Java. They trade alfo in flaves, ambergris, fwallo, or fea flug, tortoifefhell, fmall pearls, black loories, large red loories, birds of Paradife, and many

---

* I faw no gold ornaments wore by the Papua people ; but in the hills, pointing towards them, they declared that buloan, meaning gold, was to be found.

many kinds of dead birds, which the Papua men have a particular way of drying.

The Dutch permit no burgher of Ternate, or Tidore, to fend a veffel to the coaft of New Guinea. They are not willing to truft thofe burghers, while they put a juft confidence in the Chinefe; that they will not deal in nutmegs, as formerly mentioned. The Chinefe have a pafs from the Sultan of Tidore, and wear Dutch colours. To day I found our muftard well fprouted.

On *Friday* the 10th, fine weather and foutherly wind; went to Manafwary ifland, which I have fometimes called Long Ifland. There was a good party of us, and we fearched for the nutmeg tree, as fome Papua men faid it grew there. We returned about funfet, without finding it.

Saturday the 11th. Had ftill fair weather, and eafterly winds; went again to Long Ifland, in queft of the nutmeg tree. I promifed a reward to whoever fhould find it. Found fome trees, that the Batchian officers faid were nutmeg trees; but they had no fruit. The weather being dry, faw on the hills many fires and fmokes, which I was told were made by the Haraforas, for purpofes of agriculture. Found on the ifland, clofe by the beach, a Papua burial place, rudely built of coral rock. On it was laid the wooden figure of a child, about eight years old, reprefented completely clothed. A real fcull was put into the upper part, on which ears were cut in the wood.

Sunday the 12th, fine weather, and S.E. winds; went round Manafwary ifland. To day found

I   the

the variation of the compaſs, by the medium of ſeveral amplitudes taken aſhore, to be 01° 30′ E.

Monday the 13th, all day long cloudy weather, with variable winds.   This being the firſt day of the Mahometan year, Tuan Hadjee and all the Mahometans had prayers aſhore.   In compliment to them, I fired twelve guns, ſix aſhore, and ſix on board.   After prayers, they amuſed themſelves in throwing the lance, and performing the whole exerciſe of the ſword and target.   Tuan Buſſora was the moſt diſtinguiſhed for alertneſs.

On *Tueſday* the 14th, fine weather, and S. E. winds ; went to Manaſwary iſland, with a numerous party ; landed on different parts, and made the tour of it a ſecond time.   We ſaw no wild hogs, but by the prints of their feet, perceived plainly where they had been : within the iſland, about a quarter of a mile from where we landed, we reached a riſing ground.   The iſland is about five miles in compaſs, every where full of trees, among which is good walking, there being no underwood.

On *Wedneſday* the 15th, fine weather, with S. E. winds ; went again to Manaſwary.   About a mile from where we landed, found a nutmeg tree; we eagerly cut it down, and gathered about thirty or forty nuts : there were many upon it, but they were not ripe.   Tuan Hadjee and all the Molucca people aſſured me it was the true nutmeg, but of the long kind, called Warong ; the round nutmeg, which is cultivated at Banda, being called Keyan.

I preſently

I prefently found many more nutmeg trees, and many young ones growing under their fhade. I picked above one hundred plants, which I put up in bafkets with earth round them; intending to carry them to Balambangan, whither I now pro-pofed to return as faft as poffible. Gave the re-ward I had promifed for finding the nutmeg tree, being five pieces of baftas.

On *Thurfday* the 16th, the fair weather conti-nued, with eafterly winds: faw many great fires on the mountains of Arfak. As the Papua people had not yet returned with the provifions ftipulated, and I was unwilling to lofe the fair winds, that had blown fome time from the eaftward, being alfo afraid of N. W. winds returning ; againft which it were imprudent to attempt, and impoffible to work up the coaft to Waygiou ; I therefore gave up to the Dory people, the debt of thirty pieces of Surat cloth, and a bar of iron, with which I had trufted them : this rejoiced the old men.

On *Friday* the 17th, had ftill eafterly winds, with fine weather. To day fome of the people found a nutmeg tree not a hundred yards from our Shed Houfe. We cut it down, but the fruit was not ripe ; it was juft fuch a tree as I had found and cut down at Manafwary ; and the people of Dory faid there were many fuch trees about the coun-try ; at the fame time they did not feem to know that it was an objeⅽt of confequence, and regard-ed it no more than any wild kind of fruit, that is of no general ufe : whereas on the plantain, the coco nut, the pine apple, and the bread fruit

of two forts, they fet a proper value. They allowed that to the eaftward, at a place called Om-
berpon and Mandamy, were many nutmegs gathered, but I could not learn what was done with
them, or to whom they were fold.   Sometime
before this, I had afked Tuan Hadjee and Tuan
Buffora, what they thought of going farther down
the coaft.   They both objected to it, as they likewife did to making any inland incurfion, to vifit
the Haraforas houfes. The Papua people alfo did
not feem willing that we fhould have any intercourfe with the Haraforas, who, I believe, are
fomehow kept under, or at leaft kept in ignorance
by the Papuas.   When I afked any of the men of
Dory, why they had no gardens of plantains and
kalavanfas, which two articles they were continually bringing from the Haraforas ; I learnt, after
many interrogatories, that the Haraforas fupply
them with thefe articles, and that the Papua people do not give goods for thefe neceffaries every
time they fetch them ; but that an ax or a chopping
knife, given once to a Harafora man, makes his
lands or his labour fubject to an eternal tax, of
fomething or other for its ufe.   Such is the value
of iron ; and a little way farther eaft, I was told
they often ufed ftone axes, having no iron at all.
If a Harafora lofes the inftrument fo advanced to
him, he is ftill fubject to the tax ; but if he breaks
it, or wears it to the back, the Papua man is
obliged to give him a new one, or the tax ceafes.

Tuan Hadjee, when before at Dory, had gone
among the Haraforas. He faid many had long
hair, but that moft of them were Coffres, as the
Papua

Papua men are. He alſo told me they built generally on trees, their houſes, to which they aſcended with great agility, by a long notched ſtick, and often pulled their ladder after them, to prevent followers. The Papua men not inclining I ſhould have any knowledge of the Haraforas, put me in mind of the Malays at Nattal and Tappanooly, on Sumatra, not wiſhing to let Europeans have intercourſe with the Batta people, where the gum benjamin and camphire grow.

Being ready to go from Dory over to the iſland of Manaſwary, where I propoſed to ſtay a day before I ſailed for good, and the people of the village, cloſe to which I had lain, (ſeeing our motions, I ſuddenly perceived, what I imagined, to be a diſtruſt of us, as few children were to be ſeen about the Papua tenement that day: whereas, heretofore, they uſed to come every day on board of us, with fruit, fiſh, &c. to ſell. About noon, when we ſailed, not a man accompanied us over to Manaſwary iſland. Some time after, two men came over, one of them a kind of linguiſt. I cauſed to be fully explained to him, the nature of my giving up the debt, and that nobody would ever call upon the men of Dory for it. At the ſame time, I made him a Capitano, by giving him a frock and drawers of chintz, and firing off three guns, this being the Dutch ceremony. He returned to Dory very well pleaſed, and very vain of his dreſs.

Saturday the 18th. Employed in getting ready for ſea. Took up a good many nutmeg plants, and felled another nutmeg tree ; the fruit was ſuch as we had got before. Tuan Hadjee faid it would be a month or fix weeks ere the fruit would be fully ripe. He and the reft talked fo much about its being of the right fort, tho' it was long, and not round, like the Dutch nutmeg, that I no longer doubted it.

About noon, our Capitano linguift returned. With him came many boys and women, and two men from Dory, who brought us fifh, plantains, kalavanfas, &c. which were purchafed from them as ufual; all jealoufies being removed laft night.

The promontory of Dory, the fea coaft of which extends about fourteen leagues, is of middling height : the grounds every where afcend gradually. It may be faid, like Malay countries in general, to be covered with wood; but it differs in one re-fpect : there being no underwood, it is very eafy travelling under the fhade of lofty trees. The country abounds with fmall frefh water rivulets; here and there is very good grafs, but in no large tracts that I faw. It is very temperate, being fo near the high mountains of Arfak, where the clouds feem always to fettle, fo that it is by far the beft country hitherto vifited on the voyage.

What I fhall now fay of the coaft of New Gui-nea, to the eaftward of Dory, and of the iflands off the coaft, is from the information not only of the Moodo of Aiou, but of fome of the old men at Dory.

From Dory I could not fee Schouten's ifland, which I was told lay to the northward, confequently

quently there muft be a wide paffage between it and the main ; a paffage however not very obvious in the map of this coaft, accompanying Dampier's voyage in the Roebuck, in 1699. Captain Dampier faw Schouten's ifland, and coafted its north fide, which, as I have faid, abounds with kalavanfas, and is full of inhabitants. In fight of Myfory, which poffibly may be Schouten's ifland, lie, as I was told, the iflands Saba and Sao, in an eaft direction. Saba, by the Moodo of Aiou's account, is about as large as Gibby. From Saba and Sao are brought large red loories, alfo black ones.

Farther, in a fouth eaft direction, lies the ifland of Padado, as large as Aiou Baba ; alfo the ifland of Awak, each under its particular Rajah. Still farther is Unfus, * an ifland about the fize of Gibby, it is four days fail from Sao, and near it are the fmaller iflands of Bony and Yop.

Along the coaft of New Guinea eaftward, are the countries of Oranfwary, one day's diftance by water from Dory ; Wariapy two days ; Warmaffine four days ; Yopine five days ; Mandamy fix days. Over againft Wariapy, lies the ifland of Omberpone, behind which is a harbour. Beyond Mandamy, are places on the coaft called Wopimy, Yowry, Manfuary, Morry, then Waropine, the refidence of a powerful Rajah. Oppofite Morry, fpreads a number of fmall iflands, abounding in

* Unfus, poffibly Meanfu, mentioned by Mr. Dalrymple, in his collection of voyages, p. 39.

coco

coco nuts and kalavanfas. Beyond Waropine appears the ifland Krudo, where iron is almoft unknown ; and here prevails the cuftom of boring the nofe : the inhabitants are fometimes called Komambo. Krudo is five days fail from Sao. At Krudo, and the iflands near it, may be got much tor-toifefhell, as indeed every where on this coaft ; but it requires time to collect a quantity, and the mer-chant muft advance the commodities of barter. This the Chinefe do, and are feldom cheated by the Papuas.

From Waropine, above mentioned, is faid to be a . long land ftretch to the head of a river, or a branch of the fea, which comes from the fouth coaft of New Guinea. I have been told that the inhabitants of Ceram carry iron and other goods up this inlet, and trade with the inhabitants of the north coaft, for Miffoy bark. They are deemed alfo to fpeak different languages : but I could learn nothing of the coaft eaft of Waropine.

As to the character of the inhabitants of thofe places, eaft of where we lay, I have the greateft reafon to think it was fierce and hoftile, that they are numerous, and have a vaft many prows : at the fame time, they are faid to deal honeftly with the Chinefe, who trade with them, and advance them goods for feveral months before the returns are made. They trim and adorn their hair, but bore the nofe, and wear earings like the mop-headed people of Dory.

The places on the north coaft of New Guinea, weft of Dory, are, Toweris, which is reported to have

have a harbour ; Warpaſſary and Warmoriſwary, near the Miſpalu iſlands, behind which is ſaid to be good anchoring. I ſaw them both : they are flat low iſlands. Beyond Miſpalu, that is, farther weſt, is Worang; alſo Pulo Womy, which was repreſented to me at Dory, as an iſland, a little bigger than Maſmapy, and to have a harbour behind it. Then comes Pulo Ramay, and next to it Salwatty, which bounds Pitt's Strait on the ſouth, and on its ſouth ſide, with New Guinea, forms the ſtrait of Golowa.

The above intelligence is the beſt I could procure. Thoſe who gave it, not having a true idea of a harbour, and ſometimes thinking that place deſerving the name, into which a boat of theirs could go, excuſe me from depending on their accounts. In the names and diſtances, reckoning by days, they could not ſo well be miſtaken ; and I have the greateſt reaſon to believe, they anſwered my queſtions, not only with ſincerity, but as well as they could. During my ſtay here, Tuan Buſſora daily ſupplied us with ſmall fiſh, like ſprats, he being very expert in caſting the net : which fiſh broiled, with freſh baked ſago bread, and a diſh of tea, were our breakfaſt. We ſeldom ate in the middle of the day ; but had always, about noon, a diſh of tea, coffee, or chocolate, and ſometimes a young coco nut. At ſunſet, we regularly boiled the pot, ſtewing whatever we had ; ſometimes greens and roots only, but always mixed with the emulſion or milk of a full grown coco nut, raſped down. This the Malays call guly (curry): and, thank God, we were all in good

health,

health; but we failed not to bathe daily, nor was there want of pleasant brooks.

CHAP. IX.

Departure from Dory Harbour——Put into Rawak Harbour for Provisions—Description of it—Anchor at Manouaran Island—Put into Piapis Harbour—Description of it—Leave it, and row to windward, intending to anchor at Pulo Een——Find it every where rocky and steep—Bear away, in order to go to the Southward of Gilolo—Pass between the Islands of Gag and Gibby—Pass between the Islands of Bo and Popo——Description of them.

1775.
February.

I WAS very glad to find, before we sailed, that the people of Dory had an opportunity of being convinced, we intended them no harm; and that, by giving up the debt above mentioned, I did not mean to entrap them, or carry them off, as is sometimes done by the Mahometans of the Moluccas, who, I was told by Tuan Hadjee, fit out vessels with no other design. I sailed in the evening, and found, when I got out of the bay, that the current set strong to the westward, against the wind, which, from a favourable S. E. gale, had shifted to the westward.

Saturday the 19th. We had squally, thick, and rainy weather, with westerly winds. The vessel was so uneasy, and pitched so much by a short sea, occasioned by the windward current, that she made a good deal of water. I wished to get into port again;

again; but the current. fet us ftrongly to windward. To my great fatisfaction, however, came fair weather in the afternoon; and we had a light breeze at N. E. the current favouring us. At funfet, we were paft the promontory of Dory, and the Beehive bore fouth; the Cape of Good Hope bore at the fame time weft, fifteen leagues. During the bad weather, I had the misfortune to have many papers wet, as the rain got almoft every where.

Monday the 20th. At dawn the promontory of Dory, appearing like an ifland, was but juft feen. We had variable winds all day, with fultry weather before noon. At noon it was cloudy, and we had no obfervation. At funfet the Cape of Good Hope bore S. S. W. In the evening we had frefh land wind at fouth; fteered N. W. the current being in our favour.

In the morning of the 21ft, found ourfelves about five leagues off fhore, and the Cape of Good Hope bearing S. E. by S. Our latitude at noon was 00° 40′ N. the Cape then bore S. E. about fixteen leagues diftant; the wind was N. E. and we fteered N. W. by W. The night being pleafant, and the water fmooth, we rowed moft part of it, the people finging as ufual.

On *Wednefday* the 22d, in the morning the high land of New Guinea was very confpicuous, although twenty leagues diftant; at the fame time we could fee Waygiou, bearing from S. W. to W.

In confequence of the lofs of the Borneo corocoro, we had five of the Batchian people upon

wages,

wages, and maintained in all twenty-nine perſons aboard the galley, beſide the crew of the Banguey corocoro, which amounted to nineteen. I became, therefore, afraid of running ſhort of ſago bread, now our only diet, except a very ſmall quantity of fiſh. Dory afforded us neither fowl nor goat. A little wild hog, which I got there now and then, and which I eat aſhore, was all the refreſhment I could procure, except fiſh, greens, and fruits. I was told, that on New Guinea were no four footed animals, except hogs, dogs, and wild cats; I ſaw no domeſtic ones. This being our ſituation, Tuan Hadjee repreſented to me, it was hard to proceed in the attempt of weathering Morty, with ſo ſmall a ſtock of proviſions; and it was dangerous to put in any where on the eaſt of Gilolo, where Dutch panchallangs and corocoros were conſtantly cruiſing, as, no doubt, they had heard of us; and that Morty, where ſago grew in abundance, had few, if any, inhabitants. He, therefore, adviſed me to put into Rawak harbour, on the N. E. part of Waygiou, where proviſions were certainly to be had. At the ſame time he ſaid, I was very lucky in getting off the coaſt of New Guinea, from Dory harbour, which he had always conſidered as a dangerous navigation for a ſmall veſſel. Being fully ſenſible of the juſtneſs of what Tuan Hadjee had ſaid, I immediately bore away for Rawak harbour, ſteering S. W. with the wind at E. N. E, and at noon we were in 00° 10′ N. latitude. Early in the afternoon we got ſight of Rawak iſland, it bearing weſt eight leagues. At the ſame time ſaw from the deck, Abdon, one of the Aiou iſlands; rowed and

ſailed

failed all night for the harbour of Rawak; the
people kept finging, as ufual, their Mangaio fong, and were refrefhed with a difh of tea.

On *Thurfday* the 23d, we got in about five in the morning, and found here the Moodo of Aiou, who had with him only one of his wives, with her little boy, befides fervants. We foon filled our water jars, and bought fome fago bread, from boats that came from a village called Kabory, the houfes of which were plainly to be feen, bearing S. E. by. E. from where we lay. To day the winds have been moftly north eaft.

Friday the 24th. Had the winds at N. W. with fine weather. In the morning, the Moodo of Yowl, and one of the king of Tidore's officers, who was then in a boat trading for fwallo, came on board, to make me a vifit. I gave each a piece of coarfe calicoe. Afternoon, many boats from Kabory and from Wargow, which lies beyond it, came with fago bread, which I bought : I bought alfo fome raw fago from the Moodo, afhore, where I faw many of my Aiou acquaintances. In the evening I founded all about the harbour, went in the boat through the narrow, but bold ftrait, that divides the ifland Rawak from the main ; and landed at a pleafant fmall river on the main land of Waygiou, where our people had filled water. The watering place on the ifland of Rawak is a pond, not very clean, juft behind the few houfes that are there : the houfes on the land were built low ; a few built on pofts, in the water, were higher.

The ifland of Rawak, which makes the harbour, lies on the N. E. part of the ifland Waygiou, about five miles E. S. E. from Manouaran; which ifland has been already mentioned. Rawak is of a fingular figure, the fouth part projecting towards Waygiou, in a narrow promontory, fomewhat lower than the northern part of the ifland, which is high, and has a remarkable hill, covered with the aneebong tree, the heart of which is an excellent cabbage. The eaft part of the ifland is alfo a narrow promontory, which I call the Dolphin's Nofe, from its fhape. A fhip from the eaftward muft keep clofer to it, than to the oppofite fhore, off which runs a reef of rocks. The channel is there above a mile broad, with good mud foundings, from fifteen to ten fathom. A little beyond the Dolphin's Nofe, is a good road; and ftill farther, in five fathom, the water is very fmooth; but even there, a veffel lies open from the E. by S. half S. to the E. by N. Should too great a fea come in thence, a fhip might run out by the ftrait, keeping clofe to the ifland, which is bold, and anchor behind the ifland, in fandy ground.

While I ftaid here, I bought about two thoufand cakes of fago, each weighing a pound, or a pound and a quarter; fome fmaller, weighing three quarters of a pound; but it was all hard baked, and kept well. We bought alfo fome fifh, and feveral turtle. Some of my people, who were not Mahometans, and eat turtle, cut the meat up fmall, and ftewed it in green bamboos. No goats or fowls could we find. Rawak ifland lies in latitude 00° 13′ N. longitude 128° E.

Saturday the 25th. Early in the morning, being ready to fail, I found Mapia miffing, whom I had
bought

bought of the Moodo, at Aiou: I fent afhore,
to enquire about him ; but to no purpofe. I fuppofe he had met with fome old acquaintance, who
had feduced him to leave me.

We weighed at nine in the morning, with the
wind about N. E. by E. and went out between
the iflands of Rawak and the main. About noon
I anchored clofe to Manouaran, and fent the boat
on fhore. They filled fome jars with very good
water, from a kind of pond or dead river, hard
by the beach, whilft I lay in feven fathom, fandy
ground. In that pofition, the extreme to the
weftward, which I call Shoe ifland, was juft open
with the weft point of Manouaran, and the land
abreaft (the higheft on Waygiou) concealed the
Third Peak, or Buffalo's Horn, while the entry
into Offak harbour appeared towards the weft.
Rawak ifland, bearing S. E. is alfo very confpicuous. That part of Manouaran, which is next to
the ifland, and where I anchored, is low, and very eafy of accefs. The weft part is fteep and
rocky ; above that fteep part, is grafs, with fhaggy
trees intermixed. This kind of ground extends
to the fummit, which is almoft flat. The whole
ifland looks at a diftance like a faucer, bottom up.
Afternoon we weighed, wind at N. E. During
the night we lay up N. W. but made only a W.
by N. courfe, as the current fet to leeward.

On *Sunday* the 26th, had rainy fqually weather,
with variable winds : found the current fet ftrong
to the weftward ; and, when we had an offing,
it fet to the S. W. We made feveral tacks to little

tle purpofe; at laft, we bore away for Piapis harbour, which I was juft abreaft of.   At that time,
Pulo Een bore N. W. and I was at noon in the latitude of 00° 18′ N.   About two P. M. I got into
the harbour of Piapis; and anchored in two fathoms, fandy ground, clofe to the high rocky ifland
of Sipfipa.   We found lying here a boat bound to
Gibby; but neither houfe nor inhabitant.

Monday the 27th, fair weather, with northerly
winds: weighed, and rowed up to the fouth eaft
bay, and anchored at the mouth of a pleafant frefh
water river.   Tuan Buffora was very lucky in
fifhing with the caft net.

On *Tuefday* the 28th, the wind at N. N. E. with
fair weather; filled all our water jars, and got
ready for fea.

On *Wednefday* the 29th, weighed in the morning, and rowed out of the S. E. bay, but the wind
blowing frefh at the harbour's mouth, we rounded
the rocky promontory, and anchored in the fouth
bay.   It being about the change of the moon, the
weather was very fqually, and unfettled.

Thurfday, *March* the 1ft, wind at N. N. E.
The boat I mentioned, bound to Gibby, failed.
I made the Noquedah a prefent, as he knew our
veffel was the fame that had been repaired at Tomoguy.   After he failed, I vifited the mouth of
the harbour, where I found irregular foundings,
and overfalls.

On *Friday* the 2d, hauled the corocoro afhore,
on an ifland in the S. bay, on which was a pond
of

of frefh water. Had all day long variable winds, and a good deal of rain; it being the time of fpring tides, we got, at low water, much kima on the coral reefs, of which we made very good curry; ftewing it with the heart of the aneebong, or cabbage tree, which we found abundant in the woods. But I come to the defcription of Piapis harbour.

On the N. coaft of Waygiou, lies an ifland, remarkable for a pretty high table land, called Pulo Een, or Fifh ifland, already mentioned. It bears N. N. W. from the mouth of Piapis harbour, fifteen miles; fome rocky iflands, with low trees and bufhes upon them, and fome iflands like buttons lying between. By keeping the faid ifland in the above direction 'N. N. W. you cannot mifs the entrance of the harbour.

The hill, which in the defcription of the N. E. coaft of Waygiou, I have called the firft peak, may be feen far beyond Pulo Een: it is alfo a good object to fteer for, as it is near the harbour's mouth. A perpendicular rock named Sipfipa, making the mouth of the harbour to the eaftward, has fome ragged rocks contiguous, on which are fome withered trees and bufhes. Off the rock of Sipfipa, are three fpots of breakers, even with the water's edge, one without another. The fea generally breaks upon them; but in very fine weather, at high water, they may poffibly not fhow themfelves: it will be neceffary to give them a birth.

In fteering for this vaft harbour, which has two capacious bays, keep rather towards the weft

K   fhore,

fhore, on account of the faid three fpots of breakers, near which is a remarkable fugar loaf rock, about the bulk of a pigeon houfe, or hay cock. Within piftol fhot, is ten fathom water. Having paft it, you may, with a wefterly wind, anchor in a bay juft within it; or, proceed up what I call the fouth bay, if the wind favour. But, if the wind is fcant, you may round a certain rocky promontory, into a commodious bay, which I call the S. E. bay, at the top of which is good frefh water, and a great deal of tall ftraight timber, fit for mafts.

In either bay are good mud foundings; on Sip-fipa ifland, is a pond of frefh water; the ifland in the fouth bay, upon which I hauled the corocoro afhore to clean, has alfo a pond; and fome young fago trees grew clofe to it. In going up the fouth harbour, leave this ifland on the right. Piapis harbour lies in latitude 00° 5′ N. longitude 127° 24′.

On *Saturday* the 3d, we rowed early out of the harbour; juft without it we had foundings thirty-five fathom, muddy ground. Made fail, lying up N. N. W. wind at N. E. but made only a W. N. W. courfe. We then ftruck our maft, and, as the wind was moderate, rowed to windward, thinking to anchor at Pulo Een. I gave to each rower, a red handkerchief for encouragement. About five in the afternoon we came up with Pulo Een, and faw many aneebong or cabbage trees growing on the ifland that lies weft of it. Found the bottom every where rocky, and fo fteep that we durft not anchor. We, therefore, put off
again,

again, rowing and failing all night. We lay up north, but made only a N. W. courfe, the current fetting us ftrong to the fouthward. Finding it impoffible to get to the northward of Gilolo, without going near Patany Hook, where the Dutch have conftant cruifers, either floops, panchallangs, or corocoros, I bore away in the night.

Sunday the 4th. In the morning we had the paffage between Gag and Gibby open, the wind being at N. N. E. Had an obfervation at noon, but it was not to be trufted : Gag bore then S. E. three leagues, and Gibby N. W. five. Got our fwivel guns loaded, and our fmall arms in order.

Gibby is a much larger ifland than Gag; it is alfo higher, appearing as two hills, and has many inhabitants.

On *Monday* the 5th, we fteered S. W. part of the night, then W. S. W. I expected to find the current fet to the weftward, but was miftaken. In the morning I found the current had fet us to the fouthward, and that we had fhot in between the iflands Bo and Popo. I immediately hauled as much as I could to the weftward, but could not get to the northward of Bo. At noon were in 01° 10' S. latitude.

The Banguey corocoro went to a fmooth landing place, and picked up a great many excellent kimas (cockles) about the bignefs of a man's head; nor failed to give us our fhare. At funfet we anchored in thirteen fathom water, fandy ground, clofe to a fmall ifland, with coco nut trees on it.

When

When we were at anchor, an ifland, pretty large, the top of which is like the back of a hog, bore N. W.

Prefently came on board feveral boats : in one of them was the Papua man, whofe boat had formerly carried Tuan Hadjee from Gag to Tomoguy, and with whofe fon I had like to have there had a quarrel about a wooden anchor.

Bought a great quantity of dried fifh, which came very feafonably, as we were badly off for any provifions, but fago bread, and a very few fpoiled fifh. By the affiftance of the country people, we this evening filled moft of our water jars, intending to put immediately to fea, as the wind was fair.

Here I was informed that the Dutch had got notice of our having repaired at Tomoguy.

The two clufters of iflands, Bo and Popo, lie nearly in the fame parallel of latitude, 01° 17′ S. the longitude of Bo is 126° 10′ ; of Popo, 126° 25′. They are about five leagues afunder. Bo confifts of fix or feven iflands. When lying clofe to the fouthermoft part of the fmall ifland, near to which we anchored, the iflands of Popo (almoft fhut in) bore about E. by N.

Coming from the weftward, the firft of the iflands of Bo, that you meet with, is a low flat ifland, about four or five miles round ; the fecond is an ifland fomewhat higher, with a table land, it

being

being flat atop. The next, and largeft, is alfo
higheft ; and has been already mentioned : its outline, when bearing N. W. refembles a hog's back,
or the roof of a long hayrick. You may anchor in
fifteen fathom, fandy ground, clofe to a fmall
fandy ifland, which has fome coco nut trees upon
it. Farther eaftward, are two or three fmall iflands,
hard by that which is eaftermoft in the view. Off
the eaftermoft point, is a coral bank, with two
fathom water, about two miles from the fhore.

Thefe iflands, which have a good many inhabitants, can fupply plenty of coco nuts, falt, and
dried fifh. Had I ftaid till next day, we might
have got fome goats ; but the wind being fair, I
was unwilling to lofe it.

The iflands of Popo I paffed at fome diftance :
they are higher than the iflands of Bo. To the
weftward of the clufter, but almoft contiguous to
it, are about nine or ten low fmall iflands ; to the
eaftward, on two iflands, are two hills, which, at a
diftance, look like two tea-cups, bottom up. Thefe
iflands are alfo faid to be well inhabited ; and here
refides a Rajah.

CHAP.

CHAP. X.

Departure from Bo—Contrary Winds---Anchor at
an Ifland near Liliola, and not far from Pulo
Pifang ; but can get no frefh Water---Bear away
for the Kanary Iflands---Find them uninhabited---
Proceed to the Ifland Myfol---Arrive in Ef-be
Harbour---Tranfactions there---Valentine's Account
of the Birds of Paradife---Account of Cloves growing
on Ceram and Ouby---Strict Watch of the Dutch
near Amboyna---Arrival of a Corocoro from Ti-
dore, belonging to the Sultan---We learn the Dutch
have fent after us to Gibby---Account of the Ra-
jah of Salwatty---Defcription of the Ifland Goram,
and fome Places on the Weft Coaft of New Guinea,
from old Voyages.

1775.
March.

ON *Tuefday* the 6th, having finifhed our bufinefs
the evening of the fifth, we failed at midnight from
the fouthermoft ifland of Bo, and fteered weft,
with the wind at N. much rain in the morning.
The hill fhaped like a long hayrick, then bore
N. N. E. and Pulo Pifang bore W. S. W. five
leagues.

At noon we had no obfervation. The current
fetting ftrong to the fouthward, made me give
up the hope of getting round Gilolo.

Wednefday the 7th. Many calms and ripplings
of currents Pulo Pifang, in the morning, bore
about

about N. N. W. Towards noon, the wind coming
to the S. W. we hauled up N. W.

Thursday the 8th.   In the morning saw Ouby,
bearing west, and Pulo Pisang N. by E. about six
leagues distant.   At noon we observed the latitude
to be 01° 48' S.   At sun-set Pulo Pisang bore N. E.
by N.

Friday the 9th.   The night being calm, we
rowed to windward, at the rate of three knots an
hour.   By break of day, Pulo Pisang, bore N. E.
eight leagues ; and Pulo Lyong, (an island near
Ouby, appearing with an even outline) bore
W. N. W. about ten leagues.   I am told, that
between it and Ouby is a good passage, which the
Dutch ships use.   Tapiola at the same time bore
north ; the water was smooth, and many porpoises
blowing near us.

Saturday the 10th.   Having the wind at S. W.
steered N. N. W. and got Pulo Pisang to bear
E. N. E. the wind then came to the N. W. and
blew fresh.   The corocoro losing much ground,
we lay to for her all night ; the wind then veered
to the southward ; but, on her account, we could
not make sail.

Sunday the 11th.   In the night, the tide or current favouring us, we drove up under Tapiola ;
but I durst not venture to anchor near, as it was
rocky.   The tides and winds were uncertain near
the island, and I could not anchor but among the
rocks, close on shore.   The island is of some height,
but

but not fo high by far as Pulo Pifang ; and near it
we found an eddy wind, fometimes blow from the
S. E. although the true wind was from the N. W.
therefore I rowed towards a fmaller ifland, that
bore about weft half a mile from Tapiola. This,
in fhape, refembles a cat couching ; the head of
the cat being the north extremity of the ifland.
It has a fine fandy beach ; fo at noon I anchored
under its lee, among rocks, in two fathom water,
and got a rope faft afhore. We foon after parted
twice from our wooden anchor ; and then rode by
the grapnel, in two and a half fathom, rocky
ground. Dug nine foot deep for water, clofe to a
rifing ground, two hundred yards from the beach ;
but it was brackifh, and not fit to drink.

Monday the 12th. We lay here all night, in a
very bad road. Early in the morning I fent the
boat to Liliola for water ; but fhe got none,
although water muft be there. The landing, however, proving fomewhat difficult, I was glad they
ran no rifks. The wind being ftill at N. W. and
N. N. W. and the weather looking fqually, we
weighed at eight A. M. intending for the Kanary
iflands, near Myfol, where we were certain of
finding good fhelter and refrefhments. We fteered E. by N. having frefh gales at W..N. W. The
corocoro, that had got under fail at the fame time,
foon difappeared ; but we faw her again in the
afternoon. Steered S. E. and lay to part of the
night.

In the morning of the 13th, faw Pulo Bo, Popo,
Myfol, and the Kanary iflands, all at one time ;
                                                    alfo

alfo Pulo Pifang almoft down. Pulo Pifang bore
W. by N. about twenty leagues. Loft fight of the
corocoro. Steering on, we found the Kanary
iflands covered with wood; an iflet ftood in the
paffage, with tall trees.

About noon we paffed between this Clump iflet,
or Canifter, (as I choofe to call it, from its fhape)
and the largeft of the Kanary iflands, which lies
to the weftward of it. We then anchored in feven
fathom fandy ground.

The Canifter is about a quarter of a mile round,
entirely covered with a grove of baftard pine trees,
called by Malays, Arrow, fuch as are feen near
Atcheen, and on the S. W. coaft of Sumatra, at
the mouths of rivers. The channel is very fafe,
having good foundings of feven and eight fathom,
but is not above two hundred yards wide : however
it is fhort. The Canifter muft be left to the eaftward; the apparent channel to the eaftward of it
being full of rocks, and impaffable, but by boats.
We found the Canifter to lie in 01° 45′ north latitude, and longitude 126° 40′; fighted our grapnel,
at the turn of the tide, which now was flood, and
fet towards that iflet, or to the northward.

I thought of ftaying amongft thefe iflands until
the turn of the monfoon, but was rather afraid of
the ftrong tides.

Here were no inhabitants; confequently I could
get no provifions. Tuan Hadjee, and the Batchian officers, ftrongly advifed me to fteer for the
harbour

harbour of Ef-be, on Myfol ifland, which had a
harbour behind it; and all of them had been
there.   I took their advice, as I had only one iron
grapnel to truft to, and found that, among the
Kanary iflands, was no depending on wooden anchors, in fandy ground, with a current of any
ftrength.

I therefore weighed early in the morning, of the
14th, the tide fetting ftrong with us.   The Kanary
ifland to the weftward of the Canifter (which confidered as one, proves the largeft of them all) is, I believe, divided into feveral iflands, by narrow deep
itraits, lined generally with mangrove trees, and
coral rocks.   The tide being with us, we foon came
to the weft point of Myfol, which from its fhape I
name the Dolphin's Nofe.   It lies in latitude of 2°
fouth, and about fifteen miles S. S. E. of the Canifter.   Here the ifland Myfol is of middling height,
with a pretty bold coaft; farther down towards
Ef-be ifland, near the fhore, are fome rocks and
fmall iflands, without which one muft fteer.   To
one parcel of thofe rocks I have given the name
of Cat and Kittens.   Another fingle rock I have
called the Sloop Rock, being like a floop under fail.
Onward, about four miles fhort of Ef-be ifland, is
a hill, which I call from like reafon, the Beehive:
it is but a little way from the fea fide.   The ifland
Ef-be cannot well be paffed unperceived, by the
picturefque views of certain iflets that lie oppofite.
The moft particular is a fmall ifland I call the
Crown, which muft be kept on the right hand,
and bears from the weft part of Ef-be, where is
the entrance into the harbour, W. by S. four miles:
keep

keep the ifland X and Y in one, which is the leading crofs mark direction into the harbour. Entering, you leave in the paffage, a fhaggy fmall ifland
on the left, with a reef that runs off it. Borrow
upon Ef-be ifland, keeping the lead a going: at the
entrance the channel is about a quarter of a mile
broad, with twelve and fourteen fathom water.
About noon, in running down the coaft of Myfol,
it blew fo hard, that I was once obliged to lie to
for a couple of hours, with a fair wind. Juft before it was dark, we got into Ef-be harbour, and
found a very hollow ground fwell in the paffage in
twelve fathom ; but it did not break. We had not
feen the corocoro fince the twelfth, which made us
imagine fhe had ftopt fomewhere, to get turtle eggs.

Thurfday the 16th. In the morning I fired three
guns, as a compliment to Tuan Hadjee and the
Batchian officers.—I knew the more honour I paid
them, I fhould be the more regarded by the country people ; and I underftood that many here had
intercourfe with Ceram, and poffibly with Amboyna. Willing to fee Ef-be, I went afhore with a
few people, and foon returned. I found it to contain twelve houfes. P. M. we had violent fqualls
and much rain, with the wind at W. N. W. I could
perceive a great fea at the entrance of the harbour.

Friday the 17th. To day early, moved nigher
Ef-be village, and anchored clofe to a fmall iflet.
About nine A. M. came on board a perfon, who
called himfelf the fecretaris,* and two others, feem-

* He had been employed by the Dutch as a jerrytulis or
writer.

ingly

ingly men of rank ; each came in a feparate boat,
tho' all arrived on board together.   They drank
tea, and ftaid about an hour.   They told me that
the governor of Banda had fent two months before to Linty (from which place they came, it being
about four miles off) defiring news of the Englifh
veffels which he underftood to be in thofe feas ; but
that they could give him little fatisfaction, having
only heard it rumoured that fome Englifh veffels
were near Tomoguy and Waygiou.   Yet they
added, what is not unlikely, that many Englifh
fhips coaft the north of Ceram, fteering. eaft for
Pitt's Strait, I fuppofe ; and that feveral had put
into a place called Savay, on the north coaft of Ceram, to get water.   I made them all prefents, and
faluted them with three guns at their departure.
In the night, we had hard fqualls and much rain.

Saturday the 18th.   After a very bad night, very
fine weather.   Dried our fago bread, part of which
had fuffered from the rain.

On the 19th, fine weather, and very little wind.
Tuan Hadjee went afhore to Ef-be ; faluted him
with three guns ; he foon returned on board.

Monday the 20th.   Fair weather and little wind :
went to Linty about four miles off, with Tuan
Hadjee and Tuan Bobo ; Tuan Buffora and the
other Batchian officer being in the corocoro.   Linty
is a village confifting of about thirteen houfes, many of them built on pofts in the water.   We dined
with the gentlemen who had vifited us on the 16th.
They entertained us very genteelly.   After dinner
                                                                I went

I went up a rifing ground to a Mahometan tomb, built of ftone and mortar, and whitewafhed ; whence I faw many rocky iflands that lie on this part of the coaft of Myfol, abreaft of Ef-be harbour, and extending to abreaft of this village of Linty ; the fartheft about eight or ten miles off. They are not low flat iflands, but fteep and rocky, fome with bold forelands, others with hummocs, there being twelve or fourteen in all, and (feemingly) paffages between them. Tuan Hadjee being with his friends (to whom he was liberal in making prefents of broad cloth, &c. which I had advanced him on account of pay for his * people) chofe to ftay all night, as did alfo Tuan Bobo and Tuan Buffora. I returned on board in the evening, with a black loory (the only one I ever faw) which I had purchafed ; alfo fome dead birds of paradife with their feet on. The black loory foon died. At Linty, I learnt from the gentlemen who had entertained us, that the birds of paradife come at certain feafons, in flocks, from the eaftward, or from New Guinea ; that, fettling upon trees, they are caught with bird lime, then their bodies are dried with the feathers on, as we fee them in Europe.

Here follows Valentine's account of the birds of paradife. † The Portuguefe firft found thefe birds on the ifland of Gilolo, the Papua iflands, and on New Guinea ; and they were known by the name

---

* My mind was more at eafe than it had been for fome time, when I had parted with various piece goods to Tuan Hadjee. The crew, if ill difpofed, had lefs temptation.

† Vol. III. p. 306, 313.

of *paſſaros da ſol*, i. e. birds of the ſun. The inhabitants of Ternate call them *manuco dewata*, the
bird of God, whence the name of *manuco diata* is
derived, uſed by ſome naturaliſts (Edwards, f.
110.---Margrav. Braſil. 207---Rai. Syn. av. 21. n.
7.---Briſſ. av. 2. p. 130. ſeq. and Mr. de Buffon
himſelf adopts the name of *manucode*). Fabulous
accounts mentioned that this bird had no legs;
and was conſtantly on the wing, in the air, on
which it lived : in confirmation of which, the legs
of theſe birds were cut off, when offered to ſale.
But the inhabitants of Aroo, who reſort yearly to
Banda, undeceived the Dutch, and freed them
from theſe prejudices. Another reaſon for cutting
off the legs is, that the birds are found to be more
eaſily preſerved without them; beſide, that the
Moors wanted the birds without legs, in order to
put them in their mock fights, on their helmets, as
ornaments. The inhabitants of *Aroo*, however,
have brought the birds with legs theſe ſeventy or
eighty years; and *Pigafetta*, ſhipmate of *Ferdinand
Magelhaens*, proved about the year 1525, an eye-
witneſs, that they were not without legs. However, the peculiar length and ſtructure of their ſca-
pular feathers, hinders them from ſettling in high
winds, on trees; and, when they are thrown on
the ground by thoſe winds, they cannot, of themſelves, get again on the wing. If taken by the natives, they are immediately killed, as their food is
not known, and as they defend themſelves with
amazing courage and formidable bills. There are
about ſix ſpecies of birds of Paradiſe, namely :

1. The great bird of Paradiſe from Aroo.

2. The

2. The little bird of Paradife from Papua.

3, 4 Two different birds of Paradife, which are
    black.

5. The white bird of Paradife.

6. The unknown black bird of Paradife.

7. And the little king's bird, which may rank
    among them.

1. The largeft bird of Paradife, is commonly
two foot four inches in length. The head is fmall,
the bill hard and long, of a pale colour. The head,
and back of the neck, is lemon coloured, about its
little eyes black; about the neck the bird is of the
brighteft gloffy emerald green, and foft like velvet;
as is the breaft, which is black, or wolf-coloured,
(gris de loup, wolfs-geel.) The wings are large
and chefnut. The back part of the body is covered with long, ftraight, narrow feathers, of a pale
brown colour, fimilar to the plumes of the oftrich.
Thefe feathers are fpread, when the bird is on the
wing; which is the caufe, that he can keep very
long in the air. On both fides of the belly are
two tufts of ftiff and fhorter feathers, of a golden
yellow, and fhining. From the rump, proceed
two long ftiff fhafts, which are feathered on their
extremities. Several other birds of thefe countries
have thofe long feathers, for inftance, the Amboyna arrow tail (Pylftaart), the king fifher, or Sariwak,
and one fort of the perrokeets from Papua. Its
fize is not much above that of a blackbird. The
legs are low, with four ftrong toes. The Ternate
people call them *Burong Papua* or *Papua birds*,
fometimes *Manuco dewata*, and likewife *Soffu* or
Sioffu. The Amboyna natives call them *Manu-key-*
aroo,

aroo, the bird of the iſlands, Key and Aroo; be-
cauſe the natives of the two laſt iſlands bring them
for ſale to Banda and Amboyna. At Aroo the people call them *Fanaan*. Properly theſe birds are not
found in *Key*, which is fifty Dutch miles eaſt of
Banda; but they are found at the *Aroo* iſlands,
(lying fifteen Dutch miles farther eaſt than Key)
during the weſterly or dry monſoon; and they
return to New Guinea, as ſoon as the eaſterly or
wet monſoon ſets in. They come always in a
flock of thirty or forty, and are led by a bird,
which the inhabitants of Aroo call the King, diftinct from the little king's bird. This leader is
black, with red ſpots, and conſtantly flies higher
than the reſt of the flock, which never forſake him,
but ſettle as ſoon as he ſettles: a circumſtance
which becomes their ruin, when their king lights
on the ground; whence they are not able to riſe,
on account of the ſingular ſtructure and diſpoſition
of their plumage. They are likewiſe unable to
fly with the wind, which would ruin their looſe
plumage; but take their flight conſtantly againſt
it, cautious not to venture out in hard blowing
weather, a ſtrong gale frequently obliging them to
come to the ground. During their flight, they cry
like ſtarlings. Their note, however, approaches
more to the croaking of ravens; which is heard
very plainly when they are in diſtreſs, from a freſh
gale blowing in the back of their plumage. In
Aroo, theſe birds ſettle on the higheſt trees;
eſpecially on a ſpecies of ſmall leaved Wa-
ringa trees, that bear red berries, on which
they chiefly live. (Ficus Benjamina ? Hort. Malab.
III. f. 55. Rumph. Amboin. III. f. 90.) The natives

tives catch them with birdlime, and in noofes, or fhoot them with blunt arrows; but, though fome are ftill alive when they fall into their hands, the catchers kill them immediately; and often cut their legs off, draw the entrails, dry and fumigate them with fulphur or fmoke only, and fell them at Banda for half a rix-dollar; whereas, at Aroo, one of thefe birds may be bought for a fpike nail, or a piece of old iron. The Dutch fhips, voyaging between New Guinea and Aroo, (which are at the diftance of eighteen or twenty Dutch miles) frequently fee flocks of birds of Paradife flying from the one land to the other, againft the wind. In cafe the birds find the wind become too powerful, they fly ftraight up into the air, till they reach the region where the effects of the wind are not fo ftrongly felt; and then continue their flight. The Moors ufe thefe birds as ornamental crefts on their helmets, in war, and in their various mock fights. Sometimes they tie a bird, or part of it, to their fwords. During the eaft monfoon, the tails of the birds are moulted; and, for four months of the weftern monfoon, they have tails, according to the teftimony of the people of Aroo.

2. The fmaller bird of Paradife from Papua, is about twenty inches long. His beak is lead coloured, and paler at the point. The eyes fmall, and enclofed in black about the neck: he is green like an emerald. The head and back of the neck are of a dirty yellow, the back of a greyifh yellow; the breaft and belly of a dufky colour; the wings fmall, and chefnut coloured. The long plumage is about a foot in length, and paler than in

L   the

the larger fpecies ; as in general the colours of this
fmall bird are lefs bright.   The two long feathers
of the tail are conftantly thrown away by the natives.   This is in all other refpects like the greater
fort : they follow likewife a king or leader ; who is,
however, blacker, with a purplifh caft, and finer
in colour than the reft ; though this bird is alfo different from the 3d and 4th black fpecies.   The *Papuas* of *Meffowal* relate, that thefe birds do not mi-
grate, but make their nefts on the higheft trees,
where they are found by the Alfoories.   The neck
and bill are longer in the male than in the female.
In Ternate and Tidore, this bird is called *Toffu* or
Boorong Papuwa, the bird of Papua : the Papuas
call it *Shag* or *Shague : Samaleik* is the name given
it by the people on Eaft Ceram ; and in the ifland
Serghile, in New Guinea, its name is *Tfhakke*.   Formerly this bird was thought to be found on *Gilolo*
or *Halamahera*, and the neighbouring iflands, to
the fouth and S. E. but at this day it is known to
be found only on the Papua iflands.   Thefe iflands
extend from the fouth end of Gilolo, and the north
coaft of Ceram, to the weft end of New Guinea.
The largeft of them are, the ifland of *Meffowal*
(which lies to the north of Ceram), and *Salawatti*
or *Salawat*, whofe fituation is neareft to *Serghile* (an
ifland or diftrict of New Guinea) which, in the
old Portuguefe charts, is wrongly called Ceram,
and feparated from New Guinea.   They rooft on
the higheft trees of the mountainous part, whence
they are killed with blunt arrows, by the natives
of *Meffowal*.   Others fay, the natives infect with
cocculi indici the water which the birds are to drink ;
and that, fo ftupified, they are caught with the
hand.

hand. The birds love to feed on the fruit of the *Tſhampedæh* tree, which they pierce with their bills, and out of which they extract the kernel. Some ſay, theſe birds finding themſelves weak through age, ſoar ſtraight towards the ſun, till they are tired, and fall dead to the ground. The natives draw the entrails, ſear the birds with a hot iron, and put them in a tube of bamboo for preſervation.

3. and 4. The large black bird of paradiſe is brought without wings or legs for ſale; ſo that of this ſpecies it is difficult to give an exact deſcription. Its figure, when ſtuffed, is narrow and round, but ſtretched in length to the extent of four ſpans. The plumage on the neck, head, and belly, is black and velvet like, with a hue of purple and gold, which appears very ſtrong. The bill is blackiſh, and one inch in length. On both ſides are two bunches of feathers, which have the appearance of wings, although they be very different; the wings being cut off by the natives. This plumage is ſoft, broad, ſimilar to peacocks feathers, with a glorious gloſs, and greeniſh hue, and all bent upwards; which Valentyn thinks occaſioned by the birds being kept in hollow bamboo reeds. The feathers of the tail are of unequal length; thoſe next to the belly are narrow, like hair; the two uppermoſt are much longer, and pointed; thoſe immediately under them, are above a ſpan and a half longer than the upper ones: they are ſtiff, on both ſides fringed with a plumage, like hair; black above, but gloſſy below. Birds of this kind are brought from no other place, than that part of New Guinea called *Serghile*; its inha-

L 2   bitants

bitants carrying them to *Salawat*, in hollow tubes
of bamboo, dried upon a round long ftick, in the
fmoke, and felling them for fmall hatchets or
coarfe cloth. The Papuas call this fpecies *Shag-*
awa, and likewife the birds of Paradife of Serghile:
in Ternate and Tidore it is known by the name
of *Soffoo-kokotoo*---the black bird of Paradife.
Serghile is the northermoft part of New Guinea,
tapering to a point, immediately behind, or to the
eaftward of *Gilolo*, and the Papua iflands; fo that
the point trends northerly.

4. Befides the large black bird of Paradife,
there is ftill another fort, whofe plumage is equal
in length, but thinner in body, black above, and
without any remarkable glofs; not having thofe
fhining peacock feathers, which are found on the
greater fpecies. This wants likewife the three long
pointed feathers of the tail, belonging to the larger
black fpecies of the bird of Paradife. The Alfoories,
or inhabitants of the mountains in *Meffowal*, fhoot
thofe birds, and fell them to the people of Tidore.

5. The white bird of Paradife is the moft rare,
having two fpecies; one quite white, and the other
black and white. The firft fort is very rare, and
in form like the bird of Paradife from Papua.

The fecond has the forepart black, and the back
part white; with twelve crooked wiry fhafts, which
are almoft naked, though in fome places covered
with hairs. This fpecies is very fcarce, and only
got by means of the people of Tidore, fince it is
found on the Papua iflands; efpecially on *Way-*
gehoo:

gehoo:* called alſo *Wadjoo* or *Wardjoo*. Others are of opinion, that it is brought thither from *Serghile*, on New Guinea.

6. In the year 1689, a new ſpecies of the black bird of Paradiſe was ſeen in Amboyna, carried hither from *Meſſowal*, only one foot in length, with a fine purple hue, a ſmall head, and ſtraight bill. As on the other birds of Paradiſe, on its back, near the wings, are feathers of a purple and blue colour; but under the wings and over all the belly, they are yellow coloured, as in the common ſort: on the back of the neck they are mouſe coloured, mixed with green. It is remarkable in this ſpecies, that there are before the wings two roundiſh tufts of feathers, which are green edged, and may be moved at pleaſure, by the bird, like wings. Inſtead of tail, he has twelve or thirteen black naked wirelike ſhafts, hanging promiſcuouſly like feathers. His ſtrong legs have ſharp claws: his head is remarkably ſmall; the eyes are likewiſe ſmall, and ſurrounded by black.

7. The laſt ſpecies is the *King's Bird*; ſome reckon it among the birds of paradiſe; but, according to Valentyn, it is entirely different. The late Linneus, as well as Count Buffon, reckon the King's bird among the birds of paradiſe; as it has, in general, all the characters of the bill, and the

---

* Waygiou——On Myſol, beſides the common bird of paradiſe with feet, I got a black bird, with a very long tail, and without wings; alſo, ſome ſmall birds, with wiry ſhafts in their tails, and a moſt beautiful plumage: they are in the Muſeum of Lady James.

plumage

plumage common to all the kind, known by the name of the bird of paradife.

This bird is about feven inches long, and fome-what larger than a tit-moufe. Its head and eyes are fmall, the bill ftraight, the eyes included in circles of black plumage; the crown of the head is fire coloured, the back of the neck blood co-loured, the neck and breaft of a chefnut colour, with a dark ring of the brighteft emerald green. Its wings are in proportion ftrong, and the quill feathers dark; with red fhining plumes, fpots, and ftripes. The tail is ftraight, fhort, and brown Two long, naked, black fhafts project from the rump, at leaft, a hand breadth beyond the tail; having at their extremities, femilunar, twifted plu-mage, of the moft glaring green colour above, and dufky below. The belly is white and green fprinkled, and on each fide is a tuft of long plu-mage, feathered with a broad margin; being on one fide green, and on the other dufky. The back is blood red and brown, fhining like filk. The legs are in fize like thofe of a lark; having three fore toes, and one back toe.

This bird affociates not with any other of the birds of paradife; but flits folitary from bufh to bufh, wherever he fees red berries, without ever getting on tall trees.

At Aroo the bird is called *Wowi, Wowi*; in the Papua iflands *Sopclo-o*; and by the Dutch *King's Bird*. It is chiefly brought from *Aroo Sopclo-o*, and efpecially from *Wodjir*, a well known village there.

The

The people of Aroo do not know its neft; but ſuppoſe it to come over from *New Guinea,* where it breeds; and ſtays at Aroo only during the weſtern or dry monſoon. It is taken in ſlings of *gumatty*; or, with birdlime, prepared from the juice of *ſukkom* (bread fruit, *artocarpus communis.* Forſt. Nov. Gen.) then cleared and dried; and ſold at Banda. It is uſed alſo as ornament by the natives of Aroo, on their helmets, in their mock fights, or games of *Tohakulil. Thus far Valentyn,* as tranſlated by Dr. Forſter, who favoured me alſo with the following remarks :

" Mr. de Buffon, or rather his friend Mr. Gue-
" neau de Montbeillard, gives an account of ſix
" birds of paradiſe in his Hiſtoire Naturelle des
" Oiſeaux, tom. III. edit. in 4to. tom. v. p. 207
" ---238. tab. xii. and xiii, and in the planches
" enluminées, n. 254. 496. 631, 632, 633, 634 ;
" as does Mr. Sonnerat, in his voyage à la Nou-
" velle Guinée. The firſt named *l'Oiſeau de Para-*
" *dis,* is the ſame which is called *the great bird of*
" *paradiſe,* by Valentyn : Linneus's *paradiſea apoda.*
" The ſecond is the *manucode,* which is Valentyn's
" *little king's bird,* or Linneus's *paradiſea regia.* The
" third is the *magnifique* or *manucode à bouquets* ;
" and has ſome reference to the *little* bird of *para-*
" *diſe* in Valentyn, though I think there is ſtill a
" great difference between them. The fourth is
" the *ſuperbe* or the *manucode noir.* The bird re-
" preſented in the planches enluminées, is either a
" young bird, or one moulting, or perhaps a
" female : for the *large black bird of paradiſe* of
" Valentyn, is ſaid to have ſome long ſhafts in his
tail;

" tail ; and Mr. Gueneau de Montbeillard fuppofes
" that the fpecimen in the Paris cabinet has by
" fome accident loft thofe long plumes.   The fifth
" is the *fifilet* ou *manucode e fix fileto*.   I fhould
" almoft be tempted to fuppofe that Valentyn's
" *fmall black bird of paradife*, is this very fpecies, but
" that the fpecimens feen by Valentyn, had been
" deprived of the three long feathers on each fide
" of the head, either by accident, or purpofely by
" the natives.   The fixth bird mentioned in the
" Hiftoire Naturelle des Oifeaux, is the *Calybe*,
" which feems to be an obfcure fpecies, fince the
" fpecimen is very imperfect, from which the
" defcription is made; and I have good reafons
" for fufpecting that it has likewife loft fome long
" plumes off the tail.   Upon the whole, it muft
" be obferved, that Papua and New Guinea are
" countries, which, when fearched by an able na-
" turalift, will enrich fcience with many new and
" elegant objects.   The birds of paradife there-
" fore living in a country very little frequented
" by Europeans, it has not been hitherto poffible
" to procure more accurate accounts of thofe beau-
" tiful and curious birds ; and it is hoped that this
" however imperfect account, will be acceptable
" to the lovers of natural hiftory, till fomething
" more perfect can be obtained."

During my ftay at Myfol, it was natural for me
to afk about the clove and nutmeg.   I was affured
that neither was produced on that ifland ; but that
cloves grew on fome part of Ceram, the high
mountains of which were to day plainly to be
feen ; that the clove grew alfo on the ifland of
Ouby,

Ouby, which we had more than once been in fight
of; and that on Ouby lived many runaway flaves
and others, from Ternate, and elfewhere, who
would have no communication with ftrangers,
except fome Buggefs prows whom they could
truft, and to whom they were faid to fell cloves,
the produce of the ifland.

This account of Ouby agreed with that I had
received from Tuan Hadjee and the Batchian
officers ; Ouby being claimed by Batchian : but the
Sultan makes no farther ufe of it, than fifhing for
pearls on its coafts, where no doubt any ftranger
may do the fame. The Dutch have a fmall fort
on the weft fide of Ouby, and keep there faft
failing corocoros always ready, to carry advice of
whatever happens remarkable. When I was ply-
ing for many days, as has been related off Pulo
Pifang, I afked Tuan Hadjee's opinion about
ftanding on with our ftarboard tacks, and fetching
Ouby, where, under the lee of the ifland, we
could row up along fhore. His anfwer was,
that we fhould certainly be difcovered, that advice
would be inftantly fent to Amboyna, and the
ifland Bouro, by fmall prows, and then we fhould
be way-laid by armed corocoros, of which Amboyna always keeps many in readinefs. Here in Ef-be
harbour, we were not above fifty leagues from
Amboyna ; but we trufted to the fidelity of thofe
we were amongft, that no advice of us would be
fent to the Dutch, to whom they did not feem to
be warmly affected, as they informed us of many
feverities, and even robberies committed by their
cruifing

cruifing panchallangs and corocoros; nor concealed the Papua people offending in their turn,
with their bows and arrows. In March and April,
the Papuas of New Guinea and Salwatty, are apt
to affemble in great numbers; and make war on
Gilolo, Ceram, Amboyna, Amblou, and as far as
Xulla Beffy. About the year 1765, the Papuas
plundered the·ifland of Amblou, near Bouro, and
carried off many of the inhabitants.

Tuefday the 21ft. Southerly winds; Tuan Hadjee not yet returned.

Wednefday the 22d. In the morning Tuan Hadjee came on board; we failed this afternoon, and
met juft without the harbour's mouth, the Banguey corocoro, with whom we had parted company: put back, hauled her afhore, and breamed
her bottom that night.

Thurfday the 23d. Fine weather; fent to the
main land of Myfol for ratans to the corocoro;
fhe wanting fome repairs in her outriggers, &c.

Friday the 24th. Rainy weather, and wefterly
winds; a corocoro appeared in the evening with
one of the Rajahs of Myfol on board. Next day,

Saturday the 25th, In the morning I faluted the
Rajah with three guns, and prefented him with a
fathom of fcarlet cloth, and two Tappies; * prefented likewife two Tappies to each of his Manteries.

* Surat cloth.

The

The Rajah came from the north fide of the ifland.
Rain in the night, and fqualls from the S. E.

Sunday the 26th. Came on board, in a corocoro, the fon of the deceafed Rajah of Ef-be. As he
was quite a youth, the uncle governed. I faluted
the young Rajah with one gun, and prefented him
with a piece of Kincob, † and two Tappies.

Monday the 27th. Fine weather in the evening.
Came into the harbour a large corocoro from
Tidore, belonging to the Sultan. She had an
Alfrez (Enfign) on board, and two Malay foldiers;
the enfign being alfo a Malay. She entered the
harbour, paddling with many hands; which put us
on our guard.

Next morning, *Tuefday* the 28th, I received the
Enfign on fhore, near to which we lay, and faluted
him with three guns. The Enfign told me the
Dutch had fent to Gilolo a floop with Europeans,
in queft of us.

Wednefday the 29th. The Gogo (an officer fo
called) came on board in a corocoro. I faluted
him with one gun, and made him a prefent. Thefe
two days the wind has been foutherly, with fqually
weather and rain.

Thurfday the 30th. Having repaired the corocoro, we launched her. The two Batchian
officers and Tuan Buffora have now been three
days amufing themfelves at Linty. Eafterly
winds: which made me willing to be gone.

† Another manufacture of Surat.

Friday

Friday the 31ft. The Tidore enfign, who yefterday had gone to Linty, returned. I prefented
him with a Palampore and a hundred flints; nor
failed to fend by him a handfome prefent to his
mafter.

About ten in the forenoon we were all ready to
fail. This morning Tuan Hadjee was vifited
by the confort of the Rajah of Salwatty, whofe
hufband had lately been circumvented by the
Dutch, and fent to the Cape of Good Hope. I
alfo paid my refpects to the lady, and made her
a prefent. She was a well-looking woman, and
had three female attendants. She prefented Tuan
Hadjee with a fmall corocoro; and from him I
learnt the following account of her lord.

Some time about the year 1770, a number of
Papua boats from New Guinea, the iflands Aroo,
Salwatty, and Myfol, near the time of the vernal
equinox, when the feas are generally fmooth,
affembled, to the number of more than a hundred,
and failed up the ftrait of Patientia, which divides
Batchian from Gilolo. They committed no hoftilities; but the Dutch, apprehenfive of what they
might do, fent to them, and made the chiefs prefents of cloth, &c. upon which they difperfed, and,
after fifhing a few days, and hunting in the woods,
they went home. However, the Rajah of Salwatty ftaid behind; but neither he, nor any of his
people, did any mifchief.

The Dutch, willing to get the Rajah into their
power, fell on the following ftratagem. They fent
a meffen-

a meffenger to him with a paper, figned and fealed by the governor of Ternate, telling him, it was a pardon and remiffion of his falla (offence) for having come with an armed force into the Dutch territories ; and that he, in particular, was more lucky than the other Papua chiefs, who had return-ed home without fuch a formal abfolution. At the fame time, he was invited to come and fee Ternate, where the governor would do him all kind of honour fuitable to his rank ; and in cafe he fhould fancy any thing in the Company's ware-houfes, he had a bag of dollars prefented him. This was the bait. The Coffre chief, fenfible the dollars could buy him nothing in his own country, whither he certainly might have carried them, and having heard of the fine things to be bought from the Dutch at Ternate, could not refift the temp-tation of laying out money, got unexpectedly, and for nothing. He therefore confenting, went, ac-companied by ten or twelve people into the fort, and waited on the governor, who fhowed him civility and refpect. He then laid out his dol-lars.

Prefently a guard was turned out ; and they thought themfelves fo fure of their prifoner, that they did not even fhut the gates. When it was announced to him he muft furrender, he whifpered his people, (who were ready to mangamo (*run a muck*) upon the occafion, to fave their mafter, or fell their lives dear), not to ftir in his defence. but to fave themfelves ; which, while the Rajah was delivering up his crefs, (dagger) they immediately did ; and, running out of the fort, got on board

their

their corocoro, and efcaped. The Rajah is now
prifoner at the Cape. Poffibly the Dutch allowed
his people to get away.

Before I leave the harbour, it may not be amifs
to give an account of what I could learn of the weft
coaft of New Guinea from the beft information.

The ifland of Goram is faid to have thirteen
mofques, and is fituated about a day's fail E. by N.
of Banda. Contiguous is a fmall ifland called Sal-
wak, between which and Goram is faid to be a harbour. N. E. of Goram, one day's fail, is Wonim.
In Keytz's voyage to Auftralafia, mention is made
of Onin, which I take to be Wonim, being twenty leagues N. E. of Goram. There is alfo mention
made of places called Afs, Effi, Kubiay, Adi, Ca-
ras. Keytz procured a linguift at Goram. In
Venk's voyage, of the year 1663, Onin is miftaken
for a man's name. Venk names, right or wrong,
a place called Kumaky, on the weft coaft of New
Guinea. The ftrait, between New Guinea and
Salwatty, is called Golowa.

The people at Ef-be told me, that a day's fail
fouth of Wonim, a gulph ftretched far into the
land of New Guinea, where the tides run very
ftrong ; that at the top of this gulph, lay two
places, one called Buntunan, the other Lufurajah :
from the latter, they faid a road croffed New Guinea, to the oppofite or north fhore, whence Miffoy
bark* was tranfported.

* This does not agree with the fuppofition, that New Guinea
is divided into iflands, as in many charts it appears.

Near

Near the mouth of this gulph, is a harbour, named Bury. Beyond it, or to the southward of it, is Kabſay, Leſkayay, Warandamo, Lakamaro, and beyond that Habſy, where are ſaid to be people who wear large turbans, and wide ſleeves.†

Commodore Watſon, in the Revenge frigate, not many years ago, ſailed along the weſt coaſt of New Guinea. Near Wonim, are two iſlands, Balamafully, and Galapy.

The harbour of Ef-be, lies in latitude of 2° 12′ S. and longitude 127°, it is perfectly land locked. Freſh water is very acceſſible on the iſland, or may be had in a little river on the main land of Myſol, where I found, two miles up, ſeveral ſmall canoes, belonging probably to the Haraforas : for I ſaw neither houſes nor people.

I was informed at Linty, that not long ago, the Dutch ſent an armed force to ſubdue Goram : it conſiſted of Buggeſſes, who were beat off by the inhabitants.

† It is not impoſſible that a colony of Arabs may have ſailed this way, in former days, and that theſe may be their poſterity.

CHAP.

C H A P. XI.

Departure from Ef-be Harbour---Stop at the Kanary
Iſlands--Account of Round Harbour---Searched for
Nutmegs---Leave the Kanary Iſlands---Paſs between
the Iſlands Bo and Popo---Paſs Gibby---Tuan Buf-
fora goes off in the Night with Tuan Hadjee's Coro-
coro---Anchored near the Iſlands Syang and Eye, and
got freſh Water---Departure thence---Saw the Iſ-
land Gilolo---Saw the Iſland Morty---Saw the Iſ-
lands of Kabruang, Salibabo, and Tulour---Arrive in
Leron Harbour on Salibabo---Tranſactions there.

1775.
March.

BEING all ready to ſail, about ten A. M. of
the 31ſt, as has been ſaid, we rowed out of Ef-be
harbour. We preſently ſaw a large corocoro, coming from towards the iſland Ceram. This put us
on our guard ; but ſhe ſteered another way. In
the evening we were got abreaſt of the Beehive,
which lies about five miles W. N. W. from Ef-be
harbour. Sounded thirty-three fathom muddy
ground.

1775.
April.

On *Saturday, April* the 1ſt, calms, with rain in the
night ; had a current in our favour, ſetting weſt.
The morning being very clear, we could ſee Ceram, which appeared not above twelve leagues off.
By noon, the weſtermoſt Kanary iſland, which is
the largeſt, bore N. N. W. about four leagues, we
being then in latitude 2° 10′ S. afternoon we loſt
ground with the ebb tide.

On

On *Sunday* the 2d, gained in the night, with the flood tide ; rowed a good deal in the morning, and got to the eaftward of the great Kanary, where we anchored in five fathom clear fand, within mufket fhot of the fhore, the Dolphin's Nofe bearing S. E. by S. five leagues. The boat's crew found a good watering place in a pond, at the fouth end of the great Kanary. While we ftopped here, Tuan Hadjee fitted up the fmall corocoro, which had been prefented him by the confort of the Rajah of Salwatty: much as I difliked the equipment, I complied with it, finding he was refolved. Got a great many Kanary nuts, the kernels of which (generally two or three, but always in three cells) are full of oil, and as big as a fmall almond ; but more lufcious.

1775.
April.

Monday the 3d. Weighed about ten, A. M. and ftood over to Long Ifland, where we anchored, within a land locked harbour, in feven fathom, muddy ground. To day we had the wind at weft. The fmall harbour lies on the left hand, as you pafs from the fouthward, between Long Ifland and Turtle Ifland. The ftrait is about a mile broad, with good foundings, eighteen and twenty fathoms.

The paffage into the harbour, which is a circle of about eighty fathom diameter, is bold, and a mufket fhot acrofs. In the middle of the harbour is a round coral rock, dry at low water, and bold all round. A firft rate might lay her fide to it, lying in fix fathom water, muddy ground. Table Ifland, appears higher than Long Ifland.

M   To

To the eaftward of Turtle Ifland, are many fmall
low iflets covered with trees.

Tuefday the 4th. Wind at Weft. Rowed northward into a creek, where we lay clofe to the fhore,
and had a clear fpot to land upon; whereas, in
the harbour before mentioned, which I fhall call
Round Harbour, it was every where very muddy
and fwampy in landing. From this creek we went
into the woods, and cut a new foremaft and bowfprit of bintangle wood, which is light, yet ftrong,
and of a colour like fir. Found abundance of ratans, many of which we cut for our ufe. We alfo
fearched for nutmegs and cloves, but found none.
Sultry weather. To day, four of our people amufing themfelves in the boat, which could carry ten,
overfet her on purpofe, and turned her bottom up :
having afterwards righted her, all four laid hold of
one end, and, by fuddenly ftriking out their feet
behind, and forcing the boat forward, a deal of water ran out of her, over their heads. She being
thus lightened a little, one man went in, and baled
her dry. I have often obferved one of my people
free a fampan, (canoe) by (being in the water)
pulling her fuddenly backwards and forwards, making the water fplafh out. Thus they cannot be
drowned, if overfet.

Wednefday the 5th. Wind ftill at weft : went a
founding about Turtle Ifland, where we had gathered many Turtle eggs.

Thurfday the 6th. Variable winds and calm :
founded about Clump Ifland. Tuan Hadjee and
                                        Tuan

Tuan Buffora feemed much afraid of meeting with the Dutch.

Friday the 7th. Variable winds and calms with thunder and lightning to the fouthward. Caught quantities of fifh in Round Harbour, whither we fent the boat at night. The people burnt torches, and ftruck the fifh with lances, from the boat, in fhallow water. We got more turtle eggs; but were not fo lucky as to catch a turtle, tho' we faw many prints of their fins. During our ftay here we found the iflands unfrequented; nor had they ever feen Britons before.

Saturday the 8th. Much rain and calms. Caught fome fifh in Round Harbour, but not fo many as yefterday. To day, Mr. Baxter, my mate, having ftruck Capez, a perfon belonging to Tuan Hadjee, it had like to have made an uproar among the people, feveral looking angry and feizing their arrows; but immediately on his, at my requeft, making an apology to Tuan Hadjee, the affair was made up.

Sunday the 9th. Calm moft part of the night, with a fine clear morning; failed at ten. Wind S. W. fteered N. W. refolving to go round Morty. Having a fevere head-ake, I could not obferve. We found the current fet to the northward. About funfet we paffed between the iflands of Eo and Popo.

Monday the 10th. In the morning could fee Gag, bearing N. N. E. alfo Pulo Pifang, Eo, and Popo, all at the fame time.

At

At noon we were in 00° 50′ S. latitude. We then saw Gibby bearing from N. by E. to N. E. by N.

Tuesday the 11th. In the night paffed between Gibby and the two low iflands of Yo and Utu, that lie to the eaftward of it. Of them, the ifland near-er to Gibby, is about two miles round. At the fouth point of the larger is faid to be a harbour. The paffage between Gibby and the two iflands may be about five miles broad. The N. W. point of Gibby bearing weft fix leagues, we could not fee Patany Hook, on Gilolo.

I imagine Gibby to be about four or five leagues long, and about twelve round; being narrow, and divided into two hills, with a low neck between. From the more northerly hill, a long low point ftretches towards Gilolo; and in the faid hill ap-pears a remarkable gap or cut, when it bears about N. half W. Off this N. W. end of Gibby, from the fouthward, appears alfo an ifland; behind which, as I was told by Tuan Buffora, whofe fa-mily lived at Gibby, fome French fhips had lately lain, and got from Patany many nutmeg and clove plants, which they carried to their iflands of Bour-bon and Mauritius. † This perfon went off in the night, with the fmall corocoro that Tuan

† The French have fince carried them to the iflands Mahe or Sechelles; and fome were even fent to the Weft Indies.

Tuan Buffora had, in converfation, informed me, that the eaft coaft of Gilolo was better inhabited than the weft. The weft coaft being more immediately under the eye of Dutch fe-verity, the inhabitants poffibly get to the eaftward, to enjoy more freedom.

Hadjee

Hadjee had fitted up. I cannot help imagining he expected to be able to get afhore, and afterwards to overtake the veffel, as he left a flave on board, and his wearing apparel. Neither of my Europeans knew of his going off, until fome little time after he was gone; and I did not choofe to lie to for him, as the wind was then frefh and fair; befides that, hereabouts were faid to be many Dutch cruifers.

At eight A. M. we faw low land, bearing N. E. Towards noon, the wind came to the northward, with which I flood N. W. finding the current fet N. E. for we faft approached the low land we had difcerned at eight in the morning. Still approaching the low land in the afternoon, I wifhed much to get to it; but, in the night, the wind coming thence, I fteered to an oppofite quarter, N. N. W. and N. W. Towards morning I put about, and flood N. E. right for the land, the wind coming from the N. N. W.

Wednefday the 12th. At day light I faw again the land mentioned yefterday. There were two iflands, low and flat: the more northerly was the fmaller. As I expected anchorage near them, and did not like to keep the fea with uncertain winds, in the track of Dutch cruifers, I promifed a reward to twenty rowers, if I reached them. This made them exert themfelves, and at ten A. M. I got within four miles of the iflands: the wind then coming fair, I flood on; at noon had no obfervation; P. M. anchored on a bank of great extent, depth ten fathom, fand and long weeds. Towards evening, the wind dying away, we rowed back towards
the

the two low iflands. Sent the boat to the fmaller, named Pulo Eye, for water; but, it being late, there was not time to dig. Anchored in the ftrait between the iflands, the tide running three knots: caught fourteen fifh in the night, each weighing feven or eight pounds.

Thurfday the 13th. In the morning I went afhore to the larger ifland, called Syang. On cutting an arrow plant, (a fpecies of pine) I found frefh water drop from it; I then dug, and got good water. The weather threatening, I hafted on board, and rowed behind a low fandy iflet, not above an acre in content. It had a few bufhes on it; and, by the frefh prints of turtle fins, we were guided to fome of their eggs. This iflet lies on the welt fide of the ifland Syang, with two fathom water, fandy ground, behind it in fome places: in other places it is rocky. We touched upon the rocks; but, the water being fmooth, we got no hurt. P. M. it was fqually to the N. W. which, however, came to nothing. Had it come to blow at N. W. we lay very fnug behind the fmall ifland, where no fquall could affect us. Dug for water: fome rain water, which was fweet, ran off the furface into our wells.

Friday the 14th. This morning we found the water in our wells brackifh: weighed about two P. M. rowed from behind the little fandy ifland, and anchored in feven fathom abreaft of where we had firft dug for water, being the northermoft part of the larger ifland. Had much rain, with winds at S. E.

On

On *Saturday* the 15th, weighed at one A. M. there being appearance of fine weather. We were immediately carried to the eaftward, entirely out of our courfe, by a tide or current. We therefore rowed and failed back to Pulo Eye, and anchored at feven P. M. in five fathom rocky ground, two miles from the fhore, its fouth extreme bearing E. S. E. We had hard fqualls from the eaftward, with rain; ftruck our maft.

Sunday the 16th. Weighed, and ran behind Pulo Syang, and anchored in feven fathom fand and rocks, oppofite the watering place, it bearing E. by N. three miles diftant. The trees there appeared green, but low; fome tall timber trees, ftripped of their bark, being behind them. We fent our boat afhore, and filled our jars with good water at the well we had firft dug. In attempting to weigh our anchor from this place there being a great fea and a frefh gale at E. N. E. we parted our cable, and then fteered N. N. W. the veffel making much water.

On *Monday* the 17th, moderate weather, wind at E. and S. E. By noon we had run from Pulo Syang eighty-four miles on a N. W. by N. courfe, and were in the latitude of 01° 55′ N. We could then fee fome high land, bearing W. N. W. it was part of the great ifland Gilolo. Steered north, the wind at S. E. by E. The fea being fmooth, we did not make fo much water as before. At funfet we faw plainly the land: it appeared in two bluff points, bearing from W. by N. half N. to W. S. W. We faw alfo a point of low land
bearing

bearing N. W. Steered N. N. E. when the wind
permitted, not choofing to keep near the land.

Tuefday the 18th. Calms, rain, and variable
winds. By an indifferent obfervation at noon, we
were in 02° 39ʹ N. the N. E. point of Gilolo bearing W. N. W. where an almoft table land jets out,
and promifes a bay to its fouthward. At one P. M.
faw the ifland Morty bearing N. N. W. Rowed
a good deal in the night, and rewarded the rowers.
I remarked the north eaft promontory of Gilolo to
be rugged land.

Wednefday the 19th. Light airs and calms. At
three A. M. a frefh breeze from the S. W. by S.
Steered N. E. and N. N. E. Towards noon it
was dead calm: we then rowed a little while in latitude 03° 29ʹ, the north part of the ifland Morty
bearing N. W. five leagues; the fouth part of it
S. W. half S. fix leagues. Could fee, at the fame
time, the north eaft promontory of Gilolo bearing
S. by W. very diftant. I reckon the north part of
Morty to lie in 03° 40ʹ N. It was calm fome part
of the night.

Thurfday the 20th. Having rowed a good deal
all night, in the morning found the current fet us
to the N. W. Morty then bore from S. S. W.
to S. S. E. the north part of Gilolo bearing
S. W. very diftant. At noon we were in latitude
04° 05ʹ N.

Morty, to the eaft, north, and north weft,
floping gently to the fea, and terminating in low
points,

points, bids fair for good anchoring ground. The
ifland is pretty high, but rifes no where fuddenly:
the outline, taken on the whole, is not uneven,
though fome portions are. At funfet Morty bore
from S. E. by E. to S. S. E. ten leagues.

On *Friday* the 21ft, rowed and failed in the
night, it being fine weather. We fteered N. W.
and N. W. by W. as the wind permitted. About
ten in the morning, faw land bearing W. N. W.
ten leagues diftant. At noon, were in the latitude
of 04° 41′ N. then difcerned other land, bearing
from N. W. to W. N. W. forming in faddles and
hummocs. The land firft feen was the ifland of
Kabruang, which makes like a peaked hill. Salibabo, clofe to it, has a table land; and the land
appearing in hummocs is Tulour, or Tanna Labu,
which Valentine * calls Karkalang. At funfet we
lay to, fearing the current might drive us paft
Salibabo, where was (one of Tuan Hadjee's people
told me) a good harbour at a place called Leron,
and whither we propofed to go for provifions.

Saturday the 22d. At two in the morning,
made fail, and ran between the iflands Kabruang
and Salibabo, into the harbour of Leron. Anchored in ten fathoms muddy ground, having the
fea open only from S. by E. half E. to S. E. by E.
We had fince morning hoifted Dutch colours, and
fent the boat afhore as a Dutch one. Immediately
after we had anchored, came on board to queftion

---

* Since my being in England, I have feen Valentine's map
of Leron harbour, and found it very exact.

us,

us, a blind Chinefe, who fpoke very good Malay. I prefented him with a fathom of coarfe chintz. In the afternoon I went on fhore in the corocoro with Tuan Hadjee, and the two Batchian officers, to vifit the two Rajahs, fo many being on Salibabo. I gave each a piece of Tappies, and they permitted the people of the village to fell us provifions. I found that the people of this ifland were at war with the inhabitants of Kabruang, the ifland oppofite, and diftant only five or fix miles. I was fhocked at landing, to fee a man's head, lately cut off, hanging by the hair from a branch of a tree, under which we paffed; the blood yet dropping from it on the fand.

Sunday the 23d. Frefh northerly winds; got into the inner harbour, and anchored in three and a half fathom water, muddy ground. Here I found we lay much fmoother, than where we lay yefterday in ten fathom. To day many fmall canoes came on board; we bought kalavanfas, potatoes, fome rice, and two goats, all very reafonable in their price, which we paid in coarfe calicoes, red handkerchiefs, &c. Thefe iflands being well cultivated, abound with inhabitants and provifions. To day we had a good deal of rain; a great fwell without, made high breakers on a point of rocks, which forms the harbour on the right hand coming in, and on which a few bufhes grow. We obferved great rejoicings afhore, and feveral Dutch enfigns difplayed. Sent Mr. Lound the gunner about ten A. M. to examine a prow or boat that lay for fale about two miles off, to the N. W. of Leron; fuch feeming an expedient purchafe, as the

galley

galley was very leaky. I found fome difficulty in agreeing about the terms that afternoon, becaufe fhe wanted fome repairs; fo in the evening, when we went on board, confulting with Tuan Hadjee and the Batchian officers, we refolved to have nothing to fay to her, and to be gone immediately in our own veffel; for we dreaded a rupture with the people of Leron, who began (we were told) to fufpect our galley a Mindano piratical cruifer.

Monday the 24th. At break of day, a fmall canoe with only one man came from Kabruang, to fee who we were. Of this though we did not inform him, he feemed in hafte to return, without landing on Leron, the two iflands being at war. Leron is a very good harbour: but, in going into it, it would be proper to fend a boat a head, and examine the entrance.

The people of thefe iflands are of the Malay colour, with long hair. They are under Sangir, which is fubject to Ternate. They are much oppreffed by their Kolanos, or chiefs; and for trifling offences, fold for flaves. Their arms are, lance, fword, target, and dagger. They manufacture a coarfe kind of cloth, made of the wild plantain tree, called Abaka; the fruit of which is bitter, and full of black feeds. They had many hogs, but I bought none.

C H A P.

C H A P. XII.

*Departure from Leron—Paſſed by ſeveral ſmall Iſlands
—Saw the Iſlands Belk and Serangani—Paſſed the
Harbour of Batulakki, on Magindano—Alſo, the
great Bay of Sugud Boyan—Stopt at a Sandy Iſland
—Got Sight of the Iſland of Bunwoot—Paſſed
Timoko Hill, and entered the River of Magindano
—Remarks on the Monſoons in the Eaſtern Parts
of India, in low Latitudes.*

HAVING therefore reſolved to continue in
our own veſſel, leaky as ſhe was, rather than run
any hazard in changing her for another, which
was neither launched nor fitted, I weighed at ſunriſe, with a ſcant wind at N. E. Going out we
made much water, as there was a head ſea, and I
was obliged to carry ſail, to clear the iſland Salibabo. Mr. Baxter having yeſterday purchaſed a
boy about fifteen, for an old ſcarlet coat, the
latter in the night jumped overboard and ſwam
aſhore, leaving the purchaſer to boaſt of his bar-
gain. Being now clear of the ſtrait between
Kabruang and Salibabo, we ſtood on N. W. by
N. with the wind at N. E. by E. towards night
had much rain, with a chopping ſea ; made much
water : lay to till morning.

Tueſday 25. Fair weather, after a very bad night,
from many cauſes ; at eleven A. M. ſaw a ſmall
iſland with a hummoc, bearing N. W. eight miles ;

at

at noon, were in latitude 05° 00' north, lying up N. W. wind at N. E. the corocoro far aftern. At the fame time, a very high hill bore S. W. by S. half S. I take it to be the north part of Sangir.

P. M. faw four other fmall iflands at different times to the northward ; one, rocky, made like buttons ; one was flat, one made like an obtufe cone ; and one had a treble hill.

On *Wednefday* the 26th, at midnight, could fee the ifland, with a hummoc mentioned yefterday, bearing S. E. at noon were in 05° 13' by an in-different obfervation ; it was then almoft calm. The weather being very cloudy to the northward, over Magindano, and the wind at north, fome part of the night we lay to : I fufpect the current fet to the weftward.

Thurfday the 27th. It looking very gloomy to the northward, with much rain, ftowed all our fails, and lay to until morning ; had no obfervation. The wind in the afternoon chopped about to W. and W. N. W. We thought we faw land bearing N. E. fteered for it ; faw a butterfly : at night thunder and lightning over the land.

On *Friday* the 28th, wind at N. W. fteered N. N. E. and N. E. made much water ; at day light difcovered Pulo Serangani, bearing E. by N. at the diftance of about twelve leagues. It appear-ed like a blunt fugar loaf ; at the fame time, we could fee other land to the northward of it, being part of Magindano. Wind at W. S. W. fteered

N. and

N. and N. N. E. had much rain, thunder, and lightning, with a chopping fea. Lay to fome part of the night.

On *Saturday* the 29th, fteered N. N. E. and N. E. under our lateen mizen bent as a forefail, having rent our proper forefail. In the morning, the ifland of Serangani bore S. E. we fteered directly thither, and anchored near it about ten A. M.

There are two iflands ; the more wefterly is very high, making a fugar loaf ; its north coaft is bold. A fpot of land runs off its N. E. point, which we doubled, and anchored in feven fathom, muddy ground mixed with fand ; a certain flat table point bearing weft, half a league off, and the ftraits mouth between the eafter and wefter ifland being fhut in. Tuan Hadjee went afhore, and, in about an hour, returned with a pilot, who carried us farther into the ftrait, that feparates the iflands, fteering S. E. and brought us into nine foot water among rocks ; however, we lay in a clean fpot of fand, about thirty fathom wide, and got out two wooden anchors, which we fixed between the coral rocks, it blowing frefh at N. W. but in the evening it foftened a little.

Several canoes came on board from the more wefterly ifland, with coco nuts and fowls ; they proffered alfo for fale, fome pieces of yellow wax, which I am told abounds in thofe parts. That ifland is partly cultivated, and is properly called Belk. The eaftern has not near fo good an ap-

pearance,

pearance, neither are there any coco nut trees to
be feen, which are fo numerous on the weftern
ifland.

Next morning, the 30th, I went afhore on a
little iflet, hard by the weftern Serangani, (called
Moleron) where we found many lemon trees, and
gathered a good deal of the fruit, which was, however, very fmall; on this ifland, we found alfo
many Mahometan graves. Trees were planted,
as if to fhade the graves. They had few leaves,
but bore white flowers, tinged with yellow infide,
about an inch long, which yielded a moft fragrant
fmell : Malays call it Bunga Mellora. We filled
our water on the weftern ifland, near Moleron :
this day the winds have moftly been from the
N. W.

Monday, May 1ft. Fine weather, with the wind
at fouth; weighed and got from amongft the
rocks and fhoals, with which we were almoft furrounded. At noon we approached the coaft of
Magindando, which we found to be twelve miles
diftant from the iflands of Serangani : at three
P. M. we were abreaft of the harbour of Batulakki,
which may be known by a remarkable rock, about
the fize of a large dwelling houfe. It is of a pipe
clay colour, with a few bufhes atop. This large
rock, and a fmall rock contiguous, which appears
like a boat bottom up, muft be kept on the left,
going into the harbour. Between the large rock
and the main, is a reef of rocks, over which, boats
may pafs at high water. In the harbour is ten
fathom water, as I was told. A little way to the
northward,

northward of it, are two cleared fpots on the hills
of a conical fhape : off the harbour, I founded
thirty-three fathom water, muddy ground.

Tuefday the 2d. Fine weather. To the northward of this harbour, is the entrance of the great
bay of Sugud Boyan, or harbour of Boyan. North
of Sugud Boyan, and clofe to the fea, is high land,
of a pretty even out-line, its flope to the fea terminating in a fair beach. I was affured there was
anchoring ground ; but it is near the fhore. Tuan
Hadjee informed me, that the Dutch had fome
years ago endeavoured to fettle at Batulakki, having fet thither a fhip, and a number of panchallangs
from Ternate ; but, that they were drove off by
the people of Mindano, who carried away a ftone
they had left with their mark upon it.

Wednefday the 3d. Fine weather, with the tide or
current in our favour, ftill failing along a fmooth
fandy beach, to the northward of the entrance off
the bay of Sugud Boyan. At noon, the weather
being cloudy, we had no obfervation. At fun fet,
Serangani was juft out of fight, bearing S. E. by S.
Came on board feveral boats, from a place called
Tugis; they hoifted fmall white flags. The Mindano people in thofe boats, paid great refpect to
Tuan Hadjee, whom they had known before.
At his defire, I made them fome fmall prefents.
In the night we paffed a bluff head land, about
a league N. W. of Tugis. On either fide this
head land, the natives faid there was good anchorage. They informed me withal, that the fame
head land being in one, with a fugar loaf hill juft
within

within it, leads at fea to a fhoal on which is only three fathom water, upon fand and rocks.

On *Thurfday* the 4th, faw a fpot of fand clofe to the fhore, and near a flat point. I approached it in the boat, and found many funk rocks about it. I then returned on board, foon after the tide fetting S. E. with the wind at N. W. I ftood off, and lay to, not chufing to go near this fpot of fand, (which might be about an acre) on account of the many rocks about it. In the evening, the wind coming off the land, we lay up along fhore.

Friday the 5th. Fine weather : about funrife, the land wind veered to the northward, and we lay up no better than weft. The wind then fhifted to S. W. foon after to W. N. W. About ten A. M. we unexpectedly faw the fandy ifland mentioned yefterday. Finding the tide had driven us a good deal to the fouthward, I ran behind it, leaving it on the left, and anchored in five fathoms clear fand. I then fent to the main land, and got water. We weighed at funfet, and failed between the main and the fandy ifland, where we found overfalls, from twenty to two fathoms, and then to thirty-five fathoms rocky ground, about two miles from the beach. All night we had a fine land wind at N. E. with a new moon.

In the morning of *Saturday* the 6th, faw a fmall ifland with a hummoc, bearing north, near the main land. Steered N. N. W. with the wind at S. W. by S. At nine A. M. we perceived the low trees of a bay, lying to the N. E. of the faid ifland.

N   At

At night the tide was in our favour, and we had a fine land breeze, steering N. and N. by W. The sun being to the northward these several days, we had no obfervation.

Sunday the 7th. Fine weather, and a favourable gale at E. and S. E. Before day light we passed the north part of the bay observed yesterday: at seven A. M. we discovered the island of Bunwood, bearing N. N. E. Part of it appeared like what seamen call a gunner's coin or wedge. Dark and cloudy was the weather, till near noon; it then cleared up, and Tapian point bore N. N. E. three leagues. It is rather low, but not flat; and lies in latitude 7° 15′ N. Afternoon we had a fresh gale at south, and passed Tapian point about three. At half past four we were abreast of Timoko hill: we left it on the right; as we did a hill, inland a little way, which is clear from wood atop, being intirely covered with grass; and is called Kablallang, about five I entered the river Pelangy, commonly called Magindano river, and had barely two fathom water on the bar.

Having so far prosecuted the voyage, before I conclude this chapter, I could wish to say something of the nature of the winds and currents in low latitudes, east of Atcheen Head; which may be termed in general as far as the Moluccas, a Malay region---The Malay tongue, soft and easily learnt, being understood and spoken all along the coast of the islands, which in the map occupy this vast space.

The

The winds, which blow from the fouth and weft, in the bay of Bengall, and in the China feas, commonly called the S. W. Monfoon, blow N. W. on that part of Sumatra, north of the line; as the hills there alter the direction of the wind, which at Atcheen Head is S. W. and follows the fituation of the coaft, which is N. W. Again, fouth of the line, the S. W. monfoon coincides with the perpetual trade wind, and becomes S. E.

Between Borneo and Celebes, between Celebes and Gilolo, and without Java and Sumatra, the monfoons, that in the China feas are S. W. and N. E. may, with propriety, be called N. and S. or rather N. W. and S. E.

Captain Wilfon, of the Pitt, Indiaman, in this idea, profecuted and made good his paffage from Batavia to China, againft the monfoon. In evidence of fo great merit, that track is often kept. When the fhips get paft Pitt's Strait, into the fouth fea, near the iflands Palaos,* they find the current fet ftrong to the northward at full and change. The purfuers of this track, I would advife to fteer without Java, rather than within, or to the northward of it; unlefs, indeed, the fhip has bufinefs at Batavia. On the fouth coaft of Java, during the N. E. monfoon, the winds are ftrong from the N. W. and W. the current fetting the fame way, and in this track, the road of Carang Affem, on the ifland of Bally, affords moft excellent refrefhments. Being there on board the Bonetta ketch,

---

* Of this circumftance I was informed by Captain Affleck, of his Majefty's fhip Argo, who made the paffage in 1764.

N 2

in the year 176:, I found plenty of bullocks, at two dollars, and hogs at one dollar each: ducks alfo in great quantities. I left Banditten Ifland on the left, fteered for Bally Peak or Hill, and anchored in ten fathom, fandy ground, out of the tide, about half a mile from the fhore. As there are no foundings, or at leaft, very deep water, juft without where I anchored, I would recommend to the navigator to fteer boldly for the houfes of Carang Affem, and anchor as I did, keeping the peak about N. by E. This I choofe to be more particular in mentioning, as the India Directory, from wrong information, fays, there is no anchorage hereabouts. The fhip Experiment was alfo here, fome years after me. When I anchored, the natives, who are Gentoos, came on board, in little canoes, with outriggers on each fide. On the edges of the canoe, for the bottom was too narrow, I put a gang cafk, with which the owner paddled into a frefh water river, and, within twenty minutes, brought it full of water; for which fervice I paid ten or twelve China cafh, with a hole in each, of which I bought four hundred for a Spanifh dollar.

This agreeable officioufnefs of the natives prevented my rifking our boat on fhore. Afternoon the Rajah of Carang Affem did me the honour of a vifit. He fung as he came on board, in a fmall boat, with one attendant. His nails were remarkably long. In the road lay feveral prows, loaded with rice, from the adjacent ifland Lomboc, which is alfo inhabited by Gentoos; and on the fides of the hills of Lomboc are, I am informed, large pools or tanks of water, for the purpofe of watering

ing

ing their rice fields, after the manner of the Gentoos of Indoftan, from whom they are certainly
defcended.

The ifland Bally, on the fouth fide, is well cultivated, and many of the grounds are inclofed; it
is full of inhabitants, who fpin a great deal of cotton yarn, which the Chinefe chiefly export to Bencoolen, and other parts, as well as checkered cloths,
like Bengal Lungys made of it. The Chinefe carry alfo in floops and prows, from Bally to Fort
Marlbro, pickled pork and dried (jerked) beef,
which Malays call ding-ding. If a fhip refrefh-
es here, and the captain has a little patience, he
will come off remarkably cheap. Iron, cutlery,
and opium, are the articles of trade; but no quantity can be fold, as filver and gold are fcarce. They
have cotton exceeding cheap; but they do not
pack it well; putting it in bafkets, like thofe called
at Batavia, canifters. The natives are rather of a
better character than the Mahometan Malays; but
I did not truft myfelf afhore.

Here, not only women often kill themfelves, or
burn with their deceafed hufbands; but men alfo
burn in honour of their deceafed mafters. Thofe
who determine on this, are not limited to time:
they name, perhaps, a diftant day; and, in the
mean while, their intention being made known,
there is no honour the natives can think of, but
they pay to this devotee. He is venerated and ca-
reffed wherever he goes. On the fatal day, by the
fide of a great fire, a loofe ftage of boards is erected;
on this he dances, working himfelf up to a fit; he then

fkips

ſkips to the end of a plank, which tilting, he falls headlong into the flames. This I learnt from one of my men, Iſhmael Jerrybatoo, a man of veracity, who had ſeen it.

A ſhip having refreſhed at this moſt eligible place, may continue her voyage, leaving Bally to the weſt, and after making the Paternoſters, haul up for what is called the Bugeroons, or the Strait of Salayer. By no means go to the ſouthward of Salayer, which is full of ſhoals. The track then is, to leave Bouton on the left, and Ceram on the right; but I queſtion whether it were not preferable to haul up to the northward of the Kanary iſlands; leaving them and Myſol on the right, left the ſhip ſhould fall to leeward.

Some ſhips go through the Strait of Golowa, ſome through Pitt's Strait, and ſome through a Strait ſtill farther north, called, in certain maps, Auguſta's Strait, which has the iſland Waygiou on the north ſide of it.

I cannot find any ſhips have gone north of Waygiou, into the South Sea, coaſting the north ſide of that iſland, where I found three good harbours, Piapis, Offak, and Rawak. All the charts I have ſeen, leave the north coaſt of Waygiou undetermined by a dotted line.

However deſirable it may be to put into theſe harbours, yet I would not adviſe a ſhip to go into the ſouth ſea, by the north of Waygiou; as, ſo far north, ſhe may meet the wind at N. E. whereas,

whereas, farther fouth, in Augufta's, Pitt's, or Golowa Strait, the wind, *during the N. E. monfoon,*
is more likely to blow from the weftward, according to the general rule. Nor do I doubt, but on
each fide of thefe Straits there may be very good
harbours and inhabitants. Salwatty may be better
inhabited than Waygiou ; for I fent to the former,
whilft I lay near Waygiou, for a ftock of fago
bifcuit, which was prefently purchafed as has been
told.

A VOYAGE

People of Moa. Jamna, &c. with one of their Boats.

A

VOYAGE

TO

NEW GUINEA.

BOOK II.

CHAPTER I.

Of the Ifland Magindano---Account of the Rivers Pe-
langy, Melampy, and Tamantakka---Town of Se-
langan---Coto Intang.

THE word *Magindano* is compounded of *Mag,* 1775,
related to, or near akin; *in,* country, and *dano,* May.
lake:* fo the whole means, kindred fettled in the
country about the lake.

The ifland extends from the latitude of 5° 40'
to 9° 55' N. and from the longitude of 119° 30' to

---

* Francifcus Combes, the Jéfuit, fays alfo, in his Account
of Mindanao ; " Porque Mindanao quere decir hombre de
" laguna."

125° E.

125° E. It is of a triangular form, having three remarkable capes or promontories; one, near Samboangan, where the Spaniards have their chief settlement, to the weftward; Cape Auguftine or Pandagitan, to the eaftward; and Suligow to the northward. The ifland may be divided into three parts; each under a diftinct and independent government. The firft divifion is under the Sultan, who refides at the town of Mindano or Selangan, by far the largeft and moft ancient: it formerly comprehended the greateft part of the fea coaft. The fecond is under the Spaniards, comprehending a large portion of the fea coaft, to the weft, north and north eaft, where they have planted colonies of Chriftians from the Philippines, called Bifaya. The third is under the Illano or Illanon, Sultans and Rajahs, a fort of feudal chiefs, who inhabit the banks of the Great Lake or Lano, and thence a good way inland, towards the hills. The Illanos poffefs alfo the coaft of that great bay, fituated on the fouth fide of the ifland.

The ifland of Magindano may be about 800 miles round; as large as the kingdom of Ireland. The Spaniards, though they have fubdued the north coaft of the ifland, never conquered the whole.

They fometimes call it a Philippine, in order to enlarge their own dominions; yet one of their moft credible authors calls Magindano, an ifland *adjacent* to the Philippines. *

* To the diftrict of the Philippines and their confines, thofe of Mindano are adjacent.

Le Recapitulada, lib. 6.   Dalrymple's Proofs, p. 28.

A French

A French author, D'Avitay, fays exprefsly, Mindano is not a Philippine ifland. *

The Illano and Magindano tongues are much the fame ; but, I am told, there are fourteen dialects fpoken in the ifland ; and that fome of the dialects are greatly different from others. There is firft the Magindano and Illano, which nearly coincide.

2. The Dya,	9. The Matigdrog,
3. The Manubo,	10. The Bangil Bangil,
4. The Belam,	11. The Matima Pulo,
5. The Tagabaly,	12. The Matima Pute,
6. The Kalagan,	13. The Telandrig,
7. The Eagubo,	14. The Alang.
8. The Manfaka,	

The Magindano tongue is copious and energetic : it has many of the Chinefe idioms, as I was told by the Sultan, who, by converfing much with Chinefe, though not in the Chinefe, but in the Magindano tongue, was able to judge of this circumftance ; about which I particularly afked him.

They have a name, which they give to their fons during childhood, and another for manhood : in this they refemble the Chinefe. In their manners and cuftoms are other particulars in which they refemble that nation ; fuch as, yellow being the royal colour ; guefts at feafts of ceremony having all different tables, and, in proportion to the greatnefs of the ceremony, the tables loaded.

* Hiftoire General de l'Afie, p. 909.

They

They are fond of mufical gongs, * which come
from Cheribon on Java, and have round knobs on
them ; others without knobs, come from China.
Their ladies, when compleatly dreffed, put me in
mind of Chinefe pictures, and of thofe ladies, whom
by chance I have feen in chairs, in the ftreets of the
fuburbs of Canton.

Before the difcovery of the road to India, by the
Cape of Good Hope, it is certain that fhips found
their way to China, from the two Arabian gulphs,
as alfo from the coaft of Malabar.

Even many hundred years before the time of
Marco Polo, the famous Venetian traveller, Eben
Wahab, in the year 898, travelled to China, † he
mentions, that in China is Canfu, the city of Arabian traders.   The capital of that empire was
then called Cumdan, two months journey from
Canfu.   No wonder then that fome of the Arabs
found their way to the ifland of Magindano.

The Arabians were formerly great difcoverers,
and feldom failed to conquer the lands they had
difcovered.   Their religion contributed to their
influence whitherfoever they reforted.   Their frequent ablutions, tending to cleanlinefs, efpecially
in a warm country, recommended a felf-evident
virtue, of which the practitioners only know the
luxury.   Their abhorrence of fwine's flefh, makes
thofe who not only handle, but eat that animal,

---

* A gong is an inftrument of brafs, fomewhat like a tabor or
drum, with only one head.

† Harris's Collection, pages 522, 529, 535.

become

become contemptible in their eyes, and poſſibly ſoon
after in their own: for, who can bear to be deſpiſed ?

The trade alſo of ſuch an iſland as Magindano,*
where the uncivilized inhabitants wanted iron, &c.
was a great inducement, as the returns were in
gold, wax, and cinnamon. No wonder therefore,
that the moors ſoon ſought and found ſuch footing.

Voyages in thoſe days were not ſo ſafe or ſo frequent as in theſe. For this reaſon, no doubt, the
merchants ſtayed long at a place, took wives, built
houſes, &c.

The town of Magindano ſtands about ſix miles
from the bar of the river Pelangy, on the right
hand going up, juſt where the river Melampy joins
it. The Pelangy is then about the width of the
river Thames at London bridge. The Melampy
is a river about half as broad as the Pelangy ; and,
as you go up, it ſtrikes off to the right, whilſt the
Pelangy on the left, retains its breadth for many
miles.

A good way higher at Kabantallan, the Pelangy
ſends forth a branch bigger than itſelf, called the
Tamantakka, which diſcharges itſelf into the ſea,
about three miles ſouth of the Pelangy or Magin-

---

* Mindano omnium maxima regio, eſt cinnamomi commen-
data. Auri quoque Fodinas habet, portuſque, ac navium ſta-
tiones commodiſſimas. De Bry, vol. iii. fol. 35.

Canela de Mindanao tan vivo el picante como lo mejor de
Ceilan.
　　　Combes's Account of Mindano, 1667. p. 9.

dano bar. The remarkable hill of Timoko, an
only hill at the fea fide of a pretty large plain, lies
between the mouths of the two rivers.

The Tamantakka has three fathom water on its
bar, at high water in fpring tides ; while only two
fathoms are on the bar of the Pelangy.

The bar of the river Tamantakka being more
expofed to the weftern fea, than the bar of the Pelangy, and confequently more liable to a fwell, makes
that river's accefs lefs fafe than the Pelangy's ;
altho' there be more water on its bar.   The mouth
of the Pelangy, being much fheltered by the ifland
of Bunwoot, affords a fmooth bar almoft at all
times. No wonder then that the fmall river is
preferred to the greater, as the largeft veffels on
either, never draw above fix or feven foot water.

From the fouth fide of Magindano river, runs
alfo a fpit of fand, the extremity of which may be
brought almoft in one with the S. W. part of Bunwoot ; and then is fifteen fathom water. If the
tide does not anfwer, a veffel may anchor here in a
good road, juft without the bar : for, it fhoals fuddenly from ten to two fathoms, coming from fea
on the bar. Within, is two and a half fathom
water, and in certain places three fathom at low
water, half a mile from the bar. About five miles
from the bar, or one mile from the town, is fhoal
water ; fo that a veffel drawing above twelve foot,
cannot get over it. Abreaft of the town, is two
fathom and a half depth at low water.

A good

A good way to the eaftward of Magindano are two lakes. The fmaller, called Buloan, runs into the larger Liguaffin, and the latter communicates with the Pelangy: but the fource of the Pelangy lies a great way farther N. E. Thefe two lakes are feveral miles round, but they are much inferior in extent to the great Lano in the Illano country, already mentioned, and of which more hereafter.

The town, that goes properly by the name of Magindano, confifts at prefent, of fcarce more than twenty houfes. They ftand clofe to, and juft above where a little creek, about eighteen foot broad, runs perpendicular into the Pelangy, from a fmall lake about one mile diftant, and about half a mile in circumference.

This fmall lake is called the Dano; the creek I have juft mentioned, is the Rawafs (or river) Magindano; and from the banks of the lake or Dano, a little earth is taken, upon which the Rajah Moodo * muft ftand, when he is confecrated Sultan.

The Rajah Moodo is elected by the ftates, and fucceeds the Sultan; fimilar to the king of the Romans fucceeding the emperors of Germany. A Watamama † is alfo elected, who becomes Rajah Moodo, when Rajah Moodo becomes Sultan.

Clofe to the Rawafs (river) Magindano, and oppofite the few houfes making the town of that name,

* Rajah Moodo, young king.
† Watamama fignifies male child.

ftands

ftands the town of Selangan, * which may be faid
to make one town with the other, as communicat-
ing with it by feveral bridges over the Rawafs. It
extends about one mile down the fouth fide of
the Pelangy, forming a decent ftreet for one half
of the diftance.   The fortified palace of the Sultan,
and the ftrong wooden caftles of the Datoo's,
Topang and Chartow, take up one fide of the
river, the other fide is occupied by individuals.
By Datoo Chartow's Fort, which is the third fartheft
from that of his father the Sultan, runs another
fmall river, like that which is called Rawafs Magindano.   It alfo difcharges itfelf into the Pelangy,
and Datoo Chartow has led it round three fides of
his fort, the Pelangy wafhing the fourth fide.   His
caftle feems ftronger than either Topang's Fort, or
the Sultan's palace.

Below this, the town extends about half a mile,
in feveral irregular ftreets, where many Chinefe re-
fide.   In the town of Selangan altogether, may be
about two hundred houfes; below the Sultan's palace, about twenty yards, is a brick and mortar
foundation remaining of a Spanifh chapel.

But in a country thinly inhabited, and where
ground is of no value, Mahometans efpecially,
choofe not to croud together ; each defiring a houfe
on the bank of a river.   Peculiarly is this vifible
here, where, upon the winding banks of the Pelangy, the Melampy, the Tamantakka, and by

* Called Siligan, by Pierre D'Avitay.
    Description Generale d'Asie, p. 910.

the

the fides of the many creeks that interfect the
ground between thofe capital rivers, at the diftance of almoft every three hundred yards, fometimes we fee a fingle houfe, fometimes a group of
houfes, with gardens of coco nut, mango, and
plantain trees, fugar canes, and rice fields, for
many miles up thofe rivers : particularly the Tamantakka, which being the greateft, its banks are
bold and dry. They are too fond of bathing in
frefh water, to wifh the neighbourhood of the fea,
though there are fome villages of falt makers, who
live always clofe to it. Their manner of making
falt, will be related hereafter.

As the country, through which thofe rivers lead
often in a winding courfe, is a plain of about twelve
miles broad, extending N. E. forty or fifty miles
as far as the fource of the Pelangy, and S. E. as
far as the lakes of Liguaffin and Buloan, they travel
moftly by water in fampans or canoes of different
fizes ; and many veffels of forty and fifty oars are
built along the banks of thofe rivers. Wherever
is a houfe, there is a fmall portion of the river fufficient for bathing, railed in, againft Alligators :*
a practice no lefs requifite at Selangan, where
houfes are built by the river fide.

The river Semoy, between Magindano river
and Pullock harbour, iffues from the Pelangy, and
runs through a plain. I have obferved, in going
up the Tamantakka, that it is bounded to the

* They have alfo in the water two neceffaries, one above,
and one below the bathing place, to ufe as the tide comes up
or down.

O   fouthward

southward by clear hills gently rising to no great height from its banks. They are diversified with woods, and clear spots of the coarse long grass, which the Malays call Lalang, Kutch Grass.

Though I have described the towns of Magindano and Selangan as making one, the name Selangan carries it generally over the other, among the people of the country. It stands on the south side of the Pelangy, where it is joined by the Melampy, about six miles from the bar.

In the south west monsoon, when much rain is in the river, fresh water may be had just within the bar. The strongest current is with the ebb tide, which may then run about four miles an hour, especially after rain ; and, during this monsoon, the tide seldom or never runs up. The highest tide is then about two days after the full moon, near eight in the morning. An east or west moon makes high water. During the north east monsoon, the highest tide is in the night, near eight o'clock ; and, during this monsoon, the tide runs up about two or three miles an hour, a good way above Selangan. In both monsoons, the tides rise about six inches higher on the full moon than on the change ; then rise on the bar about six foot, and at town about six foot and a half perpendicular. This rise sometimes overflows a little the adjacent grounds ; to obviate which inconvenience, the paths are in many places raised ; as is, particularly at Selangan, the street which passes the three capital houses.

On

On the point of land, where the river Melampy runs into the Pelangy, is a fort called Coto Intang, or Diamond Fort. Here, a few years fince, Kybad Zachariel, fome time ago elected Rajah Moodo, or fucceffor to the Sultan, has built alfo a town.

The fort is upon the extreme point of land, in extent about fix acres, ftrongly palifadoed with round trees five and twenty foot high. This fort commands both rivers; and towards the Pelangy, the broader and more confiderable, is a platform twelve foot from the ground. The floor is of ftout plank, ftrongly fupported by pofts and beams. On this are mounted five pieces of cannon, fix and nine pounders; and, being covered over head, the platform is not fo fubject to decay as gun platforms generally are in this country, becaufe moftly expofed to the weather. Guns are mounted under the platforms.

When I was there, Rajah Moodo was conftruct-ing three folid baftions of clay and logs of wood intermixed, cafed round with piles. The baftions were fquare, about ten foot high, and at three corners of his fort; the covered baftion already mentioned making the fourth.

The fort is nearly fquare, and the covered baf-tion, contiguous to Rajah Moodo's dwelling houfe, is under the ftout floor already mentioned. On the ground are feveral pieces of heavy cannon, even with the water. All round the fort are mounted many brafs fwivel guns, the fwivel being ftuck into the pofts; alfo fome brafs rantackers. The

O 2　　　　　　rantacker

rantacker is a gun fometimes fix foot long, and carries a half pound ball, refembling Marfhal Saxe's amufette.

On each baftion of the fort, is a large Spanifh bell, with a ratan made faft to the clapper. Two fentinels watch all night at each bell, and toll three ftrokes about every ten minutes, each bell anfwering regularly round to the firft. A Mindano Moor, and a Bifayan Chriftian, are always put together to watch.

From the gate, which is on the middle of that fide of the fort next the land, and which is nearly perpendicular to both rivers, leads a broad and ftraight ftreet, for the diftance of above half a mile. It is fo well raifed, as never to be overflowed; and is moated on both fides. At the end of this ftreet, a canal, cut from river to river, bounds the town, which having been built but a few years, confifts of about a hundred and fifty houfes, and is daily increafing. Beyond the town are gardens and rice fields.

On the fide next the Pelangy, dwell many Chinefe families; moftly carpenters, arrack diftillers, and millers. They grind the hufk off the rough rice (paddy) between two ftones, much more expeditiously than the Magindano people beat it off in a wooden mortar.

In that part of the town of Coto Intang, which borders on the Melampy, live a few Chinefe; but many Magindano mechanics, veffel builders, and merchants.

1775.
May.

merchants. They build their veffels of various dimenfions, and employ them in trading from one part of the coaft to the other; often in cruifing, amongft the (Bifayan) Philippine Iflands, for flaves and plunder. They cruife alfo as far as the coaft of Java, and the iflands of Celebes and Borneo, feizing whatever prows they can mafter. Thefe veffels are always very long for the breadth, and very broad for their draft of water.

C H A P. II.

Geographical Sketch of Places on the Banks of the Rivers Pelangy and Tamantakka, by Tuan Fakymo-lano---Defcription of the Saltpetre Cave---Rajah of Boyan.

ON the Pelangy, above Coto Intang, are the nigris (countries) of Katib-tuan, Labungin, and Batanig, on the left hand going up; then Kaban-tallan on the right, where the Tamantakka ftrikes off; alfo Limopog on the left: Utandan, with a hill on the left, oppofite to Boyan * on the right, where is a river; Kabolokan on the right, where are hills: Pelangy Lamo, (*old Pelangy*) on the left, oppofite Udfudun, on the right, where is a river that goes to the lakes of Liguaffin and Buloan. In thefe are many teal and ducks. Then Babuin-

* The Chinefe fettled at Mindano are not permitted to trade higher than Boyan; the Mindanoers being jealous of their fuperior abilities in trade.

gad

gad on the right, a little below Lagungan on the
left; Dupilas on the left, oppofite Makatudog on
the right. A little higher, on a fmall river, is
Maliduggou, where grows much coco. Then,
Kabakan on the right of the Pelangy, where a little
river difcharges itfelf into it. Dalapuan on the
right; Mulita on the left. Ulupelangy on the left,
Sanipan on the right; Gillang, with a river, on the
left, and Selag on the right, near the fource of the
Pelangy, where is much cinnamon.

On the banks of the river Tamantakka, are the
nigris of Kabug, by the fea-fide, where they make
falt; Demapatty, Tamantakka, Dywan, Ampuyan, Tanuel, Batu, Sagil, Dalikan, Tapidan,
Butillan; and then you come to Kabantallan,
where the two rivers meet. At Tapida is a fmall
river, up which are the places called Bunwoot and
Talaian. A little below the lake Leguaffin, is a
river which leads to Gunong Salatan* (fouth hill),
where the Subanos or Haraforas † get more gold
than they can difpofe of; trade being fo dead at
Magindano. Of this I have been affured by the
Sultan.‡

As I am now upon the Tamantakka, the faltpetre
cave, near a creek running into that river, having

* The chart of thefe countries and rivers, drawn by Fakymolano, is depofited in the Britifh Mufeum.

† Called fometimes Oran Manubo.

‡ This is different from Valentine's account, who fays there
is no gold on Magindano. I have feen lumps weighing above
an ounce.

excited

excited my curiofity, the reader may not be difpleafed with an account of the vifit I made.

I paffed in a canoe from Magindano up the Melampy two miles ; I then ftruck off on the right
through many narrow winding creeks, about three
miles; and got to Ampuyan, on the banks of the
river Tamantakka, four miles above its bar. I
then afcended the Tamantakka, about fix miles
in a winding courfe to Tapidan. I ftayed all
night at the Rajah's, whom I acquainted with my
intention of going next morning to the faltpetre
cave. He entertained me very politely, as he
knew my connexions ; and early next morning
we fet out, accompanied by fome of his people.

At Tapidan, a river fets off to the right from
the Tamantakka. Having mounted it about half
a mile, we found running into it a fmall brook of
a fky blue colour, with a very offenfive fmell and
tafte. This brook comes from the hill, where
opens the Saltpetre Cave. After paddling up about
a mile, I left it on the right, and entered another
brook of common frefh water. This with fome
difficulty (it being very fhallow) brought me to the
foot of the hill.

Having climbed the hill a quarter of a mile pretty fteep, I came to a hole, twelve yards to the right
of the path way, and about ten foot diameter. I
then defcended by means of fome poles laid flant-
ing about thirty foot, to a circular area of twenty-
five diameter. Exactly above the center of this
area is a hole about fix foot diameter, which, befides

fides the paffage we came down by, gave light into it.

I then defcended about fix yards through a floping paffage, which in height and width will admit only one man at a time, and that ftooping, into a magnificent round hall, with a flat floor of earth. From the top hung fomewhat like ificles; but from the fides feemed to fpring half ificles, which, rifing from the height of five or fix foot to the dome, looked like the cluftered columns of Gothic architecture. The dome may be twenty-five foot high, and the hall is thirty foot in diameter.

From the hall, I paffed on the fame level into a crooked gallery, in length about two hundred yards. It was feven or eight foot broad, and from fix to eight or ten high. The fides and top looked like dirty freeftone; the floor was perfectly level, and, in moft places, miry to the ancles. Around us flew an infinite number of fmall bats,* from which I defended myfelf by the lighted torch I carried in my hand. Many of thefe birds of darknefs clung by little hooks at their wings to the fides of the paffage. I might have gone farther, but declined it.

Returning, I faw the entrance into another paffage, and felt a very fmall draft of air, which

* Combes fays, in the caves of Mindano are bats as large as fowls, and that faltpetre is made of their excrement.

On Sumatra are faltpetre caves, in the Sultan of Mocomoco's dominions. Mr. Terry, refident of Cattown, in 1770, offered to work them; but the governor and council of fort Marlbro' gave him no encouragement.

made

made our torches burn. This paſſage, I was told, went a good way, and gave another outlet; but at a diſtance reported ſo great, that none of my guides had ever ventured to explore it. As I went in barefooted, I found the miry ſtuff ſtick to my feet. Being very glutinous, it was not eaſily waſhed off. To make ſaltpetre, they mix one meaſure of this ſtuff with two of wood aſhes; and then filter through it the water of which the ſaltpetre is made. The gunpowder they make here is very coarſe grained, and has but little ſtrength.

Many of the countries above Boyan are ſubject to the Rajah of Boyan. He is a Mahometan, and his ſubjects, called by the Magindano people, Oran Selam de Oolo (inland Muſſulmen), may be about twenty thouſand males.

While I was at Magindano, the Rajah of Boyan paid a viſit to Rajah Moodo. He had an iron gun, at leaſt a ſix pounder, in a large ſampan or canoe. All his boats were covered; and numerous were his attendants, male and female; the former armed with ſword, ſhield, and lance. All day they were aſhore at Rajah Moodo's; but at night retired to their canoes. The viſit laſted a week. The ſight of us ſeemed to ſtrike ſurprife.

In caſe of war, the Rajah of Boyan is obliged to ſupply Magindano with a certain number of men. The Rajah of Boyan can have no connexion with any body out of the river, without leave of Magindano. As all egreſs muſt be by water, the

Sultan

Sultan has him in a manner locked up ; unlefs indeed he go by the lake Buloan, and the harbour
of Sugud Boyan, between which is a communication by land over a flat country; as will be fhown
hereafter.

About twenty miles above Coto Intang, where,
I am told, the tide runs little or nothing, the
grounds are overflowed, as in all fimilar flat countries, during the wet feafon. There, the grounds
are richer than where the water runs off with the
tide, and afford a much greater increafe of rice.
At Coto Intang they plant rice in May and June,
and reap when the dry feafon begins, which is in
November.

C H A P. III.

*Defcription of the Coaft of Magindano, Weft of the
Bar of the River Pelangy—Harbour of Kamaladan—Farther Defcription of the Coaft.*

ABOUT eight miles to the northward of Magindano bar, on the right (or Kawannan) looking
down the river, is the hill of Pollock ; which is
remarkable, not on account of its height, but as it
ftands on a promontory, at the end of a neck of
land, which is a kind of peninfula. The natives
call the point Watta Maliga, or red ftone; between it and the bar of the Pelangy, the river Semoy difembogues itfelf into the fea. Here the
coaft

coaſt is ſteeper than to the ſouthward of the Pelangy.

The hill of Pollock is peaked, but is not above
two hundred foot high.   Behind it is the noble harbour of Sugud or Pollock.   The word Sugud
means harbour, and it is ſo called by way of eminence.   There can hardly be a better, as is obvious from the chart publiſhed by Mr. Dalrymple.
Next is the river Sampanitan, and next to it Tukapangan or Pangan Point : here the Illano, or Illanon diſtricts begin.   Next is the ſmall harbour of
Lubugan, the depth five and ſix fathom muddy
ground : it is open only from the W. by S. to the
W. by N. but a reef on the north ſide ſo breaks the
little ſea that can come in, that the harbour is tolerably good, though not to compare with Pollock
harbour on the eaſt, or with Tetyan harbour on
the weſt of it.   About a mile to the weſtward of
the ſaid harbour of Lubugan, ſtands a village, called
Luſine.   In paſſing, I obſerved it paliſadoed round.
The points Tukapangan, Banegan, and Matimus,
(ſalt) may be approached in ſafety.

The harbour of Tetyan, or Bridge harbour, is
ſo called from the ſmall iſland being joined to the
main by a kind of natural pier, juſt covered at
high water.   Near it is the village Bungabung,
waſhed by a ſmall river, with a tolerably ſmooth
bar, if it do not blow hard from the weſtward.
Freſh water is to be got a little way up the river;
the bar is almoſt dry at low water.

There is no danger in entering the harbour of
Tetyan, but what may be ſeen.   Keep the land

on

on board boldly, and round barrel rock: a ſhip of any ſize may lie behind the peninſula.　Here re-ſides the Rajah of Bungabung.

From this, the coaſt, trending away to the northward, affords no harbour until the iſland of Ebus, called Eos in Mr. Dalrymple's chart; and here the country makes a very agreeable and rural figure.　The land riſes gently from a beach of dark coloured ſand, and exhibits manly cleared ſpots beautifully intermixed with trees.　Some miles weſt of Bungabung, the ground for about a mile from the beach, appears black and ſtony; and for a mile or two along the ſea ſide, ſhows ve-ry little verdure.　Of this I the more particularly take notice, as it is unuſual in a Malay coun-try; and as it gives me an opportunity of rela-ting the manner in which it is ſaid to have hap-pened.

About ten years ago, one * of the mountains, ſix or ſeven miles inland from this part of the coaſt, broke out into fire and ſmoke, with all the fury of a Volcano.　It ejected ſuch a quantity of ſtones, and black ſand, as covered great part of the cir-cumjacent country, for ſeveral foot perpendicular. Large ſtones loaded many places, even at the ſea ſide; and at Tubug, near Pulo Ebus, I have ſeen freſh ſprings burſt out, (at low water) from amongſt black ſtones, of many tons weight, in various parts

* Combeſes account of Mindano, p. 9, mentions a dreadful eruption before 1667 ; it was heard as far as Manilla, alſo at Ternate.

of

of that dry harbour. I was told that a river was
formerly there, where is not the leaft appearance
of one now.

At prefent there feems to be a good deal of
mould intermixt with the black fand, which is
favourable to vegetation; and the country hereabouts is now covered with long grafs, called
lalang. In fome places are reeds eighteen foot
high, in others low trees and bufhes. This varied
landfcape has an afpect the more peculiarly pleafing from the fea, that Malay countries in general,
from Atcheen-head to New Guinea, are burden-
ed with unintermitted woods. Here, in time, a
wood may re-appear: for, in any warm country,
alternate rain and funfhine, with few long dry in-
tervals, muft greatly promote vegetation.

During the eruption of the Volcano, the black
fand was driven to Mindano, the afhes as far as
Sooloo, which is about forty leagues diftant; and
the Illano diftricts fuffered fo much, that many colonies went to Sooloo, even to Tampaffook and
Tawarran, on the weft coaft of Borneo, in
fearch of a better country, where many of them
live at this day. *

The dry harbour of Tubug, about two miles
fouth of the ifland Ebus, is the chief place for af-
fembling Mangaio or piratical prows. It is about

* In the Sooloo capital, called Bowan, is a quarter where
fome Illanon inhabit.

twenty-

twenty-eight miles N. by W. of the bar of the Pelangy. Not fifty yards from the harbour, on an eminence ftands the houfe of the Rajah, ftrongly palifaded round ; and mounted with twenty brafs fwivel guns, carrying each a ball about a pound weight : all the guns were Spanifh. There are alfo many iron guns, very large, but mounted on bad carriages, placed on rotten platforms. The fwivel guns were ftuck into the pofts, that came up to the windows.

About two miles farther north is the village Brafs, on a beautiful river, oppofite Ebus. This ifland is about half a mile from Brafs, and, by its fituation, keeps the Bar of Brafs ever fmooth. Ebus, in circuit, about a mile and a half, or two miles, confifts of pleafant hills, covered with long grafs, and has but very few trees. Towards the fea, it is bounded by an almoft perpendicular rock, at leaft a hundred foot high. It has good water, and feveral gardens of fweet potatoes. This ifland forms within it, a harbour large enough for a fleet of fhips of any fize : they may lie in five and fix fathom, almoft clofe to the ifland.

What I am going to fay farther of the coaft of Magindano, to the weftward and northward, is chiefly from the information of Fakymolano ; except the account of Kamaladan harbour, which is from my own obfervation.

From the ifland of Ebus the coaft trends to the northward, into the great Illano bay ; but I fhall name

name the Illano diſtricts, * from Tukapangan
point, where I have ſaid they begin.

Bungabung in Tetyan harbour; the Rajah's
title Balabagan—Lalabuan—Tubug. Braſs over
againſt the iſland Ebus, behind which is a harbour
already mentioned. Lamitan—Se Leangan—Se
Maruga—Dagoloan—Kalibon—-Pekulang—-Tu-
koran.——Here reſides the Sultan Buzar, who is
head of the above named diſtricts; but I never
was farther than Braſs and Ebus.

At Tukoran, the Illano boundary ends, and the
Magindano diſtricts begin again; of which ſome
are crowned lands.

Dupuliſan—Labangan—-Miaſſin—-Dinas, belonging to the preſent Sultan—Lukuvan—Babudy
—Gaſſakan—Tabina—Tambatuan, near Point
de Flechas, † ſometimes named Baganean Point,
which is about ſeven leagues E. S. E. of the little
iſland called Malebagas, at the entrance into the
harbour of Kamaladan.

Many of the countries above mentioned, belong
to the family or branches of the family of Magindano. The inhabitants hold their poſſeſſions by a
kind of feudal tenure, being vaſſals to their lords.
The diſtricts I have named, are all on the ſea
coaſt.

---

* A fiſh with valuable teeth being caſt aſhore in the Illanon
diſtricts, the Mindanoers aſſerted their ſovereignty of the whole
coaſt, ſeizing the fiſh by force of arms.

† Some have told me that Point de Flechas, and Baganean
Point, are two different but adjacent points.

About

About feven leagues W. N. W. of the Point
Bagancan, opens the fpacious harbour of Kamaladan, governed by Datoo Affem, brother in law to
the Rajah Moodo. His place of refidence is called
Se Tappo.

Ten miles S. S. W. of the harbour, lies the
ifland of Lutangan. I am apt to think this the
ifland named St. Iago, in a Spanifh manufcript
map, exhibited by Mr. Dalrymple. It belongs to
Rajah Moodo, and abounds with cattle. I have
coafted the eaft fide of it, where I found irregular
foundings, and fhoal water two or three miles from
the fhore.

I fhall now give a defcription of the harbour of
Kamaladan.

Having paffed Baganean Point, which lies in latitude 7° 25, you will fee the iflet of Malibagas :
when it bears N.W. or S. E. it is like a jockey's cap.

When it bears eaft two miles, you will difcover
a point bearing north, which makes the S. E. part
of the harbour of Kamaladan. At the fame time
or perhaps fooner, according to the height of the
fhip, clearnefs of weather, &c. you will perceive
fome rocks, juft above water, bearing N. N. W.
About N. by E. from this fpot of rocks, and two
miles diftant, are two iflands ; one in fize about the
third of the other. I left both the iflands and the
fpot of rocks, on the right, failing through a wide
and clear channel, with nineteen and twenty
fathom

1775.
May.

fathom water, muddy ground. There feems alfo to be a very fair channel on the other fide of the rocks, and of the two iflands. Having paffed thefe iflands, you may fteer N. and N. by W. for the town Se Tappo, avoiding the weft fhore, where is a fhoal, a little way off. Incredible is the quantity of fmall oyfters to be had in this harbour, on the rocks, at low water. I now return to the defcription of the coaft of Magindano weftward, learnt from Fakymolano.

Beyond the ftrait parting the ifland Lutangan and the main, which ftrait is faid to be fhallow, and unpaffable by fhips, lies the ifland Pandalu-fan : to the northward runs a very bad fhoal. You then pafs the ifland of Batian, into the bay of Se-bugy. Here provifions of all kinds are much cheaper than at Mindano; and here are built many ftout veffels, good timber being in great plenty. Sebugy is in the jurifdiction of Rajah Moodo.

Near Sebugy is a pretty large lake; alfo a fmall river, of which a certain portion is hot, the water being cold above and below it.

Having paffed Sebugy, you come to Selanfan, the river Tapila, and the harbour of Sampang Mangaio.

Oppofite to Tapila is the pretty high ifland of Buloan, faid to have a harbour behind it ; and far-ther on is the ifland of Bangahan, or Bangan, re-fembling alfo Ebus; reported to have a harbour behind it. Still more to the weftward is the river

P   Tikboo,

Tikboo, and the country of Bitaly; whofe lord or fuperior is, Oran Caio Sampangady, of the family of Mindano. Then you come to the river Curuan, boafting much gold * and clear extended plains of grafs, abounding with deer : over againft Curuan are fome fmall iflands, behind which the anchoring is good. Behind Curuan is high land, of great extent. After Curuan comes Panabigan, where is a hill, that produces brimftone. Here is the Spanifh boundary. Next to Panabigan is the Spanifh Saboan Padang, and then Samboangan.

Samboangan is the moft confiderable fortrefs the Spaniards have on this ifland. It is built of mafonry, and has a high wall, clofe to the fea. It is not very capacious, the church and many of the houfes being without the walls; but the cannon of the fort commands them, and can fo far oppofe any approach, that may be made that way by an enemy. There is a clear plain of fome extent, towards the land. A fwamp alfo on one fide of the fort, adds to its ftrength.

Towards the fea is no harbour, only an open road ; but many iflands, around, make the road a very good one. On fome of thofe iflands, the Spaniards keep a breed of hogs.

---

* Zacharias, governor of Samboangan, is reported to have got in Curuan river, nine catties (20 ounces each) of gold duft, in twenty days, with a hundred men. The chief places for gold, under Magindano, are Curuan, Tikboo, Labangan, Tubuan, and Eu, near Kalagan. Under the Spaniards are, Emilou, Cagayan, Suligow, Capafahan, Buluan, Adon, Ebon, Leangan, and Epunan.

The

The tides on the fprings are pretty ftrong in the offing, and the paffage between Samboangan and the ifland Bafilan, which belongs to Sooloo, being narrow, the Spaniards prevent Chinefe junks from paffing this way to Magindano.

The garrifon is faid to confift of about forty or fifty American Spaniards, a few native Spaniards, and about a hundred Bifayans, or natives of the Philippines. Their pay is two Spanifh dollars a month ; but provifions are reafonable, though not fo abundant as in fome of the Philippine iflands. The Spaniards at Manila tranfport convicts to Samboangan, as England did to America.

A little way beyond Samboangan is a fmall harbour, called the Kaldera.

Rajah Moodo has taken from the Spaniards, in fome late wars, certain places to the northward of Samboangan, called Sebuky, Sedoway, and Seuky. Thefe places remain in his poffeffion. They are faid to produce much caffia.

Next to Seuky is the Spanifh fort of Dapitan, built on a hill, by the fea fide, and fo, at leaft, naturally ftrong.

Eaft of Dapitan is the point of Batafonkil ; and, farther on, about five leagues, lies Mifamis, at the entrance of the bay of Siddum or Panguyl, as it is called in a Spanifh manufcript chart, publifhed by Mr. Dalrymple.

This

This bay is of great depth, in a perpendicular direction, right inland from the north coaft of Magindano. Many fmall rivers difcharge themfelves into it ; and in thofe creeks the Illano cruifers conceal themfelves from the Spanifh guarda coftas. One of the rivers is called Infyawan, and runs from the foot of a very high hill in the Illano country, into the bay of Siddum.

A little beyond the eaft part of the coaft, that makes the entrance into this deep bay of Siddum, is the town of Eligan, which contains about a hundred and fifty houfes. The river, on which Eligan ftands, comes from the great Lano, in the Illano country ; of which more hereafter.

Beyond Eligan is Cagayan, where is faid to be a very good harbour ; that of Eligan being not fo recommended.

Cagayan fort is of ftone towards the land, and of wood towards the fea. Within it are ieckoned above one hundred houfes ; and, without it, near three hundred. At Cagayan is alfo a confiderable river, which goes far up into the country. The country is faid to produce gold : and the Bifayans on the coaft, who are Chriftians, live on a friendly footing with the Mahometan mountaineers, as well as with the Haraforas.

Almoft due north of Cagayan, is the ifland of Camagian ; where is much trade for wax, gold, cocoa, and caffia.

Next is Buluan, which has a good harbour, and a river that comes from a lake. Then Banaka's Point.

Point.   A little way beyond it lies Suligow, or Surigow: this is the ifland of Mindano's N. E. point, with a good road in either monfoon.   Here are a fort and town; alfo a river from a lake.   In the offing, where the paffage is narrow, between the Philippines and Mindano, the tides are faid to run ftrong. *

Next lies Catil, which has a fort; then Tandag, which had a fort; but it was taken and burnt by the people of Magindano, not twenty years ago: many Spaniards and Bifayans perifhed in the flames, as they would not accept of quarter.

Both Tandag and Catil have bad roads in the N. E. monfoon, becaufe they lie on the windward part of the ifland at that feafon.

Here ends the Spanifh jurifdiction, and begins the great diftrict of Kalagan, which is under Magindano; and of which farther mention will be made.

* This I learnt from Mr. Grior, who experienced it in the fhip Royal Captain, where the tide broke the palls (keys) of the capftan.

CHAP.

C H A P. IV.

The Hiſtory of Magindano.

1775.
May. NOTHING of the hiſtory of this iſland is on record, before the Moors, or rather the Arabs, came to it, about three hundred years ago. The country was perhaps then in the ſame ſtate as that part now, which is inhabited by the Haraforas.

The following ſhort account of the hiſtory of Magindano, is drawn from original records, in the poſſeſſion of Fakymolano, elder brother to Paharadine the preſent Sultan, and father to Kybad Zachariel, the preſent Rajah Moodo; they are wrote in the Magindano tongue, and Arabic character. I took it down from Fakymolano's own mouth, who dictated in Malay.

Before the arrival of Serif Alli, * the firſt Mahometan prince who came from Mecca to Magindano, the latter had kings of her own. For the towns of Magindano, Selangan, Catibtuan, and Semayanan had, or aſſumed, the right of taking from the banks of the Dano, that portion of earth, on which the ſovereigns were to be confecrated: a ceremony already hinted in the geography of Magindano.

* Combes, in his account of Magindano, written in Spaniſh about the year 1667, ſays little or nothing of the princes of the iſland ; only that they were of the falſe religion.

The

The towns of Malampyan and Lufuden, are faid to have been the firft who joined Serif Alli : the other four foon acceded. Serif married a daughter of the laft king of the royal line, and on this marriage founded his title to the crown.

His fon was Mahomet Kabanfuan, whofe fon was Makallan, the father of Bankaio.

Bankaio had two fons, Buiffan, furnamed Captain Laut, who fucceeded him ; and Salicola.

About the time that Kabanfuan fon of Serif Alli reigned, a perfon named Budiman, was Pangaran of Sooloo. Budiman had a grandfon, who became his fucceffor ; his name was Bonfoo, and he was related to the family that governed at Borneo : which family came alfo from Mecca, and the head of it was brother to Serif Alli.

Bonfoo had two children ; a daughter Potely, by a wife : and a fon, Bakliol, by a fandle or concubine.

Bakliol the baftard, robbed his fifter Potely, of her right, threw off his dependance on Magindano, and affumed the title of Sultan, his forefathers having been only Pangarans * of Sooloo.

Solicola married Bakliol's fifter, Potely (a word which fignifies princefs, or lawful daughter to a man of great quality) and had iffue, one daughter

---

* Pangaran, a title much ufed on Sumatra, and inferior to Sultan or Rajah.

named

named Panianamby. Panianamby married Kudarat, fon to Buiffan, the Captain Laut already mentioned, who was her firft coufin.

Kudarat had iffue, Tidoly and Dolidy. Tidoly
fucceeded his father, and had two fons, Abdaraman
and Kuddy.

Abdaraman married Sembafin, the daughter of
Maholanding, an Illano prince's fon : Maholanding had married Timbang-Sa-Riboo (weigh a
thoufand) daughter of the king of Sangir.

Abdaraman had feveral fons. Seid Moffat fucceeded him ; but, being an infant, Kuddy his
uncle ufurped the government, and went to Semoy,
carrying with him the effects of the deceafed
Sultan. Thence he invited the Sooloos to fupport
him againft the lawful heir.

The Sooloos, ufing fmaller prows or veffels than
the Magindano people, eafily got into Semoy
river, where the bar is fmooth, though fhallow.
Finding Kuddy there, with only a fmall force, they
cut him off, and plundered his camp ; and, as
they were carrying away fome pieces of cloth,
they faid fcoffingly to his attendants, Surely you
won't grudge thefe to cover the body of your dead
king. By this treacherous act, the Sooloos poffeffed
themfelves of a great many pieces of heavy cannon, which Kuddy had tranfported from Magindano to Semoy.

The

The Sooloos being returned home with their booty, Seid Moffat's party got the afcendant; but, the civil war had fo diftracted the ftate, that he never had domeftic peace. The Sooloos, confcious of their iniquity, and fearful of the refentment of Magindano, who, fhould fhe have exerted her force againft their fmall ifland, would again have brought it into fubjection, took pains to foment her difturbances. Sahaboodine and Badaroodine, brothers and fons of Bakliol, and Bantillan, Sahaboodine's fon, then governed the councils of Sooloo.

Annuel, younger brother to Seid Moffat, was fupported by the Sooloo party againft him; and, after many fkirmifhes, where both fides were much weakened, Seid Moffat was affaffinated by Molenu, the fon of Annuel.

Seid Moffat left two fons, Fakymolano,* father to Kybad Zachariel, the prefent Rajah Moodo, and Paharadine, the prefent Sultan.

Fakymolano and his brother were obliged to leave Magindano, and to retire a few miles to the banks of the Tamantakka. The country then fuffered much. The great palace at the town was firft plundered, and then burnt. In the conflagration many of the houfes of Magindano were deftroyed; alfo great part of the town of Selangan. The groves of coco nut trees were alfo moftly deftroyed;

* I have feen a letter from the King of Spain, directed to Fakymolano, King of Tamantakka, defiring him, amongft other things, to permit the preaching of the Chriftian Faith. His Catholic Majefty avoids giving the title of *Sultan of Mindano*.

as being convenient, and at hand, to make pali-
fades for temporary forts.

After a tedious defultory war, of feveral years
continuance, Molenu being worfted, fled up the
Pelangy to Boyan. Fakymolano then got poffeffion
of all the lands about Magindano, and peace was
made foon after, about thirty years ago. Molenu
died a natural death, leaving by concubines, two
fons, Topang and Uku, alfo a natural daughter
Myong.

Fakymolano had about this time given up the
Sultanfhip to his younger brother Paharadine, on
condition that Kybad Zachariel, his own fon,
fhould be elected Rajah Moodo.

Topang and Uku, for fome time after the peace,
vifited Fakymolano and his fon; but, afterwards,
on Paharadine's marriage with Myong, their fifter,
they grew fhy, as the Sultan took them greatly
into his favour. Topang had from his father large
poffeffions, which made him formidable to Rajah
Moodo; he was alfo clofely connected with the
Sooloos, and had married Gulaludine's daughter of
Bantillan, once Sultan of Sooloo.

By this time Rajah Moodo had got himfelf well
fortified at Coto-Intang,* which is within mufket
fhot of the Sultan's palace, and within cannon fhot
of the ftrong wooden caftle of Topang; both of
which lie on the fouth fide of the Pelangy.

* Diamond Fort.

The

The Sultan Paharadine has no children by his confort Myong; but had by a concubine, a fon named Chartow, now arrived at maturity. Whether Myong, who is faid to have entirely governed the Sultan, favoured Chartow, or her elder brother Topang, is uncertain; but fhe was believed the caufe of the coolnefs that prevailed between the Sultan and Rajah Moodo; who, though duly elected, and acknowledged lawful fucceffor, yet, when I came to Magindano, in May, 1775, had not vifited his uncle for above a year. Fakymolano, Rajah Moodo's father, lived, at that time, juft without the gate of his fon's fort. *

C H A P. V.

Arrival at Coto Intang---Reception by Rajah Moodo ---Vifit the Sultan---Mifunderftanding with Tuan Hadjee, whofe People I difcharge---Set about decking, and otherwife repairing the Veffel---Vifit the Ifland Ebus---Write to the Sultan of Sooloo---Invited to fup with Rajah Moodo---Devotion of the Crew of a Mangaio Prow---Sultan of Sooloo's Anfwer---Tuan Hadjee quits Mindano abruptly--- Method of making Salt---Vifit the Ifland Bunwoot.

O N *Friday* the 5th of *May*, 1775, I entered the river Pelangy, as has been faid. Having got about two miles within the bar, I was vifited by a boat from Rajah Moodo, who had learnt by fome fmall canoe, the arrival of a veffel, with Englifh colours.

Datoo

Datoo Enty, a natural fon of Rajah Moodo, was in the boat. He invited me ftrongly to go to his father's fort, Coto Intang, and not to the Sultan's. I told him, I could not then determine to which I fhould go firft, but that, certainly, I would wait upon his father, Rajah Moodo. Datoo Enty, and one of his attendants flept on board the galley that night; his boat being made faft aftern. I treated them with tea and fago bread.

About feven next morning, by favour of the flood tide, got in fight of the town of Selangan, and immediately after I faw a white enfign, bordered with a checker of blue, yellow, and red, hoifted on a flag ftaff, in a wooden fort, palifaded with very ftrong piles, and fituated in the fork, where the river Melampy ftrikes off to the right, from the Pelangy. Datoo Enty told me, that was his father's fort; repeating his inftances, that I would pafs the Sultan's, and go thither directly.

At this time, being near abreaft of the Sultan's fort, where juft fuch colours as before defcribed, were hoifted, a Buggefs man (whom I had known at Balambangan, Noquedah of a trading prow) came on board, and told me, from the Sultan, that Balambangan was taken by the Sooloos; faying alfo, that I had much better ftop there, than go to Coto Intang.

The caution he gave with an air of myftery, expecting it would work on my fears. I lay upon my oars for a moment, in which time the flood tide carried me abreaft of the Sultan's. I anchored, and faluted with five guns, which were returned.

turned. I then inftantly weighed, on which the Buggefs Noquedah went afhore; the flood tide prefently bringing me up to Coto Intang, I faluted with five guns; and thefe were alfo returned.

The veffel clofe to the fhore, it being high water, I ftepped out; and was welcomed to Mindano by Datoo Bukkalyan, brother in law to Rajah Moodo.

Having walked about a hundred yards into the fort, I found Rajah Moodo, and his father, Fakymolano, feated on European chairs: they received me very gracioufly; alfo Tuan Hadjee and the Batchian officers. Nor can I but acknowledge, in juftice to Tuan Hadjee, that it was greatly owing to his advice, that I paffed the Sultan's, and landed here firft.

Rajah Moodo was a man of good ftature, piercing eye, and aquiline nofe; Molano, of low ftature, fmiling countenance, and communicative difpofition.—Chocolate was prefently ferved. After fome little converfation, I told Rajah Moodo, that I had a letter from the chief of Balambangan for the Sultan, with a prefent, which I propofed to deliver that day. He faid, it was very well, that his brother in law fhould accompany me thither; and immediately ordered the boats. I croffed the Melampy at ten o'clock, and, after waiting in the Sultan's hall, about fifteen minutes, I beheld his entrance. The Sultan can fpeak good Malay; but chofe to converfe with me by an interpreter, the Buggefs Noquedah before mentioned.

After

After delivering my letter and prefent, the Sultan declared me fafe at Magindano, whether on his fide the river, or on Rajah Moodo's; adding, that Rajah Moodo was to be his fucceffor. We were then treated with chocolate, on a table, decently covered with European broad cloth. The Sultan, Rajah Moodo's brother, and I, fat on chairs; the interpreter on a ftool. He invited me to come often and fee him; and, after afking me many indifferent queftions, fuffered me to take my leave. Tuan Hadjee and the Batchian officers did not come with me, but paid their vifit in the afternoon. By the frefh foutherly winds all day long, I found the S. W. or rainy monfoon was fet in.

Three days afterwards I paid a vifit to the Sultan. Myong, the Sultana, at the far end of a long room, did not deign to caft a look upon me. On taking leave, the Buggefs linguift afked me, when I had got into the ftreet, if I chofe to vifit Datoo Chartow, the Sultan's natural fon; as I was afraid of giving offence to Rajah Moodo by fuch a ftep, I excufed myfelf.

From that time, to the beginning of Auguft, though I frequently croffed the Melampy, to wait on the Sultan, I declined going to the houfes of Chartow, or Topang, knowing that Rajah Moodo was jealous of them both. The Sultan had the character of a weak man; and Rajah Moodo, being in poffeffion of the crown lands, which his father Molano had made over to him, when he refigned the Sultanfhip to his brother, held the

finews

finews of power, Paharadine's own lands not being
fo confiderable.

I knew myfelf a ftranger to their manners and
cuftoms, and was unwilling to rifk intercourfe
with perfons of their rank, in whofe company, I
made no doubt, but a political topic would have
been ftated fooner or later, by adherent or dependant, in order to draw from me an anfwer, that
might entangle me in the fequel; it requiring no
penetration to perceive that, being idle, they were
fond of politics, news, and every kind of fmall
talk. They in general fpeak Malay; and what
might have paffed in converfation with Chartow or
Topang, had I accepted of their invitations, which
were frequent, would probably have been handed
about with alterations, according to the fancy of
the relater.

I had a profpect of ftaying among them many
months, until the monfoon fhould fhift for my return to Borneo, whither I heard the Englifh had
retired, after quitting Balambangan : for had I pretended to encounter the monfoon, I fhould, in all
probability, have been obliged to put into Sooloo.
Various was, therefore, my ground of circumfpec-
tion ; particularly, when I underftood the jealoufies and heartburnings among them.

Rajah Moodo, to whom I luckily attached myfelf at firft, lodged me very well in his own fort,
and hauled up my veffel on the dry land. He, on
all occafions, fhowed me civility, and gave me affiftance.

fiftance. Befides, his court * (if I may fo call it) was crowded, in comparifon of the Sultan's ; which demonftrated to me his fuperior power.

I fhould therefore have probably left the country, without feeing either the Datoo Chartow, or To-pang, if an unexpected reconciliation had not happened between the Sultan's and Rajah Moodo's family; which fhall, in its place, be related. As matters ftood then, had I gone but once to their houfes, I could not afterwards have fignified, what I fometimes, as by accident, did in the hearing of Rajah Moodo, that I had never feen Topang or Chartow ; and I had reafons to think on thofe oc-cafions, that he was not difpleafed with what he heard.

Fakymolano, whofe houfe ftood juft without his fon Rajah Moodo's fort, was almoft every day at breakfaft with him. He had acquired a great cha-racter for wifdom and bravery, during the late civil wars; and had brought them to a happy conclufi-on. But from the weaknefs of his brother's go-vernment, who was entirely governed by Myong, many frefh difturbances were expected.

On the 10th, Rajah Moodo, with his father Fa-kymolano, did me the honour of a vifit ; and pre-fented me with a young bullock. Rain in the night. Next day fair weather ; dug a dock for the

* Every perfon entitled to fit down, is treated with choco-late : but Kanakans, (vaffals) meffengers, and others, lean on their knees, while they deliver what they have to fay ; and then retire.

veffel,

veffel, againft the enfuing fpring tides. Doing this piece of duty, I found Tuan Hadjee's people very unruly, fupported, no doubt, in their difobe-dience, by their mafter, who feemed much chang-ed in his behaviour to me, fince affured of the ta-king of Balambangan, which to day, the 12th, was confirmed. In the afternoon, the Banguey corocoro arrived under Batchian colours. Abreaft of Rajah Moodo's fort, the crew took the opportu-nity of playing with their paddles, throwing them up into the air, and catching them by their handles as they fell. When fhe was fecured along fide of the fort, I fent and caufed Englifh colours to be hoifted upon her ; at which Tuan Hadjee looked difpleafed.

To day, the 13th, I fent to cut fago leaves for covering the galley. Had frefh foutherly winds. Wrote a letter to Rajah Moodo, acquainting him, I was bound to Balambangan, there to hoift Eng-lifh colours ; and afked fome people from him, as I thought to get rid of Tuan Hadjee and his tu-multuous crew. Rajah Moodo foon after paid me a vifit, and excufed himfelf, alledging that fuch a ftep might caufe a mifunderftanding between Ma-gindano and Sooloo. Tuan Hadjee was prefent at this converfation, and took an opportunity of faying before Rajah Moodo and his father, in a flighting manner, that he was not at all obliged to the Englifh Company, but that he had greatly affifted them. I told him, in the fame prefence, that I apprehended he was a Captain of Buggeffes, in the Englifh Company's fervice, and that as fuch,

Q   he

he had received pay. This vifibly provoked him, but he durft not contradict me. Fakymolano and his fon fmiled at this little altercation. Next day I paid off and difcharged all Tuan Hadjee's vaffals and dependants.—Tuan Imum the prieft, who feldom minded any orders, but was always very obfequious to his mafter; Saban a ready fellow, very dexterous at cutting down a tree and making oars or paddles: he and Marudo, another ufeful fellow, were Gilolo Coffres and flaves to Tuan Hadjee. Abdaraman, a Gilolo Kanakan: a capricious young man, who fometimes ftaid on board the galley, and fometimes in the corocoro, being under no command: Andrew, a good quiet flave, that Tuan Hadjee had borrowed: and laftly, Dya, a fulky, morofe rafcal of the Malay colour, with long hair; one I never liked, as he ufed to relate adventures that redounded very little to his credit, and, at the time when there was a demur at Tomoguy, about our proceeding to New Guinea, affected to fleep, as I was told by Mr. Baxter, with his crefs ready drawn by his fide. The goods I had advanced Tuan Hadjee in Ef-be harbour, balanced great part of their pay; as alfo what was due to five Batchians, who had been upon wages, ever fince the lofs of the Borneo corocoro. At the fame time, being in poffeffion of Tuan Buffora's flave and wearing apparel, as he was a Molucca man, I delivered every article to Tuan Hadjee before witneffes.

On the 15th, in fettling accounts with Tuan Hadjee, I was greatly aftonifhed to find he claimed the Banguey corocoro as his own. It is true he made

made the purchafe at Tomoguy, on our joint account, and, as an indulgence to him, I permitted
him to be half concerned; but I had advanced
him full one half of the purchafe, fhe having been
bartered for goods. I told him, as he and I had
lived fo long together without the leaft difpute, I
was refolved at this time to have none; and defired the affair might be fettled by Rajah Moodo.—
Accordingly it was brought before him, and the
calicoes, &c. advanced by Tuan Hadjee and by
me for her purchafe and equipment, fo nearly balanced, that half of her was adjudged mine. Tuan
Hadjee, by his looks, fpoke his difappointment;
and, on my telling him, he muft either fell me his
half, or purchafe mine; whether he thought I
meant to impofe on him, or did not underftand
my propofal, for the firft time, I obferved him
grow angry, which, confidering in whofe prefence
we were, doubly amazed me. Nay, he went fo
far as to fay, to the amazement of every one,
billa corocoro, tida mow bili, tida mow jual, fplit the
corocoro, I will neither buy nor fell.

Senfible that Tuan Hadjee, fince our laft arrival, wanted to part with me; and fufpecting
from what had happened on the 13th, when he
fpoke flightingly of the Englifh, that he was capable of ingratiating himfelf with Rajah Moodo
at my expence, I feized the opportunity of morti-
fying him, for the rafhnefs of his laft expreffion.
As it put me in mind of the judgment of Solomon,
I told that memorable ftory to the no fmall entertainment of the company: upon which Tuan
Hadjee got up, and, without making the ordinary
felam, went abruptly out of the hall.

Q 2 Next

Next day Tuan Hadjee being in a better humour, I fettled with him, and purchafed his half
of the corocoro. On the 17th, fome nutmeg plants,
which Mr. Baxter had preferved with great care,
were taken out of his apartment. Thofe were
found to have been taken by fome of Tuan Hadjee's followers, and prefented to Rajah Moodo, in
Tuan Hadjee's name. Mr. Baxter made a heavy
complaint, telling me he had given fome cloth to
one of Tuan Hadjee's people at Manafwary
ifland for gathering them. I informed him it was
a delicate affair, advifing him to fay nothing about
it ; and he followed my advice.---The nutmeg
plants I had brought from New Guinea, having
been touched by falt water, were fpoiled : thofe,
of which Mr. Baxter was thus deprived, were in
better prefervation. I faw them afterwards growing in the garden of Rajah Moodo.

On *Thurfday* the 18th, I fignified to Rajah
Moodo, that I had fomething to fay to the Batchian officers, which I wifhed to impart in his prefence. They were accordingly fent for, and
Tuan Hadjee came with them. Fakymolano
was alfo prefent at this meeting in Rajah Moodo's
hall.

I addreffed Tuan Bobo, and Tuan Affahan, acknowledging how much I was obliged to them, for
fo far accompanying me, and affuring them, that
were it in my power, it was greatly my inclination, to reward them as they deferved. I regretted
that, being far from any Englifh fettlement, and
likely to ftay at Mindano fome months, all I
could

could do was to prefent them with the Banguey
corocoro, to fupply, in fome degree, the one
they had loft on the coaft of New Guinea; adding, if they propofed returning to Batchian, I
would do them farther juftice, in writing by them
to the Sultan.

They thanked me for the prefent of the corocoro; but avoided intimating whither they intended to go. I plainly perceived, they in every thing
were directed by Tuan Hadjee, who on this occafion fpoke not a word. I had, however, the
pleafure to hear Rajah Moodo, and his father,
exprefs fatisfaction at what I had done.

On *Friday* the 19th, Rajah Moodo did me the
honour of a vifit, and drew on paper, a fketch
of the ifland Lutangan, which lies near Kamaladan harbour: it belongs to him, and abounds
with cattle.

Next day, the 20th, a cold foggy morning;
the fun broke out about ten. I examined the
veffel's bottom, fhe being now raifed upon blocks;
and found it much worm eaten. Neverthelefs,
fet about decking her, employing Chinefe carpenters, at one Kangan (half a dollar) a day.

On *Sunday* the 21ft, the Batchian officers hauled
up the corocoro, with which I prefented them: her
bottom proved quite found, owing, doubtlefs, to
my having frequently hauled her afhore.

Early on the 22d, we had much rain, afterwards
fine weather. Embarked in a covered boat, with
Datoo

Datoo Enty, Rajah Moodo's fon, to vifit Tubug,
and the ifland Ebus, which have been mentioned
in the account of Magindano. Mr. Lound, the
gunner, went with us, Mr. Baxter ftaying behind,
to look after the repairs of the veffel, At night
we went down the river with the ebb tide, and
found it perfectly fmooth on the bar. We then
made fail, with a frefh land wind, and flept com-
fortably enough in the boat. At funrife of the
23d, we entered Tubug harbour, near high water
time, and found many Illanon Mangaio prows.
We then waited on the Rajah, whofe wooden
fort, on an eminence, clofe to the harbour, was
well furnifhed with brafs fwivel guns, taken from
the Spaniards. He had alfo many iron guns,
pretty large, but mounted on miferable carriages,
that ftood on rotten wood platforms. I made him
a prefent of a piece of calico. After noon, the
harbour was dry; I then meafured a Mangaio
prow, and found her only four foot broad, three
and a half foot deep, and forty-two foot long;
fhe had outriggers, mounted fix brafs rantackers,
and had thirty men. The Rajah, who paid great
refpect to Rajah Moodo's fon, killed a goat, and
entertained us very genteelly at fupper, his lady
fitting by. We flept on mats in the houfe, and,
embarking early, proceeded to the village Brafs,
oppofite which lies the ifland Ebus, pleafantly di-
verfified with hill and dale.

The village Brafs confifts of about twenty
houfes, at the mouth of a fmall river, that runs
through a fandy plain, of fome extent : the
fmoothnefs of its bar is owing, as has been faid,

to

to the ifland Ebus, lying before it. Here we faw
a very fmart Mangaio prow, without outriggers;
fhe kept rowing for fome little time, as if to exercife the crew, in a fmooth harbour made by the
ifländ. After walking a little on Pulo Ebus, we
embarked, and returned to Magindano on the
25th, having flept in the night of the 24th in
Lubagan harbour.

On *Friday* the 26th, I was vifited by Molano,
and Rajah Moodo. They drank tea with me, and
commended much the Batchian fago bread, which
was of a reddifh colour, and preferable to any I
had met with. Soaked in tea, it fwelled like a
curd, and was very palatable.

Next day, the 27th, I croffed the water, and
vifited the Sultan, who received me with much lefs
ceremony than before; and I had the honour of
drinking chocolate with him and the Sultana Myong.

On the 28th, I began to lay the deck upon the
veffel. To day Tuan Imum, whom I had difcharged (as has been mentioned) failed for Sooloo
in a boat belonging to Rajah Moodo. I took
the opportunity of writing by him to the Sultan.
In the evening I was vifited again by Fakymolano
and Rajah Moodo. The fine weather from the
22d continued till *Monday, June* the 12th. We
then had a good deal of rain. On the 1ft of *June,*
I was invited to fup at Rajah Moodo's, with my
two officers. On the table were about twenty
china plates, which might be called fmall difhes,
tolerably filled with fifh, fowl, and roafted goat.
Rajah Moodo fat by, did not eat with us; but

drank

drank chocolate, his ufual fupper. Next day the
cold victuals were fent to my apartments.*

* Man being every where man, hofpitality muft prove fimilar in countries and times, that refpectively could never hear of
each other. Nor can the Afiatics be more fuppofed to have
borrowed from the Romans, than the Romans from the Afiatics, the practice of not only treating their guefts at enter-
tainments, but of indulging them with the fragments to be
carried home : a practice, by its very benevolence, expofed to
abufe, as we fee it humoroufly painted by Martial, II. 37. of
which epigram a friend has favoured me with the following
verfion.

In Cæcilianum.

Quicquid ponitur, hinc & inde verris ;
Mammas fuminis, imbricemque porci ;
Communemque duobus attagenam ;
Mullum dimidium, lupumque totum ;
Murænæque latus, femurque pulli ;
Stillantemque alica fua palumbum.
Hæc cum condita funt madente mappa,
Traduntur puero domum ferenda.
Nos accumbimus, otiofa turba.
Ullus fi pudor eft, repone cœnam :
Cras te, Cæciliane, non vocavi.

To Cecilian.

Whate'er is ferv'd, thou fweepeft thine :
The parent's udder, porket's chine ;
Heathcock for twain of focial foul ;
The mullet half, the fturgeon whole ;
The lamprey's flank, the pullet's thigh ;
The ringdove, dripping with her fry.
When all within the napkin fmoke,
Thy boy bears home the motley foke.
We ftare reclin'd, an idle crew !
For thou haft left us nought to do.
Reftore, if yet be fhame or forrow,
I did not afk thee for to-morrow.

Monday

Monday the 5th. I went up the river Melampy in a Mangaio veffel about thirty tons burden. She rowed with fixteen oars of a fide; and was full of people, the intended crew with their friends. They were going to burn each man a bit of wax candle on a heap of coral rockftones, rudely piled under fome fpreading trees clofe by the river. This they declared the tomb of their great anceftor the Serif, who came firft from Mecca. In a few days the veffel went a cruifing, as I was told, to the ifland of Tulour, and the coaft of Celebes, againft the Dutch. She belonged to Watamama.

Tuefday the 6th. Went with Datoo Enty to Timoko Hill. Found a harbour clofe to the north end of it, fhoal at the mouth. We carried dogs with us, and ftarted deer; but thefe were too fleet. On *Thurfday* the 8th, went to Buckalayen, where Rajah Moodo's fifter is married to a Datoo. The village is in a narrow winding creek, which iffues from the river Pelangy, about a mile and a half below the town of Selangan.

In the evening, I received from the Sultan of Sooloo a letter, in which he laid the blame of the capture of Balambangan upon Datoo Teting. I received a letter alfo from Datoo Alamoodine, with a prefent of fugar candy and jerked beef.

Friday the 9th. Finding Tuan Hadjee about to go away, I afked him for his balance due to the Company; which he refufed to fettle.

Saturday the 10th. Tuan Hadjee and the Batchian officers failed.

Monday

Monday the 12th. Much rain. On the 14th, hauled the veffel upon the dry land, by means of a crab, or fmall capftan. I was told to day, that Tuan Hadjee failed without taking leave either of Molano, or of Rajah Moodo ; which gave great offence : he had taken leave of the Sultan only. Fakymolano, whom I had acquainted with his behaviour at Tomoguy, faid I was well rid of him.

Friday the 16th. Fine weather, after much rain. On the 18th, one of my people having ftruck another in the prefence of Fakymolano, whom I imagined he did not fee, I put him in irons ; but releafed him next day, at the requeft of Rajah Moodo.

Had fine weather for a few days ; then had continual rain for three days ; then fair weather again, the wind blowing from the land every night, and generally frefh from the S. W. in the day.

Wednefday the 28th. Went over to the ifland Bunwoot, accompanied by Datoo Enty. Stopt all night juft without the bar of the Pelangy, at a village, whofe inhabitants make falt in the following manner.

They cut down a quantity of wood always near the fea fide, and rear over it a fort of fhed, of the leaves of trees of the palm kind, fuch as the fago, the nipa, or others. This pile is then fet on fire ; but, as any flame iffues, they throw on falt water, to check it. In this manner they continue, till the wood be confumed, there remaining a quantity of afhes ftrongly impregnated with falt.

falt. The fhed is made to open and fhut, to let in funfhine, and keep off rain.

Thefe afhes they put into conical bafkets, point downwards ; and pour on frefh water, which carries off the falt into a trough. The lye is then put into earthen pots, and boiled till it become fometimes a lump of falt, fometimes falt in powder. They often burn in this manner feaweed, of which the afhes make a bitter kind of falt. At Manila, falt is made as at Madrafs, by the heat of the fun ; and might be fo at Mindano, during the N. E. monfoon ; but the people have not yet got into the way.

Thurfday the 29th. Found the ifland of Bunwoot in fome parts bordered with fharp pointed rocks, at the fea fide. It is all over covered with tall timber ; but is clear both of underwood, and of grafs.

Friday the 30th. Returned from Bunwoot. Until the 6th of *July*, we had rain, which prevented our working on the veffel fo much as I wifhed. From the 6th to the 9th, fair weather.

Whilft on the ifland Bunwoot, we faw feveral wild hogs, one of which I certainly wounded ; but he carried off the ball, being remarkably ftrong and fwift.

CHAP.

C H A P. VI.

Account of Subadan Watamama—His Sickneſs and Death—Arrival of a Spaniſh Envoy from Semboangan—Particular Account of a Mangaio Prow —Datoo Utu parts with his Wife Fatima—— Rajah Moodo viſits the Sultan—Deſcription of his Palace.—Interview with Datoo Topang.

SEID MOFFAT, beſide Fakymolano, and Paharadine the preſent Sultan, had a natural ſon named Palty. Palty was dead ; but had left a ſon, named Subadan, on whom was conferred, by Rajah Moodo's party, the title of Watamama.

Subadan was not legally declared Watamama ; nay, I have heard that Chartow and Topang treated with contempt his aſſuming that title, and ſpoke of him accordingly. He had married Fakymolano's daughter, his firſt couſin, by whom he had a daughter, Fatima, who was married to Utu, a youth of fifteen, Rajah Moodo's ſon, and her own ſecond couſin.

Conſidering the connection Rajah Moodo had with Subadan Watamama, it was expected that, when the former came to be Sultan, the latter, waving his own right, would allow his ſon-in-law Utu to take the title of Rajah Moodo.

On the 7th of *July*, Subadan Watamama fell ſick. His diſorder was an impoſthume. Making him a viſit, I found him in the great hall, on a

large

large bed, which feemed dreffed up for fhow, and had a number of filk bolfters, embroidered with gold at the ends, fome of which fupported the patient. The hall was full of vifitors, difperfed on the floor in companies of three and four together, each company fitting round a brafs falver, covered with faucers of fweet cakes and cups of chocolate. I obferved that many of this various company had their feet wafhed at the bottom of the fteps, by a perfon pouring water on them, whilft they rubbed one foot againft the other. This ftruck me a little; fo I pulled off my fhoes at the door. I then picked my way among the feveral companies, and went ftooping with my right hand almoft to the ground, as is their cuftom, to avoid treading on their clothes. I fat down crofs legged near the foot of the bed on a clean mat, and afked the patient how he did. He feemed to be very low and feverifh. Fakymolano fat clofe by me, and afked me to prefcribe for the invalid. I told him a purgative would be of fervice; at the fame time, I faw a Chinefe fhred fome green leaves, and then mix them up in a bafon, with common coco nut oil.

The Chinefe approaching with his mixture the bed of the fick, the curtain was dropt; of which hang two rows, fometimes three, in the houfes of perfons of rank, their beds being remarkably large.

In the fame hall, not far from me, fat an elderly woman, employed in cutting flices off a large cake of wax, with an inftrument heated at a charcoal fire, as one would flice a loaf of bread. Thefe

Thefe thin pieces of wax were handed to another perfon, who immediately wrapt up in each flice a ftrip of white calico, about a foot in length. This rolled between two boards, became a very fmall wax candle to fupply the company. Having drank chocolate, I took my leave, accompanied by Molano.

Next morning I went to vifit Watamama, with whom I found Molano. I carried with me a little medicine, mixed up in a bafon, and found his wife and his daughter Fatima attending him. The former would by no means allow him to tafte the medicine ; notwithftanding her father urged it. At laft Fakymolano was pleafed to fay, Let you and me, captain, drink this phyfic ; I am certain it is good. So faying, he poured one half into another cup and drank it off : I drank the remainder. Afternoon, when I faw Fakymolano, he fmiling took me by the hand, and faid, Captain, your phyfic is very good.

July the 27th, Watamama died. I was at work upon my little veffel, when I heard the difmal yell fet up by the females of the houfe, whilft I faw a number of meffengers from it, no doubt, to carry abroad the news. At the fame time, I heard the carpenters in his court yard redouble the ftrokes of their axes, in making his coffin of thick planks ftrongly dovetailed. They had indeed begun it two days before his death ; but the ftrokes then were neither fo loud nor fo frequent ; though, I am certain, the fick man muft have heard them.

I had

I had visited him often, beside the time mentioned above; and I cannot help saying, he died in state.

Early next morning, the coffin was carried empty to the grave in a burial place not two hundred yards from his house. About noon, the corse, covered with a white sheet, was born out on the bedstead on which he died; part of the slender wooden wall of the house being taken down to let it pass. The bedstead was then, by bamboos under it, and about twelve umbrellas over the body, transported mostly by young men, his near relations, to the grave. The corse was then put into the grave, about five inches deep in the earth; the stout coffin, without a bottom, was laid over it, and the earth thrown in, to about three foot above the upper part of the coffin. Then over all was poured water, from china decanters, their mouths being bound over with clean white calico, through which the water strained.

A great company attended the funeral; but no women. In the company was Chartow, who eyed me stedfastly. Neither Topang, nor his brother Uku, was there.

From the time of Watamama's death till his funeral, were fired many guns; but not regularly. During the funeral, with Rajah Moodo's permission, I fired half minute swivels.

Next day a kind of shed was built over the grave; and, a temporary floor of boards being
laid,

laid, the widow of the deceafed lived there about a week; * during which time, his more diftant relations made very merry at the houfe; feafting upon bullocks, which they kill but on certain occafions. They alfo by book fang dirges in honour of the defunct, and for the repofe of his foul.

All this while I was employed in decking the Tartar Galley, and repairing her bottom, into which the worm had got pretty deep in fome places. On the 9th, I finifhed the calking, and fixed to her a catwater. On the 12th, I heard at Rajah Moodo's, that an Englifh fhip had been at Sooloo, and that her bottom was covered with copper. This circumftance evinced the truth of the report. On the 20th, I finifhed the veffel's ftern port, and got a mainmaft ready. We have had frefh wefterly winds in the day, with a good deal of rain; and generally land winds in the night, for the moft part of this month. On the 25th, came in a prow from the Spanifh fettlement of Samboangan, with an Envoy on board, who brought letters from the governor there to Rajah Moodo. This Sinior Huluan was a native of the Philippine iflands, and in rank an enfign. During his ftay, a ferjeant he brought with him, daily exercifed Rajah Moodo's guards, in the ufe of the mufket and bayonet. Thefe guards were captives from the Philippine iflands, called Bifayan, and were in number thirty. The envoy, with his ferjeant and fix Manila foldiers, lodged without the fort.

* I once vifited her under the fhed. She received me kindly, and fent home after me a piece of beef, about four pound weight.

From

From this time, to the end of the month, the weather grew fairer, with moderate wefterly winds. On the 29th, my cook Panjang, died of a flux. Great was my lofs of a faithful fervant, and much was he lamented by his fhipmates, confiderably decreafed fince my difcharging Tuan Hadjee's vaffals, in whofe place Rajah Moodo lent me people occafionally. I buried Panjang on the oppofite fide of the river, and confoled myfelf with reflecting that he was the only perfon I had loft.

On the 31ft, came in a large prow belonging to Datoo Malfalla, Rajah Moodo's brother in law, from a cruife on the coaft of Celebes. She had engaged a Dutch floop, and was about to board her, when the Dutch fet fire to their veffel and took to their boat. Notwithftanding the fire, the attackers boarded her, and faved two brafs fwivel guns, which I faw, and even fome wearing apparel. The veffel being hauled up, I had the curiofity to meafure her. She was from ftem to tafferel 91 foot 6 inches, in breadth 26 foot, and in depth 8 foot 3 inches. Her ftern and bow overhung very much what may be called her keel. She fteered with two commoodies or rudders; had ninety men, and could row with forty oars, or upwards of a fide on two banks. The manner was this: the twenty upper beams, that went from gunnel to gunnel, projected at leaft five foot on each fide. On thofe projecting beams were laid pieces of fplit cane, which formed a gallery on each fide the veffel for her whole length; and her two ranks of rowers fat on each fide, equally near the furface of the water, the two men abreaft having full room for their oars, which are far from lying horizontally,

zontally, but incline much downwards. This veffel
brought to Mindano about feventy flaves.

Tuefday, the 1ft of *Auguft*, we had a very
frefh gale at S. W. which almoft entirely blew
off the attop roof that covered the veffel. The
3d, nailed on the irons to hang the rudder by,
laying afide the commoodies. The 6th, I fent
the boat up the river, to buy rice; this article
paffing current in the market for common expences. On the 7th, I faw brought to Coto Intang
a handfome young man, a Spaniard, as a flave to
be fold. His name was Bohilda. I purchafed him
for fix peculs of iron, from an Illano man; which
was reckoned a great price.

About this time I learnt that Tuan Hadjee had
been at Tukoran, and married Rajah Moodo's
wife's fifter, daughter to the Sultan there. Before he
left Mindano, and before the coolnefs arofe between
him and Rajah Moodo, he had, it feems, promifed
to return to Selangan by the beginning of the N. E.
monfoon, and proceed in fome veffel of Rajah
Moodo's, againft the Dutch in the Molucca iflands.
For, fince the Dutch had fome years before committed hoftilities on Mindano, a kind of piratical
war was carried on.

During Watamama's illnefs, I obferved his
daughter Fatima, a beautiful young lady, about
nineteen; her hufband Datoo Utu, Rajah Moodo's
fon, a youth not above fifteen years of age. Whatever might be the difproportion in their years, I
never heard that they had lived unhappily together,
till during the ficknefs of Watamama. Fatima, in
perhaps

perhaps a peeviſh humour, had ſaid ſomething harſh to her young huſband; who took it ſo much to heart, that he went home to his father and mother, telling them he would never live with her more. This I learnt ſometime afterwards, being prompted to enquire by Rajah Moodo's hinting to me one day, with apparent concern, that his ſon had quarrelled with his wife Fatima; to which my natural anſwer was, that little miſunderſtandings would now and then happen between young married people, but that this, I hoped, would ſoon be made up.

On the 7th of *Auguſt*, I waited on Rajah Moodo, and told him, I was going over the water to viſit the Sultan. Sir, ſaid he, the Sultan is very ill, and has juſt ſent for Fakymolano and myſelf, deſiring to ſee us. Then replied I, Sir, I defer my viſit, not offering to accompany the Rajah; neither did he aſk it.

Fakymolano, and Rajah Moodo, were on this occaſion attended by the Spaniſh Envoy, his ſerjeant, and ſome of the new diſciplined guards.

Rajah Moodo returned about ten, in ſeeming high ſpirits; and told me he had been very happy in embracing many of his near relations, whom he had not ſeen for a long time. He gave me alſo to underſtand by diſtant hints, that this was a device of the Sultan's to make up matters.

Next day, his thirty Biſayan guards were dreſt in compleat uniforms of blue broad cloth, turned up with red, and trimmed with white buttons of

tin,

tin. They had all grenadier caps, with this motto;
Yo el Rey : I the king.

About four in the afternoon, it was ſignified to
me, that Rajah Moodo deſired my company to
viſit the Sultan.   We croſſed the Melampy in two
large canoes, ſtrongly joined, though ſomewhat
ſeparated, by tranſverſe planks. This floating ſtage
carried over above forty perſons.

The Sultan's palace is a tenement about one
hundred and twenty foot long, and fifty broad.
The firſt floor riſes fourteen from the ground.
Thirty-two ſtrong wooden pillars ſupport the houſe
in four rows, eight in a row.   The intercolumnia-
tion, or filling up between the two outer rows, is
exceſſively ſlight ; being of ſticks ſo put together,
that both light and air intervene.   Through ſome
windows cut low, are pieces of iron cannon pointed outward.   Above ſix foot, which height the
ſlender ſticks do not ſurpaſs, the tenement is well
matted all round.   In the lower part nothing was
kept, but boats under cover, with their furniture.

The firſt row of pillars inward, is about ten
foot within thoſe which ſupport the outſide, and
covered with ſcarlet broad cloth to the top ; where
at the height of about twenty foot from the firſt
floor, they ſuſtain the beams and rafters, on which
reſts a ſubſtantial, though light roof, made of the
ſago tree leaves.   From the tops of the inſide pillars, palempores with broad white borders extending them, were ſmoothly expanded, and made a
noble cieling.

A move-

A moveable ſlight partition divided the whole into two unequal parts. The firſt part being about one third of the whole, was well floored with planks on ſtrong beams : here were ſix pieces of cannon mounted. The inner apartment was not floored, but covered with ſplit aneebong, a kind of palm tree, in pieces going the whole length of it, about five inches broad, and placed half an inch, or an inch aſunder. This contrivance of floor for the inner apartment, ſeemed preferred to the ſolid floor of the outer, as admitting the freſh air from below ; and covered, except in the paſ-ſage, with matting, and a few carpets, it render-ed the palace remarkably cool.

Between the two fartheſt pillars of the farther apartment ſtood the bed, on a ſtage of plank, a foot high, which projected about two foot beyond the bedſtead : this was covered with mats, and proved a convenient ſeat all round, except on the back part.

From the roof depended the teſter, to which were fixed three rows of curtains ; the inmoſt of white calico, the next of blue, the outermoſt com-bining breadths of ſilk, of the moſt contraſted colours.

Towards the head of the bed were arranged yellow pillows or bolſters ; ſome as large as an or-dinary bale of Engliſh broad cloth, ſome ſmaller, and all filled, with the plantain dry leaves, which made them light. Their ends of ſcarlet cloth, were embroidered with gold. Of the pillows, ſome fome were fhaped like prifms, and lay neceffarily on a fide. I imagine thofe large pillows are fometimes ufed to lean againft, though no fuch ufe was made of them at that time; they lying then all near the head of the bed, which was about eight foot fquare.

That fide of the inner apartment, which was oppofite the bed, had much the appearance of a china fhop. Below ftood a range of about thirty china jars, each capacious of, at leaft, twenty gallons; above them, a fhelf fupported another row of fmaller jars; the next fhelf exhibited a row of black earthen water pots, with brafs covers, in which the water contracted a coolnefs for the refrefhment of guefts. A fourth fhelf, attainable only by a ladder, held falvers and cufpadores. Towards the farther end ran a crofs row of fhelves, containing fimilar furniture, the largeft jars being always the loweft: behind, were the retired apartments. Oppofite the row of fhelves, that went partly along the hall, ftood two rows of red coloured china chefts, one upon another, the lower row the larger; but each containing chefts of equal fize. A ramp of mafonry was the afcent, but only to one door of this vaft apartment. A palifade of ftrong pofts furrounded three fides of it, the river wafhed the fourth.

Rajah Moodo was accompanied by one of his natural brothers; there was alfo Muttufinwood, an officer of polity, called fometimes *Gogo*, as in the Molucca iflands: Datoo Woodine, an officer who fuperintended the prows and veffels belonging to

Rajah

Rajah Moodo; with fome *Manteries* * and *Amba Rajahs.* †

In the outer hall were drawn up about twenty of the Bifayan guards, with the Spanifh ferjeant at their head.

The fultan fat on the ground, in the inner hall, filling the center of a fquare, well fpread with mats. Rajah Moodo was feated about eight foot from him, towards the door. The company was ranged before the Sultan and Rajah Moodo, and on the latter's right hand, making two fides of the fquare above mentioned. The third fide, being open, difplayed afar the Sultana Myong, and fome ladies fitting by the foot of the bed. Near the fourth fide, a curtain of party coloured filk was dropt, the Sultan's back being towards it. I had the honour of being feated on Rajah Moodo's right hand, and next to me fat the Spanifh Envoy.

One of the company was Marajah Pagaly, ‡ the Sultan's natural brother. Topang, and his brother Uku, prefently came in ; the former gaily dreft, in new filver brocade : nobody there was fo fine.

After the Sultan had fpoke fomething, with a low voice, in the Magindano tongue to this affembly, confifting of about twenty perfons, feated on mats, fpread upon the floor, he faid to me, in

* Mantery, a kind of juftice of peace.

† Amba Rajah, proteƈtor of the people's privileges.

‡ Pagaly Mama, fignifies brother ; Pagaly Babye, fifter.

Malay,

Malay, ſomewhat louder, Captain, you brought
good fortune, when you arrived; there was darkneſs, now there is light. I perfectly underſtood
his expreſſion; and anſwered, Sir, I rejoice to hear
ſuch news.

Out of reſpect to this aſſembly, I left my ſhoes
at the door; † as did the Spaniſh envoy. I had
lately been accuſtomed to do ſo at Rajah Moodo's,
but it was never required of me. They, who
walk with ſlippers, always leave them without,
when they are to ſit down.

At this viſit, whenever the Sultan, or any other
ſpoke to Kybad Zachariel, they named him Rajah
Moodo, rather loud, and with a pauſe. This
circumſtance ſufficiently acknowledged his title.

---

† Among the Romans, it was uſual for each gueſt to leave
his ſlippers or ſandals, with a ſlave, when he went in to ſupper.
One merry inſtance may ſuffice, tranſlated by the hand to which
we had before been indebted.   Mart. Ep. XII. 88.

> Bis Cotta ſoleas perdidiſſe ſe queſtus,
> Dum negligentem ducit ad pedes vernam,
> Qui ſolus inopi præſtat, et facit turbam.:
> Excogitavit homo ſagax, et aſtutus,
> Ne facere poſſet tale ſæpius damnum;
> Excalceatus ire cœpit ad cœnam.

> That his ſandals he loſt twice poor Cotta complain'd,
> While a negligent ſlave at his feet he retain'd;
> Who, remiſs as he was, made up Cotta's whole train:
> So he ſhrewdly bethought, nor bethought him in vain.
> That he might no more ſuffer a damage ſo odd,
> He reſolv'd to proceed to his ſupper unſhod.

Eight

Eight or ten large yellow wax candles being lighted, and put into brafs candlefticks, before each perfon was placed a large brafs falver, a black earthen pot of water, and a brafs cufpadore.

The falver was loaded with faucers, prefenting fweet cakes of different kinds, round a large china cup of chocolate. My chocolate and the Spanifh envoy's appeared in glafs tumblers ; and our water pots were red. The fame diftinction was obferved at Rajah Moodo's, to us Chriftians.

About ten o'clock, as feveral had retired, and Rajah Moodo was talking with the Sultan, in the Magindano tongue, I got up alfo to go away. Leave is taken, with a fmall ceremony ; a lifting the right hand to the head, with a fmall inclination of the latter.

At the foot of the ramp, I found Topang and the Spanifh envoy in converfation. Topang fqueezed me hard by the hand, and fo forcibly conducted me with the Spaniard to his manfion, that I could not refift. Being fat down, after a little paufe, he faid ; How comes it, Captain, you have been fo long at Magindano, and I have not feen you at my houfe ? Recollecting immediately the figurative fpeech the Sultan had that evening made to me, I anfwered : Datoo Topang, fince my coming to Magindano, it has been fo dark that I could not find my way. He made no reply. After a fhort paufe, I expoftulated in my turn : Datoo Topang, how came it, that your brother Datoo Uku durft take an Englifh veffel ? Alluding to Mr. Cole's fchooner, which he had

taken.

taken. He replied : *Bugitu adat deſini barankalli:*
" ſuch is here the cuſtom ſometimes."

I was in a manner forced upon the viſit ; however, I ſtaid chocolate, which I ſaw preparing, and
then decently took my leave. Of at leaſt forty
perſons preſent, none were ſeated, but the Datoo,
his lady, the envoy, and myſelf, who filled four
chairs, at a table. His conſort was Galaludine,
the daughter of Bantillan, once Sultan of Sooloo :
a very pretty woman.

When I got back into the ſtreet, it ſtruck me, that
my viſiting Topang, a ſtep I was reſolved never to
take, would be told to Rajah Moodo next day,
with circumſtances perhaps little to my advantage. I was then cloſe by the Sultan's palace,
going home with only three attendants. Judging
by the lights, that the company was not broke up
there, I ſcaled the ramp. Rajah Moodo ſeeing
me, beckoned. I immediately ſat down by him,
and related what had happened at Topang's. He
laughed heartily, and ſeemed fully convinced that
the viſit was unintended on my ſide. The Sultan,
hearing the ſubſtance of my relation, appeared no
leſs entertained. I had reaſon to be thankful, that
I had ſo opportunely prevented Rajah Moodo's
jealouſy.

Next day Topang ſent me, by an old woman,
in a private manner, a preſent of about half a
pound of ſweet ſcented tobacco, and deſired to ſee
me. I returned a few cloves, (an eſteemed preſent here) but declined the invitation.

C H A P.

C H A P. VII.

*Celebration of a Feſtival at the Sultan's Palace—
Entertainment—Potely Pyak viſits the Sultana—
Certain Salutations—Dances—The Sultana returns
the Viſit. The Spaniſh Envoy affronts Rajah
Moodo, who forgives him.*

ON *Friday*, the 10th, the day was uſhered in at
the Sultan's, by beating of gongs, large and
ſmall, and firing of great guns. At one ſide of
the ſtreet, was erected the tripod maſt of a large
Mangaio covered with alternate rounds of red,
white, and blue calico, a foot broad each to the
top ; and booths for the accommodation of ſpectators were raiſed on three ſides of a ſquare, leaving
room for the ſtreet that paſſed cloſe to the Sultan's
palace; the long front of that edifice making the
fourth ſide. The floors of theſe temporary ſtruc-
tures were four foot from the ground.

1775.
Auguſt.

All this was prelude to a feſtival given by the
Sultan, in honour of Chartow's daughter, and his
own grand-daughter, Noe's coming of age to
have her ears pierced, and her beautiful white teeth
filed thin when ſtript of the enamel, in order to be
ſtained jet black.

This rite is performed on the Mindano ladies
at the age of thirteen ; and the ceremony is ſump-
tuous in proportion to the rank of the perſon.

From

From all quarters were numbers invited. I ſaw many Illano prows enter the river; particularly one, compoſed of two canoes, fixed parallel to each other.

The figure of a camel was put on board; two feet in one canoe, two in the other. The camel is an animal much reſpected by Malay Mahometans, as they never, perhaps, in their own iſlands ſaw one alive. In the body of the camel was a perſon, who gave movement to its neck, and it ſometimes lolled out a long red tongue. There was alſo an entertainment, that put me in mind of what we read in ſtory of tilts and tournaments.

Behold, a champion, armed cap-a-pe, with a braſs helmet, a lance, ſword, target, and creſs. On his helmet nods generally a plume of feathers; ſometimes a bird of paradiſe.

Thus accoutred, he enters the ſquare before the Sultan's with a firm ſtep, and look of defiance. He preſently ſeems to diſcover an opponent, advances towards him; ſteps back, jumps on one ſide, and then on the other; ſometimes throws down his ſpear, and draws his ſword, with which, fore ſtroke and back ſtroke, he cleaves the air.

When he is thus ſufficiently tired, and worked up to an apparent frenzy, the ſpectators ſhouting, according as his agility pleaſes, his friends ruſh in, and, with difficulty overcome his reluctance to quit the combat. The female ſpectators often applaud as loud as the men.

I obſerved

I obferved a boy of about ten years, who had
worked himfelf up to fuch a frenzy. When his
friends took him off, he fo ftruggled in their arms,
that I feared, he would have fallen into a fit.

The Sultan and Fakymolano entered the fquare,
to fhow their agility: Fakymolano preceded.
Their attendants, however, took care that they
fhould not too long exert their exhibition of youth.
The Sultan returning to his palace, paffed me,
where I ftood on the ramp. He feemed much fatigued. Datoo Utu alfo appeared, and gave great
fatisfaction. I had prefented him with a bird of
paradife, which he wore in his helmet. He made
his lance quiver in his hand.

Uku, Topang's brother, the perfon who took
Mr. Cole's fchooner, alfo exhibited with abundant
agility. Neither Rajah Moodo, Topang, nor Chartow, appeared in the fquare: they were contented
with being fpectators.

At night, little boys difplayed their nimblenefs
in the outer hall, at the Sultan's: they would fometimes fall fuddenly plump upon both knees, and
feem to fight in that attitude. They brandifhed
their little fwords with fury, and their targets jin-
gled with ornaments of brafs.

During this merriment, which lafted ten days,
a number of guefts were daily entertained with
fweet cakes and chocolate. Rajah Moodo's guards,
directed by the Spanifh ferjeant, fired mufketry;
as did about fixteen foldiers of Topang's, and the
fame number of Chartow's. Rajah Moodo's foldiers

diers went through their firing beſt. Neither the Sultan nor Fakymolano ſeemed to have any guards. I ſuppoſe, that Chartow's were the Sultan's, and Molano little minded pomp or ſhow.

In the mean while I got the Tartar galley tolerably repaired, having alſo painted her. On *Wedneſday* the 16th of *Auguſt* I launched her, and brought her abreaſt of my apartments, in the fort, where we rigged her as a ſchooner. Mr. Baxter, who was an excellent ſeaman, took pains to make her look very ſmart.

On *Saturday* the 18th, I croſſed the Melampy, along with Rajah Moodo, at his deſire. He bid me go on to Chartow's houſe, where I ſhould ſee Noe, the young lady, getting ready for the grand proceſſion, which was to be that day. I was accompanied by my two officers. We were immediately treated with chocolate and ſweet cakes. I obſerved a female, who ſerved the chocolate, talking of her maſter Chartow, title him Rajah Moodo.

The Sultan, and Myong the Sultana, were there. The Sultan came on a fine white horſe, which he had from Sooloo. The Sultana was in diſhabille, very buſy at the farther end of the hall, giving orders for dreſſing out ten handſome young ladies: they were loaded with gold ornaments. They wore heavy bracelets of gold; of the ſame metal large earings and criſping pins in their hair; which was clubbed in the Chineſe faſhion. Gold moſtly embroidered the ſlippers, to which their garments reached. They had no need of ſtockings.

ings. Each held a fmall batoon, or roller of wood, covered with yellow filk, and tied at either end with red filk ribband. They alfo wore each a yellow ribband fafh, about two inches broad, over the fhoulder, as little miffes do fometimes in England. All this while Noe did not appear.

Thefe ten young ladies got upon a wooden vehicle, mounted on four low wheels. It had a tefter, or top, fupported by four pofts, and benches around, covered with calico, on which they fat. This vehicle went firft, and was drawn by men : then followed a fmall vehicle, in which were two dancing girls, like thofe on the coaft of Coromandel : they had nofe jewels, and tinkling ornaments on their ankles and toes.

Then followed the young lady, in a fmall kind of fhell, like what is called in India a fly-palankeen, covered with a golden cloth, on which fhe fat. It refembled a palankeen, being carried on two men's fhoulders, by fomething fixed to each end of the fhell. But this did not arch over, as does the bamboo of the fly palankeen of Coromandel. They call it prow : on examination, the hinder part bore a refemblance to the fterns of their ordinary veffels, and the forepart had a kind of ftem or beak.

On this occafion, the Sultan's two apartments were thrown into one. A filk curtain, hanging about twelve foot from the floor, and reaching within five foot of it, (to let people pafs eafily under) had an elegant effect, as it encompaffed a

large

large fpace, juft within the pillars, that were covered with fcarlet cloth.

About feven in the evening, the operation of
piercing the ears, being performed, Noe was exhibited to the company, from behind a curtain,
in a man's arms, her attendants following with a
flow pace. They then fat down by the Sultana, at
the foot of the large bed before defcribed. No
wonder, if it put me in mind of a theatrical exhibition.

On *Monday* the 20th, being invited over to the
Sultan's, I went at eight in the evening. About
half paft eight, the Sultana and ladies retiring to
the farther end of the apartment, a filk curtain
was dropped. Much about this time, I faw a number of covered falvers brought up the ramp, and
fome tables.

One of thefe was prefently covered with a number of china terrenes, each holding about three
half pints: in the middle ftood a large china ter-
rene uncovered ; containing about a gallon of
boiled rice. An old fafhioned chair was placed at
each end of the table.

I was a little furprifed, when Rajah Moodo took
me by the hand, and defired me to fit down at
one end, whilft my youngeft officer, Mr. Laurence Lound, (Mr. Baxter being out of order) was
defired to fit down at the other. Rajah Moodo
faid in his ufual manner : Eat heartily, Captain,
and do not be afhamed ; while the Sultan, ftroking

me

me gently down the back, with his right hand, joined in exhortation : Eat, Captain ; what you do not eat muſt all be ſent home to you ; pointing to the floor, on one ſide of the table, where many ſalvers were covered with confeᴄtions and ſweet cakes.

On the table ſtood ſeven rows of ten china terrenes, cloſe together, which, ſubſtraᴄting four for the large one in the middle, left ſixty-ſix diſhes for two perſons. The attendants preſently uncovered, about twenty of them, which emitted a very agreeable flavour of meats, poultry, fiſh, &c. variouſly dreſſed. The ſame attendants helped us with rice out of the middle diſh, and put china ſpoons into the diſhes they had uncovered, furniſhing each of us with an Engliſh knife and fork, and change of plates as wanted ; at the ſame time holding in little china cups, pepper, ſalt, and vinegar, aſking us now and then if we choſe any.

Whilſt at table, I perceived by the foot of the bed, another table covered much in the ſame manner, but not with quite ſo many diſhes. Dotoo Utu, Rajah Moodo's ſon, ſat alone at the head of it. Four of the ten young ladies that have been mentioned, ſtood two on either ſide the table, with large wax tapers in their hands. The young gentleman ſeemed amazed.

Preſently after, I ſaw farther behind me another table, where Rajah Moodo ſat alone ; there were not many diſhes upon it.

S   Fakymolano,

Fakymolano, Chartow, Topang, and others, were by this time gone home. Datoo Uku had not been of the company.

Not having ſeen the Spaniſh envoy to night, I enquired about him next day, and was told he had been entertained at the manſion of Rajah Moodo, by that prince's confort, proviſions being ſent from the Sultan's. Poſſibly he was ſtationed there to watch, as I dare ſay, Rajah Moodo was ever jealous of Topang's party.

Next morning, *Tueſday* the 21ſt, came to my habitation from the Sultan's, in a canoe, a great quantity of cold victuals. The contents of the ſmall terrenes, were put into eight large ones, conſequently jumbled together ; but, fiſh with fiſh, and fowl with fowl. My crew had thus a ſufficiency for two or three days. The ſweet cakes and comfits were brought on the ſalvers, which I ſaw placed on the floor at the Sultan's. I gave many of them away to ſome Chineſe of my acquaintance, who ſet a high value on the preſent, knowing whence it came.

On *Wedneſday* the 22d, Rajah Moodo's lady went over to viſit the Sultana. She had a hundred and four women in her train. At her landing, on that ſide the water where ſtood the Sultan's palace, and about one hundred yards from it, all the women in the Sultana's retinue, to the number perhaps of fifty, cried out with a ſhrill voice, YOU, exactly as we pronounce it, drawn out for about four ſeconds. This was repeated three times, with

an

an interval of about four ſeconds between the times. They then called out the monoſyllable WE, preciſely as we do, three times, and full as long as the former cry. To me it ſounded, like a kind of howl, very diſagreeable at firſt ; but cuſtom made it otherwiſe, as the two words, YOU and WE are terms, or rather ſounds of ſalutation given at a diſtance to ladies of high rank, and repeated with ſome interval of pauſe, until they got into the abode of the viſited. No man ever joins in the exclamation ; now and then a cur * in the ſtreets howls in uniſon to the no ſmall entertainment of the audience.

The above ſalutation was not uſed when the Sultan's grand child moved in proceſſion from Chartow's Fort, to the palace : ſhe might be reſpectfully ſuppoſed going home. It having been new to me to-day, ſtruck me the more.

Rajah Moodo's conſort was plainly dreſt in flowered muſlin, with large fillygree gold earings, not hanging from her ears, but fixed through a hole in the ordinary place to a piece of gold on the oppoſite ſide, as with a ſcrew. The attendants ſquatted down in heaps on the floor ; and even the

* At Sooloo, as elſewhere, the dogs often in the night, ſet up a diſagreeable howl. If one begins, or if any perſon imitates, the curs immediately ſet up their diſmal cry. Malays about Malacca and Atcheen, not fond of dogs, ſeldom keep them. The Sooloos and Magindanoers, may be ſaid only to tolerate them. A Frenchman at Atcheen, once ſtruck a native for having ſtruck his dog in a ferry boat. This coſt the life of many a Frenchman, not twenty years ago.

S 2   meaneſt,

meaneſt, the betel box bearer, had chocolate and
ſweet cakes ferved to them, after thofe of higher
rank had been fufficed. They played much at a
kind of checker board with glafs beads flat on one
fide : the beads were of different colours, white,
black and blue. The Malays and they called the
game Damahan ; which differs not much from
the French name of drafts.

At night fifteen ladies ſtanding behind one another, formed a half moon, which moved ſlowly
and circular. One lady who led, ſung three or
four minutes, the half moon and vocal leader going ſlowly round all the while. When ſhe had
compleated a circle which took up the above time,
ſhe fell into the rear, and the next ſung in emula-
tion. This continued about an hour ; and feemed
to me tedious, the firſt fong being always repeated.

The men never mix with the women in any
amuſement of this kind ; or even touch them, bow
to them, or take notice of them by look, or otherwife, as they paſs ; yet not feeming to avoid them.
Though words, ſmiles, or looks are not forbid,
they are not uſed in public as among Europeans ,
and, when women of rank walk abroad to viſit,
they aſſume a precife air and ſtep, extending with
their right hand a kind of thin ſilk, for to ſhade,
not to hide the face. A train of female attendants, often ſlaves (and the huſband's concubines)
follow. In the ſtreets, women feldom ſpeak but
to women ; and the paths being narrow, they follow one another as in a ſtring. In their houfes they
talk aloud with freedom to any body, as in Europe.

The

The Sultana in a few days returned Potely Py-ak's viſit ; but not with ſuch a train. The YOU and the WE were ſcreamed out as uſual, by the viſited, as the viſitors approached.

On the 23d, having got the Tartar Galley deck-ed and fitted as a ſchooner, I worked down the river againſt the S. W. wind, with the ebb tide, paſt Rajah Moodo's fort, and the Sultan's palace, and then ſailed back before the wind : there were many ſpectators.

They do not underſtand making ſhort tacks in a narrow river with their veſſels, as the yard on which the ſail is ſtretched muſt be dipped or ſhifted over. They were therefore the more ſurpriſed at the facility with which a ſchooner of ten tons could turn about: the Sultan and Rajah Moodo expreſſed great ſatisfaction.

On the 27th, the Spaniſh envoy having got let-ters from Rajah Moodo to the governor of Sam-boangan, took his leave, accommodated with a ſmall veſſel of Rajah Moodo's to eſcort him acroſs the Illano bay, for fear of the Illano cruiſers, to the point Baganean, called ſometimes Point de Flechas, as there the Magindano diſtricts again begin, and extend to Panabigan, near Samboangan, as men-tioned in the geography of this iſland. I ſent the governor a preſent of a curious Molucca Looriquet, with a letter ; and a Latin tranſlation of the Engliſh Prayer-book to the chief prieſt or padre.

The Spaniard, after waiting on Fakymolano and the Sultan (and, I believe, ſaluting the latter) at

Topang's

Topang's fort, anchored and went aſhore; and, going aboard again, ſaluted Topang with three guns. He then proceeded down the river.

Rajah Moodo, hearing this, was much offended with the Spaniard; and diſpatched a boat after him with a meſſenger, who demanded and brought back all his letters.

This of courſe brought back the Spaniard, who, ſenſible of the impropriety of his conduct, went firſt to Fakymolano; who next day carried him, and the ſerjeant that accompanied him, to Rajah Moodo's at eight, the hour of breakfaſt. I obſerved them both in a kind of diſhabille, wearing long drawers, and in apparent dejection.

Rajah Moodo ſent for me, to hear, I ſuppoſe the chaſtiſement he gave for the falſe ſtep they had made. He was earneſt; I never ſaw him angry. Did you not know, ſaid he to them, both in Spaniſh and in Malay, (undoubtedly that I might underſtand him) that Datoo Topang and I are at variance? He then talked to them in the Magindano tongue, in which they uſually converſed. The Spaniard ſeemed very penitent, ſpoke not a word, and had chocolate ſerved to him, but not before Fakymolana, Rajah Moodo, and I had done.

This envoy had once before waited on Rajah Moodo at Sebugy, a little to the weſt of the iſland Lutangan, upon ſome buſineſs from Samboangan. It happened at that time, that Rajah Moodo's youngeſt ſon, Se Mama, a boy about five years

old,

old, fell into the river, and Sinior Hulian proved inſtrumental in ſaving his life. Rajah Moodo, notwithſtanding the interceſſion of his father, refuſed ſeveral days to give back the letters; and the Spaniard durſt not, I ſuppoſe, return without them. At laſt the tears of the little favourite, who might be inſtructed on the occaſion, gave the Rajah an opportunity of yielding with a good grace.

C H A P. VIII.

The Iſland Bunwoot is granted to the Engliſh---Tranſactions there; and Deſcription of it---Sail for Tubuan---Mr. Baxter ſets out to viſit the Gold Mine at Marra; but immediately returns.

AFTER I had been ſome time at Magindano, and found that the country produced much gold and wax, alſo an excellent kind of caſſia, perhaps cinnamon, (of which I brought thence two boxes from Rajah Moodo, one for his Majeſty with a letter, another for the India Company with a letter, which have been delivered) I wiſhed to find near the main land, ſome iſland, which ſhould have behind it a harbour, and on it room ſufficient to eſtabliſh a fort and warehouſes. The iſland Ebus or Bos, twenty miles from Magindano river, ſeemed in every reſpect to correſpond with my idea: it has been already deſcribed. I had viſited this iſland, as has been ſaid, with Datoo Enty, and was told

told I might have a grant not only of it, but of a portion of land on the oppofite main.

I had not then vifited the ifland of Bunwoot facing Magindano river ; but when I had feen it, I found it in many refpects fuperior in fituation to Ebus, as being near the capital, and to thofe on whofe friendfhip more dependance might be had than on that of the Illano princes. Yet I did not afk a grant of it, apprehending the favour would be too great.

At laft, as I believe they learnt that I wifhed for it, a kind of proffer came from themfelves ; and Rajah Moodo faid, about three weeks before this reconciliation, that he would give Bunwoot to the Englifh, not doubting but the Sultan would acquiefce. I expreffed my fenfibility of his many marks of favour to myfelf, and affured him, it would be a greater fatisfaction to the Englifh to fettle near him than in the Illano diftricts, where, although he had the fovereignty of all iflands, and as far inland as a horn can be heard from the beach, the Illanos had much power, on which we could not depend ; while we could well depend on his protection.

On the third of *September*, the Sultan, Chartow, and Uku, Topang's brother, came to dine with Rajah Moodo, and his father Fakymolano, at Rajah Moodo's houfe. I was not invited to the re-paft, but had victuals fent to my apartments. I obferved that Topang was not there.

After

After dinner, I was fent for. The Sultan informed me, that he and Fakymolano, Rajah Moodo, and all their relations, had come to a refolution of granting the ifland Bunwoot to the Englifh Company : I thanked him. He then afked me if I intended failing to Balambangan directly, or if I chofe to ftay till they fhould fend a boat thither for intelligence.

Confidering that the monfoon was far from being fo turned as to enable me to fail direct thither to avoid the Sooloos, alfo, that I had not yet got the grant of Bunwoot, I paid him the compliment, that I would obey his commands in the matter. I perceived this pleafed them all. They advifed me to ftay till the return of the boat; but, upon my exprefling a defire to vifit Bunwoot before the boat went for intelligence about the Englifh, and, while fhe was getting ready, a mantery and fome foldiers were ordered to accompany me.

Next day, *September* the 4th, I failed for Bunwoot; but, the wind being contrary, after I got over the bar, I put into a creek clofe to the north fide of Timoko hill.

On the 5th, ftanding over towards Bunwoot, I faw the Spaniard under fail pafling to the northward of that ifland : he was attended by a fmall veffel. And, on the 6th, the mantery being rather tired of the excurfion, I returned to Magindano to get my letters ready for Balambangan, having heard that the Englifh were returned thither from Borneo, with fome men of war; and that they

they intended proceeding to Sooloo to demand
fatisfaction for Datoo Teting's taking of Balambangan.

On the 12th, the Sultan, Fakymolano, and
Rajah Moodo, figned and fealed a grant * of the
ifland of Bunwoot to the Englifh Eaft India Company. This I forwarded with my letters to Balambangan on the 21ft. But the boat finding nobody
there, proceeded to the town of Borneo Proper,
near which the Englifh were at the ifland of Labuan,
about fifteen miles from the mouth of the river
Borneo. My fervant Matthew, who was entrufted
with the packet, delivered it to Mr. Herbert. I
alfo inclofed to Mr. Herbert the Sultan of Sooloo's
letter to me. The boat had thirty men, and
mounted a three pounder, with fix brafs rantackers:
fhe had outriggers.

On the 24th, I was informed that the boat bound
to Balambangan had failed from the river's mouth.
As I had promifed to ftay till her return, I propofed, in the mean time, to go over to Bunwoot,
and furvey it. So we filled our jars with river
water, and got all elfe ready.

On the 25th, Rajah Moodo, who had before
borrowed fix of the galley's mufkets, afked of me
other four; for which he fent me four very indifferent. With this I readily put up, as, whenever

* The grant was wrote in Spanifh by Abderagani, a native
of Pampanga—once a flave, who, by turning Muffulman, had
obtained his liberty.

I went

I went from the river, I had fome of his armed foldiers on board, who behaved with civility on all occafions.

Tuefday the 26th, wefterly winds. Came on board four of Rajah Moodo's foldiers, with their arms, to attend me to Bunwoot. On the 27th, fine weather. Caft off, and rowed down the river : came too clofe to the fouth fhore within the bar. There we faw feveral wild hogs feeding at low water : they were not fhy, and might eafily have been fhot; but I did not choofe to bring pork on board. On the 28th, wefterly winds, with fome rain. Got over the bar at nine P. M. being driven out by a ftrong ebb tide.

The 29th. Fine weather. At eight in the morning, ran between the iflet Tagud Tangan and the main ifland of Bunwoot : meafured Tagud Tangan, and found it a hundred and twenty yards long, and a hundred and ten yards broad. Laid the veffel afhore, on a fmooth hard beach. Saw a number of wild hogs. On the 30th, variable winds. Went in the boat, and found a harbour within a mile of the north part of the ifland. Planted on the ifland Tagud Tangan feventeen vines, fome ferry or lemon grafs, fome parfley and clary, which I got out of Rajah Moodo's garden. Sailed out with the night tide, and founded frequently; but had no ground, with eighty fathom of line, within a mile and a half of the ifland.

October the 1ft. Sailed round the north end, and along the N. W. or outer fide of the ifland :
had

had pretty regular foundings within lefs than a mile
of the reef of coral rocks that ftretches from the
north end of it. Saw two fpots of coral rocks off
the outfide of the ifland, with three fathom water
on them. Fine weather, with regular land and fea
breezes. At noon, ran into a creek among the
coral rocks off the north end of Eunwoot.

The 2d. S. W. winds. Weighed in the morning : paffed over the rocks, and came into a fort
of bay, where I landed, and went a hunting the
wild hog, without fuccefs.

On the 3d, fine weather. Afloat in the morning : went farther round into a land-locked bay,
and moored the veffel, in eight foot high water,
muddy ground. Dug a well afhore, in black
mould and clay, mixed with ftones. It foon
filled with rainwater; but we found no fprings.
Saw many turtle doves on the high trees, but few
other birds, except fome gulls on the fhore.

On the 4th, variable winds and calms. Built an
attop covering over the after part of the veffel ,
alfo cleared fome ground on the N. E. point of the
ifland, and began to build a houfe afhore.

The 5th. Employed in furveying. On the 6th
had variable winds, with thunder, lightning, and
rain. Found in the wood fome lime trees, and one
jack tree full of fruit ; but the property was claimed by a Badjoo fifherman, who kept his ftation
near us, and daily fupplied us with fifh. To day
Mr. Baxter caught a pig, weighing about fix
pound, which the Mindanoers entreated us to eat,
and

and not to be ceremonious: this was civil. On the 7th, variable winds, with rain. Mr. Baxter, affifted by fome people and a dog, caught three fine roafting pigs.

On the 8th, variable winds, with rain. Inclofed a piece of ground, and planted in it fome vetches. Built alfo a fhed houfe on the N. E. point of the ifland.

On *Monday* the 9th, hoifted Englifh colours on the N. E. point, and faluted them with nine guns. To day came from Tukoran a prow, told us two Englifh fhips were cruifing off Sooloo.

The 10th. Variable winds. Hauled the veffel afhore, and breamed her bottom. In the garden the vetches were all fprung. Employed furveying; fome in fifhing, and fome in looking out for pigs.

During the 11th, 12th, and 13th, employed in the fame manner. On the 14th, came over from Tetyan harbour, a perfon who called himfelf brother to the Rajah of Balambangan: I prefented him with a pocket compafs. Next day, the 15th, I went with him round the ifland, and found its circumference about feventeen or eighteen miles. The Datoo, for fo we called him, ftopt to fhew me a fpring at the S. W. part of the ifland: it was but a fmall one. In our excurfion, we found very pleafant walking under the fhade of the tall trees, as there is no underwood. We frequently roufed fome black hogs, but never got near them.

To

To day, the 16th, we difcovered a fmall fpring
by the White Cliff, which is remarkable, and may
be feen from Mindano bar. Meafured the top of
the hill, near which we lay. It commands the
harbour, to which it prefents an almoft perpendicular front, about a hundred foot high, within a
fmall diftance of where a fhip may lie in five fathom water, muddy ground. I found the fummit
a flat of a hundred and twenty yards long, and
twenty-fix broad : an excellent fortification might
be built on it. I called it Ubal Hill, from a four
fruit fo named, I found there. The hill and valleys adjacent are equally clear of underwood. From
this to the 23d, I was very agreeably employed in
furveying the ifland ; fifhing fometimes, and often
hunting the wild hogs. Of this fpecies we fhould
have got many ; but unfortunately I had only one
dog, who was not able to ftop them : they made
nothing of carrying away a mufket ball. We perceived no animals on the ifland, but hogs, monkies,
guanos, and fome fnakes, about eighteen inches
long, with brown fpots, which, we were told, were
venomous.

Before I proceed, may be expected a more particular defcription of an ifland, where I fpent my
time fo pleafingly.

The ifland Bunwoot is about eighteen miles
round : its greateft breadth lies towards the S. W.
and its oppofite end tapers towards the N. E.
till, at that extremity, it is not above half a mile
acrofs.

The

The iſland is almoſt entirely covered with tall timber, free from underwood, except that in ſome places are ratans, creeping along the ground, and a certain plant, (byonos,) which reſembles a vine. It creeps alſo along the ground, and twiſts about large trees : the largeſt part of the ſtem is about the ſize of a man's leg. The Mindanoers cut it into pieces, about a foot long, which they bruiſe with a mallet upon a piece of hard wood. Thus bruiſed, it diſcharges a white juice in great quantity, which ſerves all the purpoſes of ſoap. Here grows a kind of roſe wood, called narra, many dammer trees, and the tree that produces the gum, called curuang.

Towards the N. W. ſide of Bunwoot, are many mangrove trees, extending, however, only in a ſlip along the ſhore, with a few clumps like iſlands. Theſe are all in the ſalt water. From among them, you ſpring immediately upon the firm land, by a rocky ſtep, in moſt places, three or four foot high ; there being no freſh water ſwamps which communicate with the ſea. This circumſtance makes the iſland very healthy, as the Mindano people allow, and I have experienced ; the ſoil being moſtly, from half a foot to a foot of black mold, upon ſtones and rocks ; and it is ſaid to be very fruitful.

On the N. E. end of this iſland, are few or no mangroves, and in the bay between Ranten Datoo, and Tagud Tangan, the aſcent becomes a little ſteep, whereas, on the N. W. ſide, the aſcent is gradual ; here grows a tree, the leaves of which are as tender as ſpinage ; it is called Bagoo.

From

From Ranten Datoo to Telaga point, the ifland
is both broadeft and higheft. Here you afcend by
a gentle flope, to the moft elevated part of the
ifland, which I take to be between two and three
hundred foot above the fea. The ifland from the
S. W. appears like a wedge, or what feamen call
a gunner's coin.

If the ifland has few fprings, it contains many
ponds of rain water, frequented by a number of
wild hogs, which afford excellent fport, when
hunted by two dogs at leaft : for one dog will not
ftop them. The hogs are very fwift, but not fo
large and formidable as fome on the ifland Magindano. On Bunwoot the hogs are numerous, but
have no gardens, or rice fields to feed in. Their
food is wild fruits, and what they pick up on the
fhore at low water, where they always attend in
numbers. Thofe we caught had no fat ; but thofe
we got on Magindano were plump enough, though
not to compare with tame hogs. Travelling in
the woods here is always cool, through the fhade
of the lofty trees.

There is no danger for fhips any where about
the ifland, but what may be feen ; except off the
feaward fide of it, where are fome coral rocks,
with two and three fathom, at the diftance of two
miles. A fhip may come in at either end, and
anchor to leeward of the ifland, in the S. W. monfoon ; or to windward of it, in the N. E. monfoon.
For then the water is fmooth, and it never blows
from the N. E. but it fometimes blows during that
monfoon from the N. W.

In

In the bay between Rantin Datoo and Tagud Tangan, the water is rather deep; and within twenty fathom, the ground is foul. But farther, a mile fhort of the N. E. part of the ifland, a reef projects about a cable's length from the fhore. This proves an effectual fhelter againft the S. W. fwell, and forms a kind of harbour, with three fathom and a half, clofe to the dry coral rocks, at low water fpring tides.

Some fhaggy iflets lie a little diftant from the S. W. part of the ifland, with no paffage between them and the ifland: keep therefore a cable's length without them.

As I found fuch multitudes of hogs, I conceived an idea, that fettlers on this ifland might be well fupplied with provifions, by the following method. The ifland being narrow, a wall might be built acrofs, to feparate the hogs from that quarter intended for cultivation ; fruit trees, of different kinds, fhould then be planted where the hogs are allowed to range, fuch as the nanka, the durian, &c. The hogs would then multiply and fatten, affording a never failing ftock of good meat. There are alfo great quantities of fifh.

By the 23d, we got up to town ; and found, that, during our abfence, a ftout wooden bridge had been built over the Melampy, from Rajah Moodo's fort, to the Sultan's palace.

On the 29th, I failed, with the wind eafterly, about twenty miles to the fouthward, for Tubuan river ; not far from which, I was told, had been

T   formerly

formerly wrought a gold mine: the place was
named Marra. We had regular foundings to the
fouthward of Mindano bar, from five to thirty-
five fathom, being then abreaft of Timoko hill,
and one mile from the fhore. We got into Tu-
buan-river, juft after funfet, and lay aground at
low water.

On the 30th, winds from the S. W. Gathered
the feeds of a grain, called in the Weft Indies
calalu, and by the Malays kulitis, which grew here
in great plenty. I intended to carry them over
to fow on Bunwoot. Dammed up a part of the
river, which kept the veffel afloat at low water.
The people, in wading afhore, hurt their feet very
much with a kind of fmall prickly periwinkle, that
ftuck to the pebbles.

On the 31ft, winds from the S. W. Catched
many thoufands of a fmall kind of fifh, called
Yap. Thefe yap cling to pieces of bark put into
the river, and are fo caught. Whilft we lay here,
though the feafon for the N. E. monfoon, we generally had a fea wind in the day ; and in the night
the wind blew always very cold down the valley.
On the 2d of *November*, I fent the gunner amongft
the Haraforas, to purchafe provifions ; on the 3d
he returned, having been civilly treated by them ;
and many of thofe mountaineers came to Tubuan
that fame day, bringing on rafts of bamboos,
pumpkins, potatoes, &c. which we and the people
of the village purchafed from them. One of the
Haraforas having killed a wild hog, conducted me to the place, and fold me a quarter.

In

In carrying it to the veſſel, he covered it with plantane leaves, having occaſion to paſs near the houſe of a Mindanoer, that nobody might ſee it. On the 8th we breamed the veſſel's bottom. The ſame day, I ſet out with an officer of Rajah Moodo's called Papinſhan, to viſit the gold mine at Marra ; but came back at night, finding the fatigue of travelling too great.

On the 9th, Mr. David Baxter, offering to go to the gold mine, I left him to explore it, and ſailed in the evening for Bunwoot ; where, on the 10th, I found the Datoo formerly mentioned, brother to the Rajah of Balambangan, making ſalt. On the 11th I ſowed many different ſeeds in the iſland ; ſuch as Calalu, Papas, wild ſage, and many Jack and Kanary ſeeds. In the evening ſailed for Mindano, intending to proceed ſoon for Borneo ; but not without leave of Rajah Moodo.

On the 13th, hauled aſhore at Mindano, to ſtop a leak. Recovered by Rajah Moodo's aſſiſtance, two ſlave boys, one my own, one the mate's, which had run away, and been gone three months. On the 14th, I ſent the boat to Tubuan, to fetch Mr. Baxter. On the 15th, he returned, the people who promiſed to go with him to the gold mine, having failed him. On the 16th, Rajah Moodo ordered Papinſhan and ſome others to accompany Mr. Baxter thither. On the 17th, I ſailed again for Tubuan ; but, not being able to get in that tide, I proceeded to Leno harbour. On the 19th, many Haraforas came on board with proviſions. On the 20th, I left Leno harbour, and returned to

Tubuan river. Sent the boat to found, who reported thirty and forty fathom, fandy ground, at
about a quarter of a mile's diftance from the bar.
On the 22d, Mr. Baxter fet out for Marra, and returned the 26th.

On the firft of *December*, I failed for Magindano,
where I arrived on the 3d. From the 9th of *November* till now, fine pleafant weather, and generally N. E. winds.

C H A P. IX.

*Defcription of the Coaft of Magindano South of the
Bar of the Pelangy to Tubuan River—Account
of Mr. Baxter's Journey to Marra—Leno Harbour—Farther Defcription of the Coaft round Cape
St. Auguftine—Haraforas.*

As the N. E. monfoon was fet in, I heard one
day Rajah Moodo exprefs great refentment at
Tuan Hadjee's not returning from Tukoran, as by
agreement, to go on an expedition to the Molucca
Iflands.

The coaft to the left of the bar of the Pelangy,
looking down the river, is called Bewan. So they
fay, *Angy kafa bewan:* " to go to the left :" as we
fay, going from London to Newcaftle, is going to
the northward.

After paffing the mouths of two creeks on the
left, juft without the bar, where falt is made, you
come

come to Timoko Hill, which looks at a diftance like a bowl, bottom up, and lies clofe to the fea-fide. A little to the fouthward of it are the falt works of Kabug.

From Timoko Hill to Tapian Point, is a good fandy beach. The Point is rather low, but not flat. Midway appears inland the hill of Kablal-lang : being clear of wood, it is covered with green grafs, which makes it remarkable ; and, a little to the northward of the Point, is Timowan, by the fea fhore. Having rounded Tapian Point, about two miles farther opens the river Muttubul : its bar is almoft dry at low water. About three leagues farther runs Tubuan river, which is deeper, and re-markable for a projecting fpot of fand and gravel, thrown up at its mouth by the violence of the fwell, during the S. W. monfoon. This river wafhes a plain, about eleven miles long, and one mile and a quarter broad, in a ferpentine courfe. I am told that, during the heavy rains, it covers the plain with one or two foot water.

In the month of November, when I was there, it feemed a brifk rivulet, fufficient to float down the rafts of bamboo, like the catamarans on the coaft of Coromandel ; on which rafts the Haraforas bring their rice, yams, potatoes, &c. from their plantations to the river's mouth. Their planta-tions are fcattered up and down, often far from one another : the neareft is three hours journey from the mouth of the river.

In going from the mouth, up the plain, to the farther end, which, as I have faid, is above ten

miles,

miles, you muſt croſs the river about ten times, in
an eaſt direction. The ground, through which
this path winds, as indeed moſt of the plain, is
covered with long graſs. Here and there grow
reeds and wild ſage. No timber, but on the adjacent heights. About ſix miles up, are little
riſing grounds, and groves of bamboos.

Having got to the head of the plain I found the
river make a fork ; one ſtream coming from the
S. E. the other, which I did not viſit, from the
E. N. E.

The road leads up the S. E. ſtream, moſtly in
the water, among large ſtones, between ſteep hills,
covered with tall timber.

I travelled about two miles up this road, having
three of Rajah Moodo's men to attend me, in the
purpoſe of going to Marra, where formerly ſome
Illano people dug for gold. But I was ſo fatigued
with clambering over rocks, when I had got the
two miles up this rivulet, being then about twelve
miles from Tubuan, that I was fain to come back,
and ſend in my ſtead my chief officer, who was
gratified with the opportunity.

In Tubuan river, the land wind coming down
the valley, from midnight till morning, rendered
the air much colder than I could have expected, in
the latitude of 7° N. and the quantity of water,
that ſometimes comes down, ſo carries the ſand
and gravel, as to make a projection or ſpit on the
coaſt,

coaſt, pretty remarkable to thoſe who ſail along ſhore. The coaſt here is bold, and may be approached with ſafety. At Tubuan, Rajah Moodo has a cocoa garden : I gathered of the fruit from the trees, which I had never before ſeen.

I now give Mr. David Baxter's account of his journey.

" At eight in the morning, of *Wedneſday* the 22d of *November*, I ſet out from Tubuan, accompanied by Papinſhan, a perſon whom Rajah Moodo had ordered to attend us to the gold mine : there were three attendants beſides.

" After walking up the valley of Tubuan, about ten miles, we ſtruck off S. E. to a ſmall river, up which we proceeded three or four miles. We then all bathed. We afterwards turned to the left up a hill called Tebangen ; about half way up, we reached ſome Haraforas houſes, where was a wedding, and a great company drinking a very pleaſant, though ſtrong liquor, made of rice and molaſſes. There were two large jars, and four men drank out of each. They had every man a ſmall reed or bamboo, about the ſize of a tobacco pipe ; through which, when they had ſwilled ſeveral minutes, other four came and relieved them. Here we dined : the Haraforas were pleaſed to ſee me eat pork. About two o'clock we purſued our journey up the remainder of the hill, which was high and ſteep. Four miles on the other ſide, we got to the houſes, where we were to ſtay all night ; and theſe I reckon twenty miles from Tubuan.

In

In the evening we fired a mufket as a fignal to the
people (to come in the morning) who were to go
with us to Marra. The name of this country is
Temalan.

" At three in the morning of *Thurfday* the 23d,
we fet out from Temalan, and had our landlord
for our guide. We walked for the moft part between the S. and S. E. Here Rajah Moodo's foldiers leaving us, Papinfhan and the Haraforas
held a council who fhould accompany us : for they
were all afraid, being at war with the people of
the country near Marra. However, two Haraforas went with us. At noon we ftopped at a plantation called Punagba, and eat fome fugar cane ;
we then fet out again, and croffed many low hills,
valleys, and fmall rivers ; the largeft of which laft,
is called Medapa : I thought its water tafted like a
mineral. Some rain made the roads very flippery,
the foil being clay. Having walked to day about
fixteen miles, at four in the afternoon we came to
the place we propofed for our refidence all night :
it had fix houfes, and was named Panababan. We
faw another plantation called Lanow. At this
place appeared fome coco nut trees, the firft
I have feen fince we left Tubuan. I afked why
there were not more coco nut trees, and was anfwered, that the few inhabitants did not ftay above
one or two years at a place ; which is alfo the reafon
their houfes are fo badly built, eight or ten foot
from the ground. They all feem to be flaves to
the Magindano people ; for thefe take what they
pleafe, fowls or any thing in the houfe they like
beft; and, if the owners feem angry, threaten
to tie them up, and flog them.

" On

" On *Friday* the 24th, at eight in the morning, we fet out with two new Haraforas ; becaufe the other two we had yefterday, went back. The road was very bad, as very few people travel this way. It runs moftly between the S. and S. E. We croffed feveral fmall rivers ; the name of the largeft is Kaloufoo : on the hills we faw a great many caffia trees. To day we were infefted with worms like centipedes : they bit like leaches. Like them, they could hardly be got off, and then the place bled plentifully. About two in the afternoon, we arrived at Marra, where we expected to find gold. We went to work, and made troughs of the bark of a tree, about two foot long, and one broad ; then dug where the people had worked before, from two foot deep to four. The foil was brown mold and fand ; we wafhed it feveral times ; but after feveral trials, found no gold. Neither did I find the country people wear any gold ornaments : on the contrary, they wore brafs rings.

" The ground has been wrought about twelve yards fquare, clofe to the weft fide of the river. The Haraforas declared that the former diggers found pieces of gold as large as the end of one's finger, and fome fmaller. The river is very large, and runs N. E. by N. and the land to the eaftward is very high. I think we have walked about twelve or fourteen miles to day. Our Haraforas built us fheds to fleep under ; and boiled our rice in bamboos, although it rained very hard. I had eat fome pork, which the Haraforas gave me. On this, Papinfhan faid, joking, you muft not fleep

with

with me; yet I flept in the hut they had built clofe by him. *Saturday* the 25th. Having had, fo bad luck yefterday, and very little fleep, as it rained very hard moft of the night, before funrife we got up, and began our journey back: we cut fome caffia in our way. Found the worms very troublefome: The Mindano people call them limatics. Some bit me by eight in the morning; nor did the bleeding ftop till after noon. About ten we came to Panababan, where we had flept the fecond night; and about five to Temalan, where we had refted the firft night: fo we walked as much to day, as we did before in two days. On the 26th, after croffing the river Tubuan many times, as we defcended the valley, we got on board the veffel by noon."

Mr. Baxter had got a frefh colour by his journey.—I muft own, I had a hearty laugh at his returning without any gold, though I was at the fame time difappointed.

About twenty miles S. S. W. of Tubuan Bar, juts Bamban Point. Between this and Tubuan lie feveral bays and fmall villages; if five or fix houfes together on the fea fide, deferve that name. They are all inhabited by Magindano people, who fell to the Haraforas, iron chopping knives, called prongs, cloth, falt, &c. for their rice and other fruits of the earth. For the Haraforas dread going to fea, elfe they could carry the produce of their lands to a better market. They are much impofed on, and kept under by their Mahometan lords; and are all tributary to the Sultan, or to

fome

fome Rajah Rajah * (nobleman) under him.
Their fyftem proves thus the feudal.

Bamban Point, of middling height, projects
into the fea, in a S. W. direction, and has fome
coco nut trees fcattered on its ridge, by which it
may be known : it lies in latitude 6° 45′.

About three miles S. S. E. from the faid point,
is Leno Harbour, round a bluff point with a peaked hill. Give the point a fmall birth, as there
runs off it a fhoal, near a mile in length, with
deep water clofe to it. The oppofite land is bold.

The harbour, where you lie in feven fathom
fand, opens only from the S. to the S. S. W. but
the reef off the point above mentioned, greatly de-
fends its entrance from the S. W. fwell. Though
the harbour be not very fpacious, it would conveniently hold feveral large fhips, which fhould have
all hawfers afhore. Clofe to the harbour, I found
a great pile of coral rock : the crew of every boat
that comes in, add one ftone a piece. Farther
down, at the bottom of the harbour, are many
mangrove trees. Here is a cut, or an indent into
the coral rocks, about a hundred foot broad, and
as many fathom in length, with the depth of five
or fix fathom ; where fhips of any fize might lie
fafe moored, perfectly fmooth. About five leagues
farther, lies the ifland of Dunnowan, behind
which is faid to be good anchorage ; and one
league beyond Dunnowan, a harbour called
Tuna. Near Tuna live the people called Ban-

* Rajah Rajah, fignifies perfon of rank.

gil Bangil : they do not so much as attempt to
build houses ; but live under bushes, and in hollow
trees.   They surprize the wild hogs in their pud-
dles, by covering their own bodies with mud.
The hogs in no fear approaching, fall under the
enemy's shafts.

From Tuna, S. E. about four leagues, is a remarkable sandy islet, with foul ground about it,
except just to seaward, where it may be approached within one quarter of a mile, in seven fathom
sand : this has been mentioned in the journal.

The islet (if a spot may be called so) exceeds not
half an acre.   N. W. of it three miles, is a low
point.   Inland, the mountains bearing N. W.
look like a cock's comb, seen from near the shore.
The land, between this sandy spot, and the harbour of Tuna, when bearing N. E. is like a saddle
joined to a Bungalo roof or hog's back, the saddle
lying to the northward.   I went ashore on the
islet, expecting to find turtle's eggs ; but the sand
was too hard, and mixed with broken coralines
for turtles to lay.

The coast then runs S. E. about nine leagues,
to the great bay of Sugud Boyan.   The land immediately N. W. from the entrance of the said bay,
is of middling height, and even out line.   It has
a fine sandy beach ; but no appearance of houses.

From this land, the two islands of Serangani or
Belk, bear S. E. ten leagues.   The width of the
entrance into the bay of Sugud Boyan (that is harbour

bour of Boyan) may be about five or six miles broad, as I could judge in paſſing it. There is ſaid to be but a ſmall diſtance between the lake of Buloan (mentioned in the deſcription of the river Pelangy) and Sugud Boyan, over a flat country; and in that part of the country, the indigo plant taggum grows abundantly amidſt the long graſs. After burning the graſs, the indigo ſprings afreſh. Here are many wild horſes, bullocks, and deer. Within four leagues of Serangani, is the harbour of Batulakki, with ten fathom water, by the people's account. To the northward a little way, are two clear ſpots on the hills, of a conical ſhape.

I ſaid that the left coaſt from the bar of Magindano, to the ſouthward beyond Tapian point, is called the Bewan; but I have learnt that the Bewan properly ends at Glang, which lies at the north entrance of the bay or harbour of Sugud Boyan; ſo that the Bewan diſtrict comprehends the Nigris of Kabug, Tenawan, Muttubul, Tubuan, Leno, Krang near Pulo Dunnowan, Tuna, Looan, and Glang, near Sugud Boyan.

The diſtrict of Serangani, contains the Nigris of Tugis, Balchan, Nea, Pangean, Batulan, where is the harbour of Batulakki, Louang, Balangannan, the iſlands Belk and Serangani. I never was beyond theſe iſlands: what I add, is therefore from report.

The diſtrict of Kalagan, weſt of Cape St. Auguſtine, called Pandagan, contains Kaſarradan, Dabow, and the iſland Bunwoot, inhabited by
about

about two hundred perfons ; whence Englifh Bunwoot has its name.

Then the diftrict of Kalagan, north of Cape St.
Auguftine, contains Eu, Sumoolug, Tukka, Ba-
loe.   Next is Catil, already taken notice of.   The
three diftricts, Bewan, Serangani and Kalangan,
are all under Magindano.   Off this part of the
coaft lie fome iflands abounding with turtle.

The Haraforas are thinly fcattered; and, being
all tributary, many together feldom ftay long at
one place.   This cannot be for want of water,
pafture, or fertile ground ; as with the Tartars on
the continent of Afia.   On this ifland, almoft every fpot is covered either with timber, brufhwood,
reeds or grafs; and ftreams are found every where
in abundance.   Nor can it be to avoid wild beafts;
there are none on the ifland : a good caufe why
deer, wild horfes and other wild cattle are found
in fo many parts of it.   I fufpect, that the Haraforas are often fo oppreft, that fome have wifely
got inland, beyond the tax-gatherer's ken.

In the diftrict of Kalagan is a high mountain, a
little way weft of Pandagitan, which emits at times
fmoke, fire and brimftone.   When the mountain
has not for fome time thrown out any brimftone,
the inhabitants believe that the God who rules
there is angry.   They therefore purchafe, for perhaps five or fix Kangans, an old flave; whofe
blood they fhed to appeafe the deity.

Having

Having thus given the geography of the coaſt of the iſland Magindano, partly from my own obſervation, but chiefly from the information of Fakymolano, and other perſons of credit, it will not be amiſs to ſay ſomething of the iſland inland.

C H A P. X.

Of the Great Lano or Lake—Account of the Illano Sultans and Rajahs who live on its Banks—Certain Laws of the Mindanoers—Form of Government— Taxes laid on the Haraforas—Their Dreſs.

THE Illanos have been converted to Mahometaniſm, ſince the people of Magindano embraced that religion. The boundary between them and the Magindanoers is unſettled. Sometime ago, a large fiſh, with valuable teeth, being caſt aſhore in the Illano diſtricts, near Pulo Ebus, there aroſe a diſpute, who ſhould have the teeth : but the Mindanoers carried it. This has already been hinted.

All I can ſay of this lake, is from the information of ſome intelligent perſons, who were at Mindano in November, 1776, on the marriage of the eldeſt ſon of an Illano Rajah, to a daughter of Rajah Moodo's. The feſtival laſted ten days.

Soon after my arrival at Magindano, I made an excurſion to Tubug harbour, and to the iſland Ebus, accompanied, in a covered bark, by Datoo Enty, ſon to Rajah Moodo.

Had

Had I then known this part of the iſland ſo civilized, as I found it afterwards; I mean with regard
to ſafety in travelling from place to place, at leaſt
to the Great Lano, the banks of which are full of
people, and the road from Tubug well frequented:
I ſhould certainly have viſited that lake; eſpecially,
as at Tubug, I was within a day's journey of it,
by land, and horſes were to be had.

The inhabitants of this country have generally
their name from the lake on which they reſide.
The inlanders dwell chiefly towards the eaſt, where
are ſaid to be thirty thouſand men, intermixed in
many places with the Haraforas, who ſeem to be
the primitives of the iſland.

On the N. coaſt of Magindano, the Spaniards
have had great ſucceſs, in converting to Chriſtianity
thoſe Haraforas. Their agreeing in one eſſential
point, the eating of hog's fleſh, may, in a great
meaſure, have paved the way. The Illano Rajahs, who are Mahometans, live on pretty good
terms with the Spaniards of Eligan; but I have
been told, the road is not ſo ſafe from the Lano to
Eligan, as from its oppoſite ſide to Tubug. The
diſtance is equal, being about a day's journey to
either place, and the croſſing the Lano takes part
of a day; which makes about three days requiſite
from ſea to ſea.

There is certainly a ſhorter cut from ſea to ſea;
I mean, from the bottom of the Great Illano bay,
formed by Pulo Ebus to the eaſtward, and Point
de Flechas

de Flechas to the weftward; and this is not far from the bottom of the bay of Siddum or Panguyl.

By what I could learn, the Lano is between fifteen and twenty miles acrofs, and about fixty miles round, its length lying eaft and weft.

Towards the fouth weft part, from Gunnapy to Sawir, it is high ground, and there the lake is faid to be fome hundred fathoms deep. From Sawir, towards Taraka, which lies to the S. E. and E. the land being low, is often flooded : here many fmall rivers difcharge themfelves into the lake, which has foundings hereabouts, ten, twenty, and thirty fathom, according to the diftance from fhore. On this fide are moft inhabitants.

Moraway is fituated towards the N. E. corner of the lake : near it the ground is very high, and extends weftward. The only river that runs from the lake to the fea, iffues from the foot of the heights of Moraway. This river, after a winding courfe, and one or more falls, difcharges itfelf into the fea at Eligan; where is faid to be a garrifon of twenty American Spaniards, befides Bifayans.

From Moraway to Madullum, which lies on the N. W. part of the lake, the country is hilly. Near Moraway is Watou, where a mofque of ftone, fituated on a height, is remarkable in fine weather from Byang, which is on the oppofite fide of the lake.

U   From

From Madullum to Gunnapy, may be called the weſt ſide of the lake : between them lies Madumba.

From Madumba, inland, W. by N. to the high hill of Inayawan, may be about half a day's journey. From Inayawan flows, in a N. W. courſe, a river, which pours itſelf into the ſea, in the bottom of the bay of Siddum.

From Gunnapy, weſt about ſix hours, is a ſmall lake called Dapow, whence a ſmall river leads to another lake, named Nunſinghan.

Along the eaſt ſide of the lake, from Taraka to Watou, during the N. E. monſoon, in the morning are freſh winds from the northward ; about ten A. M. they die away, and an oppoſite wind ariſes.

Along the north ſide of the lake, from Watou to Madullum, in the N. E. monſoon, blows a freſh wind from the hills, in the night.

From Gunnapy to Sawir, in the N. E. monſoon, all day the wind blows freſh at W. and W S. W.

On the lake are four little iſlands, Balak, Apou, Nuſa, and Sclangan. Many fiſhes are caught around them.

Names

Names of the Sultans and Rajahs on the Banks of the
Lano, and near it, with the number of Inhabitants
in their respective Territories.

[S. means Sultan; R. Rajah.]

		Inhabitants.	
Taraka	- -	10,000	Sultan
Ballat	- -	1,000	S.
Ramuin	- -	8,000	S.
Didagun	-	10,000	S.
Poallas	- -	5,000	S.
Bunfayan	-	10,000	S.
Moraway	-	2,000	Rajah.
Watou	- -	1,000	R.
Tampafan	- -	400	R.
Tatayawan	- -	300	R.
Linuk	- -	1,000	S.
Bagowin	- -	1,000	S.
Byabow	- -	300	R.
Gunnapy	- -	700	R.
Madumba	- -	700	S.
Madullum	- -	700	R.
Bahalud	- -	300	R.
Tugaia	- -	300	R.
Marantow	- -	700	S.
Sawir	- -	500	R.
Mafia	- -	400	R.
Mimbaly	- -	500	R.
Byang	- -	1,000	S.
Maying	- -	1,800	S.
Gatawan	- -	500	R.

U 2   Patawan

			Inhabitants.
Patawan	-	-	700 R.
Capy	-	-	700 S.
Paran	-	-	200 S.
Mony	-	-	200 S.
Kaboboan	-	-	1000 S.
Nuningham	-	-	100 R.
Palow	-	-	100 R.
Dapow*	-	-	200 R.

Total number of Inhabitants 61,300

All thefe countries produce much gold, wax, and cinnamon, falt not being made by the fun at Magindano, as at Manila; but by fire: it is therefore dear at the Lano.

Though laws † are fimilar in moft countries, each has fome peculiar: the principal of Magindano are thefe. For theft, the offender lofes his right hand, or pays threefold, juft as amongft the Mahometans of Atcheen. For maiming, death: adultery, death to both parties: fornication, a fine.‡ Inheritance goes in equal fhares to fons, and half to daughters; the fame to grand-children. Where

---

* Six hours weft of the lake.

† The induftrious Chinefe feem to be excluded from the be nefit of law: thofe in power often forcing kangans upon them, and making them yearly pay heavy intereft.

‡ The ordinary punifhment of incontinence in female flaves to their mafters, is cutting off their hair; which was a cuftom in Germany, in former days.

are

are no children, whole brothers and fifters inherit. If there are no brothers or fifters, or nephews, or nieces, or firft coufins, the Sultan claims it for the poor. It is the fame, afcending even to the grand-uncle. If a man put away his wife, fhe gets one third of the furniture; alfo money, in proportion to his circumftances. A child's name is not given by priefts, as in the Molucca iflands, and in other Mahometan countries. The father affembles his friends, feafts them; fhaves off a little lock of hair from the infant head, puts it into a bafon, and then buries it, or commits it to the water.

The form of government at Magindano, is fome-what upon the feudal fyftem, and in fome meafure monarchical. Next to the Sultan is Rajah Moodo, his fucceffor elect. Then Mutufingwood, the fu-perintendant of polity, and captain Laut * over-feer of the Sultan's little navy, are both named by the Sultan. There are alfo fix Manteries, or judges named by the Sultan, and fix Amba Rajahs, or afferters of the rights of the people: their office is hereditary to the eldeft fon.

Although the Sultan feems to act by and with the advice and confent of the Datoos, not only of his own family, but of others; yet, this compli-ance is perhaps only to fave appearances. When he can, he will doubtlefs be arbitrary.

The vaffals of the Sultan, and of others, who poffefs great eftates, are called Kanakan. Thofe

---

* The office of Captain Laut was vacant when I was at Magindano; Datoo Woodine expected to be named.

vaffals

vaſſals are ſometimes Mahometans, though moſtly
Haraforas. The latter only may be ſold with the
lands, but cannot be ſold off the lands. The Haraforas are more oppreſt than the former. The
Mahometan vaſſals are bound to accompany their
lords, on any ſudden expedition ; but the Haraforas being in a great meaſure excuſed from ſuch
attendance, pay yearly certain taxes, which are
not expected from the Mahometan vaſſals. They
pay a boiſs, or land tax. A Harafora family pays
ten battels of paly (rough rice) forty lb. each ; three
of rice, about ſixty lb ; one fowl, one bunch of
plantains, thirty roots, called clody, or St. Helena
yam, and fifty heads of Indian corn. I give this
as one inſtance of the utmoſt that is ever paid.
Then they muſt ſell fifty battels of paly, equal to
two thouſand pound weight, for one kangan.   So
at Dory or New Guinea, one prong, value half a
dollar, or one kangan, given to a Harafora, lays a
perpetual tax on him.

Thoſe vaſſals at Magindano have what land they
pleaſe ; and the Mahometans on the ſea coaſt, whether free or kanakan, live moſtly by trading with
the Haraforas, while their own gardens produce
them betel nuts, coco nuts, and greens. They
ſeldom grow any rice, and they diſcourage as far
as they can, the Haraforas from going to Mindano,
to ſell the produce of their plantations. On the
banks of the Pelangy and Tamantakka, the Mahometans grow much rice.

The boiſs is not always collected in fruits of the
earth only. A tax gatherer, who arrived at Coto
Intang,

Intang, when I was there, gave me the following lift of what he had brought from fome of Rajah Moodo's crown lands, being levied on perhaps five hundred families. 2870 battels of paly, of forty lb. each; 490 Spanifh dollars; 160 kangans; 6 tayls of gold, equal to 30 l. 160 Malons: a cloth made of the plantain tree, three yards long, and one broad. This laft mentioned cloth is the ufual wear of the country women, made in the form of a Bengal lungy, or Buggefs cloth, being a wide fack without a bottom; and is often ufed as a currency in the market.

The currency in moft parts of the country, is the Chinefe kangan, a piece of coarfe cloth, thinly woven, nineteen inches broad, and fix yards long; the value at Sooloo is ten dollars for a bundle of twenty-five fealed up; and at Magindano much the fame: but, at Magindano dollars are fcarce. Thefe bundles are called gandangs, rolled up in a cylindrical form. They have alfo, as a currency, koufongs, a kind of nankeen, dyed black; and kompow, a ftrong white Chinefe linen, made of flax; of which more particularly hereafter.

The kangans generally come from Sooloo; fo they are got at fecond hand: for the Spaniards have long hindered Chinefe junks, bound from Amoy to Magindano, to pafs Samboangan. This is the caufe of fo little trade at Magindano, no veffels failing from Indoftan thither; and the little trade is confined to a few country Chinefe, called Oran Sangly, and a few Soolooans who come hither to buy rice and paly, bringing with them Chinefe articles:

ticles : for the crop of rice at Sooloo can never be
depended on.

In the bazar, or market, the immediate currency is paly. Ten gantangs of about four pound
each make a battel; and three battels, (a cylindrical meafure, thirteen inches and five tenths high;
the fame in diameter) about one hundred and
twenty pound of paly, are commonly fold for a
kangan. Talking of the value of things here, and
at Sooloo, they fay, fuch a houfe or prow, &c.
is worth fo many flaves; the old valuation being
one flave for thirty kangans.

They alfo fpecify in their bargains, whether is
meant matto (eye) kangan, real kangan, or nominal kangan. The dealing in the nominal, or
imaginary kangan, is an ideal barter. When one
deals for the real kangans, they muft be examined ; and the gandangs, or bundles of twenty-five
pieces, are not to be trufted, as the dealers will
often forge a feal, having firft packed up damaged
kangans. In this the Chinefe here, and at Sooloo,
are very expert.

The China cafh at Magindano, naméd poufin,
have holes as in China. I found them fcarce ; their
price is from one hundred and fixty, to one hundred and eighty for a kangan. At Sooloo, is
coined a cafh of bafe copper, called petis, of
which two hundred, down to one hundred and
feventy, go for a kangan. Into the copper cafh,
fometimes is put a little bit of filver very thin,
about the tenth of an inch fquare. Thefe are double

ble cafh, and called meffuru. From one hundred
and fixty, to two hundred, of thofe meffurus, may
be had for a Spanifh dollar. I have not feen many
of the Sooloo cafh at Magindano.

Fakymolano and Rajah Moodo were willing to
admit, as a currency, a copper coin of two China
mace in weight, with the name of Kybad Zachariel on one fide, and the Company's arms on the
other; ninety-fix of them were to pafs for a Spanifh dollar: this number was pitched upon as moft
divifible. At that rate cent. per cent. would be
gained upon them; which is much about what the
Dutch gain on their doits, current all over
Java, and wherever they have fettlements among
Malays.

All kinds of Indoftan cloths anfwer well here,
efpecially, long cloth ordinary, white, blue, and
red handkerchiefs of all kinds; chintz preferably,
with dark grounds; Surat goods of moft forts,
particularly pittolies, and all kinds of European
cutlery.

Many Chinefe articles are carried from Sooloo
to Magindano, efpecially kangans, beads, gongs,
china bafons with red edges; deep brafs plates,
five in a fet; deep faucers, three and four inches
diameter; brafs wire, and iron.

On Sooloo are no Haraforas. The Haraforas on
Magindano make a ftrong cloth, not of cotton;
but of a kind of flax, very like what the Batta
people wear on the coaft of Sumatra. They alfo
wear

wear brafs rings round the wrift, and under the knee; five or fix on each arm and leg. They are fond of wearing beads about their necks, and brafs rings or beads dangling at their ears, which in both fexes are very wide, and fometimes extend almoft to their fhoulders. Into the holes of their ears, is put a leaf, rolled up like the fpring of a watch, to ftretch them.

The men tie up their hair in a fingular manner, fixing it round, or covering with it a piece of wood that is round, five or fix inches in diameter, and half an inch thick. This fo covered, lies flat on their heads, and looks graceful, the hair being tied above and below it. The women tie their hair behind, and plait it like the Jentoo dancing girls at Madrafs; and they wear a kind of petticoat. The men wear, befide the jacket, which is common to both fexes, a cloth bound about the middle, and coming up between the thighs. Their arms are bows and arrows; and, as often as they can afford to refemble the Mahometans, fword, lance, and target.

One day near Tubuan, a Harafora brought down fome paddy from the country; I wanted to purchafe it; but the head man of the village, a Magindanoer, would not permit him to fell it me. I did not difpute the point; but found afterwards, the poor Harafora had fold about three hundred pounds of paly for a prong, or chopping knife.

CHAP.

CHAP. XI.

Sent the Galley to Bunwoot to be repaired---Gale at
N. W.---Account of Noe's Portion, who is mar-
ried to Datoo Utu---Particular Account of the
Marriage of one of Rajah Moodo's Daughters.

I ARRIVED from Bunwoot at Coto Intang,
on the third December, as has been said. On the
fifth I was a good deal out of order. The vessel
wanting to be fresh calked, a clean bottom, and
some other repairs, before we attempted to return
to Borneo (for I despaired of finding the English at
Balambangan) I sent her, therefore, over to Bunwoot, to be hauled ashore. On the 6th it blew
hard at N. and N. N. W. the vessel then lay within
the bar. I was informed that such gales sometimes happen from the N. and N. W. at this
season : it might be called a breaking up of the
monsoon. The gale lasted several days, and the
vessel did not get out till the 10th, a great sea
rolling on the bar. I sent over coco nut oil, which
Mr. Baxter mixt with lime, burnt on the spot ; and
by the 19th compleated her bottom. On the
21st, I crossed to Bunwoot in the boat ; and on the
22d, we hauled off the ground. After the weather
had broke up on the 11th, we had mostly N. E.
winds, inclining from the sea in the day, and
blowing rather fresh from the land in the night :
on the 25th I entered Tetyan harbour, which has
been mentioned. I saluted the Illano Rajah of
Balabagan,

Balabagan, with three guns; he returned as many.
In the afternoon, I paid him a vifit, and returned
on board in the evening.   On the 27th, I returned
to Mindano, and made faft as ufual, abreaft of
my   apartments at Coto Intang.   Next day I
croffed through many winding creeks to Am-
puyon, on the banks of the river Tamantakka, to
vifit a Serif, who lived there, allied by marriage
to the Sultan, I having feen him frequently at
court.   He entertained me genteelly, and I faw
in his poffeffion, feveral parcels of gold duft, like
that in which I have often dealt on the ifland of
Sumatra.

On the 29th, Rajah Moodo fent me a young
bullock as a new year's gift; and on the 30th of
December his eldeft fon Datoo Utu was married to
Noe, grand-daughter to the Sultan.   A day before the marriage, the portion was carried in great
parade over the water, from the bridegroom's
father, to the Sultan's palace : finding the cuftom
was to make prefents to Rajah Moodo on fuch
occafions, fome prefenting him with a palempore,
another with a piece of chintz, and fo on, I prefented about three yards of fuperfine broad cloth,
which I had the pleafure of feeing move, with the
firft offerings in the proceffion.   I followed to the
Sultan's, where the portion was forting on the
floor in the hall, and fome clerks were taking an
account of it ; Marajah Pagaly and fome others
putting a value on each article.   Amongft other
things, was a bulfe of gold duft, which I had in
my hand.   It weighed about five or fix pounds,

and

and was valued at about twenty kangans an ounce. Valuing a kangan at half a crown, to which it comes pretty near, gold here may be about 2 l. 10 s. an ounce, reckoning one dollar five shillings.

Presently mounted the ramp two iron guns, four pounders : these were part of the portion, and valued at eight hundred kangans.

I was told that Marajah Pagaly, undervalued many of the articles, which were to make up the portion twelve thousand kangans. Some even suspected him of wanting to put a bar to the match. It is difficult, in a foreign country especially, to come at the true springs of action : but, that evening, I found Rajah Moodo dressed in a coat of mail, made of Buffalo's horn, and brass rings. In this dress, accompanied with his friends, without any of his Bisayan guards, he crossed to the Sultan's. I went over soon after, and perceived he had put off his coat of mail, which lay near him on a mat on the floor. Seeing me, he beckoned for me to sit down by him, which I did. Having taken the liberty to ask him about the valuation of the portion, Oh ! says he, with a laugh, there are four hundred kangans over.

Next evening being the 30th, came on the solemnity. A great company being assembled at the Sultan's, Rajah Moodo put the question to the company, if it should be a marriage. All answered with a loud voice in the affirmative. A priest
then

then walked into the middle of the floor, to whom
Datoo Utu got up, and advanced.   The prieft,
whom they called Serif, * took him by the thumb
of the right hand, and faid to him certain words ;
which being explained to me, were to this purpofe. The prieft afked the bridegroom if he confented to take fuch a perfon as his wife, and to
live with her according to the law of Mahomet.
The bridegroom returned an affirmative. The
company then gave a loud fhout, and immediately I heard guns go off at Chartow's caftle,
where I was told himfelf kept watch. The lady
did not appear, and fo had no queftions to anfwer.
In this they refemble the Chinefe.

Neither Fakymolano, Topang, nor Uku was
prefent. Topang no doubt confidered this as a mor-
tal blow to all his hopes ; and Fakymolano could
not be fuppofed glad at an event, which to his
widow daughter, and grand-child Fatima, muft
have been an addition to their late lofs of Watamama. I had indeed obferved, that, fince the
match was upon the carpet, Fakymolano did not
vifit at his fon Rajah Moodo's fo much as formerly.

About a week before this, having paffed by
Datoo Utu's apartments, which were in the fort,
and in the fame tenement where his father dwelt,
I remarked that the large bed, china jars, chefts,
and fo forth, were taken away. Fatima, as her
portion, had fent all to her grandfather Fakymolano.

* Serif, or Sherif, is a term of dignity beftowed on every
fuppofed defcendant of Mahomet.

I failed

I failed before the 10th day after their marriage,
and fo did not fee the conclufion of it according to
their cuftom. But fome time before this, I had
been prefent at the marriage of one of Rajah
Moodo's daughters to the fon of an Illano prince.

A great company was convened at Rajah Moodo's, amongft which were the bride and bridegroom. The prieft took the man by the right
thumb, and, after putting to him the important
queftion, the latter fignified his affent by a fmall
inclination of the head. The bridegroom then
went and fat down by the young lady, who was
feated towards the farther end of the hall, fome
young ladies her companions rifing up at his approach, to make room for him. The bride appeared difcontented, and turned from him, while
he kept turning towards her ; both being feated
on cufhions laid on mats on the floor.

The company fmiling at this, I thought it a
good opportunity to fix my German flute, and
play a tune, having afked Rajah Moodo's permiffion. The company expreffed fatisfaction ; but
the bride ftill looked averfe to her lover, who
was a handfome young man : and fhe continued
fo the whole evening. She looked indeed as I
think a woman ought, whofe confent is not afked
in an affair of fuch moment. Next evening I
found them drinking chocolate together : her looks
feemed mending ; but fhe did not fmile.

On the tenth night, fhe was with apparent∙ reluctance conducted, before all the company, by
two

two women, from where fhe fat, towards a large
bed in the fame hall with the company ; and was
put within a triple row of curtains, other two women holding them up until fhe paft. The bridegroom following, paffed alfo within the curtains.
The curtain being dropt, the company fet up a
fhouting and hollowing ; and in about a quarter
of an hour difperfed.

At the Moluccas the marriage ceremony is thus:
the woman attended by fome of her own fex,
comes into the mofque, and fits down ; then the
Imum, or, if the parties are perfons of rank, the
Calipha, holding the man's right thumb, afks him
if he will marry that woman, and live with her
according to Mahomet's law. To this he anfwers,
" I WILL."   Then the prieft afks the woman ftill
fitting, befide the like refpective queftion, if fhe
will obey. Three times muft fhe anfwer, " I
" WILL."

The woman rifing, the man and fhe pay their
refpects to the company prefent : the woman
is then conducted home. But before fhe goes out
of the mofque, the prieft gives the hufband the following admonition. " You muft not touch your
wife with lance or knife ; but, if fhe do not
obey you, take her into a chamber, and chaftife
her gently with a handkerchief." This I have
from Tuan Hadjee.

On *Monday* the 1ft of *January*, I being out of
order, my two officers went in the boat, vifited
Pollock harbour, which has been mentioned, and
found

A MAGINDANO MARRIAGE.

The material originally positioned here is too large for reproduction in this reissue. A PDF can be downloaded from the web address given on page iv of this book, by clicking on 'Resources Available'.

found it spacious, with good foundings. They also measured the distance between Mindano river's mouth, and Semoy river, as a base, to get the distance of Bunwoot. On the 4th I went to Saltpetre cave, already described. On the 5th a large prow came in, having on board the effects of one of Rajah Moodo's tax-gatherers, who was put to death by his order. Amongst other articles, I counted thirty-five slaves.

C H A P. XII.

Ask Leave to depart from Magindano—Depart privately—Character of Rajah Moodo—His Generosity—Curious about Religion—Variety of Snakes —Farther Account of the Mindanoers—Their Moderation in eating and drinking—General Character of the Mindanoers and Illanos—Journal of a Mangaio Prow---Their Song---Valentine's Account of Magindano.

ON *Monday* the 7th of *January*, I applied privately to Rajah Moodo, to the Sultan, and Fakymolano, for leave to depart. Rajah Moodo said, " Go to the Sultan ; and, if he approves of your departure, desire him to write me a note, which you will bring yourself." I went accordingly, and, after thanking him for all his civilities, I begged leave to sail: signifying also to him that Rajah Moodo wished me to depart privately, and without any firing of guns. He then wrote on a slip

X   of

of paper, that he thought it was proper I fhould go, and go privately. To day I made Rajah Moodo a prefent of half a barrel of powder.

On the 8th, I fent the galley down to the river's mouth, to lie within the bar. I heard the fmall pox was broken out near Pollok harbour. To day I vifited the Sultan for the laft time : he talked of going to Dinas or Sebugy, to avoid the fmall pox. On my return from the Sultan, I paid my refpects to Fakymolano ; he again faid at parting, " You are well rid of Tuan Hadjee." I could not help being affected at parting with this venerable per-fonage, whom I had always found open and fin-cere. I then took refpectful leave of Rajah Moo-do. He delivered to me the two letters already mentioned ; one to his Majefty, the other to the Company, with the prefents. Nobody knew what they were, but himfelf and his father Fakymolano, who wrote the letters. I thanked him for all his generous civilities, and promifed to write to him by the return of the boat, which I hoped to find at Borneo. He fmiled to his wife, Potely Pyak, as I rofe to go away ; which made me imagine, fhe knew or fufpected I was going. As I went to my apartments, I found feveral perfons who, from what they faid, feemed to imagine me bound fome whither ; and, as two of Rajah Moodo's foldiers were to accompany me, I did not difcourage the report that I was going to Tukoran on a vifit, where dwelt the Sultan, Rajah Moodo's father in law.

About half an hour after funfet, I ftepped into the boat, was on board in about forty minutes,
and

and that night got over the bar. This privacy was for fear of the Sooloos, who were numerous in the river ; and I fuſpected that Datoo Topang, their protector, thought I had ſlighted him.

Having now left Magindano, I muſt confeſs, I received, during my ſtay there, great civility and hoſpitality from Rajah Moodo ; great ſincerity and good advice from Fakymolano ; and much polite- neſs from the Sultan, both before and after the re- conciliation ; alſo from his ſon Chartow, after the reconciliation : before that, I had not ſpoke to him. Fakymolano told me Topang was not my friend, which I had long fuſpected.

Rajah Moodo, with the full ſtature of a man, has the eye, as well as the noſe of an eagle ; his underſtanding is quick as his eye : he preſerves a conſtancy of good humour, which renders his manners open, as has been before acknowledged. Once, indeed, when one of my people ſtruck ano- ther, in preſence of his father, Rajah Moodo coming in, and being told of it, a cloud overcaſt his countenance. But, as I immediately begged the favour of being allowed to puniſh him, by confinement in irons, a ſmile returned ; and he ſaid : " Do, puniſh your own way." Next day, however, he deſired the releaſe of the culprit. Another time, I was told, his armourer, or black- ſmith, a Biſayan captive, being drunk, had dared to affront the Spaniſh envoy : Rajah Moodo ſo loſt his uſual ſelf command, that, had it not been for the interpoſition of his lady, it was thought he would have put the miſcreant to death on the ſpot. Among ſecondary qualifications, Rajah Moodo had

X 2   that

that of a good mechanic: I was furprifed to fee the engines for raifing heavy pieces of timber. He alfo made drums, like thofe in Europe, and was pleafed to hear them ufed by his guards.

About a month before I failed, I was fhort of goods. Rajah Moodo was fo polite, as to offer me any quantity of kangans, to be paid at my convenience. I accepted the amount of two hundred kangans. As I was with him almoft every evening, I had much converfation, not only with him, but with his father. I found them perfectly acquainted with the circumftances of our taking Manila; and alfo, of Commodore Anfon's taking the Manila Galleon, which they named Noftra Siniora del Cabadonga. Having accidentally a copy of that great voyage, I read to Fakymolano fome particulars; the number of men in each fhip, the killed, wounded, and fo on. He wondered at the difproportion, and wrote down all I told him. I had it alfo in my power, from magazines, to relate the taking of the Havannah laft war; at the whole of which they were all furprifed.

Sometimes Rajah Moodo would afk the Spanifh envoy and me to talk about religion; glimpfing in fome things the difference between Romifh and Proteftant. If the Spaniard grew a little warm, which fometimes happened, he would laugh heartily. He talked always with profound refpect of Jefus Chrift, calling him a very great Nabbi (Prophet). He would then fay, " But God fent a great * prophet after him."

* I took particular notice he did not fay, *Nabbi laggi bazar*; a greater prophet."

I told

I told him that our Proteſtant religion was the plain and purified offspring of the Roman; and to give him an idea of it, I turned three ſtanzas of Pope's beautiful paraphraſe of the Lord's Prayer into Malay, in the following words, preſerving the title in Latin, which Sinior Abderagani, who wrote out the grant of Bunwoot, explained to him; Rajah Moodo underſtanding ſome Latin words himſelf.

DEO OPTIMO MAXIMO,

Oratio Universalis in Lingua Malaya.

I. Bapa de ſomonio, de ſomonio dunia,
    De ſomonio nigri.ſujud;
 Dery Chriſtan, dery Cafer, dery Hindoo, dery
    Selam;
    Deos, Jehovah, Tuan Alla!

II. Caſſi ſcio ari iko, makanan, dangang riſkimo;
    Somonio lain apo apo,
 Tuan tow callo by caſſi, callo tida,
    Tuan alla punio ſuko.

III. Adjar ſcio ſyang atee, lain oran punio chelaka;
    Adjar ſcio tutup matto, lain oran punio
    falla.
 Bugimano ſcio ampong ſummo lain oran,
    Caſſi ampong ſummo ſcio.

Father of all! in every age,
In every clime ador'd,
By ſaint, by ſavage, and by ſage,
Jehovah, Jove, or Lord!

II. *This*

II.   *This day, be bread and peace my lot :*
         All elſe beneath the ſun,
       Thou know'ſt if beſt beſtow'd or not ;
         And let thy will be done.

III.   *Teach me to feel another's woe,*
         To hide the fault I ſee :
       That mercy I to others ſhow,
         That mercy ſhow to me.

Any perſon who knows ever ſo little of the Malay tongue, will underſtand the above, as it is an
almoſt literal tranſlation. Fakymolano tranſlated
it into the Magindano language, and admired it
much.---He would often aſk me the abuſes of the
Romiſh religion, and why we departed from them.
I touched on this ſtring very gently ; and, when
I conſidered the Spaniard and myſelf, with ſome
few people belonging to us, as the only perſons at
court, who being reckoned unclean, were doom-
ed to drink our chocolate out of glaſs tumblers,
while every one elſe drank out of fine china ; I confeſs, it greatly abated that gall, which has for ages
dignified many perſonages, both in church and
ſtate, on the other ſide of the globe. A little ridi-
cule concerning indulgences, celibacy of prieſts,
and the like, would now and then eſcape me ; but
I qualified my freedom, by aſſuring him that the
world poſſeſſed no perſons of greater honour than
ſome Spaniards. Once, in a private conference
with Fakymolano, I told him a ſtory, which I have
read ſomewhere, of an Italian prieſt, who kept a
magazine of good works , a commodity in which
he dealt, by way of transfer from his books to
                                              thoſe

thofe afflicted mortals, whofe confciences were
out of repair; that he took care to provide, when
poffible, at the death of the godly, reaffortments
of ftock, which he fafely depofited in his ware-
houfe; but fold very dear, efpecially to thofe who
were in particular want; complaining always to
his cuftomers, that good works *(Mapia Gunawan)*
were daily more fcarce, and hardly to be had at
any rate. Fakymolano would often fay, Come,
Captain, tell us the ftory about *Mapia Gunawan.*

In the frequent converfations I had with that
communicative perfonage, I learned that Magindano has many fnakes, fome very large. The
Mamemetin fixing in trees, thence dart on the
unwary paffenger. I have heard of fuch on the
ifland Salayer, and that they will whip up a goat
from the ground: we read of fuch monftrous
fnakes being alfo on Ceylon.

There is a large fnake, called Bukkoron, found
often on Timoko hill, which, in great floods, may
be confidered as an ifland; and the fnakes carried
away by the torrents, faften where they can.
Thus, in Indoftan I have been told, of fnakes
faftening on bridges, when born down a river by
a flood. Here is alfo a fmaller black poifonous
fnake, with a white throat and red eyes. Another,
called Dolpu is very large: its blowing or fpitting
on any perfon, is poifonous, making the body
fwell. Rajah Moodo mentioned to me a man
on the ifland Lutangan, feized by an enormous
fnake, that having thrown him down, fwal-
lowed his leg and thigh. The fnake not being
able

able to get higher, the man pulled out his crefs, and cut the monfter's mouth, which then difgorged him : the man, with leg and thigh much torn, furvived. On Bunwoot, I have feen a fmall fnake, fpotted black and brown : its bite is thought to be venomous. On Magindano are faid to be Loories of the fame kind with thofe that come from the Moluccas ; but they are fo fcarce that I never faw any. The Cocatores, which abound in the rice fields, have a fmooth head, and no tuft, like thofe we fee come from different parts of India. At Sooloo, there are no Loories ; but the Cocatores have yellow tufts. There are fowls, ducks and geefe ; the latter fcarce ; yet great is the plenty of *gakey* (teal) on the lakes Liguaffin and Buloan, and elfewhere.

I forgot to mention a circumftance, that happened foon after my arrival at Mindano.

Two flaves, man and wife, that had been taken by Datoo Uku, on board Mr. Cole's fchooner, ran away from the Datoo's houfe, came to Coto Intang, and claimed my protection. I laid the affair before Rajah Moodo, who told me to keep them. The Sultan alfo hearing of it, approved. Rajah Moodo talking to the man one day, in my apartments faid, " what kind of a perfon is your " late mafter," meaning Datoo Uku, " *berenno* " *dio ?* is he brave ?" and without waiting for an anfwer, the Rajah went on, " I faw him one day on the other fide the water, peeping at me from behind the croud—why did he not come forward and fhow himfelf ?" Poth Rajah Moodo and his

father

father difapproved much of Uku's piracy, and I mentioned it frequently in pretty ftrong terms to the Sultan; but he waved the fubject, not daring (I fuppofe) to exert his authority, on account of Topang.

One night Rajah Moodo collected fome hundreds of glafs beads, and by dividing the whole, the half, and fo on continually, would tell me the original number. This I feemed defirous of being taught, which pleafed him much : his courtiers admired his ingenuity. He writes in Spanifh, and prefers, in calculation, the Roman figures to the Arabic. As he is a performer on the fiddle, I prefented him with two violins, and a german flute : he had a Bifayan, one of his guards, who played tolerably by ear on the violin. I wrote down fome minuets, and Rajah Moodo fubmitted to be taught a little by book. Having got a flight idea of it, he applied no more; but had recourfe, as before, to the ear. They wondered at my writing down and afterwards playing with my flute, fome tunes they had played on their mufical gongs, called Kallintang. Thefe inftruments had little or no variety : it was always one, two, three, four, common time ; all notes being of the fame length, and the gongs were horribly out of tune. Now and then a large gong was ftruck by way of bafs. Their ears become corrupted by fo fhocking inftruments. All proves mere jargon and difcord ; while the poor Papua people of New Guinea, who pretend to no inftruments, follow nature unvitiated, and fing moft melodioufly.

Rajah

Rajah Moodo had but one wife, Potely Pyak, daughter to the Sultan of Tukoran. His fourteen or fifteen concubines flept on mats befpreading the floor of a large hall, in which he and his lady occupied a large bed. Sometimes he went with his confort and concubines to a little garden, juft without Coto Intang, where, under a fhade, he and his friends would regale with chocolate and fweet cakes. In this garden he had fome European coleworts, which he got from Samboangan; alfo onions, parfley, fpearment, and the Spanifh rad-difh, which the Mindanoers call Lobuc, as the Malays do; but neither turnips nor carrots: there was alfo one vine. He frequently fent me part of what few growths he had. His lady fpoke good Malay, and was fond of finging a Malay ftanza, which I had the honour of teaching her.

Ambo jugo burra banfi, banfi,
Dudu debowa batang,
Ambo jugo, ma nanti, nanti,
Manapo tidado datang.

I play on a pipe, a pipe,
Repos'd beneath a tree;
I play; but the time's not ripe:
Why don't you come to me?

The complaint of an impatient lover. I learnt it at Fort Marlbro'; and a late governor there, fond of Virgil's eclogues, was faid to be the author of it. Yet the Malays have fome very pretty fongs: the following couplet the fame lady ufed to fing with me.

Inchy

Inchy piggy mandi, dekkat mulo fungy,
Scio mow be-jago, fcio mow be-nanty.

When in the flood my fair fhall glide,
Her diftant guardian I'll abide.

Alluding to a general practice in the villages of
Sumatra, where the females go a bathing in the
rivers, which they generally do once a day : the
Orang Bugin, young batchelors, attend them as a
guard.

I once faw the people of Mindano cutting rice,
which refembles barley. They cut each head
fingly with a knife, held in the palm of the hand ;
nor have they any idea of faving the ftraw, but
let it rot on the ground.

The arts are in no kind of forwardnefs here.
The women underftand plain work : the better
fort are much given to embroidery, which they
execute pretty well, with gold thread, on the ends
of fuch pillows as we have feen adorning their beds.
They have alfo a way of disfiguring fine Pulicat
handkerchiefs with forry imitations of flowers.
Their moft ufeful art is veffel building, which they
perform by dowling the planks one upon the other,
fo as never to require calking. They then fit the
timbers, the beams going without, and, as it were,
clafping the planks, like veffels called Burrs in
Bengal river. This has one bad confequence, as,
at thofe beam ends, the veffels are always leaky.
At Sooloo they build in the fame manner, and my
veffel was fo conftructed ; but, knowing where the

water

water came in, I found it not fo alarming. The gunpowder they make is large grained and weak.

They have goldfmiths, who make filligree buttons, earings, &c. pretty well, but not near fo well as Malays generally do on Sumatra and Java. Their blackfmiths are incapable of making any thing that requires more ingenuity than a common nail. Rajah Moodo had feveral Bifayan flaves; one of them could mend a gun lock : he fitted my rudder irons. Others amongft them were tolerable filverfmiths, and thofe he kept in conftant employ ; but the Mindanoers have almoft all their culinary utenfils from China, by way of Sooloo ; and I was furprized not to find here, as at Sooloo, copper currency in the market, where all was bought and fold with rough rice, and Chinefe kangangs.

Rajah Moodo beftows wives on the Bifayan foldiers in his fort, generally flaves from the fame country. They have a weekly allowance of rice. When any of thofe females have been caught going aftray, they are tied up to a poft, and chaftifed by thofe of the fame rank in the fort, who, one after another, give each her ftripe with a ratan. I have feen it inflicted ; but the punifhment was very gentle. The man had his feet put into the ftocks for two or three days.

Fond of bathing, they go into the river at leaft once in twenty-four hours. They bathe at all times of the day; but generally morning and evening.

They

They never fuffer their beards to grow, pluck-
ing out with pincers the hairs as they firft begin to
fprout : this is the general cuftom of the Malays.

They often play at football, if fo may be called
a kind of fpherical bafket about the fize of a man's
head, made of fplit ratans. About ten or twelve
perfons make a ring, and tofs the ball from one to
another : fometimes they kick it with the foot,
fometimes hit it with the palm of the hand, fometimes with the fhoulder, and often with the knee ;
keeping it up as long as they can. They amufe
themfelves at times with throwing the lance, very
feldom with bows and arrows ; but their favourite
amufement is cock-fighting, as it is univerfally to
the eaftward of Atcheen-head among the Malays.
Their perfons are rather flim, but genteelly made.
Though not athletic, they can exert great ftrength
upon occafion.

They are moderate in eating and drinking, and
delicate in the choice of the beft and fineft rice, as
Eaft Indians generally are. I have often feen
placed before Rajah Moodo, befide his difh of
boiled rice, two or three ounces of boiled pumpkin, on one tea faucer ; and about two ounces of
dried or falt fifh on another. This, with a cup
holding fomewhat lefs than half a pint of chocolate, was his dinner. Neither did he drink any
thing after it, but water ; then, rincing his mouth
and wafhing his hands. Such temperance is uni-
verfal amongft Malays. They have their falt in
lumps, like loaf fugar, which at meals they ftamp
on their rice every now and then, as a perfon
ftamps a letter.

In

In the mountains of Kalagan, on the S. E. quarter of this island, is a good deal of talc, such as comes from Muscovy. I could not learn that they had any precious stones on Magindano; but in the sea, on banks and sands, they are said to have the Teepye pearl oyster, as at Sooloo, without the art of fishing for it.

I considered myself very lucky amongst them in having no cargo to dispose of. Had I brought any thing of that kind, I much question if I could have steered so clear of party as I did: I might have gone to Topang to sell my merchandise. On the contrary, having nothing but what was to bear my expences, my freedom of mind enabled me to keep a certain line of conduct, without deviation. Nor was it less fortunate for me, that Tuan Hadjee took pet, and went away as he did. Had he remained, he might have got an ascendant with Rajah Moodo over me, as his delight, perhaps his genius, was intrigue, which I avoided as a rock or a quick-sand. Fakymolano did not like him at all.

The people of Magindano, and their neighbours, known commonly by the name of Oran Illanon, as living near the great Lano, are very piratically inclined. Neither can the Sultan of Magindano restrain his subjects from fitting out vessels, which go among the Philippines, to Mangaio, that is, cruise against the Spaniards: much less can be restrained the Illanos, being under a government more aristocratic; for, on the banks of the Lano, are no fewer than seventeen, stiled Rajahs, and

sixteen

fixteen who take the title of Sultan, befides thofe
on the coaft. When the Spanifh envoy failed
from Mindano for Samboangan, Rajah Moodo
fent a veffel, as has been faid, to convoy him
acrofs the Illano bay. This is a proof the Spaniards are not in good terms with the Illanos.
Thefe, within ten years before 1775, have done
much mifchief to the Spaniards, among the iflands
called Babuyan, at the north extremity of the
Philippines; and, at this time, they poffefs an
ifland in the very heart of the Philippines, called
Burias, where has been a colony of Illanos, for
many years, men, women, and children. The
Spaniards have often attempted to diflodge them;
but in vain: the ifland, which is not very large,
being environed with rocks and fhoals to a confiderable diftance.

Some of the veffels that they fit out as cruifers,
are very fmall and narrow. Many I have feen
fifty foot long, and only three broad; availing
themfelves, however, of outriggers, without which
they could not keep upright. They all ufe the
tripod maft, lyre tanjong, and row with great
velocity. In bad weather they throw out a wooden
anchor, and veer away along ratan cable, which
keeps their head to fea. Sometimes in an extremity, the crew will jump overboard, and,
with their bodies under water, hold by the outriggers for hours together, to eafe the veffel's
weight. and certainly the crew is moft of the
loading, for the veffels carry no ballaft, and draw
little water, in their paffage from ifland to ifland.
When the boat or prow is large, with her tripod
maft

maſt ſtruck, they hide among rocks, iſlands, or in the woods, up ſome creek. They then detach ſmall ſampans, or canoes, to ſurprize what they can aſhore, or afloat, and bring to the capital veſſel; which goes home, when ſhe has got a ſufficient cargo of ſlaves and plunder. The Spaniards not allowing the Biſayans fire arms, the latter prove leſs able to defend themſelves.

I now give the journal of a Mangaio prow, belonging to Datoo Malfalla, brother in law to Rajah Moodo, from Magindano, to the coaſt of Celebes. The prow, which left Magindano, during the N. E. monſoon, after paſſing Serangani, went to the following iſlands before ſhe reached Celebes. Firſt Kalingal, three hours from Serangani: it is inhabited, and reſembles Engliſh Bunwoot. Then, in one day to Kabio: it is uninhabited. In another day to the iſland Kabuluſu, near the north part of Sangir. Hence in one day to Karakita, which afforded ſome proviſion. Hence, in one day to Siao, near which ſhe got plenty of proviſions on a ſmall iſland, behind which is a fine harbour. Thence, to Tagulanda in half a day, thence to Banka, and thence to Telluſyang, which is near the coaſt of Celebes.

On Celebes, they take, if in Dutch territory, even thoſe of their own religion : a decent muſſulman, with his wife and four children, were brought to Mindano, by this very prow. They have particular laws amongſt themſelves, during thoſe piratical cruiſes; and keep up a certain order and diſcipline. In rowing, at which, from habit, they

are

1776.
January.

are dextrous, they have always a fong as a kind of
tactic, and beat on two brafs timbrels to keep time.
I have known one man on board my little veffel
opportunely, with fometimes a Molucca, fometimes a Mindano Mangaio fong, revive the reft,
who, from fatigue, were droufing at their oars;
and operate with pleafing power, what no proffered
reward could effect : fo cheared, they will row a
whole night.

MAGINDANO MANGAIO SONG.

CHORUS.

E, afi, magia,
Umi apan magia,
Ejondon tafalinow :
Ejondon tafalinow.

Chear up—hurrah !
Chear up—hurray !
Let's gain the ocean far away :
Let's gain the ocean far away.

Firft Man.

Elyka pulo mawatten,
Marakel fura fahan ;
Elyka pulo mawatten,
Makauma magean.

Behold yon ifland afar,
What fifhes abound in its main ;
Behold yon ifland afar,
Hafte, hafte, and the fifhes obtain.

Y   CHORUS

CHORUS REPEATED.

Second Man.

Maſikoon ſaingud Capez,
Mapia Caſtila babaye,
Makohat ſaingud Capez,
Dumayon kito panamaye.

Faſt by the Capezine land,
Caſtilian dames you will find:
My lads, to make Capezine land,
Pull, pull, with the whole of your mind.

The Malabars, in the Maſoola Boats at Madras, have
alſo their Song:

Ai li ma ten day, Ai lee ai lee,   Ai li ma ten day, Ai lee ai lee.
Chear up,   Pull away,   Chear up,   Pull away.

1ſt Man.   2d Man.
A ra kee a ray   Chirawatee ?   A ra kee van day ? Chirawatee?
Where lives   Chirawatee ?   Who goes to bring Chirawatee?

Chorus.   Slow.
A ve lu na lu   Pa kuva ma, Pa ku va ma.
Of all   The moſt comely, The moſt comely.

The Moors, in what is called country ſhips in
Eaſt India, have alſo their chearing ſongs; at work

* Chirawatee, the name of a Bramin woman.

in

in hoifting, or in their boats a rowing. The
Javans and Molucca people have theirs. Thofe of
the Malays are drawling and infipid. In Europe
the French provençals have their fong: it is the
reverfe of lively. The Mangaio is brifk, the
Malabar tender. The Greeks and Romans had
their Celeufma or chearing fong. Martial feems
to have made one, III. 67.

Ceffatis, pueri, nihilque môftis?
Vatreno, Eridanoque pigriores?
Quorum par vada tarda navigantes,
Lentos figitis ad celeufma remos.
Jam prono Phaëthonte fudat Æthon;
Exarfitque dies, et hora laffos
Interjungit equos meridiana.
At vos tam placidas vagi per undas,
Tuta luditis otium carina:
Non nautas puto vos, fed Argonautas.

*Why, my lads, more fluggifb go,
Than Vatrenus, or the Po?
Think ye through their ftill ye fteer,
Drawling oars to wait the chear?
Phaeton begins to fire,
Ethon lo! in full perfpire;
Now the noon-tide hour proceeds,
To repofe the panting fteeds.
Ye, ferene upon the wave,
Sun, and wind, and water brave.
No mere navigators now,
Ye are Argonauts, * I vow.*

* Argonauts, (in one fenfe) *fluggifb mariners.*

Y 2   Orators

Orators, as well as poets, celebrate the nautic fong. Thus Quintilian; *Siquidem et remiges cantus hortatur : nec folum in iis operibus, in quibus plurium conatus, præeunte aliqua jucunda voce, confpirat ; fed etiam fingulorum fatigatio quamlibet fe rudi modulatione folatur.* " Thus the fong chears the rowers: " nor only in thofe tafks, where, a melodious " voice leading, the exertion of numbers con- " fpires; but even the fatigue of each fooths itfelf, " by however a rude modulation."

Valentine, in his account of Magindano, fays, " The ifland is often called by the inhabitants, Molucca Bazar, (great Molucca) ;"---after defcrib- ing its fituation, he goes on : " The country ap- pears mountainous, the foil rich, with prodigious large trees: there are large rivers in the country, alfo fmall ones, and all kind of tropical fruits.

" The climate is healthy, notwithftanding there are dreadful ftorms during the S. W. monfoon. During the N. E. monfoon, there is fine weather. Of the land itfelf, lefs can be faid, it being lefs known : the towns are all without walls. The Sultan refides on the fouth fide of the country, where is an ifland named Bongat *, to the weft- ward of which, there is a large bay. The city of the chief nigri, lies ten miles up a river, and is not called Mindanao, but Catibtuan, where the king's houfe is built on two hundred large piles, with grand ftairs, and fifteen or fixteen guns regularly

* Bunwoot, I fuppofe.

mounted

mounted on carriages. Wax, rice, roots, and wild deer, are the chief articles of trade in this country, and thofe fcarce. They have a language of their own.

" If there is gold, it is very rare ; nor has any been feen fince the year 1687 ; and what appeared then, is likely to have come by means of fome Englifh, who robbed the Spaniards in the South Sea, and came thither with Captain Swan, and the celebrated Dampier. The Sultan and others having murdered Swan, ufed his gold in ornaments for their weapons, which induced the Dutch to think that gold was the produce of the ifland.

" When the Dutch were there in 1688, and 1689, they were more particular in their obferva-tions on that fubject ; and having communicated their opinion to Mr. Thim, governor of Ternate, that there was no gold, they afterwards found it wrong, and that there is fome little gold, either there, or on the ifland Serangani, of which we fhall hereafter make mention."

After giving, from report, an account of the fi-tuation of a few places, he goes on, and fays, " The Sultan is often at war with the Mountaineers, who are favages, and amongft whom gold is faid to be, as alfo, amongft the inhabitants of the N. W. fide of the ifland." He fays again, " The Mountai-neers carry their gold duft and wax to trade with the moft civilized of the Mindanoers ; that the inhabitants on the N. W. part of the ifland trade with the Spaniards of Manilla, and that the

Spaniards

Spaniards have fome forts on the S. W. part of the
ifland, but that neither the Sultan nor the inhabitants are fond of letting ftrangers have forts amongft
them." He then mentions the report of their offering to make a treaty with Dampier, and to have
allowed him to fettle. " Let this exaggerated account be what it may," fays Valentine, " it is certain, that when our people went thither in 1694,
the Sultan, his brother, and the admiral, told
them, that the Englifh had fome time before afked
leave to erect a fort, to fecure their trade, and for
which they had offered to pay four thoufand rixdol-
lars yearly, but they were flatly denied, in like
manner as the Dutch were in 1689 : wherefore I
think Dampier muft have been mifled ; though it
may be owing to the inclination thofe people have
to trade with ftrangers, but not more with the
Dutch than the Englifh ; becaufe both thofe nations are looked upon by them as being poffeffed of
great power, and they are always afraid of foreign-
ers getting a footing, left they take poffeffion of
their country. Wherefore, although on all other
occafions, they behave with civility to ftrangers,
they are deaf to any overtures about fettling. Neither do I imagine there is gold at the ifland Mean-
gis, as Dampier alleges ; if fuch fowls flew there,
it would foon appear upon the feathers of the poor
Mindanoers, which very much befpeak the contrary.

" From Ternate we have little intercourfe with
this ifland, except when a deputation of the north
ifland committee goes thither. In the year 1607
Motilif went there ; and in 1616 Joris van Spil-
bergen

bergen failed paft the ifland, on the 18th March;
and Admiral Gillis Scyft, in 1627, mentions
fomething of the iflands Magindano and Serangani,
in his General Hiftory of the Moluccas. It is certain, feveral deputations were fent from Ternate,
under Mr. Thim, and in the time of Monf. de
Long, for the purpofe of feeking gold, and to take
it where it could be found. In 1689, Lieutenant
Meindert de Roi, went out with an offer of two
thoufand rix dollars, from the Dutch Eaft India
Company, as a prefent to the Sultan, for liberty
to build a fort ; but was politely refufed.

" In 1693, Admiral Vanderduin and Mynheer
Haak were there, after making a furvey of the
iflands Tagalanga, Siaou, Sangir, &c. When he
left Siaou, he heard of fix Englifh fhips being at
Magindano : he then paffed Serangani, and arriving
at Magindano, near the river, oppofite which
lies Bongat, (Bunwoot) he failed thence to Bolak
(Pollock) harbour, where he faluted with feven
guns ; but had no return. In 1694, more Englifh
appeared, who requefted leave to build a fort;
but were refufed. They purchafed cooley lowang,
(clove bark) at the rate of fix rix dollars a pecul,
and wax at twenty-five a pecul.

" When the Dutch Admiral returned, in the
year 1694, they informed the governor of Ternate,
that no advantage could accrue to the Directors
of the Eaft India Company from that ifland, becaufe the natives themfelves carried their produce
in their veffels to Manilla, Batavia, Malacca, and
even to Siam : they alfo declared, that moft of
the gold they met with there, was brought from
Manilla,

Manilla, by the inhabitants, or Spaniards, or by
Englifh pirates. The Dutch Admiral and Mynheer Haak were very particular in their enquiries
about gold ; but there was not the leaft appearance of it. Touching at Serangani, the fon of the
king of Kandahar, on Sangir, came to them, and
told the Dutch admiral, that Serangani belonged
to his father : he brought fome rice ; but afked
dear for it: he alfo afked dear for bullocks, faying,
the Englifh had given twenty-five and thirty rix
dollars a piece ; twenty rix dollars a pecul for wax,
and twelve rix dollars for the weight of a rix dollar
of gold duft. In 1700, Captain Roofelaur was
fent by order of the States to Magindano ; but he
died, and it was reported he was poifoned. Of
forty foldiers and fifty failors, only feven returned
in health. He met with much gold, and faw there
many Chinefe junks." So far Valentine, publifhed
at Amfterdam, 1724.

I cannot leave Mindano, without acquainting
the reader, that the Sultan Paharadine told me,
his father had affured him, Captain Swan was
drowned accidentally, by a boat's overfetting ; and
that his Jerrytulis (clerk) fwam fafe afhore ; as did
the crew, (Mindanoers) with the lofs of their cloaths
and arms.

C H A P.

C H A P. XIII.

Account of the Iflands Sangir---Tulour, or Tanna-Labu---Salibabo---Kabruang---Nanufan---Karakita---Palla---Tagulanda-- Banka, and Tellufyang, from the Information of Datoo Woodine.

SANGIR was formerly independant, being governed by a prince of its own, till a quarrel broke out between him and the Sultan of Ternate. It feems the Rajah of Sangir had given to the Sultan of Ternate, his daughter, who unfortunately bore a child in fix months after marriage. This happened fince the Dutch have been in poffeffion of the Moluccas, as they now are of Sangir, which they eafily guard with a ferjeant and ten or twelve foldiers.

The Dutch difcourage Mahometanifm, and by miffionaries make many converts to chriftianity. The minifters preach in the Malay tongue to thofe who underftand it, and have fubordinate black preachers, who fpeak the language of the country. I have fome Malay fermons printed in the Roman character. They were got with other plunder on board the Dutch floop that was burnt, when attacked by Malfalla's Mangaio prow, as mentioned in the journal. The crew having fired her, took to their boat, while fome bold Mindano men jumped on board and faved many things; among the reft, two Dutch brafs fwivel guns, two pounders.

I once

I once in converfation with Fakymolano, faid to him, that Sangir being a fmall ifland compared with Magindano, and lying near it, had furely belonged to fome of his anceftors. This I did, in order to try him; but he was too fincere to deny that Sangir was always independant, till lately the Dutch had got it from Ternate.

The iflands of Salibabo, Kabruang and Nanu-fan, were under Sangir, confequently now under the Dutch; but no European was at Leron or Sa-libabo, when I was there.

Malary Rajah of Sangir, a great many years ago, had a grand-daughter named Sembaffin, who married Abdaraman, Sultan of Magindano. Her brother Manalantan, Rajah of Sangir, gave Sali-babo, and the fourth part of the ifland Tulour, to his grand-nephew Fakymolano. This gives Ma-gindano a right to fome part of the Sangir domi-nion; and on this ifland of Tulour, Fakymolano's brother was killed in a fray, in the year 1773. Poffibly he was exercifing his power too roughly: for the revenues are moft cruelly collected from thofe defencelefs iflanders, in a certain number of flaves. The inhabitants are continually accufing one another of trefpaffes, in order that the Kolano, or head man of a village, may, by trial and fine, make up the number annually demanded.

Sangir is an oblong ifland, extending from the latitude of 3° 30, to 4° 30′ north, and lying in the longitude of 122° 20′ eaft of Greenwich. It is broadeft towards the north end, and tapers fmall towards the fouth, where the coaft is indent-
ed

ed with many bays, before feveral of which lie
iflands affording good anchorage within them,
About the middle of the weft coaft of the ifland
is the town, harbour, and bay of Taroona;
oppofite which, on the eaft coaft, is alfo a town
and harbour called Tabookang, the harbour being fheltered from the N. E. by two pretty large
iflands, Pulo Noeffa, and Pulo Bookit, the latter highly cultivated. Many more harbours are
towards the fouth end of this ifland, along the
middle of which runs a ridge of high mountains,
terminated to the northward by a high volcano,
from which according to Valentine, was an eruption in 1711, preceded by a dreadful earthquake.
Valentine fays alfo, there are forty-fix iflands,
large and fmall, around Sangir, and that the king
of Kandahar on Sangir, had a claim upon part
of Mindano.

Sangir contains many Nigris: the chief are
Tabookan, Kandahar, Taroona, Maganaloo and
Sarab, in all which are reckoned about fix thoufand males, who wear breeches. It abounds in
coco nuts, as do many iflands that lie near it.
A fathom of fmall brafs wire, fuch as is ufed at
the end of a fifhing line, will purchafe a hundred
coco nuts; an ordinary knife three hundred;
and four knives a battel (60 lb.) of coco nut oil.
This I mention, as the rate of barter or exchange to thofe who may occafionally touch
there, and are not in a hurry. It has alfo bullocks, goats, hogs, and poultry; but its chief
export is coco nut oil.

While

While I was at Magindano, fometime before Watamama's laft illnefs, he fitted out a Mangaio prow, as has already been hinted. She was quite new, about thirty tons burthen, had a great deal of room on her deck, and galleries around her; but fo little room below, that fhe was continually fwagging from fide to fide: which is the cafe with all their veffels, more or lefs, and was with mine. I obferved that they launched her without any thing on her bottom. They faid they would bream and pay her bottom in about ten days.

She was declared bound to the ifland of Tulour, and the coaft of Celebes: poffibly to take fatisfaction at the former, for the death of Fakymolano's brother at Ramis. Before fhe failed, fhe rowed up the Melampy, as has been mentioned, about three miles: I went in her. At about that diftance from Coto Intang, they ftopt clofe to a grove of fpreading trees, under the fhade of which lay a rude heap of coral rock ftones, by the river fide. This was the burial place of their great anceftor Serif, who came from Mecca. Every man ftepped out holding a bit of wax candle, which he lighted, fixed on one of the ftones, and left burning, after faying fome prayers, and a felam. This performed in about twenty minutes, all came again on board.

They rowed at the rate of four miles an hour. The number of oars was fixteen of a fide ; but, as they were all fixed by ratans at the edge of the gallery, as many more might have been fixed within

within thofe : for the oars led (if I may fo fay) much up and down, and making a great angle with the horizon. She had a very high tripod maft. I faw the crew making their powder: about eight men at one time were beating in a wooden mortar. When made, the grains were very coarfe. She mounted two four pounders abreaft of each other, on her prow or forecaftle, and a great many brafs rantackers. Every man lays in his own pro-vifion, rice only. The owner gives nothing but the hull, for which he has one-third of the prizes. Mafts, fails, anchors, and cables, are made by the crew. This prow was to carry eighty men, and drew about four foot fix inches water.

Tulour, or Tanna Labu, lies in the latitude of 4° 45′ N. and longitude 124° E. It is fituated about feventy miles eaft of the north part of Sangir, and may be, fo far as I could judge, in paffing, about thirty leagues round.*

It is of middling height, whereas Sangir has fome very high mountains. The inhabitants live on the fea coaft, and have their plantations up in the country.

The following names of the villages along fhore, and the number of inhabitants I had from Datoo Woodine, who being employed by Fakymolano to go thither, kept a regifter, which I took down

---

* Valentine lays it down by the name of Karkallang, fhapes it like a right angled triangle, gives it about the fame compafs, and makes a promontory at the north jut pretty far into the fea.

from

from his mouth, as he explained it in the Malay
tongue, in which we conversed.

I shall begin at the N. W. part, where is said to
be a harbour behind an island called Gugid, and
so shall go round the island from the northward.
Next to Gugid is

		Inhabitants.
Pampang, containing	-	200
Sabay	- -	200
Carangan	- -	300
Malla River	- -	200
Issang	- -	200
Andolang	- -	200
Bulud	- -	100
Mamang	- -	200
Bamboon	- -	400
Tatoran, a harbour,	-	800
Gummy	- -	150
Karanka	- -	200
Tarukan	- -	60
Malla ⎰ Under one ⎱		
Bundad ⎰ Kolano ⎱		1000
Appan		
Gunnyo	- -	100
Babunbaru	- -	70
Tattapuan, a good harbour,		200
Saban	- -	200
Tury	- -	70
Mannaka	- -	70
Marahi	- -	70
Kiamma	- - -	40
Malla	- -	100

Anyam,

	Inhabitants.
Anyam - - -	100
Karangug - -	60
Tavrong - -	100
Bataruma - -	40
Neampai - -	150
Marake - -	200
Makalang - -	200
Bulad - -	200
Dugid - -	200
Ammat - -	400
Dappichi - -	600
Rim - - -	50
Tukadbatu - -	300
Taban 100 - -	100
Ramis, a harbour, * -	300
Pulutan - -	300
Rayhey - -	1000
Ruſſu - -	300

Males who wear breeches 9730

The iſland is under twenty Kolanos. The office of Kolano deſcends from father to ſon, but intereſt often obtains a nomination from Ternate or Sangir.

The iſland of Salilabo lies to the ſouthward of Tulour, being divided only by a narrow ſtrait, about one mile wide. It is not above eight or ten miles round, and is admirably cultivated. It contains, moſtly at the ſea ſide, the villages of

* Here Fakymolano's brother was killed.

Leron,

		Inhabitants.
Leron, containing	-	300
Morong	- -	300
Sally	- -	70
Dallong	- -	200
Tuad	- -	50
Siry	- - -	70
Karungan	- -	200
Sarunkar	- -	100
Bayor	- -	50
Muffy	- -	30
Dinkallan	- -	70
Salibabo	- -	170

Males who wear breeches, 1610

Kabruang is fomewhat fmaller than Salibabo,*
to the S. E. of it ; and is parted from it by a ftrait,
about four miles wide. This ifland is in high cultivation ; and may be feen eighteen leagues off,
being remarkable for a peaked hill, about the middle ; whereas Salibabo, at a diftance, makes like a
table land. Valentine fays, Kabruang belongs to
the king of Siao ; on it are the villages of

		Inhabitants.
Kabruang, containing	-	300
Mangara	-	500
Bulud	- -	300
Pangerang	-	50
Tuadobally	-	500
Damow	- -	200

* Salibabo and Kabruang are well laid down by Valentine.

Aras

Aras	- -	70
Bera	- -	50
Egis	- - -	40
Reoran	- -	30
Pantu	- -	30

Males who wear breeches, 2070

I learned from the blind Chinefe, who came on board to vifit me, when I went into the harbour of Leron, on Salibabo, that, about fix leagues to the N. E. of the latter, were three low iflands, of no great extent, forming a harbour. The name of the largeft ifland was Nanufa, containing male inhabitants, - - 400

The next, Kakarutan, containing 700
And the third, Karatan, containing 200

Total — 1300

The inhabitants of the ifland called Nanufa, are chiefly boat-builders. At Leron harbour, as has been faid, I had the offer of a Nanufa built boat, remarkably cheap; but as fhe wanted fitting out, and was hauled up on the fhore, I dreaded fome mifunderftanding that might arife, before fhe were ready.

Karakita and Palla are two iflands, which have been mentioned in the journal; as has the high ifland Siao; * where the Dutch entertain a fchoolmafter,

Z

* The iflands Sangir, Siao, and Tagulanda, are obliged, when Ternate is at war, to furnifh the following number of corocoros:

On

master, a corporal and a few foldiers. Provifions are in plenty, and the harbour on the east fide is good. The mountain is fometimes a volcano.

Next is Tagulanda, whence may be difcerned the coaft of Celebes. Two iflands form a harbour, in the ftrait between them. On one of the iflands is a pretty high hill. Tagulanda contains about two thoufand inhabitants: it is governed by a Kolano and a Gogo. Being Pagans, they eat pork; having alfo many goats, fome bullocks, and coco nuts in abundance. The Dutch keep here a corporal and two foldiers; alfo a fchoolmafter, for teaching the children the principles of Chriftianity. Three prongs, a kind of large chopping knives, will purchafe a bullock; and one, a thoufand coco nuts.

On Sangir,			corocoros.	men.
Tabookan	-	-	6	300
Taroona	-	-	4	200
Candahar	-	-	3	150
Manganitoe		-	3	150
			16	800

On Siao,			corocoros.	men.
Pehe	-	-	4	200
Oeloe	-	-	2	100
Tagulanda	-	-	3	150
			19	450
			16	800

Total number of corocoros and men, 35   1250

Sangir had, by Valentine's account, 4,080 fencible men, and 12,820 fouls, which agrees pretty well with Datoo Woodine's.

Next

Next is Banka, remarkable for a high hill: it has a harbour on its fouth end; is pretty well inhabited, and abounds in coco nuts, limes, nankas or jacks, fifh, turtle, and ratans. From it Celebes is more vifible than from Tagulanda. Near Banka is the ifland Tellufyang, that is, harbour of Syang, called Taliffe by Valentine. This harbour, faid to be good, is on the fouth end of the ifland, which has a hill upon it. There are fome wild cattle, no other inhabitants. Thefe iflands are much frequented by the Mangaio cruifers, not only from Magindano, but from Sooloo.

C H A P. XIV.

Of the ifland Sooloo—Claims of the Spaniards to any Sovereignty over that ifland refuted—Climate—Fruits—Government—Articles from China carried thither, and Returns---Diffipation of the Datoos---Pearl Fifhing Harbours---Cruelty to Slaves---Fray between the Sooloos and the Englifh-Buggeffes---General Character of the Sooloos---Many Inflances of their Treachery.

THE Sooloos fay, their ifland * was formerly a part of the ancient Borneo empire, founded by the
　　　　　　Z 2　　　　　　　　　Chinefe;

---

* The ifland Sooloo lies fouth weft from Mindano, and is governed by a king of its own. It is far from being large; but, its fituation between Mindano and Borneo makes it the mart of all the moorifh kingdoms. I do not find, that the Portuguefe ever pretended to fettle, much lefs to conquer thefe iflands;
　　　　　　　　　　　　　　　　　　but

Chinefe ; but the Mindanoers, as has been hinted,
affert, the Sooloos were once tributary to them.
Be that as it may, this ifland had been at war with
the Spaniards, before the year 1646 ; and on the
14th of April, of the faid year, peace was made
between them, by the mediation of the King of
Mindano ; upon which the Spaniards withdrew
from Sooloo, ftill referving to themfelves the fovereignty of the iflands Tappool, Seaffee, Balan-
guifan, and Pangaterran. The Sooloos agreed
alfo to give in fign of brotherhood, yearly, three
veffels laden with rice. This is related in Combes's
account of Magindano. The reafon of this fudden
peace was fear of the Dutch affifting Sooloo ; and
the Spaniards dreaded, that to be driven off the
ifland, might hurt the reputation of their arms.*

The treaty of Munfter was made two years after this peace, in 1648, by which the navigation
of the Spaniards is reftrained ; for the treaty fays,
" It is further agreed, that the Spaniards fhall
maintain their navigation in the manner it at prefent is, without being able to extend it farther in

but they vifited them frequently, for the fake of trade ; and in
thofe days, there was greater commerce in thefe parts, than
can well be imagined. For, while the trade was open to
Japan, there came from thence two or three fhips laden with
filver, amber, filks, chefts, cabinets, and other curiofities, made
of fweet fcented woods ; with vaft quantities of filks, quilts,
and earthen ware, from China. For thefe the merchants of Gol-
conda exchanged their diamonds, thofe of Ceylon their rubies,
topazes, and fapphires ; from Java and Sumatra came pepper.
and fpices from the Moluccas.—DALRYMPLE's PROOFS.—
HARRIS's HISTORY OF THE PORTUGUESE EMPIRE, p. 685.

* Pedro Murille Valarde's Account of the Philippines.

the

the Eaſt Indies." This is particularly ſet forth by Mr. Dalrymple; alſo, that the Sooloos made lately with the Spaniards treaties of alliance, offenſive and defenſive, as the Spaniſh governor declared in a letter wrote to the Engliſh governor of Manila. Mr. Dalrymple firſt made the Engliſh acquainted with the Sooloos, and procured from them, for the India Company, a grant of country, that ſure-ly cannot be claimed by any European power--- the north part of Borneo, and ſome iſlands north of it; of which more hereafter.

The iſland of Sooloo is ſituated in the latitude of 6° N. and longitude 119° E. from Greenwich. It is thirty miles long, twelve broad; and may con-tain ſixty thouſand inhabitants.

This iſland, lying about midway between the iſlands of Borneo and Magindano, is well culti-vated; affording a fine proſpect from the ſea, on every ſide, far ſuperior to that of Malay countries in general. Thoſe that I have ſeen come neareſt to it, in appearance, are, that part of the coaſt of Sumatra, between Atcheen Head and Pedir, the north coaſt of Java, the ſouth coaſt of the iſland Bally, the country about Malacca, part of the north coaſt of Borneo, the iſlands of Salibabo and Kabruang.

Sooloo being an iſland not very large, and the hills on it not being very high, nor conſequently the clouds ſtopt by them, it has no certain rainy ſeaſon, as have the large Malay iſlands. There is not ſuch difference in the wetneſs of the ſeaſons or monſoons, monfoons, as on continents or very large iflands; but the S. W. monfoon brings moft rain. Much falls at the change of the monfoons; efpecially the autumnal. The capital town is called Bowan, fituated by the fea coaft, on the N. W. part of the ifland, and containing about fix thoufand inhabitants. Many of them are Illanon, or Oran Illano, with whom we are acquainted, and who live in a quarter by themfelves.

A hill near the town, is pretty high, and at night generally capt with a cloud. Other hills, of inferior height, are fometimes alfo covered in the evening. Thefe clouds feed the rivulets which run from the hills. The land wind here is faint and reaches not far.

The ifland being rather fmall for its number of inhabitants, they ftudy agriculture more than do thofe of the adjacent iflands, already mentioned, where land may be deemed of no value. The Sooloos plant rice; but the crop cannot be depended on, as they are not fure of rain. They therefore cultivate many roots, the Spanifh, or fweet potatoe, the clody, or St. Hillano yam, the China yam, both red and white; fending to Mindano for what rice they confume.

They have great variety of fine tropical fruits; their oranges are full as good as thofe of China. They have alfo a variety of the fruit called Jack, or Nanka, Durians, a kind of large cuftard apple named Madang, Mangoes, Manguftines, Rambuftines, and a fruit they call Bolona, like a large
plumb,

plumb, or Mangoe, white infide. In great abundance do they enjoy a very innocent and delicious
fruit, by Malays called Lancey. The trees in the
woods are loaded with this fruit, which is large,
and ripens well: this it does not on the ifland of
Sumatra, where, perhaps, it finds too much
moifture. The Sooloos having great connexion
with China, and many Chinefe being fettled a-
mongft them, they have learned the art of ingraft-
ing and improving their fruits, while the fruits at
Magindano have remained indifferent.

The Sooloos have a very good breed of horfes,
which they train to trot faft, feldom fuffering them
to gallop. When I was there in 1773, I faw often
Datoos and their ladies ride in this manner, as
mentioned in the journal. At Sooloo are none of
thofe beautiful birds called Loories; but there is
abundance of diminutive Cocatories, and fmall
green parrots. There is no fpice tree, but the
cinnamon.

Here are wild elephants, the offspring, doubtlefs, of thofe fent in former days from the continent of India, as prefents to the kings of Sooloo.
Thofe animals avoid meeting with horned cattle;
though they are not fhy of horfes. Sooloo has
fpotted deer, abundance of goats and black cattle; but the people feldom milk their cows. They
have no fheep, except a very few from Samboangan. The wild hogs are numerous, and do much
mifchief, by breaking down fences. After har-
veft, the Sooloos hunt the elephants and wild hogs,
endeavouring to deftroy them.

This

This iſland enjoys a perpetual ſummer. Up the country, it is always cool, eſpecially under the ſhade of the teak trees, which are numerous, as on Java. This tree, ſo well known in India for conſtructing the beſt ſhips, has a broad leaf, which, bruiſed between the fingers, ſtains the hand red. The induſtrious Chineſe gather thoſe leaves, and the leaves of the fruit tree called Madang, to line the baſkets of cane or bamboo, in which they pack up the ſwallo they export in great quantities, from this place. They are attentive to dry it in the ſun, as it is apt to give with the leaſt moiſture. The Chineſe muſt gain handſomely by their trade hither; elſe they would not put up with the rough uſage they ſometimes receive from the ſturdy barons, the Datoos.

Liſt of the Articles that generally compoſe the Cargo of a Chineſe Junk, of which Two come annually from Amoy to Sooloo, and paſs to the eaſtward of Paragoa.

	Coſt in China, in Dollars.	Sell for at Sooloo.
2000 Galangs (ſalvers of braſs) ſeven to a pecul, ⸺	40	70
100 Peculs iron, in ſmall pieces, like Bengal iron ⸺	4	8
Sugar candy, a quantity, per pecul	7	10
50 Raw ſilk ditto ⸺ ⸺	400	600
3000 Pieces black kowſongs, a kind of nankeen, per piece ⸺	0¾	1
5000 Pieces kompow, white ſtrong linen	0¾	1
500 Kangans, 25 in a bundle, called gandangs, per gandang ⸺	7	10
200 Quallis, an iron thin pan, three foot diameter each ⸺	1	2
500 Neſts of quallis, three in a neſt	1	2

One

	Coft in China, in Dollars.	Sell for at Sooloo.
One million of pieces China ware, confifting of fmall terrenes and bafons in nefts, big and fmall, plates and bafons with red edges for Mindano, &c. &c. per hundred	1	2
200 Pieces of flowered filks —	6	10

Befides tea, cutlery, and other hard ware, brafs wire, gongs, beads of all colours, like fwan fhot—fire works, &c. &c.

The Returns are in the following Articles.

		Coft at Sooloo.	Selling price in China.
Black fwallo per pecul	—	15	30
White ditto —	—	10	20
Wax —	—	15	25
Teepye or pearl oyfter fhells	—	$1\frac{1}{2}$	5
Birds nefts per catty —	—	6	9
Tortoifhell, price uncertain.			

Alfo agal-agal, a fea weed ufed as gum or glue, and many other articles, fuch as Carooang oil, clove bark, black wood, ratans, fago, various barks for dying,—Caffia, pepper, native camphire, fandal wood, curious fhells for grottos—pearls, which require great judgment to deal in, alfo feed pearl from the Molucca iflands, and fpices.

The Sultanfhip in Sooloo is hereditary, but the government mixt. About fifteen Datoos, who may be called the nobility, make the greater part of the legiflature. Their title is hereditary to the eldeft fon, and they fit in council with the Sultan. The Sultan has two votes in this affembly, and each Datoo has one. The heir apparent (who, when I was there, was Datoo Alamoodine) if he fide with the Sultan, has two votes; but, if againft him, only one. There

are

are two reprefentatives of the people, called Manteries, like the military tribunes of the Romans.

The common people of Sooloo, called Telli-manhood, enjoy much real freedom, owing to the above reprefentation ; but the Tellimanhood, or vaffals of the adjacent iflands named Tappool, Seaffee, Tawee-tawee and others, being the eftates of particular Datoos, are often ufed in a tyrannical manner by their chiefs. I have been told that their haughty lords vifiting their eftates, will fometimes with impunity demand and carry off young women, whom they happen to fancy, to fwell the number of their Sandles (Concubines) at Sooloo. Varioufly do thofe iflands groan under the tyranny of their mafters.

When I was here, one Jaffier had juft returned from the ifland Tappool, where he had been fettling petty infurrections. Blood was certainly drawn from the men, and I faw fome prows arrive thence, with married women, unmarried women and children, all condemned to flavery. That day the talk was in town, " Dato Jaffier is returned from conquering his enemies." No farther enquiry was made : for thofe Datoos in their oppreffions fupport one another.

There is a law both at Magindano and Sooloo, that no Chinefe can be made a flave, but, at either place, for a fum advanced by a Datoo, or great man, to a Chinefe, and fuch advances are often forced upon them, they every twelve months
are

are obliged to pay a very high intereſt, perhaps twenty-five or thirty per cent.; the lender often refuſing to receive back the principal at the end of the year, unleſs indeed the Chineſe make appear that he is going to return to his own country; in which caſe it is never refuſed. This has already been hinted.

On this iſland, the nobles are extremely diſſo-lute. Thoſe who have more than one wife, which is not very common, keep each in a ſepa-rate houſe; but their diſſoluteneſs conſiſts in their numerous concubines and intrigues: for here women have as much liberty in going abroad as in Europe.

Malay women bathe daily in rivers or in ponds. On Sooloo and Magindano, the middle and lower ranks are leſs decent on thoſe occaſions, than the Malays farther weſt: they go into the water almoſt naked; whereas, the Malay women of Sumatra, Borneo, Celebes, and their adjacencies, wrap their bodies in a ſort of wide bottomleſs ſack, con-taining about two yards of broad cotton cloth, with the ends ſewed together, like what in Ben-gal is a lungy. This ſhrouds them from head to heel. The Sooloos have an annual cuſtom of bathing in the ſea, men and women together, but decently covered; which is alſo a Badjoo cuſ-tom, as we ſhall ſee.

At Sooloo, and the many iſlands around, which form a great Archipelago, the pearl fiſhery has been

been famous many ages.* This is the fource of their wealth, and fets them more at eafe than any Malays I ever knew, though their ifland does not generally produce fo much rice as they confume. They trade therefore to Magindano with Chinefe articles for that grain, and make great profit, as no Chinefe junks have for a long time gone thither.

The pearl fifhery, minutely defcribed by Mr. Dalrymple, proves alfo to the Sooloos, the caufe of their confequence amongft their neighbours, as being a nurfery for feamen, ready to man a fleet of prows upon an emergency. The prefent Sultan Ifrael, to whom his father Amiralmoomine had given up the reins of government, in 1773, hinted to me they have gold in their hills; but that, for the above reafon, they difcourage the fearching after it. They have often had fea fights with the Borneans, and always beaten them. Their way of fighting is feldom in the open fea, but by furprife in harbours. The prows of the Sooloos are very neatly built, from fix to forty tons burden, fail well; and are all fitted with the tripod maft. They have alfo prows much fmaller, down to fampans; but their fampans are feldom of one tree, large timber not abounding on Sooloo, as on the more confiderable adjacent iflands. The Sooloo colours are the gates of Mecca, red, on a white ground.

* In the fea between Mindano and Sooloo is a pearl fifhery, inferior to none in the Indies, either in point of colour or fize. HARRIS's VOY. p. 685.

Their

Their drudges, for the Teepye or pearl oyſter, are generally made of bamboo, very ſlight, and ſunk with a ſtone. The large pearls are the property of the Datoos, on whoſe eſtates they are found; for thoſe paramounts claim the property of the banks, as well as of the dry land. There are rich Teepye banks on the north and eaſt ſide of Tawee-Tawee. The Chineſe merchants, very ſecret on thoſe occaſions, contrive often to pur-chaſe from the fiſhermen, pearls of great value; ſo defrauding the Datoos, of what theſe pretend their property. Here are alſo many Badjoo fiſh-ermen, who by their long reſidence, are become vaſſals of the Datoos; but, as they were origi-nally from another country, and ſpeak, beſide the Sooloo, a language of their own, their ſupe-riors are more tender of oppreſſing them, than their immediate vaſſals on the iſlands.

The Sooloos have a particular way of fiſhing with hook and line. They put into the boat a number of ſtones, about a pound weight each; then wind their line with the baited hook round one of the ſtones, and throw it overboard into deep water. The ſtone deſcends, and when the fiſherman judges it has quitted the hook, he pulls this up to the ſurface with or without a fiſh. On the ſame principle do they fiſh amongſt the Mo-lucca iſlands, by fixing the hook to the leaf of a coco nut tree, tied to a ſtone, as has been related in the account of New Guinea. They alſo bruiſe a certain plant called tublee, which they then put either into the ſea or freſh water; its juice ſtupi-fies the fiſh, which then floats dead atop: this is

practiſed

practifed in all Malay countries. The Sooloo tongue has a good deal of the Bifayan or Philippine mixed with it; alfo a little of the Magindano dialect, and fome Malay words. The character is, with fome variation, the Arabic.

The better fort fpeak Malay, and thofe who trade abroad, generally underftand it. While the Englifh were there in 1773, we converfed in Malay.

The arts are in greater forwardnefs here than at Magindano: the prows are built much neater. In the common market, is alfo a copper currency, a convenience much wanted at Magindano; where, as has been faid, the market currency is rice.

The Sooloos have in their families many Bifayan, fome Spanifh flaves, whom they purchafe from the Illanon and Magindano cruifers. Sometimes they purchafe whole cargoes, which they carry to Paffir, on Borneo; where, if the females are handfome, they are bought up for the Batavia market. The mafters fometimes ufe their flaves cruelly, affuming the power of life and death over them. Many are put to death for trifling offences, and their bodies left above ground. An attempt of elopement is here feldom pardoned, or indeed at Magindano. Yet, the diftance being fo fmall from either Sooloo or Selangan, to the Spanifh fettlement, I have wondered how any ftay, as they are not clofely confined.

The

The Bisayan slaves play often on the violin, and the Sooloos are fond of European music. I have seen the Sultan Israel, who was educated at Manilla, and his niece Potely Diamelen, dance a tolerable minuet. I have also seen the Datoos go down a country dance; but, as they wore heavy slippers, they did it clumsily.

The Sooloos are not only neat in their cloaths, but dress gaily. The men go generally in white waistcoats, buttoned down to the wrist; with white breeches, sometimes strait, sometimes wide. The ladies wear likewise a fine white waistcoat, fitted close; which shows the shape; and their petticoats, which is worn over drawers, that reach the knee, comes but a little way below it. Both sexes are fond of gaming.

There are some good harbours amongst the islands, that form the Sooloo archipelago; particularly behind Bewa-bewa, west, and near to Tawee-tawee, about the islands Tappool, and Seassee, also, between Boobooan, and Tapeantana, south of Basilan, in the strait that divides it from Sooloo. Several are also behind the islands, that almost join the main island. However, before the town of Bewan, is no proper harbour; but the road is good in the S. W. monsoon, as it is on the N. W. part of the island. In the N. E. monsoon, the wind at N. E. does not blow into it; but, it is open to the N. W. from which quarter, blows sometimes a gale at the shifting of the monsoons, as in Atcheen road; which this road of Sooloo, in that respect, very much resembles.

The

The high prieſt, or Calipha at Sooloo, in 1773, was a Turk; he had travelled a good deal in Europe, and was a very intelligent man. I preſented him with a map of the world, which pleaſed him mightily. He talked much to the Sooloos, his ſcholars, for he kept a reading ſchool, of the ſtrength of Gibraltar. When he ſpoke of Conſtantinople, he called it Roma.

The Buggeſſes are a high ſpirited people. We had at Sooloo many of them in our pay, whom we had inliſted at Paſſir. One day, a Sooloo having ſtole ſomething from a Buggeſs, I ſaw the Buggeſs in full purſuit of him through the town, with a blunderbuſs in his hand; had he come up with the thief, the conſequences might have been fatal.

Some time after, when I had left Sooloo, I was told there had been a fray between the Sooloos, and our Buggeſſes; and that the latter, though much inferior in number, being only forty, had drawn out with their blunderbuſſes againſt the whole town.

A Buggeſs had been gaming with a Sooloo; the latter loſing, ſaid he would pay him next day. The Buggeſs accordingly meeting him in the paſſar or market, aſked for his due, which the Sooloo refuſing, the Buggeſs ſnatched from him a handkerchief, and ran off. Immediately ſeveral Sooloos, with drawn creſſes, purſued the Buggeſs, who fled for protection to the Buggeſs guard. A ſentinel ſeeing his brother cloſely purſued by armed men, fired amongſt them, with

his

his blunderbuſs.　Very luckily nobody was killed, but the General Almilbadar's nephew was hurt in the face, near the eye.　Upon this a mob roſe : the Buggeſſes turned out into the ſtreet, and preſented their loaded arms ; but, by the happy interpoſition of Sultan Iſrael, and Potely Diamelen, the affair went no farther.　Mr. Herbert, Mr. Alcock, and others, who were preſent, prevailed on the Buggeſſes not to fire.

Had one blunderbuſs gone off amongſt the crowd, there would have been much bloodſhed, (for theſe arms are generally loaded with a number of piſtol balls) as the Sooloos ſtood oppoſite near them, with uplifted lances.　Next day a handſome pecuniary ſatisfaction was made by Mr. Herbert, to the General's nephew, who was ſlightly hurt, and the Buggeſſes were immediately embarked for Balambangan.　Much about this time, two Dutch ambaſſadors arrived at Sooloo in a large ketch from Ternate : one of the gentlemen was Mynheer Shall.　They told Mr. Herbert, not yet gone to Balambangan, that the Sooloos had invited them.

Notwithſtanding the Buggeſſes are allowed in bravery to ſurpaſs the Sooloos, the latter have, on ſeveral occaſions, behaved very well againſt the Spaniards.　A body of Spaniards once attacking ſome Sooloos, who did not much exceed them in number, the Sooloos knelt, and with their targets before them, received the fire of the enemy, then ruſhing with their lances, defeated them.　The

A a　　　　　　Sooloos

Sooloos are not much accuſtomed to the uſe of fire
arms, but depend upon lance, ſword and dagger.

The ſtate of Sooloo is ſmall, as has been ſaid,
containing ſcarce above 60,000 inhabitants; yet
are theſe very powerful, and have under them,
not only moſt of the iſlands that compoſe that
archipelago, but great part of Borneo, ſome of
which they have granted to the Engliſh. They
have the character of being treacherous, and of
endeavouring always to ſupply by fraud, what
they cannot effect by force.

It has been related in the hiſtory of Magindano,
that the Sooloos killed their king Kuddy, when
they pretended to mean him aſſiſtance. According to Fakymolano's account, the ſame piece of
treachery was tranſacted at Borneo.

Long had a deadly hate ſubſiſted, and ſtill ſub-
ſiſts, between Sooloo and Borneo, the Borneans
alledging the Sooloos had encroached on their
territories.

About fifty years ago, a Bornean Pangaran was
at war with the Eang de Patuan (ſuch is ſtiled the
ſovereign) of the place. He had fortified himſelf
on an iſland called Pulo Chirming, at the mouth
of the river Borneo, and called on the Sooloos to
aſſiſt him. They came, but worſted by the Borneans, they fell upon the Pangaran and defeated
him. They then plundered the iſland, and ſailed
home.

Not

Not above twenty years after, the Sultan of Sooloo, Amiralmoomine, went to Samboangan on a vifit. He bought goods from Don Zacharias the governor, giving the Don his own price, made prefents to the officers of the garrifon, and loft his money to them, as if accidentally, by gaming with dice. Still refolved to ingratiate himfelf with the governor, the Sultan wanted to make him a prefent of forty male flaves, whom he had dreft in rich liveries on the occafion. Many of them were natives of Papua or New Guinea. Zacharias refufed the prefents, fufpecting the Sultan of fome defign. The Sultan then afked leave to go to Manilla. He went thither, and faid to the archbifhop, " I will " turn Chriftian, let the Spaniards take Sooloo, " fend the ftubborn Datoos to Samboangan; make " me king there, I then will oblige every one to " embrace your religion."

The Spaniards liftened to him, and he returned to Samboangan with an armada. Thence they went to Sooloo; and Bantillan, firft coufin to Amiralmoomine, was proclaimed Sultan.

The Spaniards chanced to be beaten, and the old Sultan Amiralmoomine returned with them to Samboangan. Here he defired to fend for his wife and children; which permiffion was readily granted. With the family came many of the Sooloos. On their landing, the governor found out by his fpies, that they had many concealed arms in their prows; which lay in the road oppofite the fort. He ordered the prows inftantly to be gone, made the

A a 2 Sultan

Sultan and his family prifoners, and fent them to Manilla; whence the Sultan was releafed by the Englifh arms in the late war.

The Spaniards were certainly in poffeffion of the town of Bowan, before the year 1646; I have there feen ruins of fome of their mafonry.

Only feven years have elapfed fince the Sultan of Koran, where live the people of Tedong on the N. E. coaft of Borneo, was at war with the Sultan of Booroo, on the fame coaft. One of them applied to the Sooloos for affiftance. The Datoos Alamoodine, and Noquela went; and, watching their opportunity, attacked both the Sultans, plundered them, and carried them with their wives, children, and many of their head men to Sooloo. They were fome time after fent back, on condition that they fhould become tributary, and in a manner fubject to Sooloo; which they are at this day. From this country the Sooloos get moft of the fago, and many articles, which they fell to the Chinefe; fwallo, cowries, tortoifhell, and the reft. They endeavour to preclude the Tedongers from trading with any but themfelves; for the Sooloos well underftand the benefits that arife from reftricting the trade of their conquefts or colonies: and the Datoos are all traders. Even the Sultan is a merchant.

The four inftances already given, might fuffice to afcertain the character of the Sooloos, which may however be properly crowned, by their conduct

duct to the Englifh fettlement at Balambangan
in February 1775.

When John Herbert, Efq; went thither early
in the preceding year, he found great want of
buildings, to accommodate the Company's fervants, civil and military; thofe gentlemen who
had juft been faved from the fhipwreck of the
Royal Captain on the fhoals of Paragoa, as well
as the crew of that fhip. About this time one
Teting, a Sooloo Datoo, and firft coufin to Sultan
Ifrael, came with many of his vaffals to Balambangan, offered his fervice as a builder, was employed
by Mr. Herbert, and in the whole of his behaviour,
gave fatisfaction. The Datoo, falling fick, went
home to Sooloo for the recovery of his health.
This bleffing foon obtained, he returned to the
profecution of his tafk at Balambangan.

He now brought from the Sultan and Council
letters recommending him as a truft-worthy perfon,
to erect whatever warehoufes or buildings might
be wanted. With him came two other Datoos,
Mulloc and Noquela. But Datoo Teting took
care to fhow only part of his numerous followers,
concealing the reft in the ifland of Banguey, and
even in fome receffes of Balambangan; which,
being covered with wood, as thofe iflands generally are, there was no great fear of difcovery.

Surmifes, however, had fome days begun to
fpread reports of a plot, while Teting proceeded
with fuch addrefs, that the chief and council, who
were

were not without their fufpicions, apprehended no danger very nigh.

During the night, ftrict watch was kept all over the fettlement. At dawn, the gun, as ufual, announced the morning; and for a few moments, tranquillity reigned. A houfe at fome fmall diftance fuddenly fired, proved the fignal to the Sooloos. They rufhed into the fort, killed the fentries, and turned the guns againft the Buggefs guard. The few fettlers, lately rendered fewer by death, were fain to make their efcape in what veffels they could find.

As the true cinnamon is faid to grow both on Sooloo and Mindano,* the following account of that which grows on Ceylon, will not be unpleafing here.

* Cinnamon they have as good as any in Ceylon; but nobody having any property in the trees, they tear and deftroy the bark at all feafons, which is the reafon the world is fo little acquainted with the cinnamon of Mindano.
HARRIS's VOYAGE, Vol. I. p. 685.

CHAP.

C H A P. XV.

An Account of the Cinnamon Tree in Ceylon, and its several Sorts, communicated by the chief Inspector of the Cinnamon Trade, and Manufacturer in that Island, to Albertus Seba, a noted Druggist at Amsterdam. Translated by he late Dr. Scheucher, F. R. S.

" THE first and best sort of cinnamon, which grows in great plenty in Ceylon, and is peculiar to that island, is called by the natives, *rasse coronde*, which is as much as to say sharp, sweet cinnamon. It is this choice sort which is exported yearly by the Dutch East India Company, by whom it has been prohibited under severe penalties, that any other sort whatever should be mixt with it.

1776. January.

" The second sort is called *canatte coronde*, that is, bitter and astringent cinnamon; for the Ceylonese, in their language, call cinnamon in general *coronde*; and *canatte* signifies bitter and astringent. The bark of this tree comes off very easily, and smells very agreeably, when fresh; but has a bitter taste. It is an advantage to us that this does not grow in great plenty hereabouts; because, else, one might easily mistake it for a better; as indeed, in general, it requires a good deal of skill and attention so to distinguish the cinnamon trees from each other, as not to choose now and then an inferior sort for the best. The root of this second tree yields a very good camphire.

" The

" The third fort is called by the Ceylonefe, *capiroe coronde*, which is as much as to fay, camphorated cinnamon, becaufe it has a very ftrong fmell and tafte of camphire.   It grows plentifully enough on the ifland, but not in the eaftern parts of it.   However, they find means, now and then, to fend it over privately and fell it to the Danes and Englifh, who come to trade upon the coaft of Coromandel ; for, as long as there is one port in the ifland left open, abundance of this fort of bad merchandife may be exported.   Befides there is a fort of a canella, growing upon the continent of India, about Goa, which is very like this fpecies of cinnamon tree, though it has nothing of the true cinnamon. The fame fort of canella agrees in many refpeéts with the *canella Malabarica fylveſtris*, a wild cinnamon tree, growing upon the coaft of Malabar. And although, with regard to the fhape of the tree, and the outward appearance of the bark and leaves, there is very little difference to be obferved between thefe two forts of Canella, and the abovementioned firft and good fort of cinnamon, yet the latter is vaftly fuperior in richnefs, fweetnefs, and virtue.

" The fourth fort of cinnamon is called by the Ceylonefe, *welle coronde*, that is, the fandy cinnamon ; becaufe upon chewing it, one feels, as it were, bits of fand between the teeth ; though, in fact, there is nothing fandy in it.   The bark of this tree comes off eafily enough ; but is not fo eafily rolled up into a fibular form as other forts of cinnamon are, being apt to burft open and unfold itfelf.   It is of a fharp and bitterifh tafte, and

the

the root of it yields but a fmall quantity of camphire.

" The fifth fort is called *fewel coronde. Sewel* in the Ceylonefe language, fignifies mucilaginous, or glutinous. This cinnamon acquires a very con- fiderable degree of hardnefs, which the chewing of it fufficiently proves. It has otherwife little tafte, and ungrateful fmell ; but the colour of it is very fine ; and it is not many years fince I firft took notice, that the natives, who are all blacks, mix a good deal of this mucilaginous cinnamon with the firft and beft fort, the colour being much alike, excepting only that in the good fort fome few yel- lowifh fpots appear towards the extremities.

" The fixth fort is called by the natives, *nicke coronde,* the tree which bears it having a good deal of refemblance to another tree, which is by them called *nicke gas,* and the fruit it bears *nicke.* The bark of this fort of cinnamon tree has no manner of tafte or fmell, when taken off, and is made ufe of by the natives only in phyfic. By roafting it, they obtain a water and oil, with which they an- noint themfelves, thinking, by fuch liniment, to keep off all noxious fumes and infections in the air. They likewife extract a juice from the leaves, which they fay cools and ftrengthens the brain, if the head be rubbed with it.

" The feventh fort is called *dawel coronde,* that is drum cinnamon ; in Low Dutch, *trommel caneel.* The reafon of this appellation is, that the wood of this tree, when grown hard, is light and tough ;
and

and that fort, of which the natives make fome of their veffels and drums, which they call *dawel*, is ftript of its bark, while the tree is yet growing, and is of a pale colour. The natives ufe it in the fame manner with the fixth fort.

" The eight fort is called *catte coronde* ; *Catte* in the Ceylonefe language, fignifying a thorn or prickle ; for this tree is very prickly. The bark is fomewhat like cinnamon, but the leaves differ very much ; and the bark itfelf has nothing either of the tafte or fmell of cinnamon. The natives ufe the root, bark and leaves of this tree in medicine, applying them in form of cataplafms to tumours and fwellings from corrupt blood, which they fay it cures in a fhort time.

" The ninth fort is called *mael coronde*, or the flowering cinnamon ; becaufe this tree is always in bloffom. The flowers come neareft to thofe of the firft and beft fort, called *raffe coronde* ; but they bear no fruit, which the other does. The fubftance of the wood never becomes fo folid and weighty in this, as in the other cinnamon trees above men-tioned, which have fometimes eight, nine, or ten foot in circumference. If this everflowering cinna-mon tree be cut or bored, a limpid water will iffue out of the wound, as it does out of the *European birch tree* ; but it is of ufe only for the leaves and bark.

The inhabitants of Ceylon fay there is yet ano-ther fort of cinnamon, which they call *toupat coronde*, or the three leaf cinnamon. It does not grow in
that

that part of the country which the Dutch Eaſt India company is poſſeſſed of, but higher up towards
Candia. Having never ſeen it myſelf, I will out of
regard to truth, ſay nothing farther of it.

" And thus, Sir, I have given you, I hope, a
ſatisfactory account of the ſeveral ſorts of cinnamon trees growing in this country. I can aſſure
you that you are the firſt to whom I ever communicated ſo particular a deſcription ; for, having
been almoſt theſe fifteen years employed as chief
inſpector of the cinnamon trade and manufacture
here, I have with much pains and attention, ſo
ſtrictly enquired into this matter, that at laſt I
found out all the ſorts of bad cinnamon, which
were formerly mixed with the true and good ; and
have been able to ſhew ſamples of the bark, root,
and leaves of every one of them, to our Directors ;
who, to prove their ſatisfaction that a thing of ſuch
conſequence was, after many laborious ſearches,
at laſt diſcovered, and thinking it well worth a
farther enquiry, were pleaſed to augment the
ſalary annexed to this office.

" It remains, that I ſhould inform you in how
many years the cinnamon trees grow ripe enough
to have the bark ſtript off. Here I ſhall confine
myſelf to the firſt and beſt ſort, which is yearly
exported by the Company ; and what I ſhall mention of it, may ſerve to anſwer in ſome meaſure
ſuch queries as might be made about the reſt.

" All the ſorts of cinnamon trees, the beſt
as well as the inferior, muſt grow a certain number
of years before the bark be fit for taking off: with
this

this difference, however, that fome of the trees of
the fame fort, for inftance of the beft, will ripen
two or three years fooner than others; which is
owing to the difference of the foil they grow in.
Thofe which grow in valleys, where the ground is
a fine whitifh fand (and many are fuch valleys in
the ifland of Ceylon) will in five years be fit to
have the bark taken off; others, on the contrary,
which ftand in a wet flimy foil, muft have feven or
eight years to grow, before they be ripe enough
for that purpofe. Again, thofe trees are later, that
grow in the fhade of larger trees, by which the fun
is kept from their roots : and hence it is that the
bark of fuch trees has not that fweetnefs, or agreeable tafte, obfervable in the bark of thofe trees
which grow in a white fandy ground, where, with
little wet, they ftand full expofed to the fun ; but
proves of a bitterifh tafte, fomewhat aftringent, and
fmells like camphire.

" For, by the heat of the fun's rays, the camphire is made fo thin and volatile, that it rifes, and
mingles with the juices of the tree, where it under-
goes a fmall fermentation ; and then rifing ftill
higher, between the fubftance of the wood and the
fine inner membrane of the bark, it is at laft fo
effectually diffufed through the branches and
leaves, that there is not the leaft trace of it to be
perceived. Meanwhile, that thin and glutinous
membrane, which lines the bark between it and the
fubftance of the wood, attracts, and fucks in all the
pureft, fweeteft, and moft agreeable particles of
the juice ; leaving the thick and grofs ones, which
                                                    are

are pufhed forward, and ferve to nourifh the branches, leaves, and fruit.

" What I here mention, is conformable to my own obfervation ; and I have often had occafion to demonftrate this fact to the curious. If the bark be frefh taken off, that juice which remains in the tree, has a bitterifh tafte not unlike that of cloves. On the contrary, if you tafte the inner membrane of the bark, when frefh taken off, you will find it of a moft exquifite fweetnefs, and extremely plea- fant to the tafte ; whereas the outward part of the bark differs but very little in tafte from that of the common trees; which fhows plainly, that its whole fweetnefs is owing to the inner membrane. But when the bark is laid in the fun to be dried and wound up, that oily and pleafing fweetnefs of the inner membrane, communicates and diffufes itfelf through the whole outward part of it, (firft ftrip- ped, however, while yet upon the tree, of its outer greenifh coat) and imbues it fo ftrongly, as to make the bark a commodity, which for fragrance and fweetnefs is coveted all over the earth.

" It may not be amifs to take notice alfo, how many years the cinnamon trees, when come to maturity, will continue in that ftate, fo that the bark, when taken off, fhall have loft nothing of its fweetnefs and virtue. And, to clear up this point, it muft be obferved, that the bark may yet be taken from the trees, which have ftood fourteen, fifteen, or fixteen years, according to the quality of the foil they ftand in ; but, beyond that time, they grow thicker, and lofe by degrees, their tafte and agreeable fweetnefs, while the bark contracts
the

the tafte of camphire: befides, the bark is then grown fo thick, that, though laid in the fun, it will no longer fhrink and wind itfelf up, but remain flat.

" And here it may be thought a fit fubject of enquiry, how it comes to pafs, that, confidering what vaft quantities of cinnamon have been exported from this ifland, and fold all over the world, by Europeans as well as natives, for two hundred years paft; and fince the way hither, by the Eaft Indies, has been but fome centuries explored by the Portuguefe, (long before was it difcovered and known); I fay, how, confidering this, it comes to pafs, that there are ftill fuch numbers of good trees fit to be barked, and growing yearly, on the ifland. To folve this queftion, feveral authors, defcribing the ifland of Ceylon, have committed a confiderable miftake, when they affure their readers, that, when the bark has been ftript off the trees, it grows again in four or five years, and becomes fit for ftripping anew. I can affure you, Sir, that this affertion is equally contrary to the courfe of nature, and the poffibility of obfervation. Nor do I believe, that there is, in any part of the world, a tree, which, if entirely ftript of its bark, could grow, or even vegetate longer. That part, at leaft, where the bark has been taken off, will quickly parch, and die away; but the root may meantime remain entire, and in good condition; which fhows, why fuch a number of trees is ready to be barked every year. For, although the cinnamon tree, after the bark has been once taken off, is cut down to the very root, as are in Europe

rope oaks, birches, alders, and willows; yet, the root will quickly pufh forth new fhoots, which will ripen in a fhort time; I mean, in five, fix, feven, or eight years, fome fooner, fome later, and then yield their quantity of bark. Hence it appears, how far the old roots are inftrumental to the growth and plenty of cinnamon trees; but the fruit which falls from the trees, contributes much towards the fame end: and it is particularly owing to a certain kind of wild doves, which, from their feeding on the fruit of the cinnamon tree, are called *cinnamon eaters*, that the tree grows fo plentifully in this ifland. For the doves, when they fetch food for their young, flying here and there, difperfe vaft quantities of the fruit all over the fields; which occafions the rife of fo many thoufand young trees, along the roads, that they look like a foreft. So plentifully grows here this excellent tree: I call it excellent, becaufe indeed, I know of none preferable. I need not point out to you what remarkable operations of divine providence the hiftory of the cinnamon tree affords to an attentive eye.

" Hardly is any thing fo univerfally grateful, and efteemed by all nations, as true cinnamon. The oil drawn from it by fire, is reckoned one of the ftrongeft cordial medicines: the camphire which comes out of the root, is likewife of great ufe in feveral diftempers; as is alfo the oil of camphire, a very coftly thing, diftilled from the leaves of the tree; and laftly, the fruits with their oil. In fhort there is no part of the cinnamon tree that is not of fome ufe in phyfic. I purpofely avoid fpeaking of the
large

large gains the Company makes by the yearly export of this precious commodity."

Additions to the foregoing Account, by Albertus Seba,
F. R. S.

" Having fome years ago, bought out of the Eaft India Company's warehoufes at Amfterdam, a confiderable quantity of cinnamon leaves, or *folia malabathri*, packed up in large chefts, I happened to find in one of them, the flowers of the cinnamon, as big as the Italian bean flowers, and of a blue colour. I chanced likewife to meet with the fruit; but could not find any in the other chefts.

" In 1722, and 1723, I bought of the fame company, the oil which is expreffed from the fruit of the cinnamon tree; as alfo that which is boiled out of it, which is of a very good confiftence, and white, and is by the Eaft India Company called cinnamon wax: for the king of Candia caufes candles to be made of it, which, for their agreeable fcent, are burnt only by himfelf, and at his court. However, he permits his fubjects to exprefs the juice of another fruit, not unlike the fruit of the cinnamon. But this juice, being only a thin fat fubftance, like the oil of olives, cannot be otherwife burned than in lamps.

" The Indians ufe this cinnamon wax in phyfic, and give it in luxations, fractures, falls, and contufions; that in cafe any inward part be touched, it may by its balfam heal them. They give
it

it alſo in bloody fluxes, to one dram, or a dram and a half. Outwardly applied, it makes the ſkin more beautiful, ſofter, and ſmoother than any known pomade.

" The leaves of the cinnamon tree yield a bit-teriſh oil, reſembling the oil of cloves, mixed with a little good oil of cinnamon : it is called *oleum malabathri,* or oil of cinnamon leaves. This is an aromatic, and reckoned an excellent remedy in head akes, pains of the ſtomach, and other diſ-tempers.

" The oil of the root of the cinnamon tree, is properly an oil of camphire : for of this the roots afford a good quantity. About two years, or ſome-what more, ago, I bought a bottle of our Eaſt India Company, at my own price. Several bottles were together in a box, on which was wrote in low Dutch, *deſe oliteyten ſyn tot ſen Geſchenk nyt candia geſchikt :* that is, theſe oils were ſent as a preſent out of Candia : which ſhows that they are without adulteration, nor can they be but much eſteemed. If this oil be diſtilled in glaſs veſſels, there diffuſes with it that ſort of camphire, which the Indians call camphire Baros, or camphire of Borneo ; which ſhoots in thin tranſparent cryſtals, forming, on the recipient, a beautiful variety of trees, not unlike thoſe which in very froſty weather are to be ſeen on windows. This ſort of camphire, of great efficacy in phyſic, is gathered and kept for the king of Can-dia's own uſe, who eſteems it an excellent cordial. Not only the camphire Baros, but the oil of camphire, drawn from the roots of the cinnamon tree,

B b   is

is a cordial, if taken inwardly : it ſtrengthens the ſtomach, expels wind, and has been found of great ſervice in arthritic or gouty diſorders. It is alſo a diuretic : the doſe ten or twelve drops, upon a bit of ſugar, or in a proper vehicle. Outwardly, it is applied in all arthritic pains from colds and obſtructions: rubbed on the affected part with a warm hand, it will preſently leſſen the pain, and by degrees take it off. It is now about ſix and thirty years ſince I ſerved in the ſhop of Nicholas Dumbſtdorff, at Amſterdam. That gentleman was then ſo afflicted with arthritic pains, that he could reſt neither night nor day. Though he called in the aſſiſtance of ſeveral noted phyſicians, and tried abundance of medicines, he could find no relief, till adviſed to cauſe himſelf to be anointed with the oil of the root of the cinnamon tree, of which he then happened to have a good quantity. I remember very well, that I anointed him myſelf, rubbing the oil on all the affected parts, with my hand warmed by holding it to an oven. This I did twice a day, for an hour together ; and, though when this cure was begun with him, his hands and feet were by convulſions, and the violence of the pain, ſo contracted, that they grew quite crooked and full of nodes ; yet in a fortnight's time he became ſo much better, that he could ſleep well anights, feeling neither pains nor cramps. In ſix weeks he could walk about his room ; whereas, before the anointing, he was not able to ſtir either hand or foot. This unction had proceeded three months, when the patient ſo recovered of his indiſpoſition, that he continued free from gout ever after, and lived fifteen years in good health. Nor
this

this alone do I affirm from my own certain knowledge : I have fince advifed feveral in his condition
to do the like, and with as good fuccefs. Phyfici-
ans have wrote largely on the virtues of common
camphire : but many are ftill the hidden qualities
in this efficacious medicine."

C H A P. XVI.

*Sail for Kamaladan Harbour—See fome Sooloo Prows---
Meet with Tuan Hadjee in the Banguey Corocoro—
Pafs the Ifland Lutangan—Harbour of Boobooan—
Obliged to anchor on the Coaft of Sooloo—Pafs within Liberan Ifland, on the Coaft of Borneo—Directions for that Paffage—Pafs Balambangan—Arrive
in Pelampan Harbour, behind Pulo Gaya—Meet
fome Englifh Veffels—Proceed to Abia, in queft of
the Mindano Officers, by whom I write to Rajah
Moodo—Gale at N. E.---Haul the Veffel afhore---
Depart thence, and arrive at the Englifh Factory
on Borneo.*

O N the night of *Monday* the 8th of *January*,
as has been faid, I got over the bar of the Pelangy,
accompanied by two of Rajah Moodo's foldiers.
We then fteered to the fouth of Bunwoot, loaded
our arms, and got every thing in readinefs, for
fear of being way-laid by the Sooloos. Next day
we pulled down our attop covering, and threw it
overboard. At 4 P. M. the fouth end of Bunwoot
bore S. E. five leagues : it was then fhut in with

Timoko

Timoko hill. About noon I fpoke with a prow
from Sooloo: fhe belonged to Rajah Moodo, and
was bound to Selangan.

On the 10th, had moſt of the night a very freſh
wind out of the Illano bay, which was now open.
At funrife, could fee Lutangan iſland, with a gentle rifing on it, bearing N. W. fix leagues, while
Baganean point bore N. E. half E. Baganean
point was then in one with a Sugar Loaf hill a good
way up the country. At funfet, Lutangan bore
W. half N. Stood to the northward, for Kamaladan harbour, near which Rajah Moodo had directed me to lay in rice, for our provifion, at a
village called Se Tappo, where Datoo Aſſim his
relation lived.

Variable winds during moſt part of the 11th.
We had anchored at two A. M. fix fathom fand
and mud, within two miles of a low point, which
lies to the northward of Pulo Lutangan. To the
eaſtward of this low point ſtretches a reef of
coral rocks, about three miles with two and three
fathom upon it. About noon weighed and worked up the harbour, wind at N. E. At one P. M.
came in fight, between Lutangan and the main,
four prows, with no colours hoiſted: when we
ſtood towards them, they failed and rowed from
us. We then put about, upon which one of the
fmalleſt ſtood after and fpoke to us. They were
Sooloo prows, and feemed to be working into the
harbour of Kamaladan: I aſked the maſter of the
fmall prow that fpoke to us, why the others ran
away, and why they fhowed no colours; to which
he

he made an evafive anfwer, not caring perhaps to own they were afraid. Kept working into the bay that lies before the harbour of Kamaladan, with a flood tide, by which we gained ground.

On the 12th, at three in the morning, anchored in five fathom, fandy ground, in a fmall bay on the N. E. fide of the large bay mentioned yefterday ; weighed when the flood made, and at day light perceived the Sooloo prows mentioned yefterday, bearing away towards Mindano. Kept working into Kamaladan harbour ; at ten before noon faw a corocoro near us. Sent Ifhmael the Jerrybatoo in the boat on board. He found her to be the Banguey corocoro with Tuan Hadjee, and Tuan Bobo, one of the Batchian officers : they faid they were bound to Samboangan. Ifhmael took the opportunity of afking Tuan Hadjee for the value of a flave, which the latter fome time had owed him. Tuan Hadjee replied he would foon be with the Englifh at Borneo, and there would fettle the debt. Jerrybatoo told me, that Tuan Hadjee would hardly believe I had been able to get the veffel decked and made into a fchooner. At three in the afternoon, I anchored before the village called Se Tappo, where ftands Datoo Affim's houfe. The Datoo was gone fomewhither into the Illano bay. I could not get rice as I expected, none being ready ; but I got fome fago in its ftead. Here were lying three Sooloo prows. From them I purchafed fome coco nuts and rough rice. They behaved civilly, as in a neutral port ; any where elfe I fhould not have chofen to be a night with

them

them in the fame harbour. Kamaladan harbour
was defcribed in the account of Magindano.

On Saturday the 13th, weighed and worked
out with the ebb tide. At four P. M. anchored in
a fmall bay on the weft fide of this fpacious harbour in five fathom, muddy ground. Found
abundance of oyfters on the fmooth large ftones,
with which the points of the fmall bays are lined.
About funfet we weighed and ftood out of the
harbour, I was then informed by the people I had
fent afhore in the afternoon, to cut wood, that they
had been at the homes of fome Haraforas,
who kept hogs in pens under their houfes. I regretted I had not gone afhore and feen the oddity;
as I had obferved the Haraforas at Tubuan and
Leno harbour, do not breed hogs, being perhaps
forbid, though they kill and eat wild hogs.

Standing out of the harbour on *Sunday* the 14th,
we paffed a clufter of four or five fmall iflands to
the weftward : fome of them bufhy iflands, fome
low and flat, with trees, having regular foundings,
from feven to twenty-eight fathom muddy ground.

At night, being about three miles off the S. E.
point of Lutangan, we had irregular foundings,
feven, eight, and ten fathom, fandy ground, and
coral rocks. At noon we were in the latitude of
7° 9′ N. the fouth point of Bafilan, which makes
like a Chinaman's hat, bearing S. W. by S. eight
or nine leagues. At fun-fet, Bafilan bore from
W. S. W. to N. W. by N. the neareft part being
then

then about three leagues diftant. Saw a low point
on the fouth part of Bafilan.

In the night of the 15th, we paffed the low point
mentioned yefterday ; it is part of a fmall low
ifland : we had thirteen fathom fand, within a mile
of it. Stood on fteering W. S. W. and entered a
found formed by three iflands with hummocs on
them, and feveral low fmall iflands. The found lies
about feven miles fouth of Bafilan, and is formed
by the iflands named Boobooan, Tapeantana and
Lanawan, in Mr. Dalrymple's map. The wind
coming to the N. W. worked almoft through the
found, which has fmooth water, and would hold a
number of fhips, in ten and twelve fathom deep,
fandy ground. The tide turning, we ran back,
and at funfet defcried Tonkyl, a low ifland, where
we had ftopped at the beginning of the voyage.
The eaft end of Tonkyl ftretches to the eaftward
of Belawn, an ifland with a hummoc ; we alfo faw
Duo Blod, bearing W. by N. about fix leagues.

Tuefday the 16th. Moft of the night the wind
was at N. W. which I did not expect in the middle of the N. E. monfoon : this caufed a chopping
fea. Made feveral trips near the Sugar Loaf
iflands, called Deppoolool, the tide favouring us.
In the morning, the wind eafterly brought fine
weather ; it then came again to the W. N. W.
Worked through between Tataran and Deppoolool, where the tide fets very ftrong. Paft Batoo
Mandee (Wafhed Rock) which is no bigger than
a boat ; found eight and ten fathom depth of water,
about a mile N. W. of it. The hills of Sooloo bore
now

now W. S. W. many fmall prows fteering by us
N. E. having twice paft this channel, between
Deppoolool and Tataran, I obferved in the N. E.
monfoon, the tide fet ftrong to the weftward, and
on the contrary.

On *Wednefday* the 17th, in the morning the
wind was fo fcant, that we could not weather
Sooloo.   Therefore we came to under the ifland
Bankoongan, which forms a good harbour.   We
anchored in feven fathom fandy ground, within
piftol fhot of the ifland, and one mile and a half
from the main land of Sooloo.   I fent afhore to
the ifland, and gave a fifherman to underftand,
that the veffel belonged to Magindano, being not
without my apprehenfions of falling into the hands
of the Sooloos.   At fix P. M. failed to get round by
the eaft end of Sooloo.   At eight faw a great fire
on the fhore.   All night I was very uneafy, being
upon an enemy's lee fhore.   Had I fallen into
their hands, they would certainly have kept me a
long time amongft them, being jealous of my reception at Mindano.

On the 18th, early in the morning, paffed to the
eaftward of Sooloo with a frefh gale.   Saw feveral
fmall boats fifhing for pearls to the leeward of the
ifland, where was no fwell; but, the wind blowing
in fudden fqualls off the ifland, the men were continually wet with the fpray.   Could not weather
Tappool. At fun-fet, came to near the S. end of the
ifland Pong Pong, which lies S. W. of Tappool in
twelve fathom.   There are feveral fhores to the
fouthward, and near Tappool.   Here the tides
                                                    run

run regular. Tappool abounds in cattle and coco
nuts.

At day-light of the 19th, fent the boat to Pong
Pong for frefh water: fhe returned at noon with all
the jars full. Weighed and lay up W. N. W.
At fun-fet, the weft end of Sooloo bore N. E. by
N. ten leagues: faw two low iflands a-head.

On *Saturday* the 20th, wind at N. N. E. By day
light, anchored in eleven fathom fand, clofe to a
low fandy ifland: fent thither fome hands, who
picked up many kimas of about eight or nine
pound each. The ifland is called Dafaan. Where
we lay at anchor, Tavitavi bore from S. W. to S.
Seafee S. E. and Tappool E. S. E. At eight in the
morning, weighed, and ftood to the fouthward of
many low little iflets. At four P. M. we perceived
low land bearing from N. to N. E. which I take to
be the iflands called Tajo, or the banks fo called,
where many pearls are got. At fun-fet, faw another low ifland bearing N. W. At noon, a large
prow ftood athwart us, fteering S. W. Got all
ready to receive her, fufpecting her a Mangaio.

On the 21ft, kept lying up N. W. with a full
fail ; wind N. E. by N. About midnight, had a
ftrong rippling of a current. At fun-fet, could fee
the double hummocs of Taganak bearing N. N. W.
and Baguan N. W. half N. about four leagues
diftant : fine weather, and tolerably fmooth water.
In paffing by Sandakan harbour, the ifland Bahala-
tolis is very remarkable : bearing S. it appears a
a flipper ; bearing S. W. a double flipper.

Monday

Monday the 22d. At midnight paſſed to the
northward of Baguan about two miles. In the
morning, could diſcern the iſland of Liberan and
many ſmall ones without it. About noon diſcovered a ſmall iſland bearing N. W. by N. in the
figure of a jockey cap. A dry ſand bears from it
S. S. W. about two miles. Stood to the ſouthward
of them both in twenty-three, twenty, nineteen,
and twelve fathom, muddy ground.*

I have hitherto from Baſilan, taken names of
iſlands from Mr. Dalrymple's map, which I have
found very exact, and which give the ſoundings
without Liberan ; but, as I have gone twice in a
ſmall veſſel along the N. E. coaſt of Borneo within
Liberan, and each time the ſame track, it may not
be amiſs to hint ſomething about it, in caſe ſhips
ſhould be obliged to purſue it, from circumſtances
precluding the other track without Liberan where
the ſoundings are laid down, and which, doubtleſs is the preferable.

In paſſing to the ſouthward of Liberan, keep pretty cloſe to the iſland. There are ſaid to be ſome
deer, which, on being hunted with dogs, immediately take to the water, and are then eaſily killed.
I would adviſe no one to venture after dark into
the inner channel : the outer may be navigated
with much leſs danger. If at anchor, the boat may
not improperly be ſent aſhore to the main oppoſite

* During the N. E. monſoon, the wind blows direct on this
coaſt ; but, being checked by the land, its force is never great,
and the weather is generally fair. A land wind ſometimes
prevails at night, but reaches only a little way.

the

the iſland. At low water ſpring tides, many fine
large oyſters may be found in the mud ; but, if the
time is not nicely hit, none can be had.

From Liberan to Soogoot river's mouth and point
(for a long ſpit runs off it) you croſs the bay of Labook in four, five, ſix, and eight fathom muddy
ground. In the middle of this bay, I once found
by night a ſmall ſpot of coral rocks. Though my
commoodies touched upon it, I could not, by reaſon of the darkneſs, get its exact ſituation ; but,
before and after, we had five fathom. Here the
flood tide ſets S. W. into the bay of Labook, about
three knots and a half on the ſprings. Liberan
lies in the latitude of 6° 2′ N. longitude 116° 08′ E.

In croſſing this bay with a N. W. by N. courſe
from the iſland of Liberan, you will ſoon perceive,
at Soogoot river's mouth, ſome ſhaggy pines, looking as trees generally do at rivers mouths in Malay
countries, that is, like hedge rows, and ſomewhat
disjoined from the land. Steer without them for
a flat iſland, very like Liberan : I call it Cheeſe
Iſland, from its ſhape : it lies north half eaſt ſeven
miles from Soogoot point. Steer pretty cloſe, but
to its ſouthward : many ſmaller iſlands and reefs
of rocks are without and near it. Two ſmall iſlets
bear S. S. W. and S. W. of it, about a mile and
half diſtant. The more eaſtern is a little ſhrubby
iſland ; the other, about one mile farther W. S. W.
I call Tufty Iſland, as bearing a tuft of trees. Leave
them to the ſouthward, and keep in ſix and ſeven
fathom muddy ground. You will then ſee above
water a ſmall ſand, on either ſide of which you
may

may pafs. It lies about nine miles N. W. by W.
from Cheefe ifland. You then come to Ragged
ifland, eight miles eaft of the eaft point of Semad-
dal ifland. This Ragged ifland has fome fhort
ftunted trees upon it, and many fhoals near and
within it. Here anchor may be caft, to examine
the paffage, which has fix or feven fathom water,
muddy ground : the fhoals are generally bold, and
of coral rocks. S. W. of Ragged ifland is a very
fhaggy point upon the main. Having paffed Ragged ifland, you fteer N. W. in five, fix, and feven
fathom water, muddy ground, for Pine-Tree ifland,
which has a fine white beach. From it One-Tree
ifland bears W. by N. You may fteer between
them in ten fathom. From Pine-Tree ifland the
courfe is N. N. W. and N. W. by N. to an ifland
that has a reef extending far off its eaft end : it is
fituate eight miles due fouth of the eaft part of
Malwatty : I call it Bird ifland, many birds rooft-
ing there in the night. Its weft end is bold. If a
fhip takes day light, as the water is generally
fmooth, fhe may with great fafety go this laft-men-
tioned part of the track, as the fhoals are all bold,
and fhow at a diftance ; efpecially if the weather be
clear. There is another track from Pine ifland towards Bird ifland : fteering from Pine ifland weft,
and leaving One-Tree ifland on the right hand,
you will then keep in a nine fathom channel all
the way to Bird ifland, without paffing any fhoals,
or fpots of rocks, but one, which is not far from
One-Tree ifland. Between Shaggy point and Se-
maddal ifland, but nearer the ifland, is a channel
with four fathom water. Up this channel the tide
runs three and four knots.

                                   N. W. from

N. W. from Bird ifland, about five miles, are four or five freeftone rocks, like the ruins of a building, about twenty foot high. Leave them to the fouthward, and a fpot of fand within a mile of them, to the eaftward. In the channel is nine and ten fathom. You may then fteer for Malwally, on which are two harbours, one on the S. W. the other on the S. E. fide of it. The latter is perfectly good, but has a narrow entrance. Malwally lies in latitude 7° o' N. lon. 115° 20' E.

On *Saturday* the 27th, we paft a fhoal bearing E. by S. from Maleangan, five miles from the fhore of Banguey, and five from that of Borneo ; the hummoc on Banguey bearing N. N. W. We then ftood on between Banguey and Maleangan. The beft channel is clofe to Maleangan, a fhoal lying about half a mile from it. At ten, anchored between Banguey and Balambangan. Sent the boat afhore for intelligence. She returned in two hours, having found no inhabitant, but devaftation. We then weighed, and ftood for Borneo.

In the morning of *Sunday* the 28th, could fee Matanany bearing S. S. W. had a great fwell and much rain. At funfet, Kaitan point bore S. S. W. and Pulo Gaya S. W. by S. at the diftance of eight leagues.

Monday the 29th. In the morning fteered in behind Pulo Pangir, and then proceeded to a harbour near Pulo Gaya, behind an ifland called Pelampan, no bigger than an ordinary houfe. Hither from Pulo Gaya leads a reef, covered at high water, and

dry

dry at low, in length about two hundred yards: it
bears fouth of Pulo Pangir and Kaitan point. In
this harbour, the paffage between Pulo Gaya and
the main is plainly to be perceived. It is full of
rocks ; but between them is faid to be a paffage
clofe to Borneo. Beyond this ftrait is Patatan river.
Here I learned that the Mindano prow, difpatched by the Sultan and Rajah Moodo to Mr. Herbert,
was at Tawarran on her return. On this intelligence, I weighed and ran up to Gemel point, to
the northward of Kaitan point. Difpatched three
men to Tawarran over land, to fetch my letters.
Felt here a great ground fwell, in two and a half
fathom water ; upon which I weighed and ftood
out, and found the cable almoft broken.

Tuefday the 30th. Lay to the greater part of the
night, unwilling to pafs Pulo Gaya. At day light,
made fail for the harbour behind Pelampan, where
we had lain before. Anchored in feven fathom
fand and mud, clofe to the fhore. In the evening
my people returned without any tidings of the
Mindano officers. Next morning I went afhore
to Oran Caio Mahomed, the head man of the village Inanan, diftant about fix miles by fea, and two
miles up a river from where we lay. He received
me civilly, and told me that Mr. Herbert, the late
chief of Balambangan, paffing that way to Borneo,
and being in diftrefs for money, had demanded of
him, and been paid, a debt of four hundred and
eighty dollars. The money was due to me for a
cheft of opium I had fold to the headman about
twelve months before. He prefented me with
fome rice, fruits, and other refrefhments. Oran
Caio

Caio Mahomed alſo informed me, that a new chief had ſuperſeded Mr. Herbert at Borneo, and that the Mindano officers were at Abia on their return. That evening, I ſent one of the two ſoldiers Rajah Moodo had appointed to attend me, in the boat, manned with eight people, to Abia, to learn if the information were well founded. About ſunſet, ſaw a ſail in the offing.

Next day, found the veſſel in the offing to be the Speedwell ſnow, with Mr. Herbert, bound to Madras. I went on board the Speedwell, where Mr. Herbert aſſured me he neither had ſent aſhore to Inanan, nor received any thing from Oran Caio Mahomed. The ſnow ſtretching off to ſea, I was ſoon obliged to take leave of Mr. Herbert, from whom I underſtood that a ſhip and ſloop, then in ſight, were the Antelope and Euphrates, and that Mr. Broff and Mr. Salmon were on board the Antelope, having charge of the Company's affairs on the coaſt; upon which I returned, and anchored behind Pulo Pangir.

Thurſday, February the 1ſt. Weighed in the morning, and ſaw the Antelope ſtretching to ſea. Having fired a gun, I returned and anchored again behind Pulo Pangir, in fifteen fathom muddy ground, within half a mile of the iſland. In the evening the Antelope anchored cloſe by us. I went on board to pay my reſpects to Mr. Broff and Mr. Salmon, who gave me orders to follow the Antelope to Rhio, where they ſaid they would ſtay fifteen days. Got two bags of rice from the Antelope: ſhe could ſpare no more, and ſailed next night.

night. Had alſo a ſupply of goods, chiefly blue
cloth, from Mr. Broff.

To day, the 2d, about noon, the boat returned
from Abia, with my letters, and acquainted me,
the Mindano officers were there.   The wind being
ſoutherly, weighed, and ſteered for Abia, to land
there the other Mindano ſoldier, and to ſend to
Rajah Moodo what I owed him, being two hundred kangans.

On _Saturday_ the 3d, anchored behind Uſookan
iſland.   In the evening, the Mindano officers came
on board, their prow being hauled up within Abia
river, to repair.   I ſent letters by them to Rajah
Moodo and Fakymolano, and to the former about
fifty per cent. more than I owed.   I gave alſo ten
pieces of blue cloth to the four officers, who were
men of ſome rank ; and two pieces of blue cloth
to each of the ſoldiers, who had hitherto accompanied me.   I ſent alſo four pieces of blue cloth to
the Spaniſh writer at Mindano, who had written
out the grant of Bunwoot to the Engliſh: being ſo
exhauſted, when I left that country, I could not reward him as I wiſhed.   The Mindano officers ſeemed very ſenſible of the trouble I had taken to find
them out ; and we parted very good friends.

On the 4th, towards evening, we had a great
ſwell from the northward, though we lay in a manner land locked.   In the morning the gale freſhen-
ed, and our grapnel came home.   Got cloſe in ſhore,
into nine foot at high water ; at low water, the veſſel
touched a little.   At midnight, being high water,
                                                    hauled

hauled the veffel afhore, in a fmooth bay, upon
foft fand.

On the 5th, found the flook of our grapnel
ftraightened. To night the moon was wholely
eclipfed : all day we had frefh gales, and a great
fea broke on the Point, without us : floated at midnight.

To day, the 6th, the gale abated; and the
weather fettled : cleaned and breamed the veffel's
bottom. The people of Abia came on board, and
brought us fifh and fruit. Fixed beacons on
the bar of fand, that reaches between the fouth
part of Ufakan ifland and the main, to direct our
going out at high water ; finding it impoffible, on
account of the vaft fwell, to get out to the northward of the ifland, although the tide favoured us.
About midnight got out, having touched two or
three times on the bar, which happily was foft
fand. Having got fairly over, we found a great
fwell from the northward. On the 7th, at noon,
we were abreaft of Pulo Gaya ; at fun-fet, Point
Tiga bore W. S. W. three leagues. Sailed on for
the ifland Labuan, on our way to Borneo, for provifions. Labuan is the ifland, to which the Englifh retired from Balambangan : it lies oppofite the
mouth of the river of Borneo Proper.

On *Thurfday* the 8th, at day light, I found that
I had miftaken the point Keemanees, which lies
S. W. of Pulo Tiga, for Labuan ifland, and that
I had got into the bay of the fame name, fo far,
that from feven fathom, muddy ground, the rock

C c   off

off the point bore N. W. by N. I ftood out with the land wind, and then anchored. With ten warps, of about feventy fathom each, I got round a kind of button rock, as large as a houfe, that lies off the point of Keemanees, and joins to the main by a reef of rocks, above one mile in length. We warped round in two and a half, and three fathom, fandy ground. From the faid rock, a dry fpot of fand bears W. N. W. about fix miles diftant. At midnight, I anchored in thirteen fathom, muddy ground, within five miles of the Button Rock : it bearing E. N. E. On the 9th, weighed, and fteered S. W. wind N. E. paffed a kind of table land, on the main of Borneo, leaving it on the left hand. About noon, got fight of Pulo Labuan; it makes like two hummocs of middling height, clofe together; and bears about eight leagues S. W. of Pulo Tiga.

Anchored at night. In the morning of the 10th, fteered S. S. W. for the mouth of Borneo river. The beft direction is to keep in foft ground. Paffed many fifhing ftakes, that at a diftance, look like mafts, all within Pulo Mara. At four P. M. got over the bar, on which are three fathom at high water. Rowed a good deal : at midnight got up the river, and anchored abreaft of the refident's houfe. I found here the Luconia Snow, Captain Roffin, belonging to the honourable Company.

On the 11th, at fun-rife, faluted the factory with five guns, and had the fame number returned. At feven o'clock went afhore, and waited on the refident, Mr. Jeffe, who, by the kindnefs of

his

his manner, made my fhort ftay very agreeable; nor did the behaviour of my old fhipmate, Captain Roffin, add a little to my fatisfaction. On *Friday* the 16th, came in a Buggefs prow, under Englifh colours.

After having mended our fails, and got provifions and water, I failed on the 17th, from the town of Borneo; but, at noon, the flood tide making, I came to an anchor. Weighed again in the afternoon, and worked down againft a frefh wind at N. E. When dark, the ebb being over, I came to, about a mile within the bar.

On the 18th, we had variable winds and calms the former part of the day; during the latter, the wind was at N. N. E. and N. E. Early in the morning, we weighed; and, having rowed down clofe to the bar, we anchored. At day light, weighed and got over the bar: at ten, the ebb being over, anchored. At two P. M. weighed again, and worked towards Pulo Mara. At four, found the veffel made more water than ufual: fhe had fprung a leak on the ftarboard fide, three ftreaks from the keel. Wore, and ran back to Borneo; and at eight in the morning, came to, abreaft of Mr. Jeffe's houfe. To day, juft before bearing away, we faw a China junk, under Pulo Mara.

Next day, the 19th, got every thing out, and hauled the veffel afhore. On the 20th, I employed three Buggefs calkers, who, that day, calked the ftarboard fide of the veffel, and payed it with lime and oil. We found the leak to be a large nail hole.

Next

Next day, we calked the larboard fide of the veffel, and payed it with the fame mixture. The Chinefe junk that came from Amoy, paffed us, and was moored head and ftern, abreaft of the town. I had the curiofity to go on board, and meafure her: her length over all, was one hundred and twenty foot; her breadth, thirty foot upon deck; but more below. The fhank of one of her wooden anchors, was thirty-fix foot long. On the 23d, got a haufer from the Luconia, and hove the veffel off the ground.

On *Tuefday* the 27th, I had got every thing ready for fea. In the afternoon, Mr. Jeffe and Captain Roffin came on board; alfo Mr. Kirton, Captain Roffin's chief officer, a very ingenious young gentleman, who had failed round the world with Captain Carteret, and had commanded feveral country fhips. We then weighed, and ran down the river. At fun-fet, they left us, and I faluted them with three guns. I followed my friends to the town; at eleven, took leave of them, and returned on board. As it may not be amifs to fay fomething of the north part of the ifland of Borneo, the reader will find it in the following chapter.

CHAP.

C H A P. XVII.

Of the North Part of Borneo—Its Climate—Rivers—
Harbours—Product---People called Idaan---Their
Superstition---Farther Account of Places---Advan-
tage of trading from Indostan hither---Account of
the Badjoos and the People of Tedong.

T H E climate puts me in mind of Ceylon, being, from the abundance of woods and verdure,
always cool, and not subject to hot land winds,
like the coast of Coromandel; nor to great heats,
as Calcutta in Bengal. The land and sea winds
are always cool; not but that particular circum-
stances of situation, in all countries, affect the air,
as the neighbourhood of swamps, or the freedom
of ventilation intercepted by woods.

1776.
February.

Most of this north part of Borneo,* granted to
the English East India Company by the Sooloos, is
watered by noble rivers. Those that discharge
themselves into Maludo Bay, are not barred: it
has also many commodious harbours, Sandakan,
Maludo Bay, Ambong, Pulo Gaya on the main
land, and many good harbours on the islands near
it; two on Malwally; two, if not more, on Banguey, one of them behind the island Patanuan;
two on Balambangan; and one behind Maleangan,
near Banguey.

* See Dalrymple's map of Felicia.

Of

Of the two harbours on Balambangan, called the north-eaſt and ſouthweſt, the north-eaſt is the larger; but on the ſouth ſide, where the Engliſh ſettled, the ground is ſwampy. At the entrance of the S. W. harbour, is great convenience of watering. Freſh water may be conveyed into the lower deck ports of a firſt rate, lying in five fathom, by means of a hoſe from a rivulet cloſe by. Here alſo the ſoil is rich and fruitful: at the N. E. harbour, it is ſandy and barren. Round the iſland, quantities of fiſh may be caught.

On the main land of Borneo, oppoſite Balambangan, and to the iſland Banguey, grow foreſts of fine tall timber, without underwood. Freeſtone may be had in abundance. Here are large cattle called Liſang: flocks of deer and wild hogs feed on ſpacious plains, in no fear of the tiger, as on the iſland Sumatra. The country produces all the tropical fruits in proportion, with many known in few places but Sooloo; ſuch as the madang, like a great cuſtard apple, and the balono, like a large mango. In this north part of Borneo, is the high mountain of Keeneebaloo, near which, and upon the ſkirts of it, live the people called Oran Idaan or Idahan, and ſometimes Maroots. The mountain is, in old maps, named St. Peter's Mount, and is flat atop.

I have converſed with many Sooloos concerning the Idaan, and with many of them who underſtand Malay. They believe the deity pleaſed with human victims. An Idaan or Maroot muſt, for once at leaſt, in his life, have imbrued his hands

in

1776.
February.

in a fellow creature's blood ; the rich are faid to do
it often, adorning their houfes with fculls and teeth,
to fhow how much they have honoured their author,
and laboured to avert his chaftifement. Several in
low circumftances will club to buy a Bifayan Chriftian flave, or any one that is to be fold cheap ; that
all may partake the benefit of the execution. So
at Kalagan, on Mindano, as Rajah Moodo informed me, when the god of the mountain gives
no brimftone, they facrifice fome old flave, to appeafe the wrath of the deity. Some alfo believe,
thofe they kill in this world, are to ferve them in
the next, as Mr. Dalrymple obferves. They are
acquainted with a fubtle poifon called Ippoo, the
juice of a tree, in which they dip fmall darts.
Thefe they fhoot through a hollow piece of wood,
which the Sooloos call fampit ; whence is faid to
iffue inftant death, to whoever is wounded by them.

The author of the Origin and Progrefs of Defpotifm, a book tranflated from the French, fays,
(p. 121.) " Perhaps moft nations in the world
" have originally delighted in this horrible parade
" of human victims, and this would never have
" been fuffered, if they had not been previ-
" oufly habituated to blood, by the frequent
" facrifice of animals. The blafphemous no-
" tion, that the deity can delight in blood,
" being once eftablifhed, the next blow was to
" ftrike the prieftly knife into the throats of men,
" and let loofe that purple torrent, which, accord-
" ing to their hellifh doctrine, was the moft valu-
" able and the moft pleafing in his eyes." He
then fays, " How bleft are we Chriftians, in the
" myfte-

" myfterious doctrine, that the blood of Jefus Chrift
" fhall prove a fufficient facrifice for the fins of
" mankind !"

The Idaan pen hogs, and eat pork. They carry
their rice, fruits, &c. to the fea fide, and buy falt
from the Badjoos, who make it often in this manner. They gather fea weeds, burn them, make
a lye of afhes, filter it, and form a bitter kind of
falt in fquare pieces, by boiling it in pans made
of the bark of the aneebong. Thefe pieces of falt
are carried to market, whither both the Idaan and
muffulmen refort ; and pafs as a currency for money.

The places granted to the Englifh, fouth of Pirate's point, are named Pandaffan, Tampaffook,
Abia, Ambong, Salaman, Tawarran, Inanan, and
Patatan, as far as Keemanees. In this extent of
coaft are two good harbours, Ambong, and behind
Pulo Gaya, of which hereafter. This coaft is
better inhabited than that eaft of Pirate's point,
extending a little beyond the fpacious harbour of
Sandakan, to Towfon Abia, where the grant terminates. The latter is moftly low land, and the
inhabitants live up the rivers a good way ; whereas, on the former part of the grant, the coaft is
fomewhat higher, and inhabited clofe to the fea.

The Mahometans live moftly by the fea fide,
at the mouths of rivers ; and preclude, as much
as they can, Europeans from having intercourfe,
with the Idaan and Maroots : but, at Balambangan, and on the ifland Labuan, near Borneo, the

Idaan

Idaan in their boats, brought hogs, fruits, &c. and were glad to fee the Englifh eat pork like themfelves. The north part of Borneo is faid to have been once under the dominion of China.

Mr. Dalrymple, in his plan for fettling Balambangan, gives a very particular and juft account of this country, which he calls Felicia; and adds, that the Idaan, if well ufed, would flock from every quarter, to whoever fhould fettle there. This I firmly believe, with that judicious, and inquifitive gentleman. I have feen many of them, not only at Balambangan, but on the coaft of Borneo, and have converfed with feveral in Malay;—what the fame obferver fays, about their refpecting the Mahometans, is alfo ftrictly true. They confider the Mahometans as having a religion, which they have not yet got: and I am of opinion, from the moral character which they deferve, not only that his fcheme of civilizing them could be carried into effect, but that our religion could be eafily introduced among them. The horrid cuftom already mentioned, paves the way: the tranfition hinted by the author of the origin of defpotifm, fufficiently points it out. The Idahan punifh murder, theft, and adultery, with death; and take but one wife. Had our fettling in this quarter fucceeded, in them would have been a vaft acquifition of people to furnifh us with pepper, and rough materials for exportation, from their many rivers; befide the precious articles of gold and diamonds; and the great benefit a free trade, from Indoftan hither, would bring to Bengal and Bombay. A race of Lafcars (failors) might be brought up in it, which would

would employ many veſſels, as the commodities are bulky, that return the ſalt and calicoes of Indoſtan. Theſe Laſcars, mixed with an equal number of Engliſh ſailors, would fight a ſhip well ; as has been often experienced in India, eſpecially on the coaſt of Malabar. Another advantage would have attended our ſettling in this quarter : the quick intercourſe with Cochin-China, and other places on the weſt coaſt of the China ſeas. To ſail thither, from any place already mentioned, or from Balambangan, and to return, the courſe being nearly N. W. or S. E. either monſoon is a fair wind upon the beam ; and Cochin-China would take off, not only many woollens, but many Indoſtan cottons, particularly Bengal muſlins ; as I learnt from a very intelligent Chineſe at Balambangan, who ſpoke good Malay.

The Badjoo people, called Oran Badjoo, are a kind of itinerant fiſhermen, ſaid to come originally from Johore, at the eaſt entrance of the ſtraits of Malacca. They live chiefly in ſmall covered boats, on the coaſts of Borneo and Celebes, and adjacent iſlands. Others dwell cloſe to the ſea, on thoſe iſlands, their houſes being raiſed on poſts, a little diſtance into the ſea, always at the mouths of rivers. They are Mahometans.

At Paſſir's river's mouth, are many of thoſe Badjoos, who employ themſelves chiefly in catching with hand nets, which they puſh through the mud, ſmall ſhrimps. Theſe well waſhed in ſea water, they expoſe to a hot ſun. They then beat them in a mortar, into a kind of paſte with a ſtrong ſmell, called

called blatchong, much in requeſt all over India. The Badjoos of Borneo alſo make ſalt.

Theſe laſt Badjoos may be called fixt or ſtationary, compared with thoſe who live always in their boats, and who, as the monſoon ſhifts on the iſlands Borneo and Celebes, ſhift or move always to leeward, for the ſake of fine weather, as the Tartars in Aſia ſhift their tents for the ſake of enjoying perpetual ſummer.

In their original country, Johore, where it would ſeem an old method to live in boats ; it is ſaid, that on a certain feſtival, they crouded in numbers, and made faſt their boats, aftern of the veſſel, in which was their prince ; it being their cuſtom at certain ſeaſons to do ſo : but, a ſtorm ariſing from the land, they were driven acroſs the ſouthern part of the China ſea, to the coaſt of Borneo ; and of this they celebrate the anniverſary, by bathing in the ſea on an annual day.

They have a language of their own, but no written character ; and many Badjoos are ſettled on the N. W. coaſt of Borneo, where they not only fiſh, but make ſalt ; and trade in ſmall boats along the coaſt.

At Macaſſar live many Badjoos, chiefly on the water in covered boats, and ſhift their ſituation with the monſoon, but conſider Macaſſar as their home.

When I went in 1773 from Paſſir, to viſit the little Paternoſters that lie midway between Borneo

and

and Celebes, I found many Badjoo boats, about five or fix tons burden ; all of them having the tripod maft, and lyre tanjong. Several had women and children on board. They lay at anchor, fifhing for fwallo, or fea flug, in feven or eight fathom water. They fee the fwallo in clear water, and ftrike it as it lies on the ground, with an inftrument confifting of four bearded iron prongs, fixed along an almoft cylindrical ftone, rather fmaller at one end than the other, about eighteen inches long. They always fix an iron fhot at the end of the ftone, next the point of the irons. They alfo dive for fwallo, the beft being got in deep water.

The black fwallo is reputed the beft ; but, I have feen fome of a light colour, found only in deep water, which I was affured to be of more value in China than the black ; and fold even for forty dollars a pecul. The pieces are much larger than are generally thofe of the black fwallo, fome of them weighing half a pound. The white fwallo is the worft, eafily got in fhoal water, and on the dry fand, among coral rocks at low water. Its value is about four or five dollars a pecul.

Thofe Badjoos fettled on the N. W. coaft of Borneo, near rivers mouths, ufed to fupply us at Balambangan, with rice, fowls, and other provifions.

On the N. E. part of Borneo, is a favage piratical people, called Oran Tedong, or Tiroon, who live far up certain rivers. The Sooloos have lately fubdued them, by getting the Rajah (or chief)

into

into their power.* These Orang Tedong fit out vessels large and small, and cruise among the Philippine islands, as has been formerly said. † They also cruise from their own country, west to Pirate's point, and down the coast of Borneo, as far as the island Labuan. After an excursion I once made from Balambangan to Patatan, a little beyond the island Pulo Gaya ; on my return, I put into a small bay, east of Pirate's point, almost opposite Balambangan. There appeared nine Tedong-pirates, in vessels of small size, about that of London wherries below bridge. Several Badjoo boats being in the bay at the same time, the people laid the boats close to the shore, landed and clapt on their (Ranty) iron-ring jackets for defence. The pirates kept in a regular line, put about, and stretched off altogether, not choosing to land. Had I been alone in the bay, I might have fallen into their hands.

The Oran Tedong live very hard on their cruises, their provisions sometimes being raw sago flour. They have often no attop or covering ; nay, sometimes as the Sooloos have told me, they go, especially if it rains, stark naked. The Moors of Magindano, and the Illanos, also Moors, despise these people. When they meet, however, in roads, and harbours among the Philippines where the common prey is, they do not molest one another. I have been told, that the Oran Tedong will, in certain cases, eat human flesh. If this be true, it can only be like the Battas on Sumatra, in a frantic

* See page 356.　　　† Page 17.

fit

fit of refentment. That the Battas do fo, I am
too well affured.

Their boats are fometimes fmall, and made of
thin planks, fewed together. I have heard of fome
fuch, once fhut up in a bay by a Spanifh cruifer:
they took their boats to pieces, and carried them
away over land.

The Oran Tedong make a great deal of granulated fago, which they fell to the Sooloos very
cheap; perhaps at one dollar a pecul. The Sooloos, as has been faid, fell this again to the China
Junks.

Before I leave this people, I muft mention, with
whatever reluctance, one thing faid of them, that
fpeaks the barbarity of thofe who have had no re-
vealed religion, Jewifh or Chriftian, Mahometan
or Jentoo. When the Oran Tedong get into their
hands many prifoners, to fecure themfelves, they
will lame fome of the ftouteft; nay leave them,
on perhaps a little fandy ifland, (of which are many
in the Sooloo archipelago, and among the Philippines) till they be at leifure to fetch them.
Nor do they ftick at breaking the limbs of their
captives, in cowardly fear of their own. So juftly
do the Moors defpife them for Barbarians.

C H A P.

C H A P.   XVIII.

Directions for failing down the N. W. Coaft of Borneo,
from Pirate's Point to the River---Defcription of
the Town---Return thence to Fort Marlborough.

F R O M Pirate's Point,* which lies in latitude
7° N. to Batoomandee (wafhed rock) Point, are
feveral bays, where fhips working up and down
the coaft, may anchor fafely, and get water from
the fhore. In the chart is one namelefs point, almoft half way between the two points already mentioned : it is very well reprefented in the map,
with a bay to its fouthward. Many fharp pointed
black rocks peep above water, off this point ; but
they may be approached within a quarter of a
mile ; and there is good landing to leeward, (if
the monfoon allow) with clear plains, and plenty
of deer, of which I have eaten. Juft to the fouthward of Batoomandee, is a commodious bay, at
the mouth of Pandaffan river, which has a good
bar. Farther on is the bar of the great river of
Tampaffook, on which, at times, the furf breaks
very high. Next is Abia river, the bar of which
is fmooth, the ifland Ufookan lying before it, and
will admit a veffel of fourteen foot water in the
fprings. The paffage is to the northward of Ufookan, the ifland proving, at low water, a peninfula,
leaving, confequently, no paffage between it and

1776.
February.

---

* See Mr. Dalrymple's map of Felicia, and general chart.

the

the main. Between this ifland and Ambong harbour, a bay opens, where is good riding in the
N. E. monfoon. Ambong harbour is large and
commodious, having good depth of water, with a
button like ifland well laid down, at the entrance
of it. Keep that ifland on the right hand, and
you will come into a fine harbour on the fouth fide,
clofe to fome falt houfes. From this harbour, proceeding fouthwards, you pafs the mouths of the
two rivers Salaman and Tawarran, and approach
Dallid point. From this Kaitan point bears S. W.
by W. five miles, and Mancabong river runs between. Kaitan point is bold and bluff. When it
bears eaftward of fouth, and not before, (coming
from the northward) you'll open four iflands; the
firft pretty high, called Pulo Pangir, the other
three much fmaller. The beft track to get into
the fpacious bay, before which lie thefe four iflands,
is to the fouthward of Pangir, keeping either clofe
to it, or in mid channel between it and the land
next to the fouthward of it, which is the proper
Pulo Gaya.* Pulo Gaya is an ifland fix or eight
miles round, and being very near the main land,
appears from the fea to be part of it. The channel
which feparates it from the main, is faid to have
deep water; but, that which I paffed in a boat, I
found full of rocks. It is impoffible to mifs the
paffage into the above bay; if the fhip be kept to
the fouthward of Pulo Pangir, between it and Pulo
Gaya. The next ifland, to the northward of it,
is Pulo Udar, fmaller; and the next to it, little
Udar, ftill fmaller; the fourth, and fmalleft, is

* In Mr. Dalrymple's Map, Pulo Pangir is called Pulo Gaya.

named

named Pulo Priu. Thefe three are almoft joined
to the fourth and fouthermoft, by reefs of rocks,
with an intricate channel between Pulo Pangir and
the next to the northward of it. North eaft of Pulo
Pangir runs a reef, on which a China junk was loft
many years ago: I faw on the reef, her rudder
funk in three fathom water, upon coral rocks.

In the N. E. part of this bay, are faid to be a
good harbour, and, with a fmooth bar, as difcharging itfelf into it, a river called Labatuan. To
the fouthward of Labatuan is Inanan, which has
alfo a fmooth bar, but is very fhallow. Patatan
lies to the fouthward of Pulo Gaya, and entirely
out of the bay : its bar is fmooth, but likewife
fhallow. Three or four miles up the river Patatan,
ftands the town, the houfes, about a hundred,
fronting the water. Above the town are many
pepper gardens belonging to Chinefe, in a delight-
ful country.

Farther down the coaft is Pappal river, the banks
abounding with coco nut trees, infomuch, that
during the floods, many nuts are driven to fea.
Steering on from Pulo Gaya, S. W. by W. you
approach Pulo Tiga, and the point of Keemanees.
Pulo Tiga is fo called, as confifting of three iflands,
pretty clofe, and of a gentle flope ; each having
an even outline, and a fine white beach : they
bear from Keemanees point, N. E. by N. two
leagues. This point makes a bay to the eaftward
of it fo deep, that from feven fathoms water,
muddy ground, the point bears N. W. by N.

D d   with

with fmooth water, during the S. W. monfoon.
At the point of Keemanees, appears a rock like a
houfe, with a bufh or two atop; it terminates a
very rocky point, at the diftance of a mile, off
which is but two fathom water : it muft not therefore be approached. A dry fand bears from it
W. N. W. about fix miles. Pulo Tiga lies in latitude 5° 36'. From the rocky point of Keemanees, Pulo Labuan bears S. W. about fix leagues.
The proper paffage towards Borneo river, is without this ifland ; within is fhoal water, two and a
half, and three fathom fandy ground. So, at leaft,
I found it : there may, however, be deeper water.
The ifland Labuan, beheld from the N. E. forms
the femblance of two hummocs. A remarkable
rock, like a two mafted veffel, lies W. S. W. of
it, at fome diftance from the Borneo fhore : keep
mid channel, between Labuan and this rock, fteering fouth. In this channel, you will fee low land
right a head, not unlike a clipped hedge. A little
way inland, to the right, is a peaked hill. When
this hill bears W. or to the northward of W.
haul in for the channel, which goes by Pulo Mara,
a low ifland, bearing from Labuan S. S. W. ten
miles. To the northward of Pulo Mara, runs a
fpit of fand, three or four miles. Be fure to keep
within it, in foft ground ; as on the fpit the fea
often breaks very high. The channel is then clofe
by Pulo Mara, which muft be left on the right
hand. Hence many fifhing ftakes extend towards
the river's mouth, having the appearance of fo
many mafts.

Pulo

Pulo Chirming (Glafs Ifland) bears about W. by
S. eight miles from Pulo Mara. Keep in foft
ground : but here it would be proper to get a pilot,
or at leaft to anchor, and explore the channel. In
pafling Pulo Chirming, you muft keep clofe to
the ifland, leaving it on the left, to avoid an arti-
ficial bank of coral rocks, piled, doubtlefs, for
fome purpofe : it dams up the water a little, and
is vifible at low tide. From Pulo Chirming, it is
about ten miles to the town of Borneo, in a S. W.
by W. direction. One mile from town, a fhort
reach bends almoft in an oppofite direction, round
a fmall ifland. Being up with this ifland, which
you muft leave on the right, appears a branch of
the river from the left or S. E. Keep to the right
and finifh the mile to town, whither can come up
junks of fix hundred tons.

The town of Borneo is fituate, as has been faid,
about ten miles up the river from Pulo Chirming.
The houfes are built on each fide the river upon
pofts, and you afcend to them by ftairs and ladders, as to back doors of warehoufes in Wapping.
The houfes on the left fide, going up, extend
backwards to the land, each in a narrow flip. The
land is not fteep, but fhelving; every houfe has
therefore a kind of ftage, erected for connexion
with the land. There is little intercourfe from
houfe to houfe by land, or what may be called behind; as there is no path, and the ground is
fwampy : the chief communication proves thus in
front, by boats.

D d 2

On

On the right, going up, the houfes extend about half a mile backwards, with channels like lanes, between the rows; fo that it would feem, the river, before the houfes were built, made a wide bafon of fhallow water, in which have arifen three quarters of the town, refembling Venice; with many water lanes, if I may fo fay, perpendicular and parallel to the main river, which here is almoft as wide as the Thames at London Bridge, with fix fathom water in the channel; and here lie moored, head and ftern, the China junks; four or five of which come annually from Amoy, of five or fix hundred tons burden. The water is falt, and the tide runs about four miles an hour in the fprings. Some of the houfes on the right fide of the water, are two ftories high, which I never faw in any other Malay country, with ftages or wharfs before them, for the convenience of trade. At Paffir, on the oppofite fide of this ifland, the houfes front the river; fome have ftages or wharfs in front; but there are no water lanes here as at Borneo. At Paffir, the river is frefh, and often rapid; at Borneo, the river is falt, and feldom rapid.

In thofe divifions of the town, made by the water lanes, is neither firm land nor ifland; the houfes ftanding on pofts, as has been faid, in fhallow water; and the public market is kept fometimes in one part, fometimes in another part of the river. Imagine, a fleet of London wherries, loaded with fifh, fowl, greens, &c. floating up with the tide, from London Bridge towards Weftminfter; then
down

down again, with many buyers floating up and down with them ; this will give fome idea of a Borneo market. Thofe boats do not always drive with the tide, but fometimes hold by the ftairs of houfes, or by ftakes, driven purpofely into the river, and fometimes by one another : yet, in the courfe of a forenoon, they vifit moft part of the town, where the water lanes are broad. The boat people (moftly women) are provided with large bamboo hats, the fhade of which covers great part of the body, as they draw themfelves up under it, and fit, as it were, upon their heels.

The many alligators here, do not make their appearance in the day, but at night ; and it is dangerous falling out of a boat. Yet it is furprifing, in how fmall canoes the natives will go up and down the river. The alligators lurk under the houfes, living upon any offal, that gets through a kind of lattice floor. So at Batavia, the alligators frequent the river's mouth, for what comes from the city.

Confiderable is the commerce between China and Borneo, fomewhat like the trade from Europe to America. Seven junks were at Borneo in 1775. They carry to China great quantities of black wood, which is worked up there into furniture, &c. it is bought for about two dollars a pecul ; and fold for five or fix : alfo ratans, dammer, a kind of refin, clove bark, fwallo, tortoifhell, birds nefts, &c. articles fuch as are carried from Sooloo to China. The beft native camphire is exported hence ; fuperior, I have been told, to the Barroos camphire on Sumatra.

tra. It looks no better, but is much dearer, felling for ten or twelve Spanish dollars the Chinese
catty; Barroos camphire, looking as well, being
worth no more than seven and eight dollars a catty.
The Chinese are good judges of camphire. A
great deal of this valuable drug comes from those
parts of the island Borneo, that were ceded to us
by the Sooloos. At Borneo-town, the Chinese fometimes build junks, which they load with the rough
produce of the island Borneo, and send thence to
China. I have seen a dock close to the town, in
which a China junk of 500 tons had lately been
built, worth 2500 taels, and 8000 in China. Could
these junks come readily at our woollens, they
would distribute immense quantities through the
northern parts of China.

Here are many Chinese settled, who have pepper
gardens. They do not let the vine, which bears
the pepper, twist round a chinkareen tree, as is the
custom on Sumatra; but drive a pole, or rather a
stout post, into the ground, so that the vine is not
robbed of its nourishment. The Chinese keep the
ground very clean between the rows of vine; and
I have seen them pull off the vine leaves; saying,
they did it that the pepper corn might have more
sun. I have here counted seventy, sometimes se-
venty-five, corns of pepper on one stalk; which is
more than the stalks produce on Sumatra; and I
am apt to think the chinkareens on Sumatra are
hurtful, as they not only rob the ground, but
take up much of the planter's time in trimming
the luxuriant branches, that these may not over-
shade the vine. On Sumatra, the country is full
of

of wood, as here on Borneo; fo were our planters there to adopt the Bornean method, they never could find a fcarcity of pofts; which, if made of what is called iron wood, will remain in the ground many years without rotting.

The Chinefe here are very active and induftrious. They bring all kinds of the manufacture of china, and keep fhops on board their junks, as well as afhore; but the Borneans do their beft to preclude them from dealing with the Maroots, referving the trade for themfelves. I do not find that the Maroots grow pepper. The Chinefe alone plant it. It is all fent to China. We found it dearer than at Paffir, where it was ten dollars a pecul : here it is fourteen and fifteen. I am furprifed they do not encourage the Maroots to plant this commodity. This was Mr. Dalrymple's idea in his plan concerning Balambangan.

It gives a European pleafure to fee the regularity and cleanlinefs on board the Chinefe veffels. To the latter much contributes their not ufing tar. Their tanks for water are fweet and convenient. They have the art of putting a mixture of lime and oil into their feams on the deck, &c. which hardens and keeps them tight. This is much cleaner than pitch; but, if the deck worked at fea, I apprehend this calking would break, and the junk prove leaky. Their cook rooms are remarkably neat. The crew all eat off china; and in a harbour, every one is employed without noife about his own bufinefs.

Among

Among Malay trading veſſels, prevail a languor and deadneſs : every thing they do is in a ſlovenly manner, which diſguſts Europeans. If the profits have maintained them during the voyage, they are contented ; as they make a home of every place they frequent, moving ſlowly from it, as if unwilling.   From this cenſure I except the Buggeſſes, who are really men of buſineſs.

Malays mix liquid opium with a certain herb called madat, and this they ſmoke in a large pipe. Mr. Palmer being ill at Balambangan, received benefit from thus taking opium : he had-tried to take it, as is uſual, in drops of laudanum ; but ſo, it broke his reſt.   It is a cuſtom in port, both on board Malay and Chineſe veſſels, to hang in the water, cloſe forward over each bow, a bag of lime : this impregnating the water near the ſurface, in their opinion, keeps off the worm.

The government at Borneo is of a mixed kind, as at Magindano and Sooloo. The firſt perſon is ſtiled the Eang de Patuan ; and the ſecond, the Sultan.   Then come the Pangarans (nobles) about fifteen in number, who often tyranniſe over the people. The Borneans have the character of a ſenſible, ſteady people, and are ſaid to have much primitive ſtrictneſs and ſimplicity of manners : they deteſt the Sooloos, who are gay and agreeable in private life, but reſtleſs as a ſtate, and ſtick at nothing to promote their ambition.

Having, as before related, taken leave of Mr. Jeſſe on *Tueſday* the 27th of *February*, next day, early

early in the morning, weighed and rowed down
the river. At eight A. M. came to within Pulo
Chirming. At five P. M. got over the bar: rowed
and failed paft Pulo Mara. At midnight, fhoaled
our water from three fathom mud to nine foot
fand, and perceived a ground fwell : altered
our courfe, and got off; then anchored. The
fand we had been upon, was a fpit that ftretches
three miles without Pulo Mara.

On the 29th, winds from the N. E. the firft
part of the day, and then from the S. E. Steered out between Two-Maft ifland, and the fmall
iflands S. W. of, and near Labuan. At noon,
Labuan bore N. E. two leagues ; Two-Maft
ifland W. two miles, and the extreme of Pulo
Mara S. S. E. two leagues. We then had fifteen fathom muddy ground, and were in latitude 5° 25'. Two-Maft ifland makes like a
veffel with two mafts, when feen bearing Weft
W. N. W. or W. S. W. Several rocks appear
above water clofe to it. Steered S. W. At
funfet, Labuan bore E. N. E. and Two-Maft
ifland S. E. by S. three miles. Steered W. by
N. wind N. E. In the night had a large fwell,
and a frefh gale, which carried away our cut-
water. Soon after a fea broke on our quarter;
but, the deck being flufh, it went off. Had
the veffel been without a deck, as from Balambangan to New Guinea, it would have filled her.

Wednefday,. March the 1ft. Steered W. by N.
with a frefh gale, which made a great fea. Saw
a two maft prow fteering S. W.

On

On the fixth, faw one of the Anambas, called by fome Serantan, to which I made from
Labuan 8° 6' meridian diftance weft. I then
fteered S. S. W. intending to go through the
ftrait to the fouthward of Bintang and Rhio, having heard at Borneo, that many Johore pirates
were in the ftrait of Sincapore. That night, I
ftruck foundings from thirty to twenty-eight fathom muddy ground. On the feventh, paffed
to the fouthward of Pulo Panjang; at eight in
the morning, Bintang hill bore W. N. W. and
Lingin S. W. On the eighth, ninth and ele-
venth, I worked through a ftrait to the fouthward of Bintang, and an ifland fouth of it, which
is pretty long, and makes in hummocs. The
ftrait lies nearly N. W. and S. E. and is paffable
by fhips. On the 13th, I arrived in Malacca
road; on the fifteenth, failed thence, and on the
27th, being detained by calms and contrary
winds, was no farther advanced than to the coaft
of Sumatra, in latitude 5° 54' north, where we
had the winds at N. W. On the twenty-eighth,
ftood over for Queda, where I arrived the twenty-
ninth. On the thirtieth, having got water and
provifions, I was ready to fail by feven at night.
Then, my mate, David Baxter, and Laurence
Lound the gunner, went afhore, refufing to proceed, as objecting to the veffel. On the 31ft, I
hauled her afhore, and fhifted about three foot
of bad plank on each fide. By the fixth of
April, having finifhed the repairs of the veffel,
I ftrongly invited my mate and gunner to continue with me; but they would not. On the feventh, I failed; and, on the thirteenth, arrived in
Atcheen

Atcheen Road, where I found Thomas Palmer, Efquire, late third of Balambangan, in a floop at anchor. We agreed to keep company to Bencoolen. I ftaid afhore at Atcheen, till the 17th, to recover my health, having been indifpofed fince I left Queda. We then failed in company, and that night got through the Surat paffage. On the nineteenth, I put into the harbour of Siddo, to the fouthward of King's Point, feven miles.

As fhips often make this famous promontory of Atcheen, I could wifh to fay fomething of it before I conclude, having frequently traded hereabouts. The chart of Atcheen publifhed in the directory, is fufficiently accurate as to the road, and the Surat paffage; but off Pulo Brafs are foundings, twenty fathom fandy ground, not marked in that chart, where any fhip may fafely anchor out of the currents, and wait a fhift of wind. The Surat paffage is bold and fafe for a fhip to work through in either monfoon. In the fprings, the tide runs five and fix knots; but, immediately to the fouthward or northward of this narrow pafs (which, being formed by two promontories, has no length, and is about eighty fathom in width) the tide flacks. I would advife, in working through againft the S. W. monfoon, to lay the fhip's head to the main of Sumatra, with the main topfail aback, becaufe the perpendicular rock is fteep to, the fhore of the oppofite ifland not being fo bold. In the paffage, and near it, the ground is foul.

Having got through, the tide will favour the navigator paft Pulo Gomez, between which and
Sumatra,

Sumatra, is a fafe channel with good anchoring ground : the tide will alfo favour as far as Siddo harbour, if the fhip is kept all the way pretty near the fhore, where is good anchoring. Going into this harbour, the Sugar Loaf hill and the Slipper rock are remarkable : you may keep clofe to the Slipper rock, and lie very fafe in either monfoon. Here wood and water may be had, and refrefhments as at Atcheen : bullocks much cheaper. From this, with a frefh land wind, a fhip may ftretch off, and get down the coaft of Sumatra, where fhe will find the wind W. and N. W.

Whilft in this harbour, I found the Tartar Galley fo bad, that I refolved, with all my people, to quit her. Mr. Palmer, having many fervants and others on board of his floop, one of them a daring Malay, undertook to get her navigated to Fort Marlbro', putting on board of her four horfes out of his floop's hold. As I refolved to accept his kind invitation to go with him to Fort Marlbro' in his floop, which was ftout and ftrong, I was glad the horfes were to be difmiffed. I arrived the latter end of June, with my people, whom I paid off and difcharged.

The Tartar Galley came in foon after, and was hauled afhore. At Fort Marlbro', I gave an account of the voyage to Mr. Broff and Mr. Salmon, who, on my fignifying I was going home to lay the fame before the Honourable Court of Directors, wrote to them under date the 24th of *July* 1776 : " The Tartar Galley, late under the " command of Captain Thomas Forreft, was
brought

" brought hither a few days ago, by fome Malay
" men from the northward, in a very leaky condi-
" tion; her bottom being entirely deftroyed by
" worms. She was hauled afhore foon after her
" arrival, and we fhall take the firft opportu-
" nity of difpofing of her at public fale. We can-
" not help exprefsing our furprife, that Captain
" Forreft fhould attempt a voyage he has com-
" pleted in a veffel of fo fmall a burden as ten
" tons."

A V O C A-

A

VOCABULARY

OF THE

MAGINDANO TONGUE.

The Vowel A is pronounced open as in the Word Bal.

English.	*Magindano.*
ABAFT	OLINAN
Above	Depulo
About	Malipulug
Abhor	Maligiſh
Able	Patut
Ability	Capattan
Able, I am	Sake malow
Abroad	Salewan
Abundant	Marakul
Action, work	Maghenam
Accord	Paſagdi
Adder	Nipac
Adore, to worſhip	Mugſumbyan
Affliction	Ma Lemong
Affluent	Tamug
Afloat	Makilas

Afternoon

Englifh.	*Magindano.*
Afternoon	Malolom
Agog	Mahobunug
Air	Cauang
Alive	Mocug
Allied	Kitamag pagaly
All	Langu
Always	Amug-amug
Aliment	Kannon
Alike	Magigſan
Ambaffador	Suguan
Ambitious	Mabangol
Another	Lain
Ankle	Bubun
Angel	Malaycet
Angle, to fifh	Bunet
Angle, point	Tukka
Animal	Binatang
Apparel	Nu-ug
Arm	Batkol nagaly
Arife	Boal
Arrival	Dogan Nakuma
Arrack	Alack
Arrow	Panna
Afide	Saluvat
Afk	Mangani
Affemblage	Magkatepung
Affent	Paſagdi
Affurance	Tawaial
Attend	Patungo
Attack	Magaway
Aunt	Paqui inan
Awake	Bo-at Karon

Awhile

English.	*Magindano.*
Awhile	Paedub
Aye	Wy

B

Baby	Wata
Babbler	Mugtalug
Batchelor	Dapaku-duma
Back	Dewafs
Bad	Pintas
Bag	Baloyot
Balance	Catehan
Bandage	Balotan
Bank	Bungfud
Bare	Huba
Bargain	Paholaman
Bark	Upes
Bafe	Pintas
Barren	Bagutow
Bafeful	Mugkahuia
Bafket	Salu
To bathe	Paigu
A bath keeper	Payguan
Battery, fort	Cota
Bay	Labuan, fugud
Beads	Kulintus
Beard	Bunwoot baca
Bear, carry	Sapiouwan
Beautiful	Mapia
Bed	Pakatugan
Bee	Putiokan
Beg	Mangani
Believe	Enu enu
Bell	Lingany
Belly	Tean

E e   Bench

Englifh.	*Magindano.*
Bench	Bankoo
Betroth	Magtepan
Beft	Mapia totoo
Bewail	Pugfugun
Beyond	Howannan
Big with child	Mabdos
Big	Mafela
Bind	Balud
Bird	Papanoc, hyub
Bifect	Boakon
Bite	Kagoton
Black	Maiton
Bladder	Balokan
Blame	Pakafalla
Blanket, covering	Habul
Blind	Boota
Blood	Lugu
Blunt	Dema owtong
Blow	Manludpan
Board	Tappe
Boafter	Pucaquen
Boat, great	Ouwang mafela
Boat, fmall	Ouwang paedu
Boat, fighting	Ouwang mangaio
Bold	Mabagul
Bond	Ingy
Both	Dalua katow
Bottle	Flafka
Bottom	Elalom
Bow	Bufugun
Bowl	Lajah Mafela
Boy	Paedu mama

Brain

English.	Magindano.
Branch of a tree	Sanga caiu
Brain	Uttuck tangok
Brave	Mawalow
Breadth	Maulad
Break	Mapuſſa
Break of day	Paddial
Breeches	Sallowal
Breeze	Hangin paedup
Bridle	Baſal
Bright	Mahayan
Brimſtone	Aſſupli
Bring here	Wet caſey
Brittle	Dematugas
Broad	Maulad
Brother	Pagaly
Elder brother	Caca
Younger brother	Adi
Build	Maghinan
Bundle	Balotan
Buſh	Palumpong
Butter	Mantega
Bull	Sapi mama
Button	Buttones

C

English.	Magindano.
Cabin	Salud
Cage	Waly papanok
Cake	Paniallum
Calk	Bepakul, calfatty
Camel	Wood
Canal	Canal
Cane	Baras
Cannon	Maſela lutang
Cape	Tukka

E e 2   Capſtan

English.	*Magindano.*
Capstan	Galengan
Captive	Olipun
Carcafs	Lawafs
Care	Malero
Carry	Weet
Carry to fea	Weet fa caloran
Carelefs	Mapaoy
Cafh	Poufin
Caffia bark	Upis matamis
Cat	Sika
Caft	Ebuget
Catch	Dakob
Cave	Lungib
Chain	Ranty
Chalk, lime	Apog
Charitable	Matilimoon
Cheap	Bagutow
Cheek	Puni
Cheer up, a rowing	E, afi magia
Cheft	Kaban
Child	Wata
Chocolate	Chocolatey
Circle	Bulat
Clapper of a bell	Baffal la lingany
Claw	Cokko
Clean	Magdakdak
Clear	Mahayag
Cloth	Sapot
Clove	Bunga lowan
Cloud	Auan
Club	Sampok
Coach	Caroffe
Charcoal	Ulig

Coaft

Englijh.	*Magindano.*
Coaft	Pakilidan
Coat	Bankalla
Cock	Manock mama
Coffin	Kabau
Cold	Matungow
Comb	Soo-ud
Combat	Puggawy
Come	Seeka
Comrade	Upudku
Conjointly	Magikfan ikfan
Confent	Pafagdi
Converfation	Magtalu
Cook	Towdapog
Cord	Lubid
Colt	Habyzan
Cough	Pagubo
Coufin	Igtungudminfan
Countenance	Wiahon
Couple	Satima
Cow	Sappi babaye
Coward	Matalao
Coy	Magkahoia
Creep	Magheny
Cruel	Maifeg
Small bowl, cup	Lajah Paedup
Cunning	Makafag
Current	Suig mabangul
Cut	Vtud
Cutlafs	Kampilan
D	
Dance	Magfaut
Dare	Mapangol
Dark	Maduum

Day

English.	Magindano.
Day	Cenang
Day light	Malamag
Dead	Niatty
Deaf	Demakenog
Dear	Mahal
Debt	Makaotag
Decent	Maria
Dejected	Malero figunhowa
Delirious	Quitaquita
Defire	Mnyug
Diligent	Mautol
Dirty	Mafigfik
Difh	Kaunan
Difmifs	Benokoan
Diftant	Mawattan
Dive	Tumigpu-fa-ig
Divorce	Nagbuag
Do	Maghenam
Dog	Affu
Down	Lalum
Dread	Cagelok
Drefs	Panakton
Drink	Ominum
Drop	Pagtuu
Drum	Tamboor
Dry	Mamalla
Duck	Pattu
Dumb	Bunugun
Dung	Ty

E

Ear	Deungan
Earth	Lopa
Early	Mapita

Ebb

English.	Magindano.
Ebb	Ig pagerat
Eafe	Mapia gunhowa
Edge	Maottong
Egg	Lumoan
Eight	Wallu
Elbow	Siko
Elements	Bangfa
Embrace	Magakos
End	Wulbong
Encouragement	Engyan fa tamok
Empty	Mamalla
Enlarge	Ularon
Entry	Tamba
Efpoufe	Pangarumakan
Even	Pakaladlon
Ewe	Canding-babye
Examine	Demagakrata
Expire	Meaty
Extol	Paboa
Eye	Matta

F

Face	Uyawhun
Faith	Demagpial
Fall	Meholug
Fan	Kab-kab
Far	Watan
Faft	Samoot
Fat	Malumbo
Father	Amma
Fear	Mugkagelok
Feather	Bul-bul
Feel	Anam
Feet	Ay-i

Sole

English.	*Magindano.*
Sole of the foot	Palad ay i
Feaft	Mapia kannon
Fine	Manahoot
Finger	Tindolo
Fin	Pale
Finifh	Baluy
Fire	Klaioo
Fifh	Sura, fuda
Flag	Bandela
Flat	Datal
Flefh	Unud
Float	Makilas
Floor	Salog
Flute	Plauta
Fly	Tallabang
Fool	Bunug, dupang
Foot	Siki, butis
Forget	Nalintan
Fork	Panchutfu
Fortune	Parkapia
Foul	Maligfik
Four	Apat
Free	Madika
Friend	Pagamigos
Frightful	Kadeaypan
From	See-ee
Fruit	Buoul
Full	Pakamalan
Furious	Mabunugmatoto
G	
Galley	Galera
Gall	Puddu
Gallop	Matulid

Gate

English.	_Magindano._
Gate	Puta
Gay	Kilamugamigos
Gelt	Kappoon
Get up	Tindug
Giddy	Pateug ſuloo
Gimblet	Lukub
Girl	Babye, baguto
Glaſs	Chirming
Glitter	Malega
Globe	Malpulug
Go	Angy
God	Alatalla
Good	Mapia
Tolerably good	Mapia pia
Gooſe	Ganſa
Goat	Canding
Gone	Lumakow
Got	Nakowa
Grain	Bungabunga
Grave of the dead	Kalot
Grandfather	Apu
Great	Maſela
Green	Madoolow
Grieve	Mankaledo
Grind	Galigan
Gripe	Maſakiſutian
Ground	Lupa
Grow	Oeug
Guard	Patunga
Guitar	Guitara
Gum	Tagok
Gun	Sanapan
Gut	Teenye

Hair

English.	*Magindano.*
H	
Hair	Bohok
Halt	Paguron
Hammer	Dongſu
Hand	Alema
Handſome	Maniſſan
Harbour	Labuan, ſugud
Harlot	Mabeya
Harm	Makaſaki
Haſte	Samut
Hat	Sallup
Hate	Deakomoeog
To hazard	Lawalaean
He	Sakka
Head	Ulo
Heal	Pagoyagon
Hear	Makenug
Heart	Puſung
Hearth	Sigang
Heat	Mayow
Heaven	Langit
Heel	Buull
Hell	Inferno
Help	Tabang
Hence	Dekaſec
Hen	Manock babye
Her	Sakka
Here	Sahan
Hew	Pagutudon-Waſſy
Hid	Pagtagoan
High	Malundoo
Hill	Palao
Him	Sakka

Hip

English.	*Magindano.*
Hip	Weetan
Hither	Sy
Hoarfe	Laoos
Hog	Babuey
Hold	Dakupor
Hollow	Dalla Sulud
Honeft	Maungangun
Horn	Tandok
Horfe	Kuda
Hofe	Megas
Hot	Maiou
Hour	Oras
Houfe	Wally
Hundred	Sagatos
Hunger	Pakaguton
Hurt	Palean
Hufh	Bungul

I

Jail	Belangoan
Jaw	Baggan
Idle	Mapaog
If	Kun
Ignorant	Dematow
Ill	Magafaki
Image	Pandapatan
Indigo	Pandaag
Invincible	Elallong
Inland	Saingud
Into	Lalum
Iron	Pootow
Ifland	Poolo
Judge	Kelaketa mantery
Juftice	Vucum

Keep

Englijh.	*Magindano.*
K	
Keep	Taggo
Kettle	Kaluagan
Kifs	Pugharo
Knot	Balegotal
Knowledge	Matow
Knee	Tuhud
Kneel	Maga lohod
L	
Lady	Potely
Lake	Dano, lano
Lament	Magafgan
Land	Lupa
Laft	Sowlehan
Laugh	Pakatowa
Law	Punuhan
Father in law	Panugangan
Lazy	Mapaog
Lead	Timga Maelon
Leak	Gabut
Leaft	Paedu Nean
Lee	Abunghan Angir
Left	Bewan
Leg	Botes
Lemon	Sua
Lent	Paholaman
Level	Mapanty
Letter	Sula
Liberal	Mura
Life	Moeug
Lift	Sakuat
Light	Magan
Like	Magikfanikfan

Lime

English.	*Magindano.*
Lime	Banket
Line	Kulis
Little	Paedu
Liver	Atty
Lock	Sow
Loins	Dumulug
Long	Malundo
Look	Ely
Lord	Datoo
Love	Limo
A man in love	Malimo
Louse	Kuttu
Low	Selon
Low Water	Pagerat su-ig

M

Mad	Mabunog
Maim	Pali
Make	Maginang
Man	Tow
A bad man	Alub-ito
A prejudiced man	Makabinasa
Mango	Mango
Many	Marakal
Mark	Tanda
Market	Parehan
Married	Karuma, alay
A married person	Caluma
Mask	Paglelubun
Master	Edog
Mat	Ekam
Matter	Nana
Mate	Piloto
Medicine	Gammot

Melancholy

English.	*Magindano.*
Melancholy	Lidu
Memory	Makelintan
Mice	Elaga
Mid-day	Sinang
Midnight	Magabe
Milk	Gattas
Million	Sagtos Laſſa
Mind	Quira quira
Mine	Dulangan
Mirth	Panda lamot
Miſt	Tonog
Miſer	Mazingit
Miſtake	Pakaſalla
Mix	Patinboon
Mob	Makatepong
Modeſt	Magkahoya
Moiſt	Mawaſſa
Monkey	Ubal
Moon	Ulan-ulan
Month	Sa-ulan
More	Tambapan
To-morrow	Amag
Day after to-morrow	Amiſandao
Mother	Ina
Mountain	Booked
Mouth	Semud, nagali
Mourn	Pakrlatta
Mud	Kilamun
Multitude	Marakal tow
Murder	Pagbunwoot
My	Cammoo
Myſelf	Sakeeſa

Nail

English.	*Magindano.*
N	
Nail	Lanfan
Nails of the hand	Canucu
Naked	Huba Balay
Name	Nallang
Narration	Pugtalo
Navel	Puffun
Near	Mafikun
Neck	Leog
Need	Sydalla
Neighbour	Kanakan Wally
Nephew or niece	Paqui vatan
Neft, birds	Wally hyub
Net	Pukoot
New	Bagoo
Night	Magabe
No	Dele
Noife	Safa
To make a noife	Mepafa
Noon	Sinang
Nofe	Elong
Nothing	Dalla
Now	Indona
Nutmeg	Bunga palla
O	
Ocean	Sakaloran
Oar	Pura
Oblidge	Takow
Oil	Lanna
Once	Amay
Open	Nabuka
Oppofite	Salepug

Over

Englifh.	*Magindano.*
Over the water	Salepug-ig
Oven	Mageny
Our houfe	Langoo Wally
Out	Salewan
Own	Sakki
Oyfter	Teaba

P

Pace	Mageny
Paddle	Pura paedu
Padlock	Yawe
Paid	Nebyran
Pair	Satema
Pale	Malufpan
Paper	Pappel
Pardon	Ampoo
Path	Tambak
Pay	Nabyran
Pea	Kabbud
Peaked hill	Utboon na booky
Peck	Tufikan
Pen	Pluma
People	Tou
Perhaps	Dekatowan
Piece	Tigpun
Petulant	Duaraka
Pilot	Piloto
Pipe	Koaku
Pifs	Ehe
Place	Tampat
Play	Pandalamot
Plenty	Marakal
Plump	Malumbo

Poifon

English.	*Magindano.*
Poison	Kabau
Pole	Usok
Pork	Babuey
Pot	Kulun
Pout	Pagmudut
Pray	Sumbayan
Pregnant	Mabdos
Pretty	Mapia
Presence	Arapan
Priest	Pandita
Pride	Maesog
Profit	Taban
Publication	Capayagan
Pulse	Galac
Purse	Pooio
Put	Esood

Q

Quay	Cherotcho
Queen	Potely, Sultana
Quick	Gaan

R

Race	Pagalumba
Rag	Malugbak
Rail	Kural
Rank	Masela atow
Rap	Binalan
Rascal	Mapadayo
Rat	Elaga masela
Rear	Debias
Reach	Ejondon
Red	Malega
Reed	Palunng

F f

Reins

English.	*Magindano.*
Reins	Unabin
Religion	Agamat
Reſt	Pugtalaton
Revolution	Malembul
Ribs	Gooſook
Rice	Boogas
Right	Dele ſalla
Ring	Ching ching
River	Lowaſſa-ig
Road	Tambak
Rob	Matagkow
Robber	Matagkown
Rock	Wattoo
Roof	Boobong
Round	Malimpulog
Row	Mamura
Ruin	Pakaſalla
Rub	Pahedan
Run	Palaguy
Ruſt	Tuktuk

S

Sack	Baloyot
Sad	Mugkalero
Said	Puttalog
A ſail	Lyug
Saint	Wali
Salt	Timus
Same	Magiſan ikſan,
Sat	Ungtod
Savory	Macombu
Saw	Elyka
Say	Pakſugid
Scald	Myow

Scale

English.	*Magindano.*
Scale	Katehan
Scent	Bahuka
Scold	Pugtalo marata
Scratch	Kalot
Sea ſhore	Kirin
Middle of the ſea	Kaludan
Seat	Inkudan
Secret	Mentula
See	Elyka
Seed	Eteallum
Seek	Pangelain
Send	Pugſogo-on
Sell	Igpaſſa
Seven	Petoo
Shadow	Aneno
Shallow	Kenutean
Shame	Pugkahoya
Share	Bagean
Sharp	Maoon
Sheath	Tagoban
Sheep	Carnero
Shelf	Byan byan
Shell	Opis
Shield	Taming
Ship	Kappal
Short	Pababa
Shake	Hoyong
Shout	Pagoloyan
Shore	Dedſaan
Shower	Pagulan
Shut	Lokoban

F f 2   Sick

Englifh.	*Magindano.*
Sick	Pugkafakki
Sigh	Pagenhowa
Silk	Sutilla
Silver	Pelak
Sin	Duza
Sinner	Baladuza
Sing	Pugfingal'
Sink	Tagalum kafa ig
Sifter	Pagaly babye
To fit down	Ayan
Six	Anom
Skim	Luma
Skin	Upis
Sky	Langit
Slack	Pedeet
Slave	Olepon
Slain	Niatty
Sleep	Tulug
Slip	Belakan
Slow	Paghenyan
Smalleft	Paedu kababaan
Smell	Bahooun
Smile	Maghebya
Smoke	Affu
Sneeze	Huipon
Soft	Makumok
Song	Magfenan
Sorrow	Maledo
Sour	Madfom
South	Sulatan
Sow	Babueybabye
Speak	Pugtalok

A great

English.	*Magindano.*
A great speaker	Matumpis
Spear	Belok
Spleen	Kumakop
Sport	Pugtalamut
Star	Bituun
Steal	Nakow
Steam	Lumen
Step	Lakang
Stiff	Matugas
Still	Mangokuy
Stone	Watoo
Stop	Paguning
Street	Tambak
Stream	Ig-mabangul
Strike	Panlapad
String	Lubed
Strong	Mabangul
Stupid	Bunugun
Suck	Lapſak
Sugar	Aſſukal
Sum	Cuim
Sun	Senang
Supple	Nudſtus
Sure	Matadlong
Sweat	Hulas
Sweet	Matamis
Swelling	Kalabuan
Swift	Matulin
Swim	Puglangy
Sword	Sundam
Swore	Sumumpa

Table

English.	*Magindano.*

T

English	Magindano
Table	Lamesa
Tale	Magtalok
Tall	Mapulu
Tart	Masulum
Taste	Nanam
Tax	Boiss
Teach	Paganad
Tear	Uturun
Ten	Sanpoolu
Tender	Makumo
Terrible	Terribilis
Thank	Salandu saka
Thatch	Attop
That	Inan
Theft, petty	Manabkoo
There	Sakan
Thick	Madamur
Thin	Nepis
Third	Tulu
Thirty	Tulu poolu
Thirst	Makowhow
Thought	Samalow
Thousand	Sanlibu
Thread	Bunang
Throat	Bundongan
Thrust	Alupun
Thumb	Komako
Tickle	Makattol
Timber	Kahoy
Tip	Utbong
Tire	Mabodly

To

Englifh.	_Magindano._
To	Ka, kafa
Token	Tanda
Tongue	Dela
Teeth	Nipoon
Top	Bubu
Touch	Puniutun
Town	Engwood
Tree	Kahoe
Triangle	Tulu pefagi
True	Matadlong
Turnip	Savonos
Two	Daua

V

Valour	Mabagol
Veil	Ampek
Vein	Ugat
Verfe	Pantok
Vice	Salla
Violin	Dabel
Virgin	Bagutow
Uncle	Paqui ama
Under	Lallum
Underftanding	Kalondoman
To underftand	Sabut
Vow	Sumpa

W

Wages	Bohes
Wait	Apa
Wake	Buat
Waift	Cafadan
Wall	Allud

War

English.	*Magindano.*
War	Pugawy
Weak	Sakadiumat
Weight	Timbangang
Well	Pareget
Weſt	Habagat
Wet	Nuſaſſa
Wheel	Galengan
When	Undow
Wherefore	Enu
Whence	Andow
Whip	Peſee
White	Mapute
Whole	Sateman
Whore	Mabega
Wide	Mulad
Wife	Kruma
Will	Muyog, Guinaua
Wind	Hangin, undu
Wine	Angor
Wing	Pah pak
Wipe	Pahedon
Wiſdom	Buloodon
Woe	Duraka
Woman	Babye
Won	Kataban
Wood	Kahuy
Work	Maghelan
Worm	Anay
Wrath	Mungalipungwood
Write	Mugſula
Wrong	Mugkaſalla

Year

English.	*Magindano.*
Year	Salagun
Yawn	Daghoyab
Yellow	Madulow
Young	Bagutu
Yes	Wy
Yesterday	Kagy
The day before yester-day	Kaga fandao
A young perfon	Paydido
A very young perfon	Paydidock
Sunday	Imat
Monday	Salaffa
Tuefday	Arba
Wednefday	Kamis
Thurfday	Diumat
Friday	Sapto
Saturday	Akad
January	Nayda
February	Nadi
March	Mocaram
April	Safar
May	Rabbil aval
June	Rabbil aver
July	Diumadil aval
Auguft	Diumadil aver
September	Raddiab
October	Saavan
November	Ramatan
December	Saaval
North	Utara
South	Salatan
Eaft	Timor
Weft	Habagat

N. E.

English.	*Magindano.*
N. E.	Timor laut
N. W.	Burra laut
S. E.	Tungara
S. W.	Burra dyer
1	Iſa
2	Daua
3	Tulu
4	Apat
5	Lima
6	Anom
7	Petoo
8	Walu
9	Seaow
10	Sanpoolu
100	Sangalos
1000	Sanlibu
10,000	Sanlaxſa
100,000	Sancatty
1,000,000	Sanpoolu catty

A FEW

A FEW

PAPUA WORDS.*

English.	*Papua.*
GOD	WAT
Devil	Sytan
Yes	I-o
No	Roba
I	Iya
Yoù	Suru
Fiſh	Een
Fowl	Moorſankeen
Hog	Ben
Coconut	Sery
Swallow	Pemankaku
A Man	Sononman
A Woman	Binn
A Slave	Omin
Have you any fiſh ?	Een Iſia

* In the bad weather we had croſſing the China Sea, I loſt a liſt of many words, elſe this would be more complete.

Have

English.	*Papua.*
Have you any pork ?	Ben Iſia
Don't be afraid	Wam-kawar
Don't come near	Wadaberwakini
Go	Kower, Koabur
Will you trade ?	Ofarabian
Pearls	Muſtiqua
Beads	Fin fin
Iron	Ukanmom
Greens	Caſſuff
An ax	Amkan
A Prong or chopping Knife	Sumber
Sagoe	Bariam
Baked Sagoe	Kium
Gold	Bulowan
Silver	Plat
Copper	Ganetra
Braſs	Kaſnar
A Fort	Coto
A Houſe	Rome
A Country	Nu
A Tree	Kaibus
A River	Warbiky
Water	War
Salt Water	Warmaſſin
Sweet Water	Warimaſſin
To bathe	Komaſſy
Fire	For
Hot	Rob
A Hook	Sofydine
A net	Pam
To look, to ſee,	Komamy

An

English.	Papua.
An Island	Meofs
A Hill	Bon
A Garden	Yafkaman
Sand	Yean
Cayen Pepper	Marifin
A Knife	Enfy
A Mufquet	Piddy
A Cannon	Piddybeba
A Plate	Ofo piring
A Bundle	Tataf
Large	Beba
Small	Kinik
Long	Ekouan
Short	Ekouanba
Flat	Emafin
Lean	Ebieba
Large Cockle called by Malays Kima	Koyam
A Dog	Naf
A Cat	Mow
A Rat	Py
The Sun	Rafs
The Moon	Pyik
A Star	Mak
Dampier's Pigeon *	Manipi
Bird of Paradife	Mandefor
The Unicorn Fifh	Een Ra
A Ship, or large veffel	Cappall
A Canoe, or fmall veffel	Wy

* A large blue pigeon, with beautiful feathers on its head, to be feen in many mufeums. Dampier gives a figure of it.

A Bow

English.	*Papua.*
A Bow	Myay
An Arrow	Ekay
An Oar	Koboris
A Paddle	Pura
A Sail	Sawir
A Maft	Padarin
A Rope	Kabry
An Ancor	Yor
Limes	Inkry
Rice	Bira
Sugar Canes	Cumman
Cloves	Chinky
Nutmeg	Samkow
Eaft	Wamfowy
Weft	Umbaraick
South	Wamrum
North	Amurum
A Rajah, or King	Korano
White	Pepoper
Black	Pyffin
Red	Fanadaik
One	Ofer
Two	Serou
Three	Kior
Four	Tiak
Five	Rim
Six	Onim
Seven	Tik
Eight	War
Nine	Siou
Ten	Samfoor
Eleven	Samfoor Ofer

One

Englifh.   *Papua.*
One Hundred   Samfoor Ootin
One Thoufand   Samfoor Ootin Samfoor.

The Papuas of Dory faid there were *bon for*, hills of fire, to the eaftward, but knew nothing of the names of Moa, Arimoa, or Iamna. Near thefe three iflands Commodore Roggewein fays there is a Volcano.

N. B. The Afterifk at page 219, refers to the word *Coto Intang*, in page 216.

F I N I S.

DIRECTIONS *for* PLACING *the* PLATES.

CPSIA information can be obtained
at www.ICGtesting.com
Printed in the USA
LVHW04s1302290418
575305LV00002B/168/P